Cop Shows

Cop Shows

A Critical History of Police Dramas on Television

Roger Sabin
with Ronald Wilson, Linda Speidel,
Brian Faucette *and* Ben Bethell

McFarland & Company, Inc., Publishers
Jefferson, North Carolina

Library of Congress Cataloguing-in-Publication Data

Sabin, Roger, 1961–
Cop shows : a critical history of police dramas on television / Roger Sabin
with Ronald Wilson, Linda Speidel, Brian Faucette and Ben Bethell.
p.   cm.
Includes bibliographical references and index.

ISBN 978-0-7864-4819-7 (softcover : acid free paper) ∞
ISBN 978-1-4766-1643-8 (ebook)

1. Detective and mystery television programs—United States—
History and criticism.   2. Television cop shows—United States—
History and criticism.   I. Wilson, Ronald, 1954–
II. Speidel, Linda, 1967–   III. Faucette, Brian.
IV. Bethell, Ben.   V. Title.

PN1992.8.D48S23 2015   791.45'6556—dc23   2015005669

British Library cataloguing data are available

Cover image (iStock/Thinkstock)

Printed in the United States of America

*McFarland & Company, Inc., Publishers
Box 611, Jefferson, North Carolina 28640
www.mcfarlandpub.com*

Acknowledgments

The authors would like to thank Jane Gibb for her help and support during the early stages of this book; Dr. Ana Raposo; Professor Martin Barker; Professor Teal Triggs; Professor Jeremy Till; Professor Janet McDonnell and all in the research office at Central Saint Martins; Nick Lloyd and the librarians at CSM; Professor Caroline Dakers; Nick Kimberley; and Valerie Bethell.

Table of Contents

Introduction

ROGER SABIN

STEVE MCGARRETT: Hi, I've just arrived from Hawaii.
COLUMBO: Honolulu?
STEVE MCGARRETT: No, on a surfboard!
—*Comedian Billy Howard's impersonations
on the 1975 novelty hit record* King of the Cops

When did the American public first fall in love with TV cops? Was it back in the 1950s with *Dragnet*, the first "realistic" take on policing and the classic "appointment drama"? Or the 1970s, when charismatic cops like Columbo, Kojak, and Steve McGarrett flooded the screens, when *Time* magazine devoted an issue to the phenomenon, and when dismal comedy records flourished (yes, there was more than one). Or maybe the 1980s, with the chic thrills associated with *Miami Vice* and the feminist dramas of *Cagney & Lacey*? The 1990s, with the mega-franchises that became *CSI* and *Law & Order*? Or possibly more recently, with the "novelistic" pleasures offered by *The Wire* or the Kentucky-fried irony of *Justified*?

Whatever your perspective, cop shows have been a part of our viewing lives for a long time, and have performed a function to which no other genre can aspire. Put simply, they tell us about our attitudes to crime, and hence what we think about the "social contract" that exists between state and citizen. They both transmit and reflect the politics of the moment. And as those politics change, so cop shows demonstrate that "genre" is very rarely generic. Above all, perhaps, they keep us entertained—not just when first aired on a weekday night, but as daytime re-runs and selections from DVD boxed sets, or downloaded onto our computers, tablets and phones.

This book is a history of these shows. It collects the evidence—"just the facts, ma'am"—and subjects it to close forensic analysis.[1] In so doing, the aim is modest and primarily pedagogic: to provide an accessible introduction to the topic and offer a pathway into its study. We start from the premise that TV cop shows are an important part of American culture, indeed a much-loved one (why else would anybody make a novelty record?), and that they have been unjustly overlooked. This gap is especially evident in the academy, which is not to discount the great work of Jonathan Nichols-Pethick, Jason Mittell, Jane Feuer and others, which we reference throughout the book. The target readership is therefore principally students. Possibly they will be majoring in film and television studies, but also cultural studies, media studies, American studies—and we can think of many more curricula that might be relevant. At the same time, we very much hope that the book can be appreciated by the general reader who happens to enjoy the selected shows.

This pedagogic approach explains why the structure of the book is straightforward. Case studies of shows have been selected in chronological order, from *Dragnet* to *Justified*, and subjected to analyses looking at how they contribute to the genre; how they represent class, "race,"[2] gender and sexuality; how they are constructed according to industry imperatives; how they might be considered "televisual"; how they are received by audiences; and how—if at all—they might have been controversial. Each essay concludes with suggestions of recommended episodes and further reading.[3] That's the basic idea. But it's important to note that the selection of case studies does not necessarily represent the "best" shows ever produced, and that the book is not an attempt to construct a canon. It is, however, a way—we hope—of encouraging a broader and deeper appreciation of the genre as a whole.[4]

Maybe, even, the book will become the basis for new courses in higher education. It could be argued that TV cop shows are only "teachable" at this point in history. Downloads and DVD reissues mean that it's possible to focus scholarly attention on them in a way once only conceivable in relation to film. It is true that TV *per se* has been taken more seriously in the academy in recent years (as evidenced by new journals, a burgeoning conference circuit, and new courses) and that individual cop shows have broken through as subjects for study—notably *CSI* and *The Wire*. (Would this book have been commissioned without the critical acclaim that greeted *The Wire*? We doubt it.)[5] But still the TV cop show genre as a whole remains under the radar (what about a class test for students to identify the voices on *King of the Cops*?).

Finally, it's worth noting that this is more than a "textbook." That word tends to imply a lack of primary research and a purely functional basis. By contrast, what this book does is often new. Some of the shows have indeed been written about fulsomely elsewhere, but others remain obscure (e.g., *The Untouchables, Highway Patrol*, etc.) while even huge hits like *Kojak* and *Hawaii Five-O* have garnered surprisingly little coverage. Thus, primary (archival) research has often been a necessity, while the structure of the book hopefully lends itself to identifying new patterns and associations that might not previously have been evident. (For example, can *The Wire* be understood without reference to *Kojak* and *Naked City*? We think not—though it's surprising how often shows are dealt with in isolation.) Thus the authors bring to their chapters a detailed knowledge of the field, and of cultural theory, and attempt to add fresh insights wherever possible. They concede that any mistakes are their own—though protest that this confession was tricked out of them by rogue cops who hadn't read them their rights...

The Story the Book Tells—and Some It Can't

It sounds rather grand to say that "this is the story of modern America," but in a sense that's what the book represents. Indeed, it is many stories: of a transition from narratives about lone cops to ensemble casts; from good-versus-evil to more muddied morality; from film noir–influenced storytelling to faux-documentary; from the near-invisibility of minorities to more balanced representation; from "knowing" audiences to even-more-knowing audiences. Above all, it concerns the story of the changing way we think about the police, crime and our role as citizens.

But the trouble with choosing to narrate those themes via a series of case studies is that sometimes the broader context gets missed. For example, there have been peaks and troughs for the cop show, and in hindsight we can see these as having been cyclical. The first boom came in the 1950s, with the phenomenon that was *Dragnet*, watched by a staggering 30 million viewers at its peak. The second came in the 1970s, when more cop shows were aired than at any other time. In 1973, *Time* magazine counted "29 crime shows on the network schedules, plus a few in syndication, accounting for roughly 21 of the 63 prime-time hours each week."[6] The most recent upturn came in the late 1990s/early 2000s with the success of the glossy franchise-based juggernauts *Law & Order* and *CSI*. Once again, *Time* ran a story, informing readers that "next season (2002–03) the four major networks will air at least 18 hours a week of police shows."[7]

With each boom, there was a bust (of varying severity). And each time, the media fed the backlash.

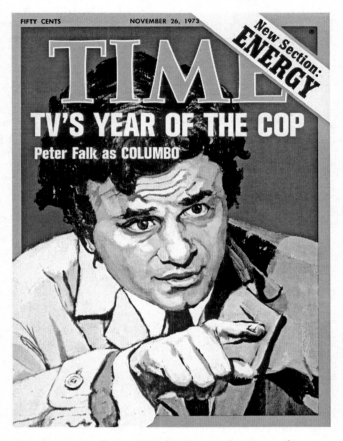

Time magazine featured Columbo on the cover of its "TV's Year of the Cop" issue of November 26, 1973 (portrait of Columbo in acrylics by Norma Wasserman; © 1973 Time Inc. Used under license).

In the late 1950s, the genre was said to be "tapped out," with calls for gentler, more family-oriented fare. In the late 1970s, it was criticized for a lack of imagination and for being too violent—again leading to demands for more "positive" programming (by 1980, none of the top 20 shows were cop shows). In the 2010s, the argument has been that the genre has become stale and boring, and that, as a result, TV companies are commissioning "quality dramas" as an alternative (note: no recognition there that cop shows might count as "quality dramas").[8] But through it all, the genre keeps bouncing back. Since that last sounding of the death-knell, for example, we've had *Longmire*, *True Detective*, *Chicago PD*, and many others.

Similar long-term patterns can also be missed, or, at least, not given the attention they deserve. For example, it's beyond the remit of this book to offer a thematic exploration of changes in representation (of gender, "race," sexuality, and class)—though the chapters do engage with this. So, to give the obvious example of gender, we can observe that the majority of our chosen shows are about lone men, usually of the macho variety (the novelty record quoted at the beginning of this introduction isn't called *King of the Cops* for nothing). This changes in more recent decades, reflecting both the rise of feminism and changing notions of masculinity, and a concomitant increase in the number of female law enforcement professionals. Thus, *Cagney & Lacey* and the later ensemble shows (*Hill Street Blues*, *Homicide: Life on the Street* and *The Wire*, especially) become symbolic of a new perspective. Another example might be the "whiteness" of most TV cops. In the early shows, ethnic minorities are marginalized, with African American characters sometimes appearing as menacing extras or as entertaining diversions—a situation complicated by ongoing discourses in the real world about "race" and "criminality." In the post–civil rights era, however, this also begins to shift, with some shows de-centering whiteness altogether: for example, *The Wire* was remarkable for having a majority-black cast, reflecting the ethnic demographics of its setting, Baltimore.

Staying with this theme, it would be glib to suggest that today we have reached a point of "equilibrium" regarding representation. Depictions of women, and of African Americans and other minorities, are still very problematic on TV (not just in cop shows), and before we label a show from the past "sexist" or "racist" (or indeed "heterosexist" or any other "-ist"), we need to ask the question: compared to what? Historical context is everything; the makers of these shows did not see them as "dubious," and one job of the cultural historian is to acknowledge such attitudes and explore their underlying cause. Our cherry-picked examples of cop shows may gesture at "progressive" or "reactionary" approaches, but cannot give the full picture, first because these labels do not tally with the genre as a whole (e.g., for every *Wire* there were many more contemporaneous shows with less enlightened attitudes), and, second, because lack of space precludes a detailed engagement with representation theory.

Similarly, when it comes to the portrayal of "the cop" him- or herself, clearly there is much more to its construction than just TV shows, and, again, this evolution is impossible to trace in a book like this. The mixture of "enforcer of authority," social worker and embodiment of ideologies has often boiled down to a question of trust and, obviously, TV cop shows have had to try to make sense of this. In Christopher Wilson's influential book *Cop Knowledge* (2000), the police themselves are seen as offering "the first drafts of a great deal of our cultural knowledge about social disorder and criminality."[9] But these drafts are constantly being challenged. For example, arguably the biggest revision (among young people especially) came in the 1960s with the advent of the counter-culture: cops were no longer "neighborhood friends" who "knew the score," but instead were sometimes characterized as brutal oppressors (for a time it seemed as if every underground cartoonist—including Robert Crumb—was depicting them literally as pigs).[10] One question might be therefore how "cop knowledge" is expressed in TV cop drama in a way that takes account of this shifting terrain.

One final aspect to the story that isn't so easy to perceive when told in case studies is the massive change that has taken place in the television industry over time—particularly the shift from what has been termed the "network era" to the "neo-network era."[11] To simplify: from roughly 1948 to 1975, three channels dominated: CBS, NBC, and ABC. These channels put advertising at the center of their business plan, which meant certain consequences in terms of the programs that were commissioned. In order to keep costs down, TV drama aimed for standardization and reproducibility ("Same time, same channel..."). This meant an emphasis on formula, so that advertisers could be sure of what they were investing in, which led, for example, to breaks every 15 minutes, music that cued the viewer into the ads, stories based on "the pleasure of returning"—often with cliffhanger endings—and content that conformed to certain boundaries of taste.

This was the basis of the modern "series" as we know it. The ads system essentially killed the idea of one-off plays (or very nearly), and set in motion a trend for westerns and then crime shows—unsurprisingly, the ad agencies associated with the tobacco companies loved these genres for their macho associations. True, there was a smattering of science fiction and hospital drama, with spy shows joining the fray from the mid–1960s, but the cop show was arguably the most enduring staple. As the contents of this book will show, in terms of "network era" programming, *Dragnet* (NBC) and *The Untouchables* (ABC) set the tone, followed by the Quinn Martin shows such as *The F.B.I.* (ABC) in the 1960s (the peak of the three networks' power), and then, with more sophisticated niche-orientated advertising in the 1970s, shows like *Starsky & Hutch* (ABC), and on into the 1980s, with *Miami Vice* (NBC).[12]

However, in the 1980s and 90s, this system started to fracture as the big three companies were challenged by newcomer networks (for example, HBO, TNT and AMC) who played by different economic rules. In particular, the rise of cable, and then digital technology, meant that the old reliance on ads could be circumvented. Thus cable subscribers could watch without the annoyance of breaks—all they had to do was pay a subscription. With the coming of "on-demand" technology, viewers, for an extra fee on top of the subscription, could watch at a time of their choosing. And later still, with the advent of downloading, they could watch where and when they chose, so long as they had a portable laptop, tablet or smart phone.[13]

Along with this came the increasing importance of DVD sales (prefigured by the VHS market, but much more lucrative). Networks that could capitalize on the idea of a "connoisseur" product were able to open up new revenue streams—hence the rise of "quality dramas" sold as items to keep (with the associated pleasures of re-playing, collecting, browsing the DVD extras, and displaying on a shelf at home). If audiences could be flattered into imagining themselves as experts, then a series could be re-sold in this format, with "boxed sets" becoming popular in the 2000s. As the *New York Times* commented, the implication was that "you are what you watch"—an idea that ran counter to the old cliché of TV as something that was mass-consumed in a passive fashion.[14]

This shift from the network to neo-network scenario, along with the concurrent drive for DVD sales, was fueled by the free market philosophies of the Reagan administration, followed by the growth of neoliberalism. The deregulation of the industry, along with its increasing globalization and new technological possibilities, set it on a new path, and in a sense this marked the point historically when it went from being a "majority" phenomenon to become niche. The same thing happened to other parts of the entertainment industry, especially the music business, and the days when the American public could enjoy a shared experience of watching the same TV drama or listening to the same pop song, were numbered. (For both reasons, the idea that significant enough numbers of people would understand *King of the Cops*, to the extent that it could chart, was an impossibility after a certain point.[15])

The shows that emerged as a result were significantly different. It was now possible to conceive a cop drama with a novelistic structure, whose content wasn't necessarily concerned with the "acceptability" of things like profanity or levels of sex and violence. These new shows were often characterized as being "more cinematic," and, perhaps, by extension, "less televisual." If one show typified this kind of aesthetic, it was *The Wire*—a bestseller on DVD, though its initial broadcast ratings were modest. As one magazine joked: "Highly addictive DVDs have been branded the scourge of well-off suburbanites…. A campaigner warns: 'This new product, Wire, is particularly dangerous because its addictiveness creeps up on you; for the first two of three episodes you're thinking "sure, I can handle this," then before you know it, it's 4 a.m. and you've finished the last disc and you're cruising the net for your next fix…. HBO's product is [the worst] because they don't cut it with adverts."'[16]

But however addictive the new products were, the old networks did not die off. The shift from "network era" to "neo-network era" certainly changed the rules of the game, but the older established companies did adapt—some better than others. Indeed, they were joined in 1986 by the fourth successful network, Fox. One inevitable consequence of the evolutionary process discussed here was that these "old model" companies themselves began to commission "quality drama." It is interesting to note that some of the shows that are commonly assumed to have been made by HBO are in fact aired by more mainstream companies (e.g., ABC's *Murder One* and Fox's *24*).[17]

All of which raises the question of whether the neo-network shows are "superior" to those that preceded them. Some critics and scholars argue that the newer shows are more sophisticated, more hip and more literary, and are therefore in a different class; others that they're simply saying the same things as old genre TV, but in a different way.[18] As a corollary, it is argued that because the new shows are being consumed via downloads and DVDs, and no longer being "tuned into" week after week, they are therefore not "speaking to the nation" in the manner of being a "cultural forum" for ideas.[19] Whichever argument(s) you prefer, it's clear that the "cultural worth" of cop shows is being debated as never before—and that conceptions of genre and taste are central to these debates.

Genre; and How "Potboilers" Became "Art"

"Genre" is one of the more difficult terms in media studies to define (see "Further Reading," below). It is true that cop shows are a genre in the sense that they are "texts" with recognizable elements that can be categorized—notably, the presence of the police as a central feature. But they can also be considered as a "sub-genre" of "crime shows," which themselves might be seen as a sub-genre of "thrillers."[20] Therefore, in writing this book, we have had to be disciplined about what we've chosen to include. The book, for example, doesn't encompass shows about private eyes (no *Peter Gunn*, *Rockford Files*, etc.), or about lawyers who solve cases (no *Perry Mason*, *Shark*, etc.). Nor is it about medics who do some sleuthing (*Quincy, ME*; *Diagnosis: Murder*, etc.) or science fiction/fantasy variants on the crime genre (*The X-Files*, *Grimm*, etc.). There are no shows that focus solely on villains (*The Sopranos*, *Boardwalk Empire*, etc.), or prison shows (*Oz*, *Prison Break*, etc.). And no comedies (*Police Squad!*, *Brooklyn 99*, etc.) or "cozies" (*Murder, She Wrote*; *Ellery Queen*, etc.).

But that still leaves quite a lot to talk about. For the sake of this study, we will indeed be calling cop shows a "genre," and concentrating on certain examples: *Dragnet*, *Highway Patrol*, *Naked City*, *The Untouchables*, *The F.B.I*, *Columbo*, *Hawaii Five-O*, *Kojak*, *Starsky & Hutch*, *Cagney & Lacey*, *Miami Vice*, *Hill Street Blues*, *Law & Order*, *Homicide: Life on the Street*, *NYPD Blue*, *CSI*, *The Wire*, *The Shield*, and *Justified*.

What will become apparent is how far these shows overlap with other genres: for example, *Hill Street Blues* with soap operas; *Law & Order* with legal dramas; *CSI* with medical shows. Indeed, the "western cop show" is almost a sub-genre unto itself (*McCloud*, *Cade's County*, *Walker: Texas Ranger*, *Justified*, and *Longmire* to name but a few). It will also be clear how genre doesn't mean one single vision of "the police." These shows offer con-

Jazz and cop shows have historically gone together—so it was inevitable that the great Henry Mancini would be invited to bring his arranging skills to the themes for *Kojak*, *Baretta*, *Hawaii Five-O*, and the rest (RCA Records, 1976).

structions of cops as public defenders, cops as Sherlock Holmes–style detectives, cops as integral members of the community, cops as two-fisted macho men, cops as working class women, and cops as people in positions of power which they abuse.

So, the point of interest is not that these shows "mirror" society—all art does that—but how they do the mirroring. Genre is evidently a very flexible idea. So, as well as the rather obvious overlap with other genres, we can say that there are several "dialogues" going on. For example, at a primary level, cop shows relate to other cop shows. The chapters in this volume are full of commentary about how they are inspired by, react to, and argue with, each other. Could *Kojak* have happened without *Dragnet*? Or *Homicide: Life on the Street* without *Hill Street Blues*?

Then there are imported dramas to consider: product from Canada, Australia and Britain has, for example, long fortified the schedules, and it is worth noting in passing that Steven Bochco (*Hill Street Blues*, *NYPD Blue*, etc.) acknowledged his debt to Britain's *Z-Cars*. (With the recent popularity of "Nordic noir" and French *policiers*, the geographical scope of influence is widening.) Similarly, other kinds of drama from other generic traditions—such as period dramas, soap operas, hospital series, and westerns—are constantly being incorporated (whether or not this results in hybrid shows).

Finally, there is the influence of documentary, obviously another distinct genre. For example, *The Police Tapes* (1977), *COPS* (1989–present) and their ilk suggested not only fresh ways of thinking about content but also about filming techniques (the "true crime" aesthetic). *Cinema verité* found its way onto TV screens via these shows to become a staple of the contemporary genre. The idea of the "dramatic reconstruction" in documentaries has also been important—compare, for example, *America's Most Wanted* (and its copyists) with *CSI*.

Such "dialogue with" and influence from other shows might encompass scripting, acting, and production values. It also involves broader politics—notably the way attitudes to authority are portrayed, and the question of representation. For example, we might ask what viewers of an average week's TV output (if such a thing exists) might come to expect of portrayals of women, the LGBT community, and ethnic minorities. As we've seen, the question of the representation of African Americans is particularly germane to the cop drama, and it's interesting to note that, despite the genre's vaunted "realism," African American characters have actually been more numerous, and demonstrated more "agency"—historically speaking—in the comedy genre.[21]

We can expand the matrix of influences even further, stretching generic cross-fertilization to other art forms altogether. The connections with novels, films, comics, and computer games are manifold. The movies are a particularly strong thread: could *Dragnet* have happened without the noir ambience of *He Walked by Night*? Or *Starsky & Hutch* without *Freebie and the Bean* and other buddy flicks? Literature, too, has obviously changed the shape of crime fiction many times: *Hill Street Blues* owes a debt to Ed McBain's *87th Precinct* novels; *Police Story* was created by Joseph Wambaugh, author of *The New Centurions*; and *CSI* certainly bears the imprint of Thomas Harris' *Silence of the Lambs*.

Which leads on to the understanding that genre is not just a classificatory system. It orientates viewers towards the shows in significant ways—performing "cultural work." So, to begin with, we tend to take things for granted about genre shows: they are, for example, expected to be serial in nature, to repeat themes week after week, to conform to certain levels of decorum, and to offer pleasures that we find hard to resist coming back to. (Usually, this boils down to production values, script and performance, but can include other elements—how many people tuned into *Hawaii Five-O* for the theme music?). As we've seen, genre shows are also, historically, bound by capitalist imperatives such as having to satisfy the demands of advertisers—"delivering eyeballs to the ads"—another "given" that audiences expect (or, at least, might have expected in the network era).

Such a positioning has led to prejudices. Genre shows have often been criticized by the "arbiters of taste" (be they reviewers in the quality press, academics, or any other—usually middle-class—commentator who has the job of "cultural judge") for appealing to the "lowest common denominator" in order to maximize revenue. Shows are said to be pot-boiler fantasies based on hackwork—repetitive, formulaic, unimaginative, schedule-fillers. From this perspective, the word "generic" becomes synonymous with "predictable" and "low class."

Historically speaking, cop shows *per se* have been seen in an even worse light because of their associations with violence, and because they are often automatically assumed to be politically conservative. Thus, to simplify the political argument, they revolve around: cops ("organs of the state," often glorified); bad guys (often villainous by dint of their nature rather than societal forces); a problem-to-be-solved (a crime); and a resolution at the end whereby social order is restored. In the words of one cultural theorist, cop shows have been stereotyped as "a constant dramatization of capitalism's logical desire to sustain itself and head off challenges to its hegemony."[22]

Enter the defenders of the cop show on the basis of "exceptionalism." Sympathetic critics have argued, in a rather backhanded way, that some rare shows do demonstrate enough signs of intelligence to be said to "transcend genre." Such judgments have been made both in the network era (particularly with regard to *Hill Street Blues* [NBC] and *Homicide: Life on the Street* [NBC]) and the neo-network era (notably about *The Wire*—a

The last shirt Stringer Bell ever wore is on the right. It was part of an exhibit called "Local Scenes on the Silver Screen: Featuring *The Wire*" at the Baltimore Museum of Industry in 2008 (photograph by and courtesy Katarina Ziegler).

show made by a company whose motto was "It's Not TV; It's HBO"). In these cases the arbiters of taste find ways in which examples "break with formula" and "defy repetition," even proposing that they might not be "cop shows" at all.

What we are talking about here is a taste judgment. For in order to "transcend genre," the cop show has to become "art." This magical transformation can best be explained by summarizing several of the threads that have already been discussed. Four interrelated tendencies can be pinpointed: first, we have seen how plots have evolved from a format (associated with the network era) of stand-alone episodes consisting of similar content for each episode, towards "story arcs" (more associated with the neo-network era) whereby plots continue though many or all the episodes of a series. This has opened up the possibility for "novelistic" tropes, such as development of character and variations of pacing, thereby rendering each episode dissimilar (to a degree) but at the same time requiring each to be watched in order to comprehend the whole.[23]

Second, there's been a move towards plots that embody "fuzzy morality," usually featuring "believable" characters, scenarios and locations; and perhaps demonstrating a willingness to portray sociocultural forces at work. In these circumstances, ethical quandaries become difficult or even impossible to resolve. Third, along with this, the "politics" of cop shows has come under increasing scrutiny. It has been argued that the newer, story-arc, "gritty," shows are more likely to challenge rather than confirm "common sense" notions of crime, "law and order," policing and "race."[24]

Lastly, there has been a stylistic evolution in terms of TV cop shows becoming less "televisual" and more "cinematic." By this, critics typically mean the borrowing of imagery, cutting techniques, camera angles, use of props, lighting, and modes of dialogue-writing, from work associated with the most in-vogue filmmakers of the moment ("films" meaning music videos and advertising as well). The most lauded dramas are thus said to exhibit a harmonious marriage of cinematography, production design and editorial direction. The idea of the "cinematic turn" is sometimes extended to shows that feature actors or directors previously associated with film. Critics point to *True Detective* (HBO, 2014) as the exemplar (director: Cari Joji Fukunaga; starring Woody Harrelson and Matthew McConaughey), but we should note that the idea has a much longer history: for example, Peter Falk was a Hollywood name by the time of *Columbo*, episodes of which were directed by John Cassavetes.[25]

These changes are interwoven, and have been interpreted by critics and hyped by marketers and branders, as ushering in a new era of "quality" in TV programming—particularly cop show programming—and thus the establishment of an "art" out of what has previously been dismissed as "genre television." In the words of cultural theorist Stephan Packard, "To go from genre to art is to move from a plurality of clearly delineated genre standards, separate traditions, towards an orientation towards the singular and always different tradition, thought of as an aesthetic experience."[26] The "rules" of genre do not have to be jettisoned for this to happen. But it is clearly about entering a new conceptual and interpretative space.

To reiterate: we don't need to take this "new creative space" on trust: there's plenty of room for skepticism. Is there, for example, really a link between commercial conditions (i.e., neo-network programming) and innovation? As we have seen, even those critics who've argued for "exceptionalism" have found it in network-era shows like *Hill Street Blues*, and when it comes to politics, many of the chapters in this book identify subversive elements in shows that might once have been classed as "potboilers."[27] In other words, we must be wary of the idea that "art" equals "progressive" and, if we reject the elevation to art, we must be equally wary of selectively using examples of cop shows to reinforce a version of the genre's history as a journey towards oppositional politics and transgressive meaning. For all its complexity, genre is neither inherently radical nor conservative.

Watching the Detectives

In all this talk of textual analysis, one factor has been omitted: the audience. More and more research within media and TV studies is currently being directed at questions involving the viewers, from "what people do with the media" to "what the media does to people."[28] By tackling the topic from this perspective, new insights emerge: for instance, about the ideological work that is being performed when shorthand representations are mobilized and about whether watching certain kinds of (usually violent) shows can have a deleterious effect on behavior. More than this, audience research can tell us what specific shows mean to individuals, the place they hold in people's lives. In so doing, it can complement other kinds of analyses in order to offer a fuller picture of both text and viewer.

One important aspect of this approach involves expectations, and how audiences bring life experiences to bear on what they are viewing. This "personal baggage" means that cop

Billboard for *Justified* (FX). "Ancillary material" is a powerful factor in the way audiences respond to shows.

shows are measured against all sorts of exterior influences. So, to add to our previous observations about what viewers might see of other shows, and other art forms, we can add what they see of "real life" and of ancillary material such as reviews, trailers, and posters.

"Real life" has to appear in quotation marks because any consideration of what might be "real" is fraught with philosophical difficulties. Nevertheless, we can generalize that viewers of cop shows are influenced by the presuppositions that they harbor about the way the world functions, especially with regard to crime and the police. For example, if we take the period of the first major boom in cop shows (1950s) then the context might involve anti–Communism and the moral panic about youth delinquency. For the second boom (1970s), we might consider the new emphasis on community policing, the institution of Miranda rights, urban decline (especially in New York) and a new awareness of drug policy. For the third boom (in the 2000s), we might list advances in DNA technology, and the post–9/11 "War on Terror."

As academic Jonathan Nichols-Pethick has pointed out, "[Critics see] stories about crime and the police as articulated with particular discourses: the mystery and horror of crime (especially murder), the cultural authority of the police officer, and the discourse of fear and moral panic in modern societies."[29] What is important, he goes on to argue, is that these discourses need to be considered alongside more wide-ranging cultural debates about what "crime" might be, and how we, as citizens, should respond to it.

Thus cop dramas often address fears expressed by communities in the face of perceived increases in crime rates, in a dual effort to provoke anxiety as well as reassure. Those shows that claim to be "ripped from the headlines" are particularly adept at this, and tend to be scheduled just before, or just after, news bulletins. In other words, within any given historical period there will be social and cultural agendas linked to crime, which get picked up by television and reinterpreted through genre-based storytelling.[30] This can lead to some rather complex emotional responses, as one t-shirt design spotted recently attests: "Fuck tha Police—Except the Ones I Watch on TV."

Ancillary material is another influence on audiences: as well as the aforementioned trailers, reviews and posters, we might include online discussion sites, "star" portraits in the press, merchandising, and—yes—to return to the example given at the start of this introduction, even humble novelty records. This is a profound part of the way genre works, because such material shapes in advance the notion of interpretation, as well as retrospectively molding understandings of meaning, creating what one theorist has termed an "architextuality."[31] To put it very simply, a particular show doesn't "start" at 9 p.m. on a Saturday night, but on a Wednesday afternoon, when we first glance at the *TV Guide* website and read about it (or before that, when we see a billboard advertising a new season).

It's worth noting too that in the 21st century, TV companies have become increasingly sophisticated about "offering something extra." Websites devoted to shows can be extensive, and offer supplementary information about characters and plot: *The Wire,* for example, was accompanied by several "prequel films" designed especially for the web. In a sense, then, a TV show is no longer just a TV show, and any budget for a new venture must include allowance for "thickening the viewer experience."

If ancillary material can be said also to include the products of fandom, then a whole other arena of meaning-making opens up. "Fans" are defined in various ways by theorists: at a basic level they are aficionados whose investment goes "above and beyond." They have clearly existed with regard to cop shows since the genre's beginning—as suggested by the range of fanzines, merchandising and ephemera relating to every show in this book currently up for auction on eBay. "Fan-power," too, is nothing new: *Cagney & Lacey* fans, for example, successfully organized to stop the cancellation of the show back in 1983.

With the advent of the web, a new era for the organization of fandom was initiated, whereby amateur interpretations and re-interpretations of shows can be distributed globally with great ease. Popular fan activity includes "fan fiction"—stories based on shows (including, for example, the "slash fiction" that exists around the characters in *CSI*), discussions on web forums, and even mini-movies made as homages and uploaded to YouTube. As a result, the shows have sometimes been reimagined, often "queered," and the boundaries between "fan" and "producer" have been blurred. (It's even true that jokey conspiracy theories exist: on the excellent "Tommy Westphall Hypothesis," which links together *Homicide: Life on the Street, Law & Order, The Wire* and others, please see the Appendix.) Not surprisingly, the networks have been paying an increasing amount of attention to fan opinion (though perhaps not to the Westphall Hypothesis), and in some cases there is evidence that this has fed back not just into the official websites, but into the plots of the shows themselves.[32]

Thus, the role of the audience should not be underestimated, and cop shows can't be understood wholly in terms of their inherent qualities. That is to say, we have to look "outside the text" as well as "inside." Shows will be interpreted differently by different audiences at different times in different contexts, and our understanding of them will always be nego-

The header to a "fanfic" website, involving slash fiction about Starsky and Hutch. Such sites operate by the credo "The characters don't belong to us, but the stories do" (art by Sonja Triebel; used with permission).

tiated. For example, the fact that counter-readings are possible may demonstrate viewers' capacity to enjoy things that, at other levels, they would disapprove of or disagree with. This may sound like common sense (we've all loved watching TV cops do hideously un–PC things), but it's rarely acknowledged. Our pleasures can never be taken for granted.

Conclusion

Introductions to books have a habit of being a bit dry. But cop shows are entertainment, not political tracts, and the authors of this volume hope we've done enough to emphasize the fun element. What's not to like about Robert Redford as a neo–Nazi in *Naked City*, Columbo shaking the claw of Robby the Robot, Kojak chatting with Liberace, and the shoot-out under the Twin Towers in *Miami Vice*? If that makes us classic "fan scholars," then we plead guilty.

For, in the end, these shows are both reflectors and transmitters of the zeitgeist. They co-opt social and political issues, push them through the mincer of a commercial system, and offer stories based on colorful characters. Stories that we, the viewers, can understand, beyond the real-life abstractions of crime statistics. As a genre, TV police drama is always hybridizing, and the stories it tells about "vics" and "perps," about good cops and bad cops, and about us as citizens are never fixed. So, if you find yourself using this book (as it was intended) to start your own "investigation" into this amazingly rich form, then take your time, cordon off the area with yellow crime tape, and be sure to follow the evidence…

Further Reading

The best introduction to the field is Jonathan Nichols-Pethick's *TV Cops* (Routledge, 2012), a theoretically sophisticated account of the "discourses of crime, community and citizenship" that puts emphasis on industry imperatives: recommended, with the caveat that it takes as its starting point 1980. For a more journalistic approach, Douglas Snauffer's *Crime Television* (Praeger, 2006) takes in the whole of the crime genre and includes useful interviews with insiders. (It also calculates the many thousands of hours that shows have notched up, emphasizing the role they've played in pop culture.) Steven Sanders and Aeon Skoble (eds.), in *The Philosophy of TV Noir* (University Press of Kentucky, 2008), take as their approach the legacy of film noir, and offer fresh perspectives on some of our case studies (notably *Dragnet*, *Miami Vice*, and *CSI*). On the broader theoretical themes touched upon in this introduction, the following are useful. Yvonne Jewkes, *Media and Crime* (second edition, Sage, 2010) gives an overview of debates, from a criminological perspective. Paul Cobley's *The American Thriller* (Palgrave, 2000) insightfully problematizes the notion of "verisimilitude" and gets to the root of narrative tropes. Jason Mittell's *Genre and Television* (Routledge, 2004) interrogates genre theory in similar penetrating fashion. Janet McCabe and Kim Akass' *Quality TV: Contemporary American Television and Beyond* (I.B. Tauris, 2007) is excellent on the neo-network revolution, while mention should be made of Charlotte Brunsdon's succinct "Bingeing on Box-Sets: The National and the Digital in Television Crime Drama" in the journal *Digicult* (November 2009). The work of the Research Unit, "Popular Seriality—Aesthetics and Practice," funded by the German Research Foundation (DFG), is well worth checking out. On representation, see the following: Melanie A. Cattrell, *Gendered Crimes, Gendered Fans: Intersections of Gender, Sexuality, and Fandom in the Contemporary American Television Crime Drama* (unpublished PhD diss., University of New Mexico, 2011); Carol Stabile, *White Victims, Black Villains: Gender, Race, and Crime News in US Culture* (Routledge, 2006 edition); and Herman Gray, "The Politics of Representation in Network Television," in Darnell M. Hunt (ed.), *Channelling Blackness: Studies on Television and Race in America* (Oxford University Press, 2005). Finally, Janet Staiger's *Interpreting Films* (Princeton University Press, 1992) is a landmark book in discussions of the role of the audience, while Matt Hills' *Fan Cultures* (Routledge, 2002) explores the complexities of fandom. For further sources, please see the Bibliography at the end of this book.

CHAPTER 1

Dragnet
(NBC, 1951–59)

ROGER SABIN

"Domm da dom domm!": the sinister brass fanfare that opened every episode of *Dragnet* was an iconic theme for an iconic show.[1] *Dragnet* holds a special place in this book. It was not only a pioneering piece of early television, it also became the template for the modern cop drama. There had been TV crime shows before, but *Dragnet* took the idea of a "police procedural" and ran with it, evolving a formula based on crime-solving rather than action, authenticity rather than sensationalism, and seriousness over wit (although this was never 100 percent true, despite what its many parodists insisted). The series was created by Jack Webb, who as well as being the star took on the roles of producer, director, co-scriptwriter, and provider of voice-overs. What *Dragnet* offered the American public was a vision of the police force as a "stabilizer" in society, made up of honest men (mostly men) dedicated both to keeping the bad guys in their place, and to the more abstract values of law and order. The show therefore also marked the start of the critical perception of the TV crime genre as politically conservative.

Each week, Sergeant Joe Friday, a Los Angeles detective, has a new case to solve. His task is introduced by the thumping theme music, and a voice-over: "The story you are about to see is true. Only the names have been changed to protect the innocent." (For the majority of episodes, the *Dragnet* stories were indeed based on actual cases.) From there, Friday and his plainclothes colleagues get on with the job in their rugged, downbeat way. Procedural tropes that audiences today take for granted took center stage for the first time: the processing of a crime scene; the work of forensics and ballistics experts; the pragmatic obsession of the police chiefs with "what's enough to go to court with," and so on. At the end of every show, the perpetrator would be brought to justice, and balance restored, followed by a close-up of the criminal's mug-shot, and a final voice-over explaining the jury's verdict. Case closed.

The fact that the focus was on the LAPD was significant, because this is the force that many historians have identified as leading the way in modernizing policing since the 1920s. When the legendary James E. Davis became chief in 1926, he emphasized statistics as a way to keep track of crime trends, and established the principle that the force should be cleaner-than-clean: he had no truck with "bad apple" cops, and sacked hundreds for "bad conduct."[2] It was Davis who initiated the idea of the "dragnet," a method of systematizing and coordinating procedures for apprehending criminals. Other chiefs followed his lead, and in the

15

1930s the force was further modernized by the adoption of an up-to-the minute radio system, reducing distress call response times to as little as three minutes. The reality of policing LA was therefore fertile ground for fictionalization. Interestingly, the force also became known for its "anti-subversive" activities, which translated as "anti–Communist"—Webb certainly knew that this political baggage went with the territory.

Culturally, *Dragnet* was formed as much by what it wasn't as by what it was. The broad background to crime fiction in the U.S. in the late 1940s was colored by a moral panic around the effects on audiences of depicting crime situations. This took in movies, novels, and TV, but especially crime comic books and magazines. Ten-cent comics like *Crime Does Not Pay* (1942), which glorified the deeds of gangsters and other lowlifes, often depicting violence in gory detail, gave the distinct impression that crime in fact paid rather well. The vast sales of such publications only added to the panic, and a backlash started with parents' groups and psychiatrists to the fore, arguing that the crime comics—and the associated genre of horror comics—were responsible for a host of societal ills, chief among them being juvenile delinquency (though, in fact, the adult readership was significant). By the early 1950s a censorship campaign was underway, and in 1955 a "comics code" was introduced, effectively banning controversial content.

Similar fears regarding TV had already led to the publication of a report by the Federal Communications Commission at the end of the 1940s. It encouraged only those kinds of shows which could be considered beneficial to family life, law and order, and "the American way." TV was not in the same category of moral panic as the comic books, but the censorious tone of the report was very similar.[3] If a new TV cop show were to be launched, then it would have been difficult, maybe impossible, not to conform. Luckily, the makers of *Dragnet* had no interest in being part of a sensationalist trend, and Webb set about distancing the show as far as possible from other kinds of "crime" entertainment.

Part of this distancing process involved looking to certain kinds of cinema: film noir was an obvious paradigm.[4] Of course, movies in this genre could be sensationalist and violent, but Webb was interested in their more "realistic" side, especially when it came to the police force. As a young actor, he had secured a supporting role in *He Walked by Night* (1948), a noir that was based on fact and filmed in a semi-documentary style. In order to be as authentic as possible, the movie made use of a police advisor, one Sgt. Marty Wynn of the LAPD. Webb befriended Wynn, and would later make extensive use of his knowledge (and that of other cops) on *Dragnet*. Other noir tropes were also perfect for what Webb had in mind—in particular, the hardboiled masculinity, the Chandleresque clipped dialogue, and the voice-overs. *He Walked by Night*, and other

The badge that says Sergeant Friday means business. It appeared every week in the credits, accompanied by the slightly sinister theme music.

noir flicks, confirmed for Webb that such a style could be used to tell stories from the police point of view, and that to focus on the criminal as protagonist (as in *Crime Does Not Pay*) was not a prerequisite for success.

But *Dragnet* was not a straightforward transference of cinematic ideas onto the small screen (though this was arguably its major innovation). There was a stage in-between, because *Dragnet* had its start on the radio. The radio version ran from 1949–57, and in the first couple of years established the format and tone of what was to come. Indeed, the TV *Dragnet* would often simply re-vamp episodes that had already been aired on the radio. Moreover, radio gave Webb the chance to develop a relationship with a supporting cast and he later insisted on bringing them with him to TV, much against the wishes of some within NBC who believed the two mediums should be kept distinct.

In one sense, the radio days were a time to experiment, and Webb used the radio shows to iron out any bumps in the formula. In particular, he developed Friday's fast-talking monotone, and played with the idea of never explaining complicated police terminology.[5] Webb also encouraged the inventive use of sound effects: he realized that such effects could be cheaply made but could "do a lot of work," enlivening even the most mundane scenes (though he never relinquished his fetishization of authenticity: even the phones had the same ring-tone as the actual phones used in the police department). Thus, the blandest police procedure could be made to sound exciting.

The economics of the show were also anchored in the radio period. Ads, of course, ruled and the tobacco conglomerate Liggett & Myers, makers of the Fatima and Chesterfield cigarette brands, sponsored the radio show and then the TV version. By the late 1940s, the medical profession was getting more vocal about the health dangers of smoking, and therefore companies like L&M were putting more dollars into their advertising to keep the public interested (including a huge drive to sell "healthier" filter-tipped cigarettes). Webb had no problem with this, and appeared in poster ads, and eventually in TV ads, momentarily coming out of character to address the audience directly. One reason was undoubtedly that he saw cigarettes as emblematic of hardboiled urban masculinity, and therefore in keeping with the show; but they also chimed with his ambitions to be seen as a jazz-loving hipster, about which more in a moment. (Note: most DVD collections of *Dragnet* omit the ads.)

How did the TV *Dragnet* develop over time? It'd be wrong to say it didn't, but a formula is a formula, and there isn't a great deal of variation in its 276 episodes. Admittedly, the opening show—about a bomb plot—was more dramatic than most, but after that it was, by and large, (police) business as usual. Friday's role developed at a glacial pace: he was always a man defined by his work, and attempts to introduce love interests in the late 1950s felt contrived. As the supporting cast came more into focus, the banter between them could be intentionally hilarious in its resolute down-beatness: what they had for lunch, what they were going to do during the weekend, their hypochondrias, etc.

Yet in their ordinariness they were showing that they were not the super-cops of pulp fiction, but part of a system. They even looked like "everymen"; partly as a result of Webb recruiting pals from his radio days, rather than established actors. The show's increasing emphasis on official terminology was no laughing matter, though, and could often tip into excess. The effect of lines such as, "We filed for violation of the state penal code, chapter 339, statutes of 1923, as amended 1947, sub 2" … could at times be almost Brechtian.

As for the bad guys, there are a significant number of *Crime Does Not Pay* style "hoods" without much hope of redemption, and today it's fun to see actors who would later become famous relishing the roles. Lee Marvin, for example, is interrogated by Friday in intense

Sgt. Joe Friday (center, Jack Webb) grills a serial killer (Lee Marvin) while sidekick Sgt. Ed Jacobs (Barney Phillips) looks on (NBC TV/Photofest).

fashion ("You tryin' a give me the treatment?")—anticipating the interrogations in *Homicide*'s "box"—and ends up spilling the beans about where the bodies are buried ("murder's a real small thing…"). In another example, Leonard Nimoy appears as a member of an armed gang, apprehended after a stakeout ("The Big Boys," 1954).

Other villains are treated in more sympathetic fashion. A teenage heroin user is forced to confront her addiction ("The Big Note," 1955). A pornographer who targets a school is shown to be a sad old guy who was once the director of silent-era feature films ("The Big Producer," 1954, a show that was daring in its subject matter and which hinted at Los Angeles' future as the center of the porn industry). A shoplifter is exposed as a middle class doctor's wife suffering from kleptomania, and even Friday takes pity and refuses to jail her ("The Big Shoplift," 1954). Along with these, there are several shows that engage with "juvenile delinquency," often portraying youths as neglected or being sucked into gang life: as we have seen, this was the moral panic *du jour*, and Webb wanted to have his say. These more sympathetic storylines can be seen as anticipating, or at least hinting at, the more liberal strain of "New Frontier" TV writing of the 1960s and the ethos of *Naked City* (ABC, 1958–59/1960–63: see chapter on same).

In order to feed the demand for new scripts, a kind of factory system had to be developed whereby cops from the LAPD would be encouraged to write about their on-duty experiences, and submit stories to the show. This was done with the full approval of the force, and indeed, the outlines of stories were edited and overseen by a cop working in the publicity unit. Until 1956, this individual was Gene Roddenberry, later the creator of *Star Trek*, who learned the craft of TV world-building from his stint on *Dragnet*. Indeed, he befriended Webb in order to learn about the behind-the-scenes mechanics of a successful TV show, and borrowed finished scripts from him to see how the stories were sculpted into their screen-ready form. (Reportedly, Roddenberry received a cut of $50 for every script accepted for production.)

One other way in which *Dragnet* developed was in its use of the language of television. Certain kinds of image-framing (especially close-ups and bird's-eye shots), intercut with stock and on-location footage of LA cityscapes, gave the show a distinct look, while the adoption of teleprompters helped actors affect an untutored approach to the dialogue (they were never encouraged to "get into the part"). The sets were minor works of art, accurate to the last detail. Entire floors of buildings were recreated on sound stages, including police headquarters at LA City Hall and a floor of the *Los Angeles Herald-Examiner* (a neat prefiguring of the way in which *The Wire* re-created *The Baltimore Sun* some 50 years later). As a report in *Time* magazine put it: "The very calendars are the same. The telephones bear the same extension numbers. Even the old-fashioned doorknobs are perfect duplicates—although it was necessary to make castings of the knobs at City Hall and have the copies struck off from them."[6] Thus, *Dragnet* was not merely "radio on the TV," and the series proved that "undramatic" did not mean un-televisual. In the same way that the show had innovated with radio soundscapes, it also took TV drama to new levels of "authenticity."

The series peaked in 1954–55, when it was rated number 2 in the Nielsen chart, with an estimated 30 million viewers weekly. As a consequence, it became part of the wider culture in a way that few TV shows would ever emulate. For example, it was parodied by comedians of every stripe: the eleventh issue of *MAD* magazine became infamous for its strip "Dragged Net!"—"My name is Detective Sergeant Joe Friday! My partner is Ed Saturday! Our Chief is Mike Sunday!" In a similar vein, the comedian Stan Freberg recorded no fewer than three *Dragnet* parodies, including "St. George and the Dragonet" (1953); while Spike Jones and his City Slickers gave us their take on the subject with the plainly titled "Dragnet" (also 1953). Not every response was humorous: the show also spawned a feature film (1954), a newspaper strip (1952–55), various paperbacks, and kids' toys (notably, a board game, a water pistol, and a *Dragnet Crime Lab*, "A complete crime detection outfit for the junior detective").

Similarly, Webb himself was catapulted to the position of major celebrity. He made the cover of *Time* magazine in 1954, and even attempted to re-model himself as a jazz-loving bohemian, and launch a singing career. His 1958 album, "You're my Girl: Romantic Reflections by Jack Webb" saw him as an unthreatening, non–rock 'n' roll, sex symbol, talking his way through the lyrics, much in the manner that Telly Savalas (Kojak) would adopt in the 1970s. In a more serious vein, Webb published a book, *The Badge: True and Terrifying Crime Stories That Could Not Be Presented on TV* (1958: it was reprinted in 2005 with a foreword by neo-noir crime writer James Ellroy). Through the 1950s and 60s, Webb continued to act and to work in movies, radio and TV, while as a producer with his own company he was an increasingly powerful player, involved in the launch of several shows, one notable late example being TV cop drama *Adam-12*.

In retrospect, the politics of *Dragnet* have been analyzed in terms of their right-wing biases. The show was recognized by the media at the time for doing the police force's PR, and when Webb died in 1982 he was given a funeral with full police honors.[7] As academic Jason Mittell puts it, "[*Dragnet*'s] ideology is not an idealized vision of society as presented in idyllic sitcoms, but the authenticated and unswerving belief in the system to continually discipline offenders and protect the innocent,"[8] Cultural historians have also pointed to the irony that some of the roots of the show's noir leanings were in Italian neo-realist movies of the post-war period, which were expressly socialist in their intent. These were an influence on, and influenced by, Hollywood noir, and much praised by movie critics (see the essays by R. Barton Palmer, listed below). Webb's ideological achievement was to take their style and reverse the politics.

However, close readings of *Dragnet* do not necessarily reveal it to be straightforwardly conservative. For example, Webb was of mixed-race descent, a jazz fan, and anti-racist.[9] Minorities were presented both in the squad room (though the LAPD's racial segregation policies were not mentioned), and out on the streets of Los Angeles: for example, Webb insisted that when Latinos were questioned, the dialogue should be in Spanish and then translated, for the sake of verisimilitude. This strategy of making visible a previously invisible minority should be seen in the context of the "Zoot Suit Riots" that took place in LA as recently as 1943, when fights broke out between white sailors and Latinos. (In the aftermath of the riots, Communists were blamed for its fomentation.) It is also true that some episodes of *Dragnet* confronted "race" head-on: in "The Big Nazi" (1958), for example, Friday goes undercover to catch a racist murderer. This is an area in which more research is required, but compared to some of the more racially intolerant programming on TV at the time, *Dragnet* looks almost progressive.

The original series closed in 1959, basically because Webb wanted to move on and do other things. By this stage *Dragnet* had become so iconic that it was an obvious paradigm to kick against. *The Untouchables*, for example, began that year (see chapter on same), and took the crime genre in another direction, with an emphasis on the kind of violence that had given the comic book censors hives a decade before. *Johnny Staccato* also debuted in 1959; a show about an ex-jazz musician/detective with a "relaxed attitude to life," it pointedly demonstrated that the good guys didn't have to be dour working stiffs (see chapter "They also served…"). Other subsequent cop shows riffed on the trope of the "dirty cop," in direct response to *Dragnet*'s perceived squeaky-clean approach.

Webb took a close interest in these developments and decided to bring *Dragnet* back in 1967, this time in color. Now Friday had a new sidekick, with Bill Gannon being played by veteran movie and TV actor Harry Morgan, who brought a lighter, semi-comedic touch to proceedings: his ad-libs were known on occasion to cause Webb to break character and laugh (something that would never have been allowed to happen in the earlier shows). The other change was a "hipper" take on crime, with a focus on youth delinquency. This is where the show demonstrated its lack of synchronicity with its times: whereas previously it had looked of-the-moment, now the exploits of two middle-aged cops among hippie-era American youth just seemed ridiculous. Today, the "Blue Boy" episode, about LSD, is routinely uploaded to YouTube in order to be scoffed at. Nevertheless, the re-boot of *Dragnet* was a ratings success, and it lasted for another 98 shows, ending in 1970.

After this, however, *Dragnet* was spent as a serious force, and Webb became an increasingly marginal figure. After his death, there were two attempts to resuscitate the show: *The New Dragnet* (1989–90), which kept the voice-overs and the mug-shots, and *LA Dragnet*, initially also titled *The New Dragnet* (2003–04) with comedy actor Ed O'Neill in the lead (casting that anticipated Ted Danson's role in *CSI*). Both shows were panned by the critics, and neither lasted more than a year.

The year 1987 saw homage from a different source; a movie that turned *Dragnet* into a comedy (Universal Pictures). Starring *Saturday Night Live* stalwart Dan Aykroyd and up-and-coming comedy star Tom Hanks, it was intended to be an affectionate satire on the show's conservatism. It riffed, in particular, on the 1960s incarnation and its obsession with youth, and featured a scene involving the cops dressed as 1980s punks. The film was a monumental misjudgment—and demonstrated by contrast just how well *MAD* magazine had done the parodying the first time around.

Since then, *Dragnet* has continued to influence the TV crime genre, sometimes profoundly. Just about every show owes a debt in some form or another, not least the two biggest franchises in the business, *Law & Order* (NBC, 1990–2010) and *CSI* (CBS, 2000–). Dick Wolf, the creator of *Law & Order,* was an unabashed *Dragnet* fan: although he knew that his show's content would necessarily have to be more violent and salacious, in keeping with audience expectations, he maintained a formula that emphasized the case over individual personalities, as well as introducing a voice-over for later episodes. ("*Dragnet* is the father of us all," he once famously declared.[10])

CSI's debt is less obvious, but academic Sue Turnbull has written a perceptive essay tracing a "bloodline" back to *Dragnet* that includes elements such as atmospheric lighting, pacing, the use of establishing shots of the city, and an emphasis on mundane work, including forensics (see "Further Reading," below). It's also worth adding that some *CSI* merchandising bears an uncanny resemblance to *Dragnet* products, notably the various toy *CSI* "forensics labs" and the above-mentioned *Dragnet Crime Lab*.

What are we to make of the original 1951–59 series today? It clearly remains a pivotal moment in TV history. By positioning itself as "the acceptable face of crime fiction," while at the same time opening up the hitherto unseen world of police work, it activated generic conventions that have endured to the present. Its sense of televisuality was also pioneering: for a show that is routinely described in terms of its adherence to documentary realism, it was highly stylized, bringing cinematic pizzazz to the small screen. As for Sergeant Joe Friday, he was the ultimate arbiter of law and order—and one of the iconic figures of the small screen.

But at the same time the show offered a perspective on how the politics of police crime drama could be manipulated in the service of an ideology. Viewed from our own particular here-and-now, the show's values, and Webb's conservatism, can seem reactionary, though, as we have seen, close readings of individual episodes reveal that this was not always entirely the case. Topicality and entertainment are never neutral, and *Dragnet* threw down a political challenge for subsequent shows to either mimic or reject. The trouble with "just the facts..." is that the facts need interpreting.

Recommended Episodes

"The Big Bar" (1954) demonstrates the appeal of *Dragnet*'s basic structure. Based on a radio show from 1949, the case involves a shooting in a bar, which then opens the way for some groovy jazz on the bar's jukebox during the investigation, followed by lots of procedural detail from the ballistics expert (played by Dennis Weaver—the future McCloud). The elements are all here, and the voice-overs are gripping: "By 4 a.m. an APB and a radiogram had been dispatched, and a manhunt was underway...." The combination of science and style is completely beguiling. "The Big Thief" (1953) emphasizes the mood of tragedy that often infused the show, and concerns a search for a gang who lure doctors to house calls, and then rob them. It ends with Friday shooting a young villain—his first kill—and trying to live with the consequences. As he distractedly lights two cigarettes at once, he mutters, "You kinda wonder if maybe there wasn't some other way...."

Further Reading

The most insightful recent research on *Dragnet* is by R. Barton Palmer: see "'The story you are about to see is true': Dragnet, Film Noir and Postwar Realism" in Solange Davin and Rhona Jackson (eds.), *Television Criticism* (Intellect, 2008), reworked from his chapter "Dragnet, Film Noir and Postwar Realism" in Steven Sanders and Aeon Skoble (eds.), *The Philosophy of TV Noir* (University Press of Kentucky, 2008). Jason Mittell's chapter on the show in *Genre and Television: From Cop Shows to Cartoons in American Culture* (Routledge, 2004), brilliantly places *Dragnet* in genre history. The Sue Turnbull essay mentioned above is "The Hook and the Look: *CSI* and the Aesthetics of Television Crime Series"; it can be found in Michael Allen (ed.), *Reading CSI: Crime TV Under the Microscope* (I.B. Tauris, 2007). The best "pop" study of Jack Webb is Michael J. Hayde's *My Name's Friday: The Unauthorized but True Story of Dragnet and the Films of Jack Webb* (Cumberland House, 2001); the other main example, Daniel Moyer and Eugene Alvarez's, *Just the Facts, Ma'am: The Authorized Biography of Jack Webb* (Seven Locks Press, 2001), is, like most authorized bios, a little fawning. For background, Robert J. Thompson's *Prime Time Prime Movers* (Little, Brown, 1992) is a "guide to important TV creators," and includes Webb; also the *Film Noir Foundation Newsletter* (see http://www.filmnoirfoundation.org/home.html) is good for noir context, and has included pieces on *Dragnet*. Finally, there are various unpublished dissertations, for example, "Images of Police Work and Mass Media Propaganda: The Case of 'Dragnet'" by Charles Anthony Varni (Washington State University, 1974).

CHAPTER 2

Highway Patrol
(Syndicated, 1955–59)
RONALD WILSON

Each episode of *Highway Patrol* opens with an authoritative voice-over narration (delivered by Art Gilmore) that stresses the social function of state policing efforts: "Whenever the laws of any state are broken, a duly authorized organization swings into action. It may be called the State Police, State Troopers, Militia, the Rangers ... or the Highway Patrol. These are the stories of the men whose training, skill and courage have enforced and preserved our state laws."

Immediately following the voice-over and the opening title sequence, an on-screen acknowledgement attests to the series' authenticity:

> We gratefully acknowledge the cooperation of Commissioner Bernard R. Caldwell and the California Highway Patrol for the technical advice and assistance, which made the authentic production of this program possible.

And finally, at the conclusion of every episode, the actor Broderick Crawford, who plays the starring role of Chief of Police Dan Mathews, appears as himself, not in character, to directly address the viewers by thanking them for watching and inviting them to tune in for an even more exciting episode next week. Before the closing credits, he provides a terse public service announcement that changes weekly, often with a gruffly ironic aside: "The clowns at the circus are real funny, but on the highway they're murder!" The use of such extra-narrative elements in *Highway Patrol* obviously served to promote and vindicate state policing efforts in the 1950s, while the series' "unique selling point" was the way it moved police television from primarily urban-centered locations to the state highways.

Highway Patrol thus extended and reinforced the conservatism of *Dragnet* (originally broadcast on the radio from 1949 and then, from 1951 to 1959, on television). Like *Dragnet*, *Highway Patrol* served as a form of public-image management, and the emphasis on police as public servants is germane to the argument put forward by cultural historian Kathleen Battles in regard to the reform image of policing during the 1930s; she suggests that law enforcement agencies used mass media (radio and, later, television), to "sharpen their own self definition as public servants whose goal was to protect citizens from crime and disorder."[1]

Such an image of the police was in keeping with the formula of "good guys vs. bad guys" prevalent on American television during the 1950s. In crime television this was established in series depicting municipal (*Dragnet*), state (*Highway Patrol, State Trooper*), and federal (*Treasury Men in Action, The Untouchables*) policing. As the opening of each episode of *Highway Patrol* made clear, the California Highway Patrol served as technical advisors, just as the LAPD had performed the same function for *Dragnet*. Indeed, the original idea for *Highway Patrol* was suggested by Commissioner Bernard Caldwell, who told the civilian public relations officer for the California Highway Patrol to "get us a show like *Dragnet*."[2]

Highway Patrol's popularity in the 1950s can be partially attributed to its mode of distribution: it was a first-run syndicated television program. The three main television networks (NBC, CBS, and ABC) controlled programming in the prime-time schedule (roughly defined as the hours between 7:30 p.m. and 11 p.m.). As a result, independent non-affiliated stations needed syndicated filmed programs to fill broadcasting hours outside the prime-time block. Since the networks in the 1950s mostly relied on live programming, filmed series allowed syndication entrepreneurs to flourish with product that could easily be placed into a programming schedule. Hal Roach, Jr., was one such pioneer; his *Racket Squad* was initially a syndicated series (1950) that was later picked up by CBS (1951–53).

But the most prolific of the first-run syndication television pioneers was Ziv Television Programs, Inc. Frederick Ziv, the company's co-founder, was originally a leader in radio syndication, producing pre-recorded half-hour radio shows that were circulated to stations across America and Canada. When in 1948 Ziv crossed over into the nascent field of television, one of his most popular radio shows, *The Cisco Kid*, a Western, became a syndicated television series. Ziv followed this with many syndicated crime programs, including *Boston Blackie* (1951–53), *I Led 3 Lives* (1953–56), and *Highway Patrol* (1955–59), all of which demonstrated his skill at maximizing audiences and keeping costs down. For example, the fact that *Highway Patrol* located the action outdoors appealed to both rural and urban populations at a time when network television programming was largely targeted at city audiences (*Dragnet*, for instance, was set in Los Angeles and rarely ventured beyond that environment). It had the additional advantage of allowing cheaper on-location shooting, which became a hallmark of Ziv series.[3]

The jurisdiction of the California Highway Patrol extended only to traffic and motor vehicle violations. For the purposes of television, it was necessary to adopt a more generic approach. As a result, the remit of the fictional Highway Patrol included such crimes as kidnapping (in one episode a computer the size of a small truck is held for ransom), extortion, drug smuggling, prison breaks, arson, robbery, assault, racketeering,

Highway Patrol's opening roadblock credits created a sense of action-packed urgency in a non-urban setting. The show is often credited with starting the trend for fast cutting.

murder, and (to some extent) motor vehicle violations. The state and area of the Highway Patrol's authority are never clearly identified, and all state trooper regalia (uniforms, cars, insignia) are indistinct. The result is that any viewer in the United States could identify with the Highway Patrol as "their" highway patrol, rather than as a distinctly recognizable regional organization.

Highway Patrol was also innovative because of its narrative structure, as stipulated in "General Information for Writers on *Highway Patrol*," the format bible that Ziv Television provided to writers for the series.[4] The aim is stipulated at the beginning: "This is basically an action documentary series. We take great care not to imitate any of the other well-known police, detective, sheriff, or district attorney type shows that are on the air."[5] By distinguishing the "action documentary" quality of the program, the producers clearly indicated that *Highway Patrol* narratives would stress action over police procedure, at the same time creating a crime series that had a factual basis. This was a definite shift away from the *Dragnet* model, though *Highway Patrol* would have its own version of Sgt. Friday in the person of Chief Dan Mathews. "Our crooks are clever; the problem insurmountable, and Mathews solves it. [*sic*] We do not like to have our criminals caught or the crime solved because thieves fall out. It must be solved by Mathews thinking and using good police work."[6]

Mathews is an intriguing character for the way in which he encompasses gruffness and sensitivity: a dichotomy perhaps reflected in his look—he has a face that says he's "seen it all," but he wears smart suits and a fedora. Broderick Crawford was 43 years old when he took the role, and had established himself as a movie actor of quality—having won an Academy Award for his performance in *All the King's Men* (1949). This reputation allowed him to bargain for a contract that paid him ten percent of the gross receipts for *Highway Patrol*—which was promptly spent on "hard living" according to the Hollywood gossip magazines. It also meant he had a certain "brand awareness" with the public, making it easier for him to be accepted as the show's anchor, despite his far-from-matinee-idol looks.

Each episode promotes Dan Mathews' "quick thinking" and "courage" as the most likely means of stopping the criminals, and Crawford brought a surprising emotional intensity to the role. Ziv's format bible is specific about his character: "Dan has no personal life, so we don't talk about wives, children, girl friends, nor does he at any time have any personal relationship with any of the characters. This does not mean, however, that he cannot know his officers and their families. It is very important that he is not written tough. He can fight and enter gunplay. He walks very well and we prefer not to have him run unless absolutely necessary."[7] The parallels with Friday are obvious, but so are the differences.

The crimes that Mathews is called upon to solve typically involve formula stories about escaped convicts, or thieves on the run after a heist. But a significant number are themed around car crime, reflecting the growth in automobile production in the U.S. in the post-war years, and the fact that many more highway felonies were being committed. Examples include "Reckless Driving" (1955), a story involving speeding and driving without a license; "Hit and Run" (1956), about a woman driver who doesn't stop after a hitting a pedestrian; "Car Theft" (1956), concerning a gang who disguise their stolen cars by swapping number plates from salvage yards; and "Revenge" (1959), about a young man who wants to kill the person responsible for the death of his father in a car crash.[8] However, it should be said that expensive stunts and explosions were a no-no, due to the parsimonious budgeting of Ziv TV.

Other subject matter touched upon "youth delinquency," the moral panic of the moment, though this was never so pronounced as in *Dragnet*. The most notable example was "Motorcycle A" (1956), about a café owner who gets fed up with visits from biker gangs—clearly a reference to the movie *The Wild One* (1953): "They come zoomin' into town just achin' to start trouble. Last year, just eight months ago, fifty of 'em swooped down on this place. Scarin' kids to death, breakin' up our property...." (That particular show featured a cameo by a young Clint Eastwood.[9]) Other youth-themed episodes included "Hot Rod" (1956), about a thief and his younger brother who make their getaway in a souped-up roadster, and several about the dangers of drugs; usually heroin, but also marijuana.

Indeed, insofar as these shows were tapping into an interest in youth culture, they can be seen as a kind of bridge into what would become known as "the American Road movie." Jack Kerouac's *On the Road* was published in 1957, and the romance of the road was increasingly becoming a trope in pop culture, culminating in the great existential road movies of the hippie era (such as *Easy Rider* [1969], *Two Lane Blacktop* [1971], and *Vanishing Point* [1971]). The politics of *Highway Patrol* were obviously hugely different to these, but in terms of its wide-open, low-budget, aesthetic, and its "highway atmosphere" (complete with truck stops and greasy spoons) there were similarities. Indeed, the figure of the highway cop was central to future films—perhaps reaching its apogee in *Elektra Glide in Blue* (1973).

Formalist properties were also notable in *Highway Patrol*. For example, other Ziv Television series (*Sea Hunt, I Led 3 Lives*) often utilized voice-over narrators to provide exposition between scenes; this had the virtue of moving the story along rapidly without the need for extraneous dialogue. The use of this device in *Highway Patrol* not only contributed to the sense of authenticity but also shaped the narrative structure. According to the "Information for Writers" document, "The opening voice-over in act one is in two parts: The first paragraph is a statement of law enforcement in general; the Highway Patrol in particular. The second paragraph talks about the crime we are about to see."[10] Thus, Art Gilmore's authoritative, third-person narration acts as a bridge between criminal activity and police investigation and links the series to semi-documentary crime films of the late 1940s such as *House on 92nd Street* (1945), *Call Northside 777* (1948), and *The Naked City* (1948).

Toy merchandise for *Highway Patrol*, such as the "Gyro Siren Car," often emphasized "modern" policing technology. Patrol Chief Dan Mathews (Broderick Crawford) is pictured on the top right.

The production of *Highway Patrol* also reflected its emphasis on action. The shooting schedule adhered to a truncated format: one or two days on location and one day on the production stage. The opening of act one would be an exterior scene "that allows footage to be shot for title, music, etc. The same applies to the closing of act two. The closing can be an interior scene if absolutely necessary but we definitely prefer an exterior."[11] This rather breathless location shooting typically occurred around the San Fernando Valley and Simi Valley in California. In one early episode, economy of means is evident in a three-minute robbery-murder-escape sequence, filmed in a single take.

The series was also notable for its editing technique, which made effective use of cut-aways and rapid edits to create dramatic urgency. The writer's guide stresses the way in these techniques should be used: "We do not use any opticals with the exception of a dissolve indicating a long time lapse, which necessitates bridge scenes. Do not indicate dissolves, fades or other opticals. Because we do not use dissolves in our format it is necessary that the writer keep this in mind and use cut away scenes to get people from one place to another, but every scene must move the story."[12] The emphasis on "cut aways" was reinforced by having scenes alternate between police and criminals. Much later, Frederick Ziv claimed that the idea of using rapid editing came about because of Broderick Crawford's acting style and vocal delivery: "He spoke so fast and moved so fast that we edited our film accordingly. Today we hear about quick cuts, but the quick cutting technique really was first put into television film in *Highway Patrol*. And if you look at previous television film, you'll find that it is not cut the way *Highway Patrol* is cut. It started a whole new trend."[13]

This technique is established in the opening title sequence of the series, which begins with a traveling shot along an open highway, the camera following a car. The "General Information for Writers" document stipulates that the music accompanying this opening shot is the "STACCATO PORTION OF THE THEME. The speed of the car to be consistent with the tempo of the THEME."[14] The traveling shot is an aerial view (most likely from a helicopter) that reveals a police barricade and then cuts abruptly to a montage of short dramatic scenes from the episode itself. This short teaser sequence, accompanied by Art Gilmore's voice-over, was a mark of the series' innovative style and made a significant contribution to its popularity.

A focus on police communication technology helped bring these formalist themes together. By the very nature of their work, the officers in *Highway Patrol* need to use in-car radios to maintain contact with each other. This established a kind of call-and-response model of modern policing that constructs the police as an organized, coherent, and efficient law enforcement agency. In that sense, there was a link with such radio crime docudramas of the 1930s as *Gang Busters*, *Calling All Cars*, and *G-Men*. Kathleen Battles has argued that "the changing relationships between time and space in police work [through the use of radio technology] found its way into the narrative structure of the [radio] docudramas as they spun their tales of criminal apprehension."[15]

Battles goes on to suggest that these radio dramas constructed the "idea of inevitable apprehension—the dragnet effect," achieved by the police use of radio and transportation technologies, which "collapsed the relationship between space and time in their practices."[16] *Highway Patrol* created a similar effect by its visual focus on cars and helicopters and its foregrounding of the constant talk heard on police car radios, on telephones and on the headquarters' intercom system.

Thus, whereas other 1950s crime television programs emphasized the footwork necessary in urban police procedural activities, *Highway Patrol*'s rural setting required greater use of technology. In this way the series constructed an idea of the constant communicative presence of law enforcement—a web from which there can be no escape, regardless of how far into the desert a felon might drive. The centralized control base for these activities is the Highway Patrol headquarters, which instigates and coordinates the pursuit of the criminals. The taut, terse quality of the two-way radio banter between the patrol and headquarters was typified by Dan Mathews' barking lines like, "Cancel the 3-11, 10-4!" This specialized language helped to underline Battles' "dragnet effect" by showing police efficiency in using modern technology to catch the criminals. The use of such jargon and Broderick Crawford's vocal delivery prompted television historian Hal Erickson to remark that "Brod Crawford did not act on *Highway Patrol*; *Highway Patrol* acted like Brod Crawford."[17]

In *Highway Patrol*, just as communication technology increased the likelihood of criminal capture, the cop cars and helicopters reflected the speed and efficiency of modern police methods. The police automobiles featured in *Highway Patrol* were 1955 Buick Century two-door sedans, the same model used by the California Highway Patrol. These models were not made available to the general public and were therefore unique to law enforcement, and had a certain exclusive glamour. The helicopters were made by Bell and were similar to those that had done service in the Korean War. In particular, the Bell 47 is today regarded as a design classic for its "dragonfly" appearance. Some of the more ambitious airborne scenes in *Highway Patrol* involved a slightly terrified-looking Chief Mathews hanging out of the door and shooting at bad guys.

Highway Patrol ran for four seasons as a syndicated series of 156 episodes. Ziv wanted to do a fifth season but according to John L. Hawkins, Broderick Crawford declined. When asked why the still-popular police series ended production, Crawford quipped, "We ran out of crimes."[18] (Thereafter, he returned to making movies, and attempted, unsuccessfully, to beat his alcohol dependency.) However, syndication enabled the series to entertain viewers long after its initial run—often under the alternative title of *Ten-4*. *Highway Patrol* was also enormously popular in international markets, particularly in Argentina, Germany, Italy, Japan, Portugal, Spain, and the UK. It aired in 17 languages in 71 countries.[19]

On the back of its popularity in the United States, where it attracted big sponsors and high ratings, a number of imitation police series were introduced. They included *Code Three* (Syndicated, 1957), *Harbor Command* (Syndicated, 1957), *Sheriff of Cochise* (Syndicated, 1956–58), *State Trooper* (Syndicated, 1957), *The Everglades* (Syndicated, 1961—concerning Florida's Everglades County Patrol), and *Border Patrol* (Syndicated, 1959). None achieved the success of the original. The cops-in-cars trope was affectionately sent-up in the sitcom *Car 54, Where Are You?* (NBC, 1961–63). Another indication of the popularity of the series was the amount of merchandising sold to young Dan Mathews wannabes: everything from comic books to toy guns, and even a replica of a two-way car radio. As for Mathews himself, he could never be marketed in quite the same way as Friday—this was one unorthodox hero who was just too unorthodox—and there would be no career in the music business for Crawford in the Jack Webb mold.

The extent of the popularity of *Highway Patrol* is also reflected in high-profile parodies. In 1960, *Mad* magazine published a satirical comic strip called "Highway Squad." The opening illustration shows a television on which can be read, "This program is dedicated to the officers and men of the highway squads throughout the nation who courageously keep our roads clear of the vicious law-breakers that terrorize decent American citizens and pedestrians with their criminal acts." The illustration below the TV set shows officers in the process of interrogating a farmer by the side of the road: "You **vicious criminal!** You were doing 10 miles an hour. Don't you know there's a school crossing 63 miles up ahead, and you're supposed to slow down to 5?!" and "What's the idea of terrorizing American motorists and pedestrians with your criminal act of throwing a **gum wrapper** from your car?!" The magazine also parodies Broderick Crawford as Lt. Don Mildew whose initial dialogue bubble is "Growl! Rowf! Arf! Arf! R-r-ruff!" followed by a squad officer commenting, "Oh! It's only Don Mildew! I guess our TV viewers are right! He does bark and growl, and it is hard to understand him!" Later Crawford helped satirize his own image on television: in 1977, the popular late-night comedy series *Saturday Night Live* provided a skit with an aging Crawford reprising his role as Dan Mathews interrogating Jack Kerouac (John Belushi):

> MATHEWS: Tell me—who was in the car with you?
> KEROUAC: Neal Cassady, Lawrence Ferlinghetti—
> MATHEWS: Kerouac? Now, wait a minute—Kerouac, Kerouac…. Hey, I think I read that book you wrote!
> KEROUAC: *On the Road*?
> MATHEWS: Yeah, *On the Road*! You know, that book makes you out a very unsafe driver, kid.

Parodies notwithstanding, the series' influence on television is best exemplified by the careers of two individuals who worked on it behind the scenes: Gene Roddenberry and Quinn Martin. Under the pseudonym "Robert Wesley," Roddenberry was a scriptwriter on the series. He had been an officer with the Los Angeles Police Department between 1949 and 1956, had worked on *Dragnet*, and was probably employed to help re-create factual situations that would be suitable for *Highway Patrol* (see chapter on *Dragnet*). Quinn Martin served as audio advisor during the first two seasons, and it is easy to see the influence that *Highway Patrol* had on Quinn Martin's subsequent television work as a producer, especially in the use of voice-over narration and the alternation of crime scenes with investigation (see chapter on *The F.B.I.*).

In conclusion, perhaps the most enduring legacy of *Highway Patrol* is its articulation of authenticity by means of its emphasis on the way in which technology made inevitable the eventual capture of criminals. This engendered an exciting, low-fi, "action documentary" aesthetic that would be much-copied. In many ways *Highway Patrol* was the logical by-product of *Dragnet* and simply extended policing to the hinterlands of the American high-ways during the Eisenhower years. But in among the police-approved, conservative mor-alizing, there are hints of something more liberal: namely, the romance of the road movie.

Recommended Episodes

The premiere episode of *Highway Patrol*, "Prison Break" (1955), is emblematic of many of the elements noted in the "General Information for Writers on *Highway Patrol*" provided by Ziv Television. Beginning with a suggested "exterior scene" the episode documents the capture of a ruthless escaped convict. The voice-over narration bridges scenes with relevant information that helps maintain the narrative momentum, while the editing moves the story forward by using quick cut-away scenes to get characters from one place to another. Every shot focuses on action of some kind: within the 30-minute time span of the program, we experience an assault on a patrolman, the hijacking of a school bus, and a final showdown with Mathews, which results in the killing of the convict. By contrast, "Reckless Driving" (1955) provides an example of *Highway Patrol*'s occasional forays into public safety aware-ness. In this episode the "criminal" is the habitual offender who has violated numerous traffic regulations. Mathews and the Highway Patrol begin a series of roadside checks on a newly constructed stretch of highway that has seen several accidents. While questioning traffic violators Mathews provides the analogy of the motor vehicle being similar to a loaded gun: "Your car outweighs this gun by four thousand pounds and it's loaded when you turn the key in the ignition…. Remember that, when your foot gets heavy on the accelerator. Think of it as a trigger on a gun—a four thousand pound gun!" Crawford's aphorism at episode's end continues the analogy: "And remember, the careless driver isn't driving his car—he's aiming it."

Further Reading

The scholarly literature pertaining to *Highway Patrol* and Ziv Television is surprisingly scant. Morleen Getz Rouse's unpublished PhD dissertation, *A History of the F. W. Ziv Radio and Television Syndication Companies: 1930–1960* (University of Michigan, 1976), remains the most authoritative account of the business side of things. It provides no fewer than 125 pages of appendices consisting of archival photo-stats of promotional materials, letters, and memoranda. In comparison, Barbara Moore's informative essay "The Cisco Kid and Friends: The Syndication of Television Series from 1948 to 1952," in *The Journal of Popular Film and Television*, vol. 8, issue 1, 1980 (Taylor and Francis), is a compact overview of the early history of syndicated television and its importance in the nascent network era. Likewise, Christopher Anderson's entry on "Ziv Television Programs, Inc." on the http://www.museum.tv website is worth reading. And even though Kathleen Battles' *Calling All Cars: Radio Dragnets and the Technology of Policing* (University of Minnesota Press, 2010) covers 1930s radio crime docudramas, her thesis concerning the image of policing and the "dragnet effect" is particularly applicable to *Highway Patrol* and the medium of television during the 1950s. In addition, the *Highway Patrol TV Website* http://highwaypatroltv.com provides a wealth of informative articles, photos, a complete episode log, and Ziv documents such as the "General Information for Writers on *Highway Patrol*" and the "Opening Format for *Highway Patrol*" script.

CHAPTER 3

Naked City

(ABC, 1958–59, 1960–63)

RONALD WILSON

Writing in 1966 three years after the series ended, television critic David Boroff stated that *Naked City* was "Chekhovian in its rueful gaze at people in the clutch of disaster."[1] Boroff's invocation of the Russian author is particularly apt because this police crime series was unlike the others represented in this volume. Although it was ostensibly a police procedural, and its only recurring characters were police detectives, the show was less about the investigation of crimes than it was about the people who committed the crimes. Often those people were ordinary folk, forced into doing bad things for good reasons. Every episode ended with the omniscient narrator (voiced by actor Lawrence Dobkin) intoning to the audience, "There are eight million stories in the Naked City ... this has been one of them."

Naked City's realistic, socially aware approach was further enhanced by the fact that 75 percent of the series was shot on location in New York City, lending it a documentary-like televisuality. This stylistic trope meant that the city itself became, in essence, a recurring character, to which each episode's opening and closing narration gave a voice. That urban narrative voice provides a link between the other "naked cities" that served as a meta-narrative for the television series' close examination of the human condition: specifically, a book of photographs and a feature film.

Both the volume *Naked City* (1945) by photographer Weegee (aka Arthur Fellig) and the Mark Hellinger–produced semi-documentary film *The Naked City* (Universal-International, 1948), directed by Jules Dassin, provide a narrative template for the television series' sense of streetwise atmosphere and urban characterization. Weegee's book is almost transgressive; its series of photos depicting the nocturnal exploits of New York City eccentrics, criminals, police officers, firemen, and ordinary citizens. Though crime photos only constitute a relatively small portion of the book, they are among the most startling in their depiction of murder victims, excited onlookers, and arrested suspects. Weegee's accompanying text is written in a conversational, ironic tone that gives the still photographs a narrative flow as the reader moves through the naked city from "Sunday morning in Manhattan" to "Harlem." Likewise, the Mark Hellinger film uses on-location photography to depict the course of a police investigation as it ebbs and flows across the urban landscape of New York. Hellinger himself provides the voice-over narration and offers a wry, down-to-earth tone throughout the film. It is the narration and the urban locations that establish a direct connection between the earlier "naked cities" and the television series.

The Naked City (at this point the title included the definite article) originally aired on Tuesday nights on ABC from 1958 to 1959 as a series of half-hour episodes. Producer Herbert Leonard, inspired by seeing the Mark Hellinger film on re-release, conceived the program as a collection of vignettes about the city itself. According to television historian Mark Alvey, Leonard imagined the series "not as a police procedural but rather as a dramatic anthology with a police backdrop ... the series was never intended as a show about detectives or their activities, but rather as a series about the city and the people of New York."[2] In this sense the original concept seems closer to Weegee's book than to the Hellinger film, which places criminal investigation at its center.

However, Leonard's concept ran counter to what the studio Screen Gems (Columbia Pictures' television subsidiary) felt the series should be: a crime-focused police show, in the manner of *Dragnet* (NBC, 1951–59) and its copyists. When Screen Gems president Ralph Cohn (nephew of Harry Cohn, co-founder of Columbia Pictures) first read the pilot script, he complained that it did not pay enough attention to the detectives. Cohn stipulated that the script would be fine for a *Playhouse 90* or even *Studio One* production (both were anthology programs of the 1950s) "but since this is a series, and basically a series about two cops ... we feel that it is important that these two characters emerge as the dominant characteristics of the pilot."[3] But Leonard resisted, and the result was a show that took the conventions initiated by *Dragnet*, and subverted them.

The writing of Stirling Silliphant further enhanced Leonard's vision. During the initial 1958-59 season, Silliphant wrote 31 of the 39 episodes, including the contested pilot. Silliphant was already a veteran writer for several anthology series, as well as for crime films such as *Five Against the House* (Phil Karlson, 1955), *Nightfall* (Jacques Tourneur, 1957), and *The Lineup* (Don Siegel, 1958). His television work displayed a fondness for self-contained stories dealing with complex characters, which would be a primary asset for *The Naked City*. (In 1960 the producer-writer team would initiate another semi-anthology series, *Route 66*, with a similar conceptual framework: two young men—the recurring characters—drive around America, encountering different occupations, characters and situations week after week.)

The original half-hour *The Naked City* (1958–59) featured a pair of detectives from the 65th Precinct. An older veteran detective, Lt. Dan Muldoon (John McIntire), was teamed with a younger idealistic detective, Jim Halloran (James Franciscus). Other recurring characters included Officer Frank Arcaro (Harry Bellaver) and Lt. Mike Parker (Horace McMahon). As previously noted, the series placed much less emphasis on police work and the police themselves than on the dramatic situations in which each episode's guest star found himself or herself—which was counter-intuitive bearing in mind Franciscus' obvious matinee idol good looks, which could easily have become a major draw for the show (he would later forge a career in movies like *Marooned, Beneath the Planet of the Apes* and *The Valley of Gwangi*). This balancing act was not easy to achieve. Stirling Silliphant characterized the show as achieving a "50/50" balance between its anthology and police series dimensions.[4] Another writer on the series, Sy Salkowitz, stated that "*Naked City* was not a cop show. It was a criminal show, because the way you wrote *Naked City* was to get into the head of the criminal and tell why he committed the crime."[5]

The early shows typically opened with a guest star committing a felony; after that, scenes alternated between the criminals and the police—a technique that had been used successfully in *Highway Patrol* (syndicated, 1955–59). (The pre-credit prologue established the nature of the crime while an accompanying voice-over provided background information

The police detectives in *Naked City* were secondary to the character-centered Chekhovian-like dramas representative of the New Frontier television of the early 1960s. The title credit was accompanied with a piercing brass fanfare.

so as to rationalize the act itself. Following the first commercial break, the detectives appear.) It was a format that would be taken up by the hour-long *Naked City*s later. As Salkowitz noted concerning the writing for the series, "You had to bring your action so that it was like a V, [the police and the criminal] starting from opposite points, and [meeting] at the bottom, [when] the criminal was apprehended."[6] Though cop and criminal eventually confront each other at the end of the episode, the proportion of scenes decidedly favored the criminals. The snappy jazz soundtrack kept things moving briskly.

Herbert Leonard himself narrated the first season episodes (in an obvious homage to Mark Hellinger's voice-over narration of the feature film). Leonard emphasized the importance of the on-location shooting in his opening remarks: "Ladies and gentleman, you are about to see 'The Naked City.' I'm Bert Leonard, the producer. This story was not photographed in a studio. Quite the contrary, the actors played out their roles in the streets and the buildings of New York itself." Thus, the image of New York was very different to that of Los Angeles in *Dragnet*, and to the "postcard effect" images so often relied upon by future cop shows (for example, the scene-setting shots in *CSI*). This vision of the metropolis was definitely not framed as a tourist destination.[7] Acknowledging both a semi-documentary style (the on-location photography) and a fictional narrative (the actors), Leonard's voice-over implies that the viewer is about to experience a unique television drama. Moreover, as the narration is developed further in the series it establishes a moral position in relation to the events that are about to unfold.

Early guest stars included Martin Balsam, Harry Guardino, Al Lewis, Lawrence Tierney,

Dina Douglas (mother of Michael Douglas), Peter Falk (the future Columbo), and Jack Klugman (the future Quincy). Storylines relied on pulp staples like extortion, robbery and mob violence, but also encompassed "hot button" topics like youth delinquency. In the 1959 episode "Hey, Teach!" detective Halloran goes undercover as a teacher to catch a teenage killer. The voice-over tells us that some kids' only aim in life is to "resist education and defy all authority," while Lt. Muldoon laments: "In my day, it was the schoolmaster who was feared, not the pupil...."

The first season of *The Naked City* was neither critically nor commercially successful. Many found the stories too downbeat and depressing. The lack of the genre structure that was typical of *Dragnet*-style cop shows and the mixture of anthology and series formats confused many critics and viewers. One of the series' early sponsors, Quaker Oats, complained to Herbert Leonard that the series was too "seamy" and not an appropriate program environment for their product.[8] Leonard stated that he had no intention of making changes and that perhaps they should pull out, which they did, to be replaced by the tobacco company Brown & Williamson. (Tobacco advertising had been a mainstay of *Dragnet*, though *The Naked City* did not offer nearly the same macho associations.)

Some critics also disliked the downplaying of the cop roles. *TV Guide* suggested that the detective "heroes" were often no more than "supporting players in a melodrama often centered around some anti-social New Yorker." The magazine further recommended that *The Naked City* "abandon its premise of featuring New York City as its star."[9] Clearly, the kind of "star" they were looking for was along the lines of Jack Webb as Sgt. Joe Friday in *Dragnet*, who had been on the front cover of celebrity magazines, and had garnered a high profile in various other media: but *The Naked City* was never going to render that kind of model of the star vehicle.

Another problem with the initial season was its half-hour length, a format which, in 1958, the networks were in the process of replacing with hour-long episodes, particularly for dramatic series. The logic was that this longer format allowed for more generation of atmosphere, narrative tension, and character development—along with allowing more space for ads. Suddenly the old *The Naked City* was looking dated. Its failure to compete in the Nielsen rankings was a sad comment that something a little bit experimental and different was not going to survive, and caused the show to be cancelled after its first season.

Yet, in the fall of 1960, to the surprise of many, *Naked City* returned to television in a one-hour format. ("The" was dropped from the title to distinguish it from both its predecessor and the feature film.) It would go on at 10 p.m. to emphasize its supposedly adult and sophisticated nature. According to Mark Alvey, ABC was spurred into financing the pilot because the sponsors, Brown & Williamson, were interested in reviving the show.[10] At first Herbert Leonard was hesitant to become involved again, primarily because he and Stirling Silliphant were working on their new project, *Route 66* (CBS, 1960–64). But Leonard agreed to be the executive producer with Silliphant serving as executive story consultant, and eventually came to relish the challenge of his new role: comparing the half-hour to the hour formats, he noted that, with the longer form "you can tell a story rather than a situation."[11]

There were cast changes. James Franciscus wanted to move to California, and anyway didn't want to stick around in a show where he was forever second-string, and John McIntire's character had been killed off by the mob late in the first season. In their place, new cops Detective Adam Flint (Paul Burke) and Lt. Mike Parker (Horace McMahon) took over.

Detective Frank Arcaro (Harry Bellaver), Detective Adam Flint (Paul Burke), and Lieutenant Mike Parker (Horace McMahon)—the only regular cast members in the series—look to be deep in thought (Screen Gems/Shelle Productions/The Kobal Collection).

The one-hour length also allowed for more notable guest stars, who included Jack Warden, Carroll O'Connor, Eli Wallach, Diahann Carroll, and Rip Torn. (Indeed, the reissue DVDs make much of the actors who played supporting roles—big and small—including a veritable roll-call of future Hollywood A-listers, for example, Robert Redford, Christopher Walken, Robert Culp, Gene Hackman, Dustin Hoffman, William Shatner, Peter Fonda, and Martin Sheen.[12]) *Naked City* seasons 2, 3 and 4 are notable for the way in which they increasingly became magnets for stars with ever-bigger reputations, thus anticipating the kind of casting that would typify *Columbo* (1968–78) and *Police Story* (1973–78).

In addition, a host of top screenwriters, many of them victims of the Hollywood black-list, worked on the series, among them Arnold Manoff (writing as "Joel Carpenter"), Ben Maddow, and Abram S. Ginnes. Leonard was in awe: "These guys were serious writers deal-ing with thematic material, humanistic stories with overt social agendas."[13] Accomplished directors such as Tay Garnett, Laslo Benedek, Arthur Hiller, Paul Wendkos, and Lamont Johnson often directed these "humanistic stories," which now ramped-up the "mitigating circumstances" trope to maximum effect.

The *Naked City* revamp proved to be a winning formula, and critical acclaim followed. The show became part of the vanguard of what Mary Ann Watson has termed the "New Frontier character drama," a label applied to various programs screened during the John F. Kennedy era.[14] In 1961 Kennedy appointed Newton Minow chairman of the Federal Com-munications Commission; in his first major speech as chairman Minow had described American network television as a "vast wasteland." In what was seen as primarily a response to Minow, the networks began (particularly in the 1961-62 season) to introduce programs that showed a heightened social awareness; they included *The Defenders, Ben Casey, Dr. Kildare, East Side West Side*, and *The Eleventh Hour*. These hour-long series were charac-terized by the liberal point of view maintained by their primarily young and idealistic central characters. Such shows became a kind of "cultural forum," in the words of academics Horace Newcomb and Paul Hirsch, and as an integral theme, the characterization of minori-ties was often more fully developed than had previously been seen on network television.[15]

Examples of "New Frontierism" in the 1960s version of *Naked City* included storylines that took a sympathetic line on middle class poverty (a family robs friends in order to keep up appearances in "Take and Put," 1961), loneliness (a woman is duped by an escort service in "To Dream Without Sleep," 1961), homeless people as victims of violent crime ("Tomb-stone for a Derelict," 1961), alcoholism and post-traumatic stress ("The Face of the Enemy," 1962), and mental illness ("Portrait of a Painter," "Today the Man Who Kills Ants Is Coming," both 1962). Which is not to say that seasons 2, 3 and 4 didn't have their fair share of tales about heists, kidnappings, and gangland slayings.

Above all, the character of Detective Adam Flint epitomized the new liberal attitude. With his heart-on-sleeve idealism, he often functions as cop, caseworker, psychiatrist, and friend. Compared to other television cops of the 1950s Flint is more interested in the moti-vation for and circumstances of a crime than in arresting the criminal. He is usually at odds with Lt. Parker who represents, so to speak, "the conservative conscience of the 65th Precinct." Though Parker is often as compassionate as Flint, he is continually more skeptical in his assessment of criminal intent. According to Mark Alvey, "In case after case, Flint's deductions, compassion, and insight are opposed by Parker, but lead to a correct solution to a crime.... Ever the voice of experience, Parker must walk the line between procedure and compassion."[16] Parker continually criticizes Flint for his "spending precious time playing Sigmund Freud" and reminds the young detective that they are not social workers but policemen. Alvey concludes, "If any one motif characterizes *Naked City*'s depiction of police work, it is Flint's charitable impulses, his commitment to lost causes and concern for under-dogs."[17]

With this ideological background in mind, was *Naked City* antithetical to *Dragnet*?[18] It is an interesting argument to make, though in retrospect, *Dragnet* was a more nuanced show than many critics have allowed (see chapter on same). The website for the Paley Center for Media contains a blog from curator David Bushman titled "*Dragnet* v. *Naked City*: A Great Debate," in which Bushman suggests that *Dragnet* was the opposite pole to

Naked City in its approach to policing.[19] Mark Alvey reinforces this idea by comparing a speech by Sgt. Friday in *Dragnet* with one by Adam Flint in *Naked City*, both concerning the role of the modern cop: unsurprisingly, Flint is "more thoughtful, and human, [recognizing] the flaws in society, and the fallibility of the policeman."[20]

Another comparison can be made concerning the use of voice-over narration in both series. In *Dragnet* this is delivered by Friday himself, who relates "just the facts" concerning a criminal case. This style of presentation is often characterized by information of the type collected in police files, offered in terse sentences relating only relevant details in the form of dates, times, locations, as well as statutes and police procedure. For example, in the opening narration to the 1956 episode "The Big Smoke," Friday states:

> This is the city, Los Angeles, California. I work here. I'm a cop. It was Tuesday, August 10th. It was warm in Los Angeles. We were working the day watch out of Homicide Division. My partner is Frank Smith. The boss is Captain Norman. My name is Friday. We had gotten a call that a 72-year-old man and his invalid daughter had been brutally beaten. There was no lead to the identity of their assailant. We had to find them [theme music cue].

Compare this with the voice-over in *Naked City*, delivered by uncredited actor Lawrence Dobkin. Here, analogy, anecdotes, and metaphors are used to address not the police, but the criminal protagonist and their circumstances. The narration is not personified and establishes a "voice of God" quality through its ability to see events through a uniquely objective perspective. Another aspect is its emphasis on parables, often multicultural in nature, that serve to parallel the circumstances of the episode's protagonist. For example, in "One, Two, Three Rita Rakahowski" (1963) the opening narration relates the sacrificial killing practices of several African tribes when their king is ill or becomes too old to serve them. This account is almost Fraserian in its documentation and is spoken over the backdrop of the New York City skyline as the camera focuses in on workers unloading stock from a warehouse onto a truck. The voice-over implicitly provides an analogy between the tribes and the characters and events that are about to transpire in the episode. There are no facts or pertinent information for the police to pursue in solving a crime or apprehending a criminal. Instead there is a story that is being related through a cultural context that sheds light on the circumstances behind the crime, with which the audience is expected to empathize. This human-interest angle is what TV critic David Boroff was referring to in his evocation of Chekhov, quoted at the start of this essay.

The three-season (second) run of *Naked City* collected numerous Emmy nominations and awards (the highest accolade for television in the United States). For all three seasons it was nominated for Outstanding Program Achievement in the Field of Drama. Paul Burke was twice nominated for Outstanding Continuous Performance by an Actor (Lead) (1962 and 1963), Nancy Malone was nominated for Supporting Role by an Actress (1963), and Horace McMahon for Outstanding Supporting Role by an Actor (1962). Among its technical achievements were Emmy awards for Film Editing (1962) and for Outstanding Achievement in Cinematography for Television (1962 and 1963: these last two awards both went to Jack Priestley). *Naked City* was not merchandized to any degree, mostly due to the fact that it had no celebrity stars on which to pin a marketing campaign. But its legacy filtered into popular culture in other ways. For example, three years after the end of the show, soul singer Jackie Wilson had a hit with the mournful "No Pity (in the Naked City)"—"Don't ask for a helping hand/cos no-one will understand" (Decca Records, 1965).

In conclusion, *Naked City*'s influence can be seen in other New Frontier character dramas that premiered in the early 1960s, in which a liberal consciousness was evident in the roles played by social workers, doctors, and psychiatrists. In terms of the cop genre, its influence was extensive and provided a new, more "humanist" dimension. Its approach is there in the location shots and the "it takes guts to be kind" ethos of *Kojak* (1973–78); it's there again in the character-play of *Hill Street Blues* (1981–87) and the liberal "cultural forum" aspects of *Law & Order* (1990–2010). It's particularly present in *The Wire* (2002–08), with its fascination for the underdog and the causes of crime. *Naked City*'s contribution, therefore, was to re-focus on the "eight million stories," thereby demonstrating that the notion of the "cop show" didn't have to mean "procedural."

Recommended Episodes

"And by the Sweat of Thy Brow..." (1962) is an excellent illustration of the social consciousness prevalent in the series, and sees Lt. Adam Flint befriend a facially disfigured young vagrant and end up getting him a job and a fresh outlook on life. Equally effective is "The Face of the Enemy" (1962) with Jack Warden as a troubled individual who steals some jewelry to give to his daughter at her wedding. He is captured by the police, but the charges are dropped when it becomes apparent that he was a decorated and well-known World War II veteran. However, he subsequently imagines himself back in combat and goes on a killing spree. The episode is unique in its treatment of post-traumatic stress syndrome (although the syndrome had not been identified as such in the 1960s), and doubly interesting for the fact that Warden was himself a war vet.

Further Reading

The literature on *Naked City* primarily concerns its importance as an example of social awareness programming in the early 1960s. David Boroff's essay "Television and the Problem Play," in P. Hazard (ed.), *TV as Art* (National Council of Teachers of English, 1966) considers the series as a progenitor of shows such as *East Side/West Side* (CBS, 1963–64), *Mr. Novak* (NBC, 1963–65), *Ben Casey* (ABC, 1961–66), and *The Defenders* (CBS, 1961–65). Historian Mark Alvey has written two online articles on *Naked City* and Stirling Silliphant for the Museum of Broadcast Communications website: http://www.museum.tv/eotvsection.php?entrycode=nakedcity and http://www.museum.tv/eotvsection.php?entrycode=silliphants.

Naked City is also the subject of a chapter in Alvey's PhD dissertation, *Series Drama and the "Semi-Anthology": Sixties Television in Transition* (University of Texas, Austin, 1995)—arguably the best source on the show. Another interesting online article is the Paley Center for Media's *Dragnet v. Naked City: A Great Debate* (http://paleycenter.org/dragnet-v-naked-city-another-great-debate), which is self-explanatory. A philosophical consideration of the series can be found in Robert J. Fitzgibbons' "*Naked City*: The Relativist Turn in TV Noir" in Steven Sanders and Aeon Skoble (eds.), *The Philosophy of TV Noir* (University Press of Kentucky, 2008). Finally there is a website devoted to the show: http://www.scc.net/~/heather/chist.html, which usefully provides an annotated episode guide to both the half-hour and the hour-long seasons, as well as a brief historical overview.

As a postscript, it would be remiss not to consider the other "naked cities" that, as this chapter suggests, were influences on the concept for the television series. A starting place would be Weegee's *Naked City* (Da Capo Press edition, 2002, an unabridged reprint of the original 1945 publication and still available). Two critical considerations of Weegee's work that contextualize it within the realm of film noir are Sumiko Higashi's "The American Origins of Film Noir: Realism in Urban Art and *The Naked City*" in Jon Lewis and Eric Smoodin (eds.), *Looking Past the Screen: Case Studies in American Film History and Method* (Duke University Press, 2007) and Mark Svetov's "Life and Death (Mostly Death) in the Street: Weegee and Film Noir," *Noir City Sentinel*, Fall 2010. On the 1948 movie *The Naked City*, see the entry in Daniel Eagan's *America's Film Legacy: The Authoritative Guide to the Landmark Movies in the National Film Registry* (Continuum, 2010).

CHAPTER 4

The Untouchables

(ABC, 1959–63)

RONALD WILSON

In an October 1960 issue, the popular magazine *TV Guide* published an article entitled "Do You Really Like *The Untouchables*?" It was written by Dr. Fredric Wertham, the notorious crusader against comic books in the 1950s. In the article the psychiatrist excoriated the American public for buying into the "culture of violence" propagated by the mass media. Wertham went on to warn how "we ha[ve] silently passed an amendment to the Sixth Commandment. It now goes like this: Thou Shalt Not Kill—but it is perfectly all right for you to enjoy watching other people do it, the more the merrier and as brutally as possible."[1]

During the 1961–62 U.S. Senate Judiciary Subcommittee's Hearings on Juvenile Delinquency and the Effects of Television Violence, Senator Thomas Dodd reinforced Wertham's view and provided another indication of the degree of violence associated with *The Untouchables*. Speaking directly to the president of ABC, Dodd castigated the network for starting the trend of action-adventure programs that carried "crime, sadism, and violence on the home screen further than anyone else. *The Untouchables*, which I would say is a typical ABC show ... is one of the goriest and most sadistic series being televised. Innocent bystanders being butchered, an old man being blinded by acid thrown by a mobster, tongues being cut out—these are typical of a series watched by some five-and-a-half million young people."[2] These remarks represent the tone of the many deeply critical responses that the series provoked during its four-season run in the early 1960s, which also included complaints around issues of ethnicity and historical representation.

Audiences first encountered *The Untouchables* as a stand-alone two-part episode of the CBS dramatic anthology series *Westinghouse Desilu Playhouse* in April 1959.[3] The episode was a fictionalized adaptation of the popular Eliot Ness–Oscar Fraley book *The Untouchables* (1957), which chronicled the 1930s campaign by Prohibition agent Ness and his elite squad of agents ("the Untouchables") to bring down mobster Al Capone.[4] In the episode, it is Ness, played by Robert Stack, who comes up with the idea of a trustworthy group of officers: "What if we had a special squad? Small, operating on its own. Every man thoroughly investigated. Drawn from all parts of the country. Men who'll spit on Capone's graft. Just a few he can't buy...."

Shortly after the airing of the episode, *The Untouchables* was optioned as a weekly series by ABC and began its regular run in October 1959 (CBS chose to pass). Broadcast on Thursday nights, the series again featured Stack as Ness, and a veritable rogues' gallery of guest character actors, including Nehemiah Persoff, Bruce Gordon, Neville Brand, Jack Weston, and J. Carroll Naish, as gangsters, hoodlums, and racketeers.

The timing of the commissioning was important. *The Untouchables* was able to attain its popular success in the late 1950s and early 1960s because it arrived at the height of the action-oriented programming trend in the network television era. The proliferation of westerns on all three networks in 1959 attests to this shift, relying as it did largely on network-sponsored filmed content. ABC, which instigated the rise of the adult western in the mid–1950s, cancelled all its dramatic live programming in the 1955-56 season, and followed this with a close collaboration with Warner Bros., resulting in the development of such series as *Cheyenne* (1955–63) and *Maverick* (1957–62). In 1958, the detective series *77 Sunset Strip* introduced audiences to a fresh young cadre of detectives, and offered another successful paradigm. The popularity of these programs assured ABC that the way to beat the competition at CBS and NBC was with their action programming strategy, and *The Untouchables* was a natural next step.[5]

According to *TV Guide*, ABC promoted the program's debut as a "New Kind of Series."[6] Part of this "newness" can be attributed to the way the channel was prepared to invest in the show to the tune of $100,000 per episode. This would set it apart from the cheap syndicated shows in the Ziv TV mold (*Highway Patrol* [1955–59], for example). However, many critics asserted that the "newness" simply amounted to ABC injecting ("hypo-ing" is the term used in Senate documents) more violent action into their programming. Previous 1950s television crime dramas such as *Dragnet* (1951–59), *Gangbusters* (1952), and *Treasury Men in Action* (1951–54) centered on the routine investigation of a crime with justice being delivered within the 26-minute duration of the program.[7] Unlike the formulaic procedural plots of these examples, *The Untouchables* presented a narrative structure that emphasized physical action rather than the quotidian aspects of police work—which would be both more expensive to realize and more controversial.

The dedicated and incorruptible agents seen in *The Untouchables* reflected the image of the federal G-Man (slang for "government man" or "government officer"), made popular in American culture during the 1930s. Ness was the moral center of the series, crusading against the criminal underworld of Prohibition America through physicality, violent action, and questionable surveillance methods. His reputation precedes him ("Are you the guy that got Al Capone?"[8]) and he has no qualms about punishing the guilty. If deductive reasoning and procedural methods were the staple of most television crime-fighters of the 1950s, Ness and his Untouchables were the opposite. In a pre–Miranda era, stakeouts, phone tapping, undercover operations, and violent raids (where shots were fired first and questions asked later) were standard.[9] Thus the show was politically conservative, but in a different fashion to *Dragnet*. In eschewing acts of interrogation and confession, *The Untouchables* privileged instead a more violent form of justice that effectively closed down any empathy for suspects and criminals.

The historicized (1930s) nature of the series also offered something "new" to television audiences.[10] The popular procedurals and private eye dramas were set in the present and reflected contemporary crime concerns such as burglary, arson, larceny, and murder. In addition, they reinforced an ideology that allowed the state immense power in its task of protecting its citizenry and the status quo. The historic setting of *The Untouchables* in Prohibition-era America differentiated the program from its rivals, not least because in focusing on federal agents and their battle with bootleggers, rum-runners, and organized crime, it incorporated generic elements from classic gangster and G-Man films.

A further distinctive characteristic was its frequent use of newsreel footage and an off-screen narrator. The choice of Walter Winchell for the voice-over of *The Untouchables* contextualized the series' "realism" through his celebrity-status association with radio, print media, and television. Executive producer Desi Arnaz explained: "Walter gave the show a feeling of truth and immediacy. His machine gun delivery was very, very important to the show. Without Walter it wouldn't have been the same."[11] Not only was Winchell well-known to the American public through his gossip columns and radio and television news shows, but he was also associated with pro-active journalism around organized crime. (It was Winchell who arranged the surrender of mob boss Louis "Lepke" Buchalter to FBI director J. Edgar Hoover shortly before World War II.) Winchell often began episodes of *The Untouchables* the same way he began his news broadcasts of real events: with a time, date, and location. As producer Josef Shaftel told *Newsweek* magazine, "All [Winchell] has to do is say: 'On the night of October 5, 1931, Eliot Ness went down to the delicatessen' and people are sure he did."[12]

The use of the third-person or omniscient narrator for *The Untouchables* provided a dual-layer narrative to the series: on one level is the documentary-like observer/investigator who is relating historical information concerning the episode (much like the voice-over narration in the successful television documentary series *Victory at Sea*, NBC, 1952–1953). On another level, Walter Winchell, the gossip columnist purveyor of infotainment, is relating the "real" story behind the supposedly factual events. And it is this aspect of Winchell's narrative voice that becomes key to *The Untouchables'* historicized presentational style. As Winchell biographer Neal Gabler observes, "his presentation of news conveyed a world of disaster and violence, a world seemingly poised on the edge, a world that reified the imminent peril that his listeners felt about their own lives and a world in which Winchell seemed always to be either at the center of every event or above events, an oracle prophesying the future and then sharing his knowledge."[13] The chaotic world that Winchell's column and radio voice presented to "Mr. and Mrs. America" fitted perfectly with the crime-ridden historic setting of *The Untouchables*.

Although *The Untouchables* was ostensibly about Eliot Ness and his agents, as historian Kenneth Tucker notes, "Frequently the Untouchables themselves were in the plot's background, while the story showcased the gangsters and their victims."[14] Episode titles such as "Ma Barker and Her Boys," "The 'Bugs' Moran Story," and "Jack 'Legs' Diamond" provide some indication of this narrative focus, and mirrored the "true crime" comic books that had so bothered Dr. Wertham a few years before (see chapter on *Dragnet*). The recurring gangsters in the series include Frank Nitti (played by Bruce Gordon), George "Bugs" Moran (Robert J. Wilke and Harry Morgan), Dutch Schultz aka Arthur Flegenheimer (Lawrence Dobkin), Charles "Lucky" Luciano (Robert Carricart), and Joe Kulak (Oscar Beregi). These bad guys really were bad, as Senator Dodd's comments above indicate, and mob history in its various mediatized forms provided a rich meta-narrative for *The Untouchables* to draw from.

The gangsters' nemesis, Eliot Ness, was not necessarily a sympathetic character, though his "straightness" was calculatedly played by Robert Stack. The actor's physicality and mannerisms, as well as his vocal delivery, create an image of complete dedication to duty, almost devoid of humanity. It is worth noting that in the original two-part program presented on *Westinghouse Desilu Playhouse*, Ness has an intimate relationship with a woman and they eventually wed. But once the regular series begins, he is denied any domestic or personal relationships. Though there are occasional references to his past and to his wife (who is

Eliot Ness (Robert Stack) and his fedora-wearing troop plan their crime-fighting strategy against Al Capone in the first episode of *The Untouchables* (Desilu/The Kobal Collection).

never seen), Ness remains throughout the four-season run an almost impersonal emblem of moral rectitude.[15] In speaking of his interpretation of the role, Stack admitted that his characterization was designed to contrast significantly with the real stars of the series: the gangsters. "I decided that my character should be a counterpoint to all the gaudy pin-striped suits, bias-cut dresses, sexy broads, loud jazz, prostitutes, and machine guns. Ness would be played *against* the flamboyance of the villains.... The strange presence and silent looks provided richness. That's where the power lay in this character."[16] Arguably, because Ness had no personal history or domestic relationships within the series, the character took on a more dynamic and symbolic role—a device that is common to many of the male lead protagonists in the shows featured in this book.

Since *The Untouchables* relied heavily on many of the narrative tropes, iconography, and characterizations of the American gangster film, it created a critical forum for issues relating to media violence, ethnicity, and historical representation. Like the gangster film in the early 1930s and its critical reception, *The Untouchables*' introduction of the mobster villain as a regular feature on American television and the constant prime-time gun battles won a popular audience but also instigated a moral panic about media violence. The show's popularity rose in its second year (1960–61), when it finally broke the A.C. Nielsen ratings top ten programs at No. 8. Hardly coincidentally, it was in the summer of 1961 that the Senate Judiciary Subcommittee began its investigations into the effects of TV violence on young viewers and specifically targeted ABC and *The Untouchables* during its hearings.

With negative articles appearing in such popular magazines as *TV Guide* and *The Ladies' Home Journal*, as well as in newspaper editorials, *The Untouchables* was thus very much in the public consciousness in the early 1960s.

The violence in the series, though not explicit, was more gratuitous and physical than television viewers were used to seeing. A memorandum from executive producer Quinn Martin that was read during the Senate hearings was remarkably candid about this: "I wish we could come up with a different device than running the man down with a car, as we have done this now in three different shows. *I like the idea of sadism* [author's emphasis], but I hope we can come up with another approach for it."[17] It was the often sadistic nature of the violence that was the particular problem, and which differentiated *The Untouchables* from other crime series. The shocking and sometimes gleefully administered stabbings, mutilations, and acid disfigurements seemed to amplify the already plentiful gunplay. Sadism had been a focal point of the backlash against crime comic books a few years before, until they had been effectively banned by the institution of the Comics Code in 1955. But the public's appetite for it did not disappear, as Martin implied, and was now being satisfied in another medium.

The formula nature of this kind of weekly visual assault was captured in a semi-humorous review in *TV Guide*:

> A unique appeal of *The Untouchables* is that the hoods, torpedoes, molls, and alky smugglers who people this show are highly consistent—both in action and in word. In practically every episode a gang leader winds up stitched to a brick wall and full of bullets, or face down in a parking lot (and full of bullets), or face up in a gutter (and still full of bullets), or hung up in an ice box, or run down in the street by a mug at the wheel of a big black Hudson touring car.[18]

Thus, *The Untouchables* became the focus of the first of the big TV panics—more serious in some ways than the previous panics around movies and comics because TV was perceived to be "in the home" and therefore not requiring a special effort to be consumed. In retrospect, we can see that worries about violence in TV cop shows have since become cyclical, focusing in particular on *Starsky & Hutch* in the 1970s, and *CSI* and *The Shield* in the 2000s. The debate always centers on whether such shows cause viewers to behave in a correspondingly violent fashion—a notion complicated by the difficulties of defining "violence" itself. Recent developments in "effects theory" in media studies have seen academic opinion swing in favor of concentrating on the ways in which viewers consume particular programs, as determined by social factors and "personal baggage" (rather than isolating violent incidents in the manner of Wertham's critique).[19] At the time of writing, it is certainly not a dead issue.

Yet violence was only one of the controversies *The Untouchables* incited during its run. Many first-season episodes featured gangsters with Italian names, usually involved with the Mafia—the preeminent subversive criminal organization. The original two-part adaptation, for example, contained a sequence where Capone places the "kiss of death" on a would-be assassin of Eliot Ness. "The Noise of Death," a first-season episode, dealt explicitly with a Mafia don (played by J. Carroll Naish) and his attempt to retain power in the syndicate. These episodes, along with the recurring character of Frank Nitti as Eliot Ness's chief nemesis, incensed many Italian-American organizations, which were concerned about stereotypes of Italians as criminals.[20] In many ethnic communities the series was pejoratively known as "Wops and Robbers" and "Guinea Smoke." The Order of the Sons of Italy and other anti-defamation groups threatened not only to blackout the program, but more

After the 1955 "Comics Code" resulted in a ban on crime comics, some comic book publishers, like Dell, found that the ban could be circumvented by producing TV tie-ins. Robert Stack takes aim in this 1961 example.

significantly, to boycott the sponsors' products. When Liggett & Myers (L&M) Tobacco Company threatened to pull its sponsorship, Desi Arnaz agreed to stop using Italian names for non-historic characters in the series. (Again, this was a recurring complaint, and would return in the context of the *Godfather* movies of the 1970s and *The Sopranos* TV series in the 2000s.)

Ness and his "untouchable" federal agents even came under scrutiny from real federal agents. The issue of historical representation was addressed early in the series with the second episode, "Ma Barker and Her Boys." The Ma Barker case was famous in the annals of American crime history because it was an FBI case that cemented the agency's reputation during the Depression-era crime wave of the 1930s. However, now it was being attributed to Eliot Ness and his men, who were Department of the Treasury agents, and *not* FBI. J. Edgar Hoover was incensed by this inaccuracy and had the series monitored for further historical misrepresentations. An under-pressure Arnaz had initially wanted episodes featuring John Dillinger, Pretty Boy Floyd, and Machine Gun Kelly, but since these too were famous FBI cases he quickly dropped the idea. During the run of *The Untouchables* Hoover received hundreds of letters from viewers thanking him and Eliot Ness for a job well done and also requesting more information about Ness and his exploits. To each he would set the record straight about the "real" Eliot Ness and his correct job title. As a further unwelcome coda, the Federal Bureau of Prisons also protested about the historical inaccuracies in an episode concerning Al Capone's transfer to the newly opened federal prison on Alcatraz Island.[21]

The fourth and final season of *The Untouchables* was a crime action series that tried to appease its critics. Executive producer Leonard Freeman eliminated the gratuitous violence, and in some episodes there was no violence at all. Attempts were made to make Eliot Ness more human and not simply a one-dimensional character. There were also attempts to incorporate the "New Frontier" writing that became fashionable during the Kennedy Administration (see chapter on *Naked City*), especially involving characters that embodied a social consciousness. Sometimes, examples of such characters were calculatedly introduced with the intention of spinning off future series based on their working lives (none of which ended up being commissioned), including Lt. Aggie Stewart of the Bureau of Missing Persons (in two episodes, "Elegy" and "Search for a Dead Man") and Doctors Garr and Gifford of the newly inaugurated Public Health Department (in "Jake Dance"). Regardless of the efforts made to assuage the moral panic concerning the series, the ratings dropped and the series was put out to pasture in the land of syndication after its four-year run on ABC.

Robert Stack went on to helm several series after *The Untouchables*, in many of which he commands an elite squad of crime fighters. In *Most Wanted* (ABC, 1976–77) he portrays Captain Link Evers, in charge of a special unit of the Los Angeles Police Department. And in *Strike Force* (ABC, 1980–81) he plays Captain Frank Murphy, head of yet another dedicated squad within the LAPD. In *The Name of the Game* (NBC, 1968–71), the first television series that he was associated with following *The Untouchables*, but not a cop show, Stack is still very much the crime-buster, playing Dan Farrell, the senior editor of *Crime* magazine, and a former FBI agent. The association of this kind of on-screen image with the actual person of Robert Stack finally merged when the actor hosted the docudrama series, *Unsolved Mysteries* (NBC, 1988–2003), cementing his authoritative persona in the popular imagination.

Quinn Martin, too, stayed with crime TV. Though Martin only served as the executive producer of *The Untouchables* during its initial season (other executive producers along with Desi Arnaz included Jerry Thorpe, second season; Alan Armer, third season; and Leonard Freeman, fourth season), the series established him as a creative and innovative producer of action-oriented fare. Because of the stylistic format associated with his work, Martin is a classic example of the television producer as *auteur*. Following the first season of *The Untouchables*, he formed his own production company, QM Productions, which had a string of successful action programs on ABC throughout the 1960s: *The Fugitive* (1963–67), *Twelve O'Clock High* (1964–67), *The F.B.I.* (1965–74: QM's longest running series), and *The Invaders* (1967–68). During the 1970s QM Productions added to the stable of popular television detective series with such programs as *Dan August* (1970–71), *Cannon* (1971–76), *The Streets of San Francisco* (1972–77) and *Barnaby Jones* (1973–80). What identifies these series as QM productions are their formatting stylistics: a pre-credit teaser, an expository prologue that often used a voice-over narrator, a segmented hour-long format that was divided into four acts, and an epilogue.[22]

In 1987 Brian De Palma's feature film *The Untouchables* starring Kevin Costner as Eliot Ness and Robert De Niro as Al Capone became a box-office hit. It loosely followed the events of the book and was acclaimed for its action sequences and playwright David Mamet's screenplay. The popular success of De Palma's film spawned two television productions that attempted to capitalize on the original series. In 1991 Robert Stack starred in the Canadian made-for-television movie, *The Return of Eliot Ness*, set in 1947 after the death of Al Capone. A considerably older and slower-moving Ness investigates the death of a former Untouchable agent, who has been framed as a corrupt cop on the take. Stack's stoic and deadpan performance re-invokes the Ness of the original series, but he is no longer the iconic G-Man as action hero. Similarly a short lived syndicated series of *The Untouchables* was produced in 1993–94; it starred Tom Amandes as Ness and William Forsyth as Al Capone. Clearly, however, these were ill-fated initiatives.

The Untouchables is significant because of its quality, its action-orientation, and the critical discourse surrounding its initial reception. By igniting a furor over media violence and ethnic representations the program became a hot spot for the self-appointed moral guardians of mass media and popular culture. In addition, it is important as an example of crime television action programming that incorporated generic elements from both the gangster films and G-Man films of the 1930s. Its legacy in the crime TV genre can thus be seen in three areas: action fare such *M Squad* (NBC, 1957–60), *The F.B.I.* (ABC, 1965–74), *T.J. Hooker* (1982–86) and possibly even on until *24* (Fox, 2001–10); gangster dramas such as *The Sopranos* (HBO, 1999–2007) and *Luck* (HBO, 2011–12); and, most obviously, period dramas such as *Boardwalk Empire* (HBO, 2010–14) and *Mob City* (TNT, 2013). Tommy guns and suited protagonists evidently have an enduring appeal.

Recommended Episodes

Perhaps the earliest episodes provide the best indication of how *The Untouchables* became both popular and controversial. The original two-part TV movie (1959) remains a wonderful piece of work primarily because of its director, veteran crime film auteur, Phil Karlson. The two episodes were later re-edited and released theatrically as a feature film under the title *The Scarface Mob* (a further indication of the generic heritage of the series). This film, with the original televised introductions by Desi Arnaz and Walter Winchell, can be found in the CBS DVD release of season one. Both "The Noise of Death" (1960) and "The White Slavers" (1960) are notable episodes; directed by Walter Grauman, they showcase how his "high octane" visual style was used in the service of some fine pulp scripting. Both are also frequently referenced in critical discussions of the series' violence and ethnic stereotyping. For anyone interested in the FBI case concerning the Barker-Karpis gang and why J. Edgar Hoover was protective of its historical legacy, "Ma Barker and Her Boys" (1959) is recommended: actress Claire Trevor puts in a fine performance as the criminal matron.

Further Reading

The literature concerning *The Untouchables* can be divided into two categories: the historical context of the series, and the social sciences' emphasis on media violence and ethnic representation. Of the former perhaps the best starting place is Tise Vahimagi's excellent monograph *The Untouchables* (BFI Publishing, 1998). Vahimagi situates the series' generic elements within the American gangster film cycle of the late 1950s and early 1960s. Kenneth Tucker's *Eliot Ness and the Untouchables* (McFarland, 2000) provides a historical background to the real (as opposed to reel) Eliot Ness and the gangsters in the series. Television historian William Boddy has written two essays dealing with the Dodd Senate hearings on televised violence in the 1960s, both of which emphasize the importance of *The Untouchables* in the investigations: "Approaching *The Untouchables*: Social Science and Moral Panics in Sixties Television" (*Cinema Journal*, 35:4, 1996) and "Senator Dodd Goes to Hollywood: Investigating Video Violence" in Lynn Spigel's *The Revolution Wasn't Televised: Sixties Television and Social Conflict* (Routledge, 2001). Ethnic representation (or mis-representation) is the subject of both Lee Bernstein's chapter "From *The Untouchables* to 'La Costra Nostra': Italian American Perceptions of the Mafia" in his book *The Greatest Menace: Organized Crime in Cold War America* (University of Massachusetts Press, 2002); and an essay by Laura Cook Kenna entitled "Exemplary Consumer-Citizens and Protective State Stewards: How Reformers Shaped Censorship Outcomes Regarding *The Untouchables*" (*Velvet Light Trap*, 63, Spring 2009). See also "Playing Good Italian/Bad Italian in ABC's *The Untouchables*" by Nathan J. Cavallero in D. Renga (ed.), *Mafia Movies: A Reader* (University of Toronto Press, revised edition, 2011). The production background to *The Untouchables* is the topic of several archival interviews and blogs. The Archive of American Television contains informative videotaped interviews with director Walter Grauman and executive producer (third season) Alan Armer. Grauman's directorial skill is the subject of a Classic TV History Blog, "Walter Grauman and the Noise of Death" (2012), http://classic tvhistory.wordpress.com/2012/03/23/walter-grauman-and-the-noise-of-death/.

CHAPTER 5

The F.B.I.
(ABC, 1965–74)
RONALD WILSON

"The mission of the F.B.I. is to protect the innocent and identify the enemies of the Government of the United States." Superimposed across the Bureau's official seal and accompanied by the brass fanfare of the show's theme, this statement heralds *The F.B.I.*'s opening credits sequence. A short scene then follows introducing the episode's guest-star miscreant—sometimes a Communist spy or out-and-out political radical, but more usually a run-of-the-mill fugitive, blackmailer, kidnapper or gangster—concluding in a freeze frame over which their FBI file number, name and federal violation(s) appear. Federal buildings representing the three branches of government—legislature (the U.S. Capitol), executive (the Washington Monument[1]) and judiciary (the Supreme Court)—then pop up, followed by the Department of Justice building (until 1974 the Bureau's home), which as the theme reaches its strident climax swells to fill the entire screen, the three panels of its central door breaking out to form the letters of the show's title. The message to viewers was clear: American democracy rests on an eternally vigilant FBI. While you're watching this show, they watch over you. The innocent have nothing to fear and the guilty nowhere to run.

Founded in 1908 as the Bureau of Investigation ("Federal" was added to its title in 1935), the FBI remains to this day indelibly linked to the name and reputation of J. Edgar Hoover, its director for almost 50 years until his death in 1972. A controversial figure for much of his career, Hoover's paranoia and fanatical anti–Communism reached fresh heights during his reign's final decade. Throughout this turbulent period of American history, ABC ran nine seasons of *The F.B.I.*, airing the show in its 8 p.m. Sunday family drama slot. The connections with the real organization, and with Hoover, were intricate and calculated, and gave the show a quality that was unique. The urbane Efrem Zimbalist, Jr., previously star of lightweight private eye drama *77 Sunset Strip* (ABC, 1958–64), played Inspector Lewis Erskine, the show's pivotal character, backed up by a series of assistants: Special Agent Jim Rhodes (Stephen Brooks, 1965–67), Special Agent Tom Colby (William Reynolds, 1967–73) and, in the show's final season, Special Agent Chris Daniels (Shelly Novack). Philip Abbott completed the regular cast as Arthur Ward, Erskine's superior, depicted as Hoover's assistant director.

But the real Hoover functioned as *The F.B.I.*'s ghost in the machine, an unseen but omniscient hand guiding both on-screen action and the production process behind it. Notoriously obsessive, by the time Jack Warner and ABC approached him with a format that met with his approval Hoover had already rejected several proposed FBI television dramas. Specially assigned agents closely monitored shooting, cast members were subjected to Bureau background checks, and certain proposed guest stars—Bette Davis among them— were blacklisted. The Bureau retained a script veto throughout the show's decade-long run, often censoring or re-writing individual scenes; according to historian Richard Gid Powers:

> Scripts ... shuttled back and forth between Hollywood and Washington, the Bureau straightened out inconsistent character details and illogical plot elements, persistently requesting that FBI legal jurisdiction be clearly established to justify every move made by ... Inspector Erskine.[2]

As its consistent prime-time scheduling suggests, *The F.B.I.* appealed primarily to a white, conservative, suburban (or rural) audience, a demographic famously referred to as the "silent majority" by recently elected president Richard Nixon when he addressed the nation in 1969 on the subject of the war in Vietnam. The second half of the 1960s witnessed widespread student protests against the escalating conflict, accompanied by the mushrooming of the hippie counterculture; coinciding with the apogee of the Civil Rights movement and riots throughout America's black inner-city neighborhoods, this led to unprecedented cultural polarization within American society. Through it all, Hoover's agents could be found at the maelstrom's center, working overtime to battle "enemies of the government," while those very same "subversives" increasingly directed their criticism towards the Bureau itself and its "rogue" director. As historian David Marc observes, "*The F.B.I.* argued for the legitimacy of the very institution that [was] being questioned most sharply during the sixties."[3] Audience reaction to the show mirrored the nation's ever-deepening cultural divide: interviewed in 2011, Zimbalist recalled:

> *77 Sunset Strip* was a universally popular series. I mean, everybody loved it; it was the favorite. *The F.B.I.*, because of the nature of the F.B.I. itself, because of the conditions in the world at the time, of the Sixties and so forth ... sharply divided [the public]. A lot of people were on the F.B.I.'s side, and a lot of people were not. We had that to contend with; we didn't have the universal audience put in our lap the way we had with the other series.[4]

Crime television in the mid–1960s came mainly in the form of escapist action-adventure entertainment. Strictly speaking, the period's only police show was *Burke's Law* (ABC, 1963–65), featuring Gene Barry as LAPD homicide chief Amos Burke, a millionaire detective who arrives at murder scenes in a chauffeur-driven Rolls Royce Silver Cloud. *Arrest and Trial* (ABC, 1963–64), starring Ben Gazzara and Chuck Connors, provided a brief respite from the prevailing silliness, though due to an unwieldy two-part 90-minute format this turned out to be short-lived.[5] Meanwhile, popular espionage shows such as *The Man from U.N.C.L.E* (NBC, 1964–68), *I Spy* (NBC, 1965–68) and *Mission Impossible* (CBS, 1966–73) took Cold War themes to their extreme, with gimmicky formulas and clearly delineated uber-villains bent on world domination.[6] *The F.B.I.* thus served a dual function: the show filled a vacancy in primetime schedules for serious crime drama, while at the same time giving Cold War action-adventure a "realistic" twist. Its producer, Quinn Martin, aimed for cinematic quality and budgeted generously for action set-pieces; he had already scored a hit for ABC with *The Fugitive* (1963–67), in which screenwriter Roy Huggins (also the creator of *Maverick* and, later, *The Rockford Files*) pioneered the segmented program format that Martin then adopted for *The F.B.I.* Like *The Fugitive*, the show begins, as we have seen, with a pre-credit teaser; its narrative structure is then broken into four "acts," the action switching back and forth between Erskine's investigators and their criminal prey, before reaching a climax (normally the arrest or death of the latter) in Act IV. Both shows concluded with an epilogue and were bookended by voice-overs from an omniscient off-screen narrator.

The F.B.I. aimed for veracity: its production team made extensive use of locations, its writers based episode storylines on genuine FBI cases, and the segmented format served to continually remind viewers that they were watching the dramatization of real events. The inclusion of

Perhaps the quintessential Quinn Martin television production (the name always denoted by a "handwritten" typeface in the credits), the ABC series focused on federal law enforcement and was divided into four acts with a prologue/teaser and an epilogue.

public service announcements (PSAs) at the end of certain episodes further blurred the distinction between Erskine's men and their real-life counterparts: in these brief codas, Zimbalist would step out of character and appeal directly to viewers for help in capturing one of the Bureau's "most wanted" suspects.[7] The strategy met with success—or so the show's own PR team claimed.[8]

Nonetheless, as production manager Howard Alston recalls, working up the show's raw case-file material up into prime-time TV drama required considerable creative effort:

> The F.B.I. gave us a lot of material, all of their closed cases. There were about a thousand or so cases, but [they] weren't very exciting…. Because the F.B.I. was dull. When you read the reports, they'd tell you they went from Point A to Point B, did such and such, and filled out the forms, and that was it. If you'd tried to do those reports and cases as an interesting hour drama, you'd have been in real trouble.[9]

The show's writers therefore cranked up the tension by turning each segmented "act" into a mini-drama in its own right, based around the thrill of the chase. Guest star criminals, including Gene Tierney, Gene Hackman, Ralph Bellamy and Robert Duvall, enlivened the action and were paid as much $5,000 to appear. Like *The Untouchables* (ABC, 1959–63), its federal policing predecessor, *The F.B.I.* employed a "cops-and-robbers" formula, where the cops prevail against worthy adversaries. According to producer Philip Saltzman:

> The villains were the ones who made the show go. Only by heightening the villain could we make the show more fascinating to the audience. You had these wonderful villains, and then you had these straight-laced, square-jawed, F.B.I. people going after them. The more difficult that became, the more interesting the show became.[10]

The benchmark for interesting, difficult villains was set fairly high at the outset: in the season 1 premiere, "The Monster," Jeffrey Hunter, familiar to viewers as Jesus Christ in Nicholas Ray's 1961 Bible epic *King of Kings*, played a serial killer who murders women by strangling them with their own hair.

By contrast, Zimbalist's restrained performance as the "straight-laced" Erskine represents a distinct shift from the mob-busting "G-Man" (slang for "government man" or "government officer") of the pre-war era, an archetype that itself evolved from detective heroes such as Nick Carter, whose serialized exploits thrilled turn-of-the-century readers of dime novels and pulp magazines. With its violent action, gunplay and frequent use of disguises, the pulp detective formula had transferred easily to Hollywood movies such as *G Men* (William Keighley, 1935), in which James Cagney plays James "Brick" Davis, an FBI agent bent on avenging the death of a friend. Conceived as an antidote to the glorification of gangster anti-heroes in movies such as *Little Caesar* (Mervyn LeRoy, 1931), *G Men* followed on the heels of several highly-publicized Bureau successes, notably the death a year earlier of bank robber John Dillinger, "Public Enemy Number One," in a shoot-out with federal agents in Chicago. Though Cagney's portrayal of the pugnacious "Brick" helped cement the G-Man's status as a mass media icon and further boosted the Bureau's fame, the movie was not a hit with Hoover. True to his pulp origins, the G-Man was an impulsive, individualistic action hero, whereas the director of the newly re-christened FBI, by then nearing the end of his first decade at its helm, saw it as a "we" organization that relied on efficiency, teamwork and scientific methods. This was the image he wanted to see portrayed in post-war popular culture.

A perma-tanned Inspector Erskine (Efrem Zimbalist, Jr.) shows his card, against the typically patriotic background of the flag and the FBI crest (ABC TV/Photofest).

Thus, Hoover, along with zealous anti–Communism, actively promoted a return to "traditional" American values and sought to remold the Bureau's image accordingly: as Powers notes, a "new commitment to domestic security (both national and familial)" characterized the FBI of the 1950s.[11] Though Zimbalist's character embodied this reformed attitude, his was not the first to do so. In the hit movie *The FBI Story* (Mervyn LeRoy, 1959), James Stewart plays John "Chip" Hardesty, federal agent and family man, whose exploits battling Klansmen, mobsters and Communists are shown in a series of flashbacks as he recounts his involvement in many of the Bureau's famous cases. As the *New York Times* observed, "The F.B.I. agent is presented as a pillar of the American home, as much as—or even more than—a pillar of law enforcement and protection against Communist spies."[12] The "house-broken" FBI man had arrived.

Hoover had personally chosen Stewart for the part in that movie, and, as he would with *The F.B.I.*, instituted background checks on cast members and forced LeRoy to re-shoot scenes he disapproved of. The film bears both Hoover's clear imprint and a striking resemblance to the later TV show, not least in its final scene, which sees Stewart drive away with his family past the Washington Monument, the White House and the Lincoln Memorial. Compare this with *The F.B.I.*'s closing credit sequence, in which Erskine leaves the Department of Justice, gets into his car (as the Ford Motor Company was one of the show's chief sponsors, he always drove a Ford), and drives past the Washington Monument before parking in a residential street. Erskine, the viewer is reminded, is an ordinary middle-class American returning home from work, just as millions of others do every day. The FBI seal then reappears on screen, followed by an expression of gratitude to Hoover and his "associates."

Other than this, however, no reference is ever made to the inspector's personal life (barring a handful of season 1 episodes featuring Lynn Loring as his daughter). Instead, the Bureau is his family: it is a closely-bonded, all-male group of which he is the leader—a set-up similar to other Quinn Martin productions (for example, Leslie Nielsen playing the pack leader in short-lived LAPD drama *The New Breed* [ABC, 1961–62] and Paul Burke fulfilling a similar role in World War II air ace series *Twelve O'Clock High* [ABC, 1964–67]). Indeed, Erskine functions as a kind of eldest son to Ward, his superior, and to the unseen Hoover, and as elder brother to his assistant Rhodes. (This dynamic shifted, however, when the older Reynolds replaced Brooks as Erskine's assistant, to be restored again only in the show's final season, when ABC replaced Reynolds, "too old" at forty-one, with Novack, a former college football star and AFL professional.) Each episode brings a new crisis that, though it destabilizes Erskine's "family," they resolve through teamwork and scientific professionalism (with great emphasis on lab reports, ballistic tests, fingerprint identification, and so on).[13] Thus the concluding epilogue always sees "family" equilibrium restored and Hoover's ethos for the Bureau reaffirmed.

The F.B.I.'s "domestic" formula can, then, be boiled down to two main ingredients: a warm and secure surrogate family group on the one hand, and, on the other, an external threat. As such, the show, as Powers notes, was "perfectly suited to an audience whose interests [were] overwhelmingly private in orientation, an audience that [had] turned away from public affairs to immerse itself in the drama of private life."[14] Or, put another way, an audience that corresponded closely Nixon's "silent majority." Erskine represented a domesticated masculine ideal acceptable to Middle America's prime-time family audience; an audience whose values, imperiled though they were by Civil Rights and the putative countercultural revolution, remained firmly those of the conservative 1950s. However, things had moved on by the time *The F.B.I.* hit its stride. For example, ten years had passed since those twin indictments of American conformity, William H. Whyte's non-fiction *The Organization Man* and Sloan Wilson's novel *The Man in the Gray Flannel Suit*, had topped the bestseller lists. Yet the "Agent in the Gray Flannel Suit" would make a fitting sobriquet for Lewis Erskine: dressed in a sober two-piece (no vests here, unlike Eliot Ness and his "Untouchables") and driving an American automobile (unlike the television private eyes with their fancy foreign sports cars), he is a model of American conservatism. Neither he nor any of his team is ever seen breaking any regulation of any kind. They don't drink or smoke, chase women or use bad language. In fact, they don't have any fun at all.

The end of the 1960s saw American society deeply divided, cultural polarity leading in turn to conservative backlash and Nixon's electoral triumph. Though Senator Barry Goldwater's humiliating landslide defeat to Lyndon B. Johnson in 1964 had been a blow to the nascent New Right, Nixon's entry into the White House four years later marked the beginning of a quarter-century of Republican presidencies, interrupted only by Jimmy Carter's 1977–81 single term and crowned by the two-term office of the New Right's poster boy, Ronald Reagan (first elected governor of California in 1967). Nixon ran for president in 1968 on a "law and order" ticket, presenting himself as a spokesman for "ordinary" Americans deeply troubled by the nation's turmoil and the permissive direction in which it appeared to be heading. Introducing the trope to which he would return a year later, Nixon declared that it was "time for the great silent majority of Americans to stand up and be counted!" ("All over this country today," he told voters, "we see a rising tide of terrorism, of crime, and on the campuses … we have seen those who … engage in violence.… It's time to draw the line and say we're not going to stand for that!"[15])

Though they were very different breeds of political animal, Nixon more than matched Hoover for underhandedness and paranoia, and both men were equally reviled by the radical Left. Indeed, by the time Hoover died in 1972, the president had largely replaced him as the counterculture's bête noire. Despite his vows to the silent majority, Nixon's first term was, if anything, marked by an *increase* in social unrest and radical dissent, the fatal shooting of four students by Ohio national guardsman during an anti-war demonstration at Kent State University in 1970 among factors leading to the increased militancy of groups such as the Weather Underground, whose terrorist bombing campaign inflicted minor, though symbolically resonant, damage to targets that included the U.S. Capitol (1971) and the Pentagon (1972). And far from a return to American family values, the early 1970s in fact saw no decline in creeping permissiveness and social liberalism—indeed, quite the reverse. A moral panic around crime and deviancy, fostered by the administration and fueled by a sensation-hungry media, with hindsight seems inevitable. Reaching its height in 1970–72, this hysteria coincided with *The F.B.I.*'s peak in ratings popularity.[16] There were several episodes that dealt directly with the president's pet folk devils—for example "Time Bomb" (1970), in which youthful Weatherman-style urban guerrillas attempt to kick-start "the revolution" by blowing up a government building. But, unsurprisingly, these shows were not exactly nuanced explorations into the causes of radical dissent. Having long drawn flak from cosmopolitan liberals for its unapologetically reactionary brand of TV law enforcement, *The F.B.I.* was now routinely mocked in the counterculture's underground newspapers and comic books as an archetypal symbol of Nixon's "pig nation."

At the sharp end, however, the distance between the show's sanitized version of Bureau activity and the reality of Hoover's often brutal methods was no laughing matter, as Yippie (Youth International Party) spokesman Abbie Hoffman made clear in 1971, complaining to a group of students that FBI agents "have been kicking in doors [and] putting guns under the chins of people … not the kind of thing you see Efrem Zimbalist carrying out every Sunday night."[17] Indeed, though Erskine and his team ruthlessly pursued criminals and Communist spies, as Marc notes, "the Bureau was never shown harassing civil rights or peace groups, or gathering files on the personal lives of public figures."[18] And though the public figures who were spied on, smeared and harassed by Hoover's men included prominent Civil Rights leaders, among them Dr. Martin Luther King, Jr., *The F.B.I.* (which include one or two black agents among its regular characters) remained silent about the Bureau's highly dubious "policing" of organizations such as King's SCLC and, as the Civil Rights movement gave way to militant Black Power, the Black Panther Party.

Viewers did, however, see an awful lot of snooping. The overall impression is of pervasive and thorough law enforcement: FBI agents seem to be everywhere, tapping phones, intercepting mail, tailing cars and donning disguises; with Erskine most likely to be found, binoculars in hand, in an empty building across the street from a suspect's home, patiently observing his prey. To contextualize this trope: in the late eighteenth century, the English philosopher Jeremy Bentham conceived the Panopticon, a type of building intended for use as a prison, school, factory or barracks, whose radial design ensured the constant visibility of its inmates to observers concealed in a central hub. Aware that they might at any time be watched, inmates would therefore monitor their own behavior, each effectively acting as their own policeman to themselves. In the twentieth century, Michel Foucault, the renegade French philosopher and social theorist, perceived the panoptic ("all-seeing") device as paradigmatic, not merely of modern penal institutions, but of what he termed "disciplinary power" itself, which aims to induce docile, self-regulating obedience in the delinquent individual.[19]

To return once more to *The F.B.I.*'s credit sequence: if the Bureau itself is understood as a disciplinary tool (and its D.C. headquarters as an immense Panopticon), then the show's pre-credit teaser can be viewed as a lesson in the operation of disciplinary power, in which the episode's criminal protagonist is observed, identified and categorized, watched by the audience from the perspective of the Bureau's all-seeing eye. As Foucault put it, "Inspection functions ceaselessly. The gaze is alert everywhere."[20] At the same time as Hoover's FBI was laying the foundations for today's "surveillance society," *The F.B.I.* was inuring the American public to the Orwellian shape of things to come. Indeed, many neocons today use appeals to fictional TV precedents to justify the extent to which the NSA currently monitors the electronic communication of ordinary American citizens: Fox News pundit and former Bush adviser Karl Rove (who began his career campaigning for Nixon) observed recently, "You cannot turn on a cop drama on television where there is not somebody who's pinging somebody's cell phone or taking a look at the phone calls made by landline or telephone booth to help solve some crime."[21]

The F.B.I.'s enduring legacy lies, then, in its importance as a pioneering example of what might be described as "panoptic television": it is emblematic of TV shows whose reliance on surveillance as a narrative trope serves to discipline viewers via constant reminders that they might themselves be being watched. Other notable examples include *The Untouchables*, in which Eliot Ness (Robert Stack) and his men often engage in undercover surveillance as they fight organized crime, and contemporary shows such as *24* (Fox, 2001–10) and *Homeland* (Showtime, 2011–present) whose post-9/11 federal protagonists are pitted against terrorist adversaries. Hugely successful non-fiction shows such as *America's Most Wanted* (Fox, 1988–2012) and *Cops* (Fox, 1989–present) can also be regarded as panoptic, as might the equally popular *Bourne* movies, with their astonishing displays of state-of-the-art surveillance technology.

By 1974, however, when after 240 episodes ABC finally pulled the plug on *The F.B.I.*, it had become something of an anachronism. The TV cop drama genre had by now entered its "golden age," and Erskine and his men would have been no match for the sexy, unconventional protagonists of Aaron Spelling's action-packed *Starsky & Hutch* (ABC, 1975–79), which debuted on the network the following year, nor the angst-ridden cops of shows such as Quinn Martin's own *The Streets of San Francisco* (ABC, 1972–79). Perhaps more importantly, *The F.B.I.* no longer had friends in high places: by 1974, Hoover was dead and Nixon, who resigned in August that year to avoid impeachment for his involvement in the Watergate cover-up, disgraced. ABC attempted to revive the show in 1981: *Today's F.B.I.* (1981–82), endorsed by the Bureau and based like its predecessor on FBI case-files, starred *Mannix*'s Mike Connors as Special Agent Ben Slater commanding an elite team of young federal agents. It flopped.

Looking back, *The F.B.I.*'s heyday had coincided with the most controversial period in the Bureau's history: while Hoover destroyed reputations and ruined lives, the show presented a whitewashed version of the FBI, portraying its agents as a straight-laced bunch of professionals who were "just doing their job." "What Jack Webb's *Dragnet* did for cops," observes television historian David Martindale, "Quinn Martin's *The F.B.I.* did for the Federal Bureau of Investigation. Each … received full cooperation from that agency's top men.… The Bureau couldn't have paid for better PR."[22] *Dragnet* was itself revived in 1967, another example of the TV industry's instinctively reactionary response to uncertain times. It was, however, Aaron Spelling and not Martin or Jack Webb, who saw a way ahead for the cop show, adjusting the genre to the meet the zeitgeist's requirements, first with the über-groovy *The Mod Squad* (ABC, 1968–73), and then with the aforementioned *Starsky & Hutch*. *The F.B.I.*'s "no fun" aesthetic remains, however, a significant thread in the contemporary genre (one need only think of Dick Wolf's *Law & Order* and its various spin-offs), though the show itself is today largely forgotten. Forgotten, that is, by everyone except the FBI itself: in 2009, and without a hint of irony, the Bureau awarded Efrem Zimbalist an Honorary Special Agent badge.

Recommended Episodes

The show's first four seasons have been made available as MOD (Made on Demand) DVDs through the Warner Archives. "The Giant Killer" (1965), featuring Robert Duvall as a demented pacifist who attempts to destroy a Thor missile en route to its launch site, provides a good introduction. The Red Menace is a theme of several episodes, for instance "The Courier" (1967), with Gene Hackman and Ruth Roman as members of a Communist spy ring. Though less frequent than domestic crime and espionage narratives, the topic of organized crime also provided storylines for several episodes. The two-part "The Executioners" (1967), with a cast including Walter Pidgeon, Celeste Holm, and Telly Savalas, is notable for its distinctly WASP-ish Mafiosi—Hoover and ABC had wished to avoid offending Italian-American viewers.

Further Reading

Much of the literature about the series is embedded in other works. Richard Gid Powers' *G-Men: Hoover's FBI in American Popular Culture* (Southern Illinois University Press, 1983) provides a cultural history of the show in relation to Hoover's efforts to change the Bureau's image. Douglas Snauffer's *Crime Television* (Praeger, 2006) provides a good overview, highlighting the show's importance and impact during the 1960s. Production history can be found in Jonathan Etter's *Quinn Martin, Producer* (McFarland, 2003), which is particularly useful for the author's interviews with production personnel. Online video interviews with individuals associated with the program (including ABC executive Leonard Goldenson, ABC Vice President of Programming Edgar Scherick, director Ralph Senensky, and actresses Doris Singleton and Suzanne Pleshette) can also be found at the Archive of American Television website: http://www.emmytvlegends.org/interviews/shows/F.B.I.-the.

CHAPTER 6

Columbo

(NBC, 1968–78)

ROGER SABIN

In November 1973, the cover of *Time* magazine was graced not by a politician or a sports star, but by the squint-eyed visage of a certain TV detective. (See photo in the Introduction.) The tag-line proclaimed "The Year of the TV Cop," and the article inside explained that *Columbo* was "the most influential, probably the best, and certainly the most endearing cop series on TV." But fans of the show knew that this wasn't really a "cop show" in any established sense. Sure, Columbo was a police officer, but there were no shoot-outs, or car chases, or tough guys talking about "APBs." Instead, the tradition to which he belonged was more akin to the mysteries of Agatha Christie, Dorothy L. Sayers, and Ellery Queen. And, in the end, that word "endearing" was so much easier to slap on a mystery than a cop show.[1]

To understand why *Columbo* was different, it's helpful to contrast it with the *Dragnet* lineage. Since its 1951 debut, *Dragnet*, as we have seen, influenced just about every other show in the cop genre, and was itself revived for a very successful second run in 1967, a year before *Columbo*'s first TV appearance. *Dragnet*'s viewers received little indication of a suspect's guilt, or whether a line of enquiry would be successful. Instead, the show focused on the drudgery of police work, and viewers could therefore never be allowed to "step ahead" of its protagonist (the lack of "pre-knowledge" was crucial). *Dragnet* was always about the bigger system of police procedure, rather than an individual detective.

But in *Columbo*, the opposite is true.[2] The charisma of the lead detective, played here by the great Peter Falk—was everything, and the viewer was invited to follow his process in the same way they might Hercule Poirot's. The joy was in watching him play a psychological game with his suspect, encouraging the little lies that cover the bigger lies that cover the murder, in order to finally trap his prey. The show followed an "inverted mystery" formula; the viewer witnessing the crime at the beginning of an episode and privy thereafter to all the relevant facts. This storytelling technique is associated with an English writer named R. Austin Freeman in the early 20th century, who set himself a *Dogme*-like set of rules for his detective stories, whose satisfaction for readers lies in following the process of detection. As such, it is the individual detective, and not some impersonal police force, who becomes the center of attention.

This leads to a second way in which *Columbo* broke with the *Dragnet* tradition: in allowing room for character-play, it opened a space for method acting. A trained method actor, Falk would ad lib, pace around, fumble in his pockets, and pull faces: a performance style neatly contrasted in a 1972 episode, "Dagger of the Mind," with the hammy Shakespearean skills of a couple of murderous actors, played by Richard Basehart and Honor Blackman. As the Columbo character developed, so the props and the mannerisms became more entrenched. There was the crumpled raincoat, the half-smoked cigar, the overheated car, and, later, the dog (a Bassett hound called "Dog"). Columbo's most famous line, "Oh, one more thing…" though technically not a catch-phrase, is used often enough to qualify as one.[3] It all amounted to a character that was essentially an actorly creation—far in tone from Joe Friday, but farther still from the cops populating the new wave of "realistic" movies such as *The French Connection*.

Many of the actors guest-starring opposite Falk as Columbo's adversaries were equally adept at "the method." Watching names such as Patrick McGoohan, Robert Culp, Leonard Nimoy, Roddy McDowall and many more play off Falk was where the fun really started—in stark contrast to the *Dragnet* mode of impassive, autocued, performance. If this "method" dimension made the show more cinematic than most TV drama, then the directing kept pace—with dolly pans and editing techniques (such as the use of split-screens) that were unusual at the time. The fact that *Columbo* gave early breaks to Steven Spielberg and Jonathan Demme is no coincidence: other guest directors included Ben Gazzara, Patrick McGoohan and John Cassavetes. Episodes lasted either a full hour or were 90-minute "TV movies," again contributing to the show's cinematic feel.

Finally, unlike *Dragnet*, *Columbo* was conceived as a fantasy. We've seen that Columbo and his foes were imbued with a distinct theatricality, but it is important to note that the setting of the show was equally artificial. The Los Angeles of *Columbo* was a very different LA to that of *Dragnet* and other cop shows—a dreamlike blur of soft colors set against brilliant sunshine, bringing to mind the kind of West Coast airbrush art that graced the era's soft rock LP covers. Columbo's suspects were drawn from the city's wealthy, and their ostentatious homes, typically featuring shimmering blue swimming pools, provided another level of exoticism ("Gee whiz! Nice place ya got here!"). These suburban mansions functioned as the updated stately homes of the Christie/Sayers tradition—ethereal visions of American (usually Nouveaux Riche) splendor.

With this fantasy aura came the banishing of anything resembling "real" politics. Columbo's creators always rejected an interpretation of the working-class-cop-in-middle-class-surroundings scenario as a subversive attack on the American class system. In this reading, the plebeian Columbo is a brown smudge in the context of his opulent high class surroundings ("as welcome as a turd in the swimming pool," as the saying goes—a saying too coarse ever to be uttered in the show itself). If *Columbo* was about class war, then it was in the same way that Agatha Christie's stories were about class war. Given that the rest of the aforementioned 1973 issue of *Time* magazine concerned Vietnam, Watergate, the Middle East, and the oil crisis, it's little wonder that the American public craved a bit of escapism.[4] Similarly, the issue of "race" was present, but only tangentially: Columbo is an outsider in the sense of being from immigrant (Italian) stock, and thus fitted into a vogue for "ethnic" TV cops and private eyes (including a Greek—Kojak; a Pole—Banacek; and African Americans—Shaft, Tenafly, etc.). Otherwise, black characters rarely featured, and LA's Latino population was all but invisible (unlike in, say, *Dragnet*).

These four elements—structure, acting, cinematic aura, and fantasy setting—marked out *Columbo* as a new direction in cop shows. We can quibble over how far there were precedents. For example, the "inverted mystery" format was already popular on the big screen (e.g., *The Killers* [1946], and familiar to viewers via the imported BBC series *Dial M for Murder*). Similarly, the 1960s had seen cinematic direction and method acting find their way into various TV genres. As for Falk's bumbling detective act *per se*, critics have pointed out that the "le surveillant" character in Henri-Georges Clouzot's *Les Diaboliques* (1955) comes pretty close, while author William Peter Blatty has claimed it was closely modeled on the detective in his novel The Exorcist (even though this was only published in 1971).[5] Nevertheless, and in spite of such caveats, at the time of the *Time* cover story, *Columbo* was evidently perceived as a fresh template for the cop show genre.

Columbo's origins were mundane. The show's creators, William Link and Richard Levinson, the prolific Universal TV producer-writer team (also responsible for *Mannix* and *McCloud*), had been attempting to get it off the ground since the late 1950s.[6] Columbo himself first appeared in a 1960 episode of *The Chevy Mystery Show*, played by Bert Freed. Levinson and Link then wrote the character into their 1962 Broadway play *Prescription Murder*, with Thomas Mitchell in the role. In 1968, NBC aired *Columbo*, a TV movie based on the play, starring Peter Falk, in rotation with *McCloud, McMillan and Wife*, and others, on *NBC Mystery Movie*. A second TV movie, "Ransom for a Dead Man," followed in 1971, setting the stage for the show's first full season.

Falk got the role partly by accident: first choice Bing Crosby turned it down, and second choice Lee J. Cobb was unavailable. Though initially wary—he viewed TV with suspicion, as being somehow inferior to film or stage work—Falk quickly saw the potential for a method actor of a show that sought to subvert the *Dragnet* clichés. He was, by his own admission, a strange looking guy, with one eye missing due to a childhood tumor; the resulting squint, captured on the cover of *Time*, as much a part of Columbo as any of the props. Those props, too, had Falk's imprimatur—Columbo's wardrobe, including his trademark crumpled coat, belonged to him.

Due to his perfectionism and desire for more creative control, Falk's relationship with Levinson and Link was of the love-hate variety. His previous roles in cinema (*Pocketful of Miracles, The Great Race*, etc.) had earned him a reputation for hard work and professionalism, and he expected those traits to be respected—and finally remunerated—when he moved to TV. While starring in *Columbo*, he continued to appear on the big screen, notably in low budget art flicks directed by his long-time friend, indie auteur John Cassavetes (e.g., 1974's *A Woman Under the Influence*). These movies were part-bankrolled by Falk's paycheck from *Columbo*, which swiftly rose to $150,000 per episode—making him one of the highest paid actors in the TV business. Again, this *modus operandi* caused friction with the show's producers, who, according to a piece by them in *American Film* magazine, spent years having to bite their lips (it's entitled "How We Created Columbo—and How He Nearly Killed Us"[7]).

How was *Columbo* received? Success was not immediate—it took two pilots to get off the ground, and was significantly into its run when *Time* ran its cover story. Levinson and Link recall NBC's "major 'conceptual concerns'" with their narrative approach: "How could we have made the terrible blunder of keeping our leading man offstage until twenty minutes into the show?"[8] These worries were exacerbated by the fact that *Columbo* wasn't cheap to film. As each show was a one-off, the producers were denied the economic benefits of standing sets and a regular cast—Falk himself was the only point of continuity.

But success is a great pacifier, and by the end of Season 1 it was clear that the network had a monster hit on its hands: by 1973, the show was drawing 37 million viewers per episode, a figure due partly to its unthreatening nature, which allowed NBC to schedule it

A dapper Columbo (Peter Falk) as he appeared in the pilot episode (compare with his later, crumpled look on the front of *Time* magazine, reproduced in the Introduction), here quizzing a twisted psychiatrist (Gene Barry) (Universal TV/The Kobal Collection).

at any time and make the most of repeats. Also, syndication was easy—*Columbo* became huge in Europe (the BBC initially copied NBC by creating an anthology series of their own, called "The Detectives," with *Columbo* in rotation with *Ironside*, *Cannon* and others), while in Japan, Falk was overdubbed by popular actor Asao Koike. Novelizations, board games, and toys soon followed, and TV impressionists and stand-up comedians had fun with one of the most easily imitated characters in pop culture—all that was needed was a cigar and an old raincoat. (Johnny Carson's own somewhat feeble attempt can be viewed on YouTube.) Other humorists leaped on the bandwagon; "Clodumbo" was a favorite with readers of *MAD* magazine.

How did the show develop over time? It's clear that the early movie-episodes were more disciplined, and more tightly scripted. Episode 1 of the series ("Murder by the Book," 1971) is notable for its director, the 25-year-old Steven Spielberg, and its writer, Steven Bochco, later of *Hill Street Blues* fame. The story involves a pair of mystery writers, one of whom kills the other using a method of dispatch invented for their next book. Amusingly, these characters were parodies of Bochco's bosses, Levinson and Link (similarly, when *Columbo* was revived in 1989, the first new episode was a story about a movie brat murderer, based on Spielberg). Falk later recalled the episode fondly—especially working with Spielberg, whose technique he perceived as "comforting" for actors: "I'm rehearsing a scene where I'm walking up a street talking to a guy and it suddenly dawns on me there's no camera around that I can see. Steven was shooting me with a long lens from across the street. That wasn't common [in TV at the time]."[9]

A looser approach developed as the show progressed, due largely to Falk's growing creative role. He progressively won more screen time for his method technique, and greater input into the actual making of the show—especially directing. Quirks became style; for example, by the mid–1970s, *Columbo* was famous for its pauses—which, once again, distinguished it from the barreling momentum of shows in the *Dragnet* tradition. (Sometimes, these were used purely for their entertainment value. In one episode from 1972, "Blueprint for Murder," directed by Falk, Columbo has to persuade City Hall to pay for the excavation of a building in his search of a corpse, and in order to do this, has to stand quietly in lines at various government offices, unable to circumvent the bureaucracy, to his mounting frustration, and to the viewer's mounting amusement.) Similarly, the show's directing style was finessed; the lesson learned from "Murder by the Book" was that a spontaneous feel could be engendered by filming actors when they weren't directly cognizant of the fact—a technique also used by Cassavetes.

As the show evolved, casting grew more inventive, with big-name stars (albeit one or two somewhat past their prime) more than happy to star opposite Falk as guest villains. The list of "*Columbo* killers" is astonishing, and included (along with the aforementioned McGoohan, Culp, Nimoy, Basehart, Blackman and McDowall) Martin Landau, Jack Cassidy, Nicol Williamson, Rip Torn, Robert Vaughn, Vera Miles, William Shatner, Dick Van Dyke, and—perhaps inevitably—John Cassavetes.[10]

In a typical show, the star killer (bourgeois, cultured, smartly dressed) would "help" Columbo (working class, Italian, shabby) in his investigation, to the point of becoming over-confident and giving themselves away. Guest stars relished the opportunity to explore the fury, panic and bewilderment that accompanied their characters' dawning realization that the irritatingly dogged detective was in fact their nemesis. Indeed, there was a culture on-set of "keeping things alive," with Falk ad-libbing and expecting others to keep up—a kind of friendly joust that guest actors would appreciate (McGoohan recalled that working on *Columbo* was among his happiest acting experiences—he starred on four occasions and won two Emmys for his performances).

Sometimes the shows would be sculpted around the guest villain. Thus, for example, in "A Stitch in Time" (1973) Leonard Nimoy plays a murderous surgeon who is "always in control"—thus riffing on his Spock persona. Similarly, in "Forgotten Lady" (1975) Janet Leigh, star of Hitchcock's *Psycho* (1960), plays an aging actress who will kill for the chance of a comeback: we see her alone at night obsessively watching her younger celluloid self—the clip featured is from 1953's *Walking My Baby Back Home,* a musical in which Leigh herself actually starred. Such "postmodernist" referencing of a celebrity's own life was daring at the time, and underlined that the show's vaunted "playfulness" wasn't always as flippant as some critics imagined.

Perhaps the most famous example of this trope involved Johnny Cash in a 1974 episode entitled "Swan Song." Cash plays an adulterous gospel singer who murders his black-mailing wife (Ida Lupino) and

Columbo meets Robby the Robot in the episode "Mind over Mayhem" (1974). "Stunt casting" was a feature of the show, but it sometimes went too far.

then fakes an airplane crash to cover his tracks. He gets to sing a few songs, and act like a sinner, and there are lots of biblical references. In the end, he says to Columbo that he would have confessed anyway because the guilt was "beginning to get to me."

Once again, the episode's storyline bore a close relationship to its guest star's biography and relied on a sophisticated response from its audience. It's easy to forget how big a star Cash was: in 1969, one in every five records sold in the USA were by him, and he was outselling the Beatles. On his prison albums, the bedrocks of his fame, he identified with the prisoners, so casting him as anything other than a baddie was unthinkable. His life story— his poor roots, his (brief) incarceration, his drug addiction, his Christian beliefs, etc.— were all known to the American public via media profiles and his TV show. By 1974, when the *Columbo* episode aired, he was in full born-again mode, touting his friendship with Billy Graham, and identifying himself as a gospel singer. The show never got more "meta" than this.

Finally, over time, *Columbo* "grew into itself," with its tone becoming increasingly emphasized. The mystery format had from the beginning set it apart from regular cop shows, but now its innocuousness became its strength. When in one 1975 episode ("Forgotten Lady") Columbo admits, "I can't stand the sight of blood," and gets caught out for not keeping up with his firearm practice, it can be interpreted as the character speaking for his audience, and taking a dig at what was perceived as a rising tide of unnecessary violence on TV—perhaps the biggest panic in this regard since the furor surrounding *The Untouchables* in the early 1960s. In a 1978 episode, "Make Me a Perfect Murder," the theme is made explicit, with a witness despairing of "violence on television."

The violence issue was of genuine concern in some quarters, and, as ever, the debate focused on the perceived "effects" of narratives. The *Time* article cited a report for the National Institute for Mental Health about rising levels of fear in America's cities, while at about the same time a Surgeon General's report claimed to provide evidence linking screen violence and aggressive behavior. In 1975 the National PTA adopted a resolution demanding that networks and local TV stations reduce the amount of violence in programs and commercials, while other lobby groups demanded that companies pull their ads if nothing was done. A CBS high-up noted that there was now "a thirst for positive, nonviolent drama."[11] This was not good news for cop shows, and before long *Starsky & Hutch* and others were "toning down."

But *Columbo* had no such worries, and capitalized on its gentler aesthetic—thereby reassuring advertisers. Indeed, for some actors it was an attraction—Patrick McGoohan, a devout Christian, made it clear he abhorred explicit violence. Even the fact that the shows lasted longer than the average cop show came to be seen as a sign of good taste, supposedly denoting longer attention spans and greater "maturity" on the part of viewers who belonged to the older—and, it was assumed, more affluent—demographic that advertisers were keen to reach.

The show concluded in 1978, not because it was unpopular, but because Falk wanted to do other things. He had continued to make movies (*Murder by Death*, *The Brink's Job*, etc.), and never felt the urge to exploit Columbo in the same way as Jack Webb had Joe Friday or Telly Savalas had Kojak. He'd taken the character as far as he could go, and felt it was time to "hang up the mac."

However, that wasn't the end. Eleven years later, in 1989, with Falk now 62, ABC revived *Columbo*. Now there was a whole new roster of celebrity killers, and new ideas about how the show should be shaped for a post–*Hill Street*, post–*Miami Vice* audience. In some episodes, Columbo has a love interest (including Faye Dunaway), and in some he even carries a gun. Shows now lasted two hours, with Falk very much in control of the production side (his salary per episode was now reportedly in the range of $300,000—ironically, he now owned one of those porticoed LA houses with a swimming pool). But although ratings remained solid, the new run was a creative disaster, with critics bemoaning the tweaks to the formula as padded and narcissistic.

There was also a misjudged spin-off called *Mrs. Columbo* (1979–80), starring Kate Mulgrew (later better known as Captain Janeway in *Star Trek: Voyager*). In the original series, Columbo would often talk about his wife, but she never made an appearance. When she did, as a detective in her own right, she turned out to be rather dull: in the words of one critic, "Her vulnerability was just that: awful, terminal vulnerability."[12]

Right up to the end of Falk's life, in 2011, there was talk of a *Columbo* revival. However, he now suffered from Alzheimer's, the crueler tabloid newspapers making much of the fact that the guy who played the cop with the bad memory now couldn't even remember the cop. The fan base has remained strong, however, and William Link continues to write *Columbo* short stories.

In terms of *Columbo*'s legacy, there were two obvious patterns. First, the show gave rise to the era of "character cops." It had proved that there was an appetite for policemen with a bit more personality than Joe Friday, and in the immediate wake of the initial episodes there were a number of quirky creations—notably Cannon (portly, with expensive tastes), and most famously, Kojak (if Columbo was a shabby cop in elegant surroundings, Kojak was the opposite: an elegant cop in shabby surroundings). The trope endured, and we can detect traces of Columbo's eccentric sleuthing method in *CSI*'s Gil Grissom and *The Wire*'s Lester Freamon—indeed, in the 21st century, it's almost a given that a star cop will have some kind of character flaw (alcoholism, OCD, depression, etc.) or more positive personality trait (odd hobbies, amusing pets, etc.).

Second, *Columbo* was responsible for opening up a space in the schedules for the sub-genre that became known as "the cozies"—typified by *Murder, She Wrote* (another Levinson and Link creation) and *Diagnosis: Murder*. These are non-threatening cop, mystery and detective shows that feature "special guest stars" and which are perfect fodder for syndication and Sunday afternoon repeats. As the success of *Miss Marple* (BBC, 1984–92) reminds us, they in a sense reanimate the spirit of Agatha Christie. *Columbo* had always been very clear about its tonal parameters, and the cozies are all about never crossing the taste barrier.[13]

In conclusion, *Columbo* proved emphatically that the *Dragnet* formula wasn't the only way to approach the cop genre. By taking a gentler, more meandering, path, it remade the English "drawing room mystery" for TV audiences of the 1960s and 70s. It showed the appeal of non-realism at a time when other cop shows—notably *Kojak*—were going in the opposite direction. When *Time* called *Columbo* "endearing," the magazine was actually highlighting a carefully crafted formula that had several layers—from the pleasures of recognizing guest stars to the often quite sophisticated direction and acting. At the center of it all, there was Columbo himself—in *Time*'s words, "deceptively plodding, cunningly naive"—the "character cop" par excellence.

Recommended Episodes

The pilot TV movie, "Prescription Murder" (1968), shows *Columbo* at a prototype stage, but with most elements already in place (even though Columbo's coat isn't rumpled, and he sports a short-back-and-sides haircut and a natty suit and tie). It's a slick mystery that privileges plot over anything else, with Columbo engaging a psychiatrist murderer in a game of cat-and-mouse—at one point he asks his adversary how to go about catching a "hypothetical" educated killer who sees his deed as an "intellectual project" (shades of Hitchcock's *Rope*, perhaps?). This postmodern knowingness has made the episode a favorite among mystery cognoscenti—though it is oddly cold compared to what the show would become. "By Dawn's Early Light" (1974), by contrast, is indicative of the show in its pomp, and is set in a military training school. It pits the slovenly detective against a paragon of self-control in the form of Patrick McGoohan, obviously relishing the role of a murderous army officer. Much glorious hamming ensues, and Columbo, in what was perhaps a nod to the anti–Vietnam War movement, makes clear his distaste for military discipline and punishment.

Further Reading

There are very few academic sources—though a search on Google Scholar reveals some intriguing oblique references in works about science, the law, and policing. The memoirs of Levinson and Link are satisfyingly detailed: *Stay Tuned: An Inside Look at the Making of Prime Time Television* (St. Martin's Press, 1981). *Mark Dawidziak's The Columbo Phile: A Casebook* (Mysterious Press, 1989) is fannish, but a good companion volume. Peter Falk's autobiography *Just One More Thing* (Hutchinson, 2007) is breezy but contains useful information. The *Columbo* (fan) website, http://www.columbo-site.freeuk.com, is terrific, and contains excerpts from the Link/Levinson book. Apart from that, the (auto)biographies of guest stars yield alternative viewpoints, and there are a few studies of the mystery genre, e.g., the relevant chapter of Alistair Wisker's *Crime Fiction: An Introduction* (Continuum, 2009).

CHAPTER 7

Hawaii Five-O
(CBS, 1968–80)
BRIAN FAUCETTE *and* BEN BETHELL

For many years the longest running cop show in television history (until finally overtaken in 2003 by *Law & Order*), *Hawaii Five-O* starred the lantern-jawed Jack Lord as Steve McGarrett, one of TV law enforcement's greatest tough-guy protagonists. Like many of the era's procedurals, the show prided itself on its depiction of police work in authentic detail. But set against the lush backdrop of America's fiftieth state, it had a distinct edge over its rivals. With a lead character—more action-adventure hero than by-the-book detective—who broke the *Dragnet* mold, suffusing the cop genre with the ultra-modern glamour of 1960s spy fiction, *Hawaii Five-O* ran for twelve years, achieving top ratings for eight of its record-breaking seasons. It also became a pop-culture phenomenon: surf-rock group the Ventures reached number four on the *Billboard* Hot 100 in 1969 with a cover of the show's theme tune (later a favorite with amphetamine-fueled dancers at the UK's legendary Wigan Casino discotheque), while fans devoured spin-off novels, and *MAD* magazine mercilessly lampooned Lord and his co-stars. McGarrett's catchphrase, "Book 'em, Danno," his episode-concluding instruction to dutiful sidekick Danny Williams (James MacArthur), remains widely used. As does "Five-O" as generic slang for police officers, employed by New York street gangs from the early 1980s and later popularized by rap acts including Nas, the Fugees and, recently, Nicki Minaj.

Formally annexed by the United States in 1898, Hawaii won statehood only in 1959. This followed a decade of labor unrest by longshoremen and agricultural workers culminating in 1954's nonviolent "Democratic Revolution," which broke the stranglehold on political power enjoyed by the islands' plantation-owning oligarchy. Identified by the architects of statehood as key to Hawaii's future, tourism exploded after 1959. However, the rapid transition from agriculture as the islands' principal industry was already well under way by the early 1950s, during the first flush of America's long post-war consumer boom. The second half of the decade witnessed the wholesale development of such iconic resorts as Oahu's Waikiki Beach, where industrialist Henry J. Kaiser built the colossal Kaiser Hawaiian Village (today the Hilton Hawaiian Village). To promote his investment, Kaiser persuaded Warner Bros. Television to produce a version of its lightweight private-eye show, *77 Sunset Strip* (ABC, 1958–64), with characters based in the new hotel complex. Though in reality filmed on a Burbank back-lot, *Hawaiian Eye* (ABC, 1959–63) proved the most successful of three *Sunset Strip* spin-offs,[1] its stock footage of the islands beguiling TV audiences for whom the new state was an alluring novelty.

Hawaii Five-O was from the outset a far more ambitious undertaking. Costing over $750,000 to make and shot on location in Hawaii as a two-hour TV movie, "Cocoon," its pilot episode, received a Hollywood-style premier at Honolulu's Royal Theater in February 1968, and was aired by CBS in two parts later that year. The show began life as a project entitled "The Man," conceived by writer and producer Leonard Freeman as a TV vehicle for actor Richard Boone (best known as a star of big-screen Westerns). When the network rejected the script, Freeman re-tooled "The Man" and gave it a Hawaiian setting—the choice of location due principally to his mother-in-law's residence on the islands and a desire to spend more time with his family. Offered the lead role by Freeman, Boone declined, as did Gregory Peck. TV actor Robert Brown, Freeman's next choice, was then dropped at the eleventh hour by CBS, to be replaced by Lord, with whom the producer had already worked on an unsold 1964 pilot entitled *Grand Hotel*. Two years earlier, Lord had passed up the lead role in *Star Trek* (CBS, 1966–69), the part of Captain James T. Kirk going to William Shatner when producer Gene Rodenberry refused to hand Lord 50 percent of the show. With less than a week to go before location shooting for *Hawaii Five-O* was due to begin, and with Freeman and CBS now well and truly over a barrel, the actor once again demanded a partnership. This time, Lord was successful in cutting a three-way deal with the producer and the network. It was a decision that Freeman would never regret: "I'm a perfectionist and so is he," he told reporters. "Having a star like Jack is like having money in the bank. He's always on time, no bags under his eyes, and he always knows his lines."[2]

"Cocoon" owed a clear debt to Ian Fleming's James Bond novels and their cinema adaptations, the first of which, 1962's *Dr. No* (Terence Young), featured Lord as CIA operative Felix Leiter. Familiar to viewers as both a spy and a gunslinger (he frequently appeared on Western shows such as *Bonanza*, *Rawhide* and *High Chaparral*) the actor was perfectly cast as McGarrett, a combination of latter-day frontier lawman and "high-level Cold War agent, complete with top secret clearance, high tech gadgets, and state of the art intelligence."[3] The pilot sees McGarrett investigate the murder of a U.S. intelligence agent; reviewing its Honolulu premier, one local critic described Lord's character as "a first rate super sleuth who is more believable than James Bond."[4] But in contrast to the detached, debonair 007 (though like him a Navy man), McGarrett is portrayed in early episodes as a brash, hot-headed workaholic cop—the analytical master-detective of later seasons was yet to come. His characteristic obsessive tenacity is, however, already apparent: as one of the dead man's colleagues remarks, "Everybody knows that Steve McGarrett only takes orders from the Governor and God—and occasionally even they have trouble."

In the role, Lord projected a confident "playboy" masculinity of the kind associated primarily with Bond, as well as characters such as Simon Templar, the hero of Leslie Charteris's *Saint* novels (played on TV by Roger Moore [ITV, 1962–69]) and Derek Flint, the priapic American super-spy portrayed by James Coburn in *Our Man Flint* (Daniel Mann, 1966) and *In Like Flint* (Gordon Douglas, 1967). With his lacquered hairstyle and tailored suits, McGarrett resembles less a working cop than a well-heeled man-about-town. An endless succession of girlfriends and lovers serve to emphasize his playboy status. Like Bond and like Flint, he is a "lone wolf" whose "dead girlfriend syndrome" (notable fellow-sufferers include Starsky and Hutch) dictates that any episode's love interest must by its end have either fled the islands permanently or met a (usually violent) death.[5] Female witnesses or victims succumb to McGarrett's sexual magnetism and wilt before his penetrating gaze. One such is the hippie college girl with an apparent predilection for middle-aged men played in "Cocoon" by Nancy Kwan, whose career as an international sex-symbol began in 1960 when she shot to fame as star of *The World of Suzie Wong*. McGarrett discusses the murder case with Kwan's character in an ocean-side nightspot and later on a moonlit beach; *Hawaii Five-O*'s aura of romance and danger was, as we shall see, due in no small part to its use of locations. Off duty, McGarrett is seen relaxing at home in his beach house or skippering his boat across Pacific waves. Like Thomas Magnum, his successor as CBS's King of Hawaii (played by Tom Selleck in *Magnum P.I.* [1980–88]), he is depicted as the master of an exotic realm. As media scholar and former TV producer Peter Britos observes, both characters serve as "new high priests of the tropics," who in a Hawaiian context "function ideologically as Euro 'gods.'"[6]

Middle-aged, trigger-happy, promiscuous action heroes were, of course, by no means rare in the 1960s and early '70s. The period's television dramas usually revolved around white male central characters, conceived by white male screenwriters, producers and network executives as idealized embodiments of robust American masculinity. Even by contemporary standards, however, McGarrett could come across as an atavistic throwback; often labeled "fascist" by would-be countercultural revolutionaries, Lord's character still remains for many the archetypal Nixon-era "pig." It should, however, be remembered that for Freeman and the show's writers, it was McGarrett's compassion that set him apart from crime-fighting TV counterparts: CBS originally billed him as "the cop who cares."[7] And despite Lord's legendary egotism (caricatured by *TV Guide* with the precept, "I am the Lord, by God, and there shall be no other superstars before me—only featured players"[8]), *Hawaii Five-O*'s focus on a team of detectives—and, moreover, a multiethnic team—was at the time unusual. In this, the show anticipated by over a decade the groundbreaking ensemble format of *Hill Street Blues* and, later still, *Homicide: Life on the Street*.

Headquartered in a suite of offices at Honolulu's historic Iolani Palace (which, though it never in fact housed a law enforcement agency, did function until 1969 as Hawaii's state capitol) McGarrett leads the "5-O" task-force, an elite unit of the (fictional) Hawaiian State Police. The unit comprises "Danno" (played in the pilot by Tim O'Kelley, but replaced by James MacArthur following test screenings), Chin Ho Kelly (Kam Fong) and Kono Kalakaua (Gilbert "Zulu" Kauhi—always credited simply as Zulu). Fresh from appearing with Clint Eastwood in *Hang 'Em High* (Ted Post, 1968), a Spaghetti-influenced Western produced and co-written by Freeman, former teen idol MacArthur brought a baby-faced intensity to his portrayal of McGarrett's faithful subordinate. Conceived as a tough, hardworking, ordinary American, the role was just as important as Lord's. Whereas McGarrett was a character upon whom they could project escapist fantasies, viewers were meant

Iconic credits, accompanied by iconic music. Cop shows had never been this glamorous.

to identify with Danno, whose sweat-soaked shirts and "working stiff" ready-made suits are in distinct contrast to the snappy figure cut by his debonair boss. Until MacArthur's departure from the show at the end of its eleventh season, *Hawaii 5-O's* fans retained a soft spot for McGarrett's sidekick, whom they watched grow from season 1's rookie detective into a hardened cop who has pretty much seen it all.

Kam Fong, a Honolulu Police Department veteran who'd notched up sixteen years on the force before becoming an actor, auditioned for the part of the pilot's villain, Wo Fat, but was cast instead as the dependable Lt. Chin Ho Kelly. Fong's character was modeled by Freeman on fictional detective Charlie Chan, hugely popular in the 1930s and '40s and himself based, according to creator Earl Derr Biggers, on a Chinese-Hawaiian detective named Chang Apana. The imposing Zulu, well-known on the islands as a disc jockey and stand-up comedian, played Hawaiian detective Kono Kalakaua, until he fell out with Lord and quit the

Steve McGarrett (Jack Lord) radios for backup outside the Honolulu courthouse. Lord became so associated with the city that in 2004 a statue of him was erected in a shopping mall, which today gets regularly lei-ed (garlanded) by visitors (CBS TV/The Kobal Collection).

show in 1972. His replacement as the unit's authentic native element was another local entertainer, Al Harrington (in fact Samoan), who played Detective Ben Kokua for three seasons until replaced in turn by Herman Wedemeyer, a former state legislator and college football star (of European, Chinese and Hawaiian ancestry) as Detective Duke Lukela. As America's post–Civil Rights era dawned, Freeman aimed to hold Hawaii up to the rest of nation as a model of racial harmony: noting in 1971 *Hawaii Five-O's* "diversity of ethnic groups working together with no apparent problems," the *LA Times'* TV critic remarked that "it isn't just tokenism as in some other shows."[9] There was, though, never much question of the Irish-Chinese Chin Ho and his native colleagues playing anything other than second fiddle to McGarrett and Danno. And neither was the show's native support cast ever asked to do much but "drive cabs, serve as doormen, bartenders, helpers and fire-dancers, or occasionally play knuckle-headed muscle."[10]

Other regulars included Honolulu savings and loan executive Harry Endo as forensic scientist Che Fong (seasons 2 to 9) and veteran actor Richard Denning, who came out of retirement on the islands to play Governor Paul Jameson. Denning's character was based on John A. Burns, the principal architect of Hawaiian statehood and state governor from 1962 to 1974, whom Freeman had consulted while still working on the show's pilot script. "Cocoon" also saw the first appearance of McGarrett's arch-enemy, Wo Fat, the Red Chinese master-spy who, as the show's chronicler Karen Rhodes observes, functions as a Cold War update of Sax Rohmer's Doctor Fu Manchu.[11] Named for Freeman's favorite Honolulu restaurant and played as an archetypal sinister Oriental by Khigh Dheig (whose ancestry was in fact North African and who'd played a similar role in John Frankenheimer's 1962 Cold War thriller, *The Manchurian Candidate*), Wo Fat was due to be killed off in the pilot's original script. However, Lord was keen on the character and lobbied his production partner for a re-write. Though thwarted at the end of "Cocoon," Wo thus remains a perpetual thorn in McGarrett's side, resurfacing periodically in the years that follow to resume battle with his nemesis.

In the show's first full season on CBS, espionage and Bond-style action were, however, largely dropped in favor of gritty procedural storylines that took audiences to the "cheap lodgings, mean streets, boxing rings, and dirty, cluttered alleys" that lay behind Honolulu's tourist frontages.[12] Like their counterparts on the overtly liberal *Ironside* (NBC, 1967–75) and the über-hip *Mod Squad* (ABC, 1968–73), season 1's scriptwriters also relished any opportunity to tackle aspects of the era's counterculture. This might be represented by the student protesters of "Not that Much Different" or the drug-warped hippies of "Up Tight," which sees Danno working undercover to trap a renegade college professor guilty of dosing youngsters with hallucinogenic "speed." The issue of drug abuse received less hysterical— and far more affecting—treatment in season 3's "Trouble in Mind," notable for Grammy-winning vocalist Nancy Wilson's performance as a heroin-ravaged jazz singer. A season 6 episode, "Hookman" (1973, voted a favorite by fans), exemplifies the show in its heyday. McGarrett and his team are targeted by a psychopathic ex-con (played by real-life El Paso private investigator Jay J. Armes) who seeks revenge against McGarrett for the loss of his hands in an explosion during a botched bank raid (Armes, himself an amputee, had lost both hands as a teenager under similar circumstances). The unit identifies and tracks down the assassin, whom Danno in the end kills before he can reach McGarrett. There was, as MacArthur later observed, "little if any character psychology or inner personal turmoil in the scripts—we just caught the crooks."[13] His vaunted compassion notwithstanding, McGarrett remains impassive even in response to the fatal shooting of colleagues and his own narrow brush with death. As Freeman told Morton Stevens, composer of the show's immortal theme tune, *Hawaii Five-O* was "about a guy who is hard as a rock. And he's living on a rock. And he's hard."[14]

In place of backstory and deep characterization, episodes tended to focus on the unit's investigative process. In this respect *Hawaii Five-O* belongs firmly to the *Dragnet* tradition, Freeman and Lord sharing Jack Webb's obsession with the minutiae of police procedure. The show's realistic depiction of police work was complemented by its use of real Hawaiian locations. In addition to these, a disued U.S. Navy warehouse served as an ad-hoc sound stage until eventually replaced by a fully-functioning, purpose-built TV studio—Hawaii's first—which then drew other productions to the islands (and where, once *Hawaii Five-O* was finally cancelled in 1980, *Magnum P.I.*'s opulent interiors would be swiftly erected). The outlay involved in transporting cast, crew and equipment to the islands (not to mention flying "dailies" back to Los Angeles) was, as we have already seen, considerable: in regular production a single episode cost over $250,000 to make, rising to nearly twice this by 1980.[15] These costs were justified by Freeman via appeals to authenticity, which he viewed correctly as *Hawaii Five-O*'s unique selling-point.

The show's record-breaking success was doubtless due in no small part to the mystique of its novel locale. Critics were unanimous in identifying this as *Hawaii Five-O*'s key ingredient, giving what would otherwise have been a fairly standard police procedural its distinct advantage over competitors. In a fulsome 1968 write-up, *TV Guide* praised *Hawaii Five-O* as "amazingly authentic": "As befits a show which is filmed in Hawaii," the magazine enthused, "it is tremendously satisfying visually—all the way to the wave which ushers in each commercial break."[16] Color television greatly enhanced such effects. Though color sets had been commercially available since the mid–1950s, it wasn't until 1966 that the networks broadcast their first all-color primetime seasons (and not until 1972 that sales of color sets overtook those of black-and-white TVs). One of the very first shows to fully realize color broadcasting's seductive potential, *Hawaii Five-O*'s glamorous visual depiction of Hawaii gave its tourist industry an enormous boost, thus hastening the new state's transition from a plantation economy to one based primarily on servicing the needs of visitors from the mainland.

The representation of the islands as "paradise" (despite their evident crime problem) can be understood as among *Hawaii Five-O*'s principal tasks. Indeed, the show's "overt theme and unifying principle," according to Freeman himself, "was man's evil amid the beauty of paradise."[17] The islands' native population is, however, seldom treated as the source of this evil. As inhabitants of a corrupted Eden, native Hawaiians are instead pictured in Rousseauian hues. In the face of bewildering social transformation, it is with their noble yet doomed struggle to preserve their culture that the show's sympathies lie—as do McGarrett's, their "Euro 'god.'" The dispossession of native Hawaiians by the modernizing force of tourism is the subject of the first season's second episode, "Strangers in Our Own Land"; it would remain a recurrent theme in the years that followed. Correspondingly, *Hawaii Five-O* was one of the first network dramas to feature green politics in its storylines. Season 3's "The Last Eden," for instance, sees an outspoken nightclub performer (Ray Danton) framed for blowing up a sewage plant, while in season 4's "Is This Any Way to Run a Paradise?" McGarrett plays a lethal game of cat-and-mouse with an environmental terrorist (Nephi Hannemann) whose *nom de guerre* is shared with a Hawaiian war-god.

Though Rhodes sees an apparent contradiction between the show's essentially conservative, law-and-order ethos and its pro-native, anti-development agenda, the upholding of "traditional" values was in fact entirely coterminous with the preservation of Hawaii's pre-industrial, rigidly hierarchical forms of social organization. It can, moreover, be argued that *Hawaii Five-O* in no way promoted genuine forms of native self-determination but, on the contrary, served to reinforce mainland hegemony, masking inter-racial tension and making non-native rule appear a natural and inevitable state of affairs.[18] In spite of its avowed nativism, the show, for Britos, is a product of the mainland, treating the islands as "both an extension of the American frontier, and a developing space for cosmopolitan adventure," with McGarrett existing "to prevent foreign infiltration, protect American lives and property, and promote a safe haven for tourist excursion and romance."[19] Rather than participating in the Hawaiian Cultural Renaissance of the 1970s, *Hawaii Five-O* merely advocated the preservation in aspic of those elements of Hawaiian culture found charming by visitors. The show's opening credit sequence (designed by Iranian-American director Reza Badiyi) promotes the islands as an ultra-modern tourist destination. Employing rapid-fire editing and smash zooms, the montage contrasts passenger jets, high-rise luxury hotels and neon lights with golden sunsets and the native islanders themselves, represented by beguiling dark-haired maidens and an innocent young boy. Composer Morton Stevens, whose previous TV credits included *Gunsmoke*, employed insistent percussion and rousing brass to complement Badiyi's crashing surf and jiggling hula dancers, creating in the process a new "Hawaiian" sound that was completely unfamiliar to Hawaiian ears.

Hawaii Five-O's early seasons coincided with rising concern about the increasingly violent nature of television drama, an issue that dogged the show despite ratings success and critical acclaim. When Democrat Rhode Island senator John O. Pastore, chair of the U.S. Senate Subcommittee on Communications, singled it out during Congressional hearings, the show's leading man leapt to its defense: "what we're trying to say is violence begets violence," Lord declared, "that nothing is ever solved by violence."[20] (Elsewhere, he labeled the senator "a big fat windbag.") But the accusation that shows such as *Hawaii 5-O* directly influenced audience behavior simply wouldn't go away. In January 1970, a viewer was killed copying a second season episode, "Bored, She Hung Herself," in which a hippie (Don Quine) is suspected of murder following his girlfriend's death in an apparent case of yogic auto-asphyxiation. CBS subsequently pulled the episode from its rerun schedules—it has never been broadcast in syndication or released on DVD and remains to this day locked away in the network's vaults. And worse was still to come: a year later, when a Baltimore paint brush plant employee shot and killed five of his fellow workers and wounded a sixth, Baltimore PD spokesmen blamed the spree on a season 4 episode, "...And I Want Some Candy and a Gun That Shoots."[21]

By the time the show was finally cancelled, such controversy was a distant memory. The major networks had by then toned down the visceral action of much early '70s crime drama and, with the advent of VHS, anti-violence crusaders turned their attention to a new breed of low-budget ultra-violent action films and horror movies. Complaining in 1979 of the watering-down of TV violence in general, a *New York Times* correspondent noted that public morality's self-appointed guardians had managed to turn "even that arch law-and-order symbol, McGarrett ... from an attractively vengeful pursuer into a boring forensic brooder."[22] As *Hawaii 5-O* drifted toward the realm of the staid whodunit, the show abandoned Honolulu's mean streets, and with them its own social conscience. Increasingly found, as Rhodes observes, in the lavish homes of the islands' elite, the unit now operated as a "'society' law enforcement agency, looking into the problems of the rich, spoiled and bored."[23] It is to this world that McGarrett's heir, the playboy private investigator, Thomas Magnum, belongs.

Kam Fong departed at the end of season 10: in a harrowing episode for long-term fans, Chin Ho's corpse is dumped unceremoniously by mob assassins on the steps of Iolani Palace. MacArthur walked a season later. The show's final season saw Danno replaced by ex–Boston PD detective James "Kimo" Carew (William Smith) and the addition to the unit of its first female member, Detective Lori Wilson (Sharon Farrell). But new faces failed to compensate for increasingly threadbare storylines and save *Hawaii 5-O*'s ratings from terminal decline. In the final episode, "Woe to Wo Fat," aired in April 1980, McGarrett at last brings his arch-enemy to justice. By this time the master-spy has evolved into a full-blown Bond-style super-villain, complete with doomsday weapon and tropical island HQ. In the show's last shot—one of TV's greatest perpetual cliffhangers—he is seen in a jail cell, giving his trademark evil smile and producing a hidden file from inside his shoe.

In hope of a full resurrection, *A-Team* creator Stephen J. Cannell wrote and produced a 1997 TV movie, starring Gary Busey as McGarrett and featuring cameos from MacArthur and Fong in their original roles (Danno now Governor of Hawaii). Cannell's pilot was, however, shelved by CBS. Fans would wait over a decade more for *Hawaii 5-0* (the new show featuring a zero rather than an "O" in its title), which debuted on CBS in 2010 and is now in its fifth season. Freeman, tragically, did not live to see his creation's extraordinary long-term legacy, having died following heart surgery in 1974. The new show pays tribute to him in retaining (along with a barely-altered version of the famous theme tune) *Hawaii 5-O*'s original character names: Alex O'Loughlin plays ex–Navy SEAL Steve McGarrett, with Scott Caan as "Danno" Williams, Daniel Dae Kim as Chin Ho, and Grace Park as an ex-pro surfer and rookie female cop named Kono Kalakaua.

Recommended Episodes

Of the episodes mentioned in this chapter, season 6's "Hookman" is a must-see. Other key episodes include season 1's "King of the Hill" (one of only a very few in which nobody is actually killed): Yaphet Kotto (a Bond villain in 1973's *Live and Let Die* and Lt. Al Giardello in *Homicide: Life on the Street*) plays a U.S. Marine who, in a delusional state resulting from a head injury, kidnaps Danno, forcing McGarrett to go against his instincts and employ a "softly softly" approach to secure his sidekick's release. Among later episodes, season 8's "Death's Name is Sam" is well worth watching: *Star Trek*'s George Takei gives a memorable guest performance as a Honolulu PD officer drafted by 5-O to pose as the would-be assassin of an exiled Southeast Asian politician.

Further Reading

Given its longevity and popularity, surprisingly little has been written about the show. In "Symbols, Myth and TV in Hawaii, the First Cycle: An Overview" in *Oceania in the Age of Global Media*, special issue of *Spectator* 23:1 (Spring 2003), Peter Britos treats *Hawaiian Eye*, *Hawaii 5-O* and *Magnum P.I.* as a continuous "discursive arc": the approach is fruitful, and the argument developed fully in "Symbols, Myth and TV in Hawaii: 'Hawaiian Eye,' 'Five-O,' and 'Magnum P.I.': The First Cycle" (unpublished doctoral dissertation, University of Southern California, 2001). Karen Rhodes provides a useful overview, along with an episode guide, in *Booking* Hawaii Five-O: *An Episode Guide and Critical History of the 1968–1980 Television Detective Series* (McFarland, 1997). In a chapter on crime shows of the 1960s, Douglas Snauffer's *Crime Television* (Praeger, 2006) includes a section on *Hawaii Five-O*. For a discussion of the show's famous theme tune see Elizabeth Withey, "TV Gets Jazzed: The Evolution of Action TV Theme Music" in Bill Osgerby and Anna Gough-Yates (eds.), *Action TV: Tough Guys, Smooth Operators and Foxy Chicks* (Routledge, 2001).

CHAPTER 8

Kojak
(CBS, 1973–78)
ROGER SABIN

One of the most popular TV cop shows of all time, *Kojak* was built around three things: the macho charisma of star Telly Savalas, its sparky squad room banter, and its perceived "realism"—typified by the gritty multiculturalism of its New York locations. It was a new kind of cop show for a new, post–Civil Rights age. Such was its ubiquity in the culture at large that children could amuse themselves with *Kojak* board games and toys; the Clash would reference the show in one of their most famous songs; Benny Hill would do an impersonation in a plastic "bald wig"; *MAD* magazine featured the strip "Kojerk"; and the faux-friendly greeting "Oi, Kojak!" was routinely directed at passing skinheads.[1]

The show didn't start out with such a populist orientation. The pilot, made as a TV movie in 1973, and entitled *The Marcus-Nelson Murders*, was an exercise in politically-focused realism. Based on a real 1966 case, it was about the rape and murder of two young professional women in New York, and subsequent police mistakes during the investigation, which resulted in the crime being pinned on an innocent black youth.[2] The show was populated by harder-than-hardboiled cops, some of them racist, and a central character called "Kojack"—an amalgam of several cops on the real case—who is, at least, honest, but not above beating up a suspect if he feels like it. The movie's extraordinary tone was underlined when a lawyer concludes: "Law and Order is being used as a catchphrase for Stop the Nigger!" This was not the kind of line you were likely to hear in other cop shows, or indeed in later *Kojak* episodes.

The pilot was written by Abby Mann, an under-appreciated figure in TV history. He was an Academy Award–winning film writer known for his liberal politics, and a friend of Martin Luther King. From the start, he was open about his desire to use the crime genre to shine a light on injustices (one obituary would say of him that he "elevated the level" of television by his commitment to social realism[3]). Although the inspiration for the pilot was a case from the 1960s, the problem of police corruption was very much on the radar in the 1970s, and Mann was conscious that the *New York Times* was running regular exposes, and giving front page coverage to the developing Serpico court case, in which a cop testified against his NYPD colleagues.

Mann had initially assumed the show would go to Universal (NBC), but recalled later that "[they] didn't want to do it. That was the point in television [history] when you had to treat cops not just as good, but as saints. This was the time of *Dragnet* and 'All we want is the facts' [a reference to the 1967–70 remake]. Universal were scared as hell. They didn't want to show cops and society as it really was."[4] Instead, CBS picked it up. At the time, the network was trying to reorient its dramatic programming away from shows aimed at audiences in the countryside and more towards the cities (the so-called "rural purge"): Mann's project fit the plan perfectly.

Finding a suitably downbeat star was imperative. Kojack was an honest man among dishonest men, and willing to confront his colleagues, so an actor with the necessary mix of integrity and toughness would be sought. For a while, Marlon Brando was interested in the part, not least because of the story's political core, but CBS claimed he would have brought a glamour to it that was inappropriate. Instead, a character actor was cast: Telly Savalas, previously famous for playing movie heavies (a rapist in *The Dirty Dozen*, Blofeld in *On Her Majesty's Secret Service*, etc.).

Savalas thus brought with him some baggage in terms of audience expectations, but at the same time he had an undeniable New York charm; he'd grown up in the city, and had an aura of "knowing his way around." As Kojack, Savalas exuded an unorthodox sexual magnetism: this cop, despite being in his 40s and bald, was a dandy in Italian suits, who could cook, and can charm the ladies with quick-fire banter. There was also the character's, and the actor's, racial "ambiguity." Savalas was of Greek ancestry, and this was a convenient device for positioning him as a kind of mediator between the white and black communities in the story. Finally, Savalas could offer a sense of world-weariness that was crucial. In other movies of the time, Savalas had played good guys who "get the job done despite it all" (for example, "Big Joe" in *Kelly's Heroes*), and this was undoubtedly the model the casting team had in mind.

The pilot's final ingredient, and one that Mann was equally insistent upon, was a realistic setting ("the characters seemed to demand that," he said[5]). New York had to be shown in all its contemporary complexity; it was a city on the verge of bankruptcy. (In 1975 the President would reportedly refuse to bail it out: as the *New York Daily News* headline put it, "Ford to City: Drop Dead."[6]) The location shots of streets full of trash, graffiti on the walls, boarded-up houses and so on, reflected a squalid truth. CBS's rural purge was one thing, but this kind of urban grittiness was another: TV drama had never been quite this real.

In retrospect *The Marcus-Nelson Murders* can be seen as belonging to two cycles in cinema crime movies: the social conscience movie, typified by *In the Heat of the Night*, and the "authentic" urban thriller, characterized by *The French Connection* and *Serpico*—both of which were set in New York. But it was also its own thing, and offered a new, updated vision of the police force for TV audiences. It suggested, of course, that there were some (very) bad apples, but the message was that Kojack represented the best of the force; he was a cop who was "of" the streets and "for" the streets, and at a time when those streets were in crisis. As the character says, "The police force *is* the community."

The Marcus-Nelson Murders was too dark to be a major hit, but it was enough of one to get a series commissioned. From there, *Kojak* (the spelling was changed from the original), the series, took on a momentum of its own, but it was necessarily going to be different. The politics and earthiness were played down, and as a result an increasingly frustrated Mann withdrew into the background (though he continued to get a "Created by" credit). The official press release for episode 1 quoted Producer Matthew Rapf rationalizing the way things would go: "The picture [*The Marcus-Nelson Murders*], as a 'one-shot,' served us very, very well. But it was a concentrated dose of a lot of pretty heavy things. For a weekly series, we're not going away from reality or truth. If a controversial issue arises … we would do it. But we are not planning on doing controversy for the sake of it or 'message shows' to be moralizing."[7]

In the new series, the focus was on the Kojak character himself—a move that would have been familiar to watchers of single-name TV cop shows like *Cannon*, which *Kojak* replaced in schedules. There was also a new signature tune (a rousing jazz score by Billy Goldenberg) and fresh branding, with the letters of Kojak's name rising from the buildings of New York ("cop-as-community" once more). Finally, as the producer's quote above hints, the storylines became more slick and formulized—underlining that for all its "quality" elements, *Kojak* still belonged to the network era, and was inevitably driven by the old the imperative of "delivering eyeballs" to the ads.

Serialization had its creative advantages. Kojak himself could now be developed into a more rounded individual, week-by-week. Some things from *The Marcus-Nelson Murders* were kept. For example, he remained the epitome of "cop knowledge" (in the words of Christopher Wilson's book of the same name): somebody who knew his locale intimately and had a sixth sense about crime—a sense borne of, in Kojak's words, "20 years of sniffin' the garbage."[8] Also, he would continue to get emotionally involved with the cases, and often

Theo Kojak (Telly Savalas) lays down the law, "baby." Clothes were always a big part of the character, and Savalas went on to front a line of menswear ("*Telly Apparel* for the real man") (Universal TV/The Kobal Collection).

demonstrate sympathy for the villains (who were "from the same side of the street"). Similarly, his dandyism continued to be highlighted, now including wearing shades, various kinds of 1970s bling (pendants, etc.) and an up-to-the moment digital watch. The suits, as ever, were spectacular, and (latterly) supplied by the Savalas-endorsed company, "Telly Apparel for the Man" (in one episode, neatly prefiguring *The Sopranos*, Kojak's style is contrasted with that of mafia wise guys, in their terrible suits). Finally, his sexual attractiveness was sometimes played up to the level of a *Playboy* magazine Lothario: in one storyline, he ends the show with blonde twins, one on each arm; in another, he schmoozes a much younger female cop. To quote the press release for the show once more, "He's never lacking for dates."

This debonair take on cop show masculinity, hardboiled-but-with-a-sensitive-twist, was in some ways a throwback to the trendy and well-dressed stars of late 1950s/early 1960s shows like *Peter Gunn*, *Burke's Law*, and *77 Sunset Strip*. But in other ways it was very modern: Kojak wasn't by any means a "New Man"—that category was a 1980s invention—but he wasn't a Chandleresque tough guy either. He was obsessed with his appearance; old-fashioned in his hand-kissing behavior towards women but respectful of feminism; and erudite without being (necessarily) educated. He therefore occupied an interesting middle-space in the history of male representation, and this was something upon which Savalas would capitalize—as we shall see.

At the same time, Kojak also had his quirkier elements, notably catchphrases, and a fondness for lollipops (both ideas which had originated with Mann). His facility with street slang often involved him referring to people as "baby," and the words "Who loves ya, baby?" became an enduring trademark. As for the lollipops, in the first few seasons, Kojak smokes, much in the Sgt. Friday tradition, but then he quits the habit ("those things are bad for you") and takes up this sugary alternative. Bearing in mind the still-powerful tobacco advertising lobby, this was an audacious move. With his bald head, Kojak's association with an infant was obvious and humorous, and it took an actor of Savalas' wit to carry it off. This stylization of the character was in tune with other cops then appearing on TV. Perhaps the nearest comparison was with Columbo, Kojak's catchphrase contrasting with his "Just one more thing…"; his lollipop contrasting with the stogie; and his snappy suits and bling contrasting with Columbo's crumpled raincoat.

The supporting cast became more prominent as the series progressed. The character of Crocker (Kevin Dobson), Kojak's younger sidekick, only had a small role in the pilot, but now he became, at first, a gofer, forever at Kojak's beck-and-call ("Crocker!") and then a kind of surrogate son. In later episodes he would almost mimic his mentor, and even address suspects as "baby." Meanwhile, Captain McNeill (Dan Frazer) was the voice of reason, but at the same time never Kojak's "better." His is an understated role, but with deep undercurrents; as the press release explains, "They started out together and actually were partners for a few years. McNeill is aware that Theo is the superior detective, yet *he* has gone farther. Why? Because Theo's the outspoken one; ever has been and always will be." Finally, the wild-haired, but dependable, Stavros (played by Savalas' brother, George) became increasingly a kind of stooge in a double-act, the exchanges between him and Kojak being reminiscent of those between Doberman and Bilko in *The Phil Silvers Show*. It was clear at times that Savalas could barely keep a straight face while chiding Stavros for talking to the plants in the office, or for eating too much.

Thus, the dynamics of the workplace became ever more important. This was a homosocial space where the figuring-out was done, and it had to look authentic: a *sine qua non* learned from *Dragnet*. The banter between the cops was necessarily the focus, but then there were the grim dirty-green decor; the incessantly ringing phones; the extras from different ethnic backgrounds walking around in urgent fashion, clutching pieces of paper; the working lunch-breaks when Kojak, the chief, Crocker and Stavros would eat their Chinese take-aways or pastrami-on-rye sandwiches; and the constant cups of coffee gulped from styrofoam cups. All of this gave *Kojak* an atmosphere that was unique. Obviously it was glamorous in its unglamorous way, especially to viewers of the show outside the U.S.; it is interesting, for example, how satires of the show in the UK and Europe always focused on these elements.

Supporting characters also became more important in terms of guest appearances and one-offs; as in every cop show, the victims, witnesses and bad guys were replaceable every week. *Kojak* didn't go in for "stunt casting" in the manner of *Columbo*; its pretentions to realism wouldn't allow this. Yet there was one notable exception, in a final season show, when Kojak meets Liberace (playing himself), thus amusingly contrasting two rather different constructions of masculinity. More often, the *Kojak* policy was to give space to unknown actors, or those who were on the first rung of the career ladder. This was a deliberate strategy going back to the Abby Mann days, and was encouraged by Savalas, who himself had been helped as a beginner by Burt Lancaster (resulting in his casting in *Birdman of Alcatraz*). One of the pleasures of watching *Kojak* re-runs today is picking out the young faces of James Woods, Richard Gere, William Katt, Harvey Keitel, Paul Michael Glaser, and Sylvester Stallone (who ends his particular show with an anguished soliloquy that anticipates the finale of *Rambo: First Blood*).

Finally, New York continued to be a focus, but approached from different angles. The *French Connection* sensibility endured throughout the series, and some of the later episodes that riffed on prostitution and drugs offered a vision of the area around Times Square that was as disturbing in its red neon desolation as anything in *Taxi Driver*. Some storylines capitalized on recent true-life cases, for example, the "Son of Sam" serial killings of 1976–77 (the fictionalized character being referred to as a "nut" and "crackpot" by an ever-to-the-point Kojak). In other examples, the financial sector would be the setting—with the newly-built Twin Towers taking center-screen ("We're standing in the shadow of what made this country great," smirks a loan shark). Increasingly, New York's ethnic and youth-gang tensions would be referenced, but in the context of the New York Police Department having to "watch its image," Kojak's role as community cop becoming more knowing and media-savvy in the process. Filming of the show may increasingly have been undertaken in LA, but *Kojak* remained a quintessentially New York phenomenon, and the image of the city was never one informed by a tourist gaze.[9]

Thus, it would be wrong to suggest that the committed politics of *The Marcus-Nelson Murders* were completely leached out. In some senses, the show was the heir to the "New Frontier" TV writing of the early 1960s (see *Naked City* chapter), especially in the way in which the cops are shown to "care." Seasons 1 to 3, especially, held true to Mann's somber vision (Kojak says at one point: "The system stinks—but have you got a better one?"), and the writing maintained a pulpy intelligence: a 1975 episode entitled "No Immunity for Murder," about FBI interference in a case, and written by crime novelist Joe Gores, won an Edgar Award. The realism also remained key: the "technical advisor" for many shows was Salvatore "Sonny" Grosso, formerly one of the most distinguished cops on the New York force, who had been involved in the case that was the basis for *The French Connection* (for which he was also an advisor).

And what of "race," the core concern of the pilot? It was still there, because it had to be there. *Kojak* featured more black and ethnic characters than other cop shows,

A young James Woods as a psychotic kid, laying in wait for Kojak. Hint: there's only one winner. From "Death Is Not a Passing Grade" (1974).

and the language around the topic was always grittier (e.g., a crooked black politician telling a hood to beware "a dark-skinned gentleman in the woodpile").[10] However, black characters rarely exhibited any dramatic agency, despite storylines about youth gangs and unfair police tactics. In the single instance where an African American character is central, the tone of the encounter with Kojak is very different from the pilot: the blaxploitation-influenced scenario concerns one Salathiel Harms, a private eye who intrudes on Kojak's patch, and ends with Kojak grudgingly joining him in a "black handshake." Finally, as the seasons of the show progressed, Kojak's own ethnicity was modulated to become more a marker of exoticism than a political metaphor. In one episode, soundtracked by bazouki-inflected music, Kojak's niece gets kidnapped; in another Kojak tells a story about being a soldier in the war and breaking the jaw of a Nazi who'd massacred Greek partisans; in another, a rare Greek postage stamp is stolen; and so on.

Cultural historian Paul Cobley has analyzed these political threads in terms of the concept of the "Great Society" in the U.S., and the way in which American audiences were coming to terms with a post–Civil Rights perspective on law enforcement. He sums up these resonances in *Kojak* thus: "the verisimilitude of the series operated within the new tangled co-ordinates of public knowledge about racism, criminal rights, civic corruption, reform and the social determinants of poverty. American police work was shown as one activity interacting with a huge set of formidable social forces including many which had come to prominence in contemporary discourses."[11]

The cancellation of *Kojak* took a while coming. In the later seasons, the writing was less pugnacious, and the formula became tired. For one thing, the times were changing, and new kinds of cop show were more popular. Action series such as *Starsky & Hutch* made *Kojak* look old-hat, and when action storylines were introduced into *Kojak*, they invariably didn't work: an ageing Savalas was no David Soul, and it was hard for viewers to accept the sight of him running up flights of stairs and kicking down doors. The younger cops were reflecting a new era in American society, and as New York itself got the clean-up treatment (or, at least, began to, a process that did not bear fruit until the late 1980s), so Kojak's man-of-the-(oppressed)-people persona began to seem less relevant.

In addition, there was the curious fact that by 1978, Savalas had become bigger than *Kojak* itself. The trend had begun when Savalas embarked on a recording career, trading on the Kojak (sexy/attractive) image. His version of the song "If," a slice of romantic schmaltz, was an international hit in 1975. He followed it with the less successful song "Who Loves Ya, Baby," underscoring that for the public, he and Kojak were typically conflated. The result was a certain amount of confusion, and although Savalas' pop success may have been a fillip for the show in the short term, it undoubtedly contributed to its overall decline. Whereas Jack Webb had somehow kept his recording career separate, to the extent that *Dragnet*'s longevity was not compromised, and, later, David Soul developed a pop star persona that was distinct from his Hutch character, Savalas never managed—or tried—to pull off the same trick.

The conflation of Kojak and Savalas was amplified by the launch in 1977 of the afore-mentioned "Telly Apparel" line, which made a splash in the fashion world and which traded on Kojak's earthiness, as the advertising confirmed: "Telly fashions for the man are real because Telly wouldn't have them any other way. Telly's not a model or a designer, but your customers are not models or designers either."[12] The line was launched in the Big Apple (naturally) as a specifically "New York street look," despite the fact that this very concept was undergoing a transformation with the advent of punk; and it both riffed on *Kojak* and fed back into it: by the final season the costume changes were becoming very blatant (here's Kojak in sports casuals; here he is in a flared three-piece; etc.).

This kind of crossover with the fashion industry was a reflection of bigger changes that were happening in the TV and movie industries, where fashion houses were becoming more and more aware of the possibilities for exposure. In terms of TV cop shows it anticipated efforts to make "style icons" out of other stars, including the aforementioned David Soul, Don Johnson (*Miami Vice*) and Michael K. Williams (*The Wire*). It also pre-figured the "branding revolution," more broadly, of the 1980s.

The morphing of *Kojak* into a glossy star vehicle (a kind of "Telly Savalas Show") was underlined when Savalas took on the role of co-producer. This manner of commandeering more control had a long history in cop shows: Jack Webb had set the trend with *Dragnet*. By the 1970s, it had become almost the natural thing to do, especially in the wake of Peter Falk's creative take-over of *Columbo*. But whatever Savalas' aspirations for the show, it was too late: low ratings had sealed its fate.

After cancellation, *Kojak* returned in two (poorly-received) made-for-TV movies in the mid–1980s, and then a brief season of five TV movies for ABC between 1989 and 1990—the latter probably being mainly of interest here for the co-starring role given to a young Andre Braugher, later of *Homicide: Life on the Street*. Savalas never wanted the show to end, and he died in 1994 with several more *Kojak* projects in the pipeline. Perhaps inevitably, bearing in mind his association with the role, the recurrent headline for the obituaries in the papers read: "Kojak dies."

As a post-script, in 2005, there was a short-lived *Kojak* series starring African American actor Ving Rhames. This brought the question of Kojak's ethnic origins full-circle as well as anticipating the casting of a black lead in the 2013 *Ironside* remake. The show featured a much more brutal version of the character, and its style owed as much to Thomas Harris serial killer tropes and *Shaft* as to the original. With a sad lack of respect for Abby Mann's vision, and in line with many 21st century TV cops, it turned the notion of Kojak-as-community-cop on its head by having him behave like a vigilante. As one critic noted, "His violence is an effect of the system he despises and perpetuates. He is the evidence of its ongoing failures."[13]

In conclusion, none of the *Kojak* re-boots worked, and the show has largely remained lodged in the public imagination as a projection of a particular kind of masculinity (post-hardboiled), a particular place (New York), at a particular time (the 1970s). The original series can thus be seen as a crucial staging-post in the history of the "realistic" TV crime drama, and in this respect should be understood as part of a lineage that stretches from *Dragnet* to *The Wire*. It offered a new kind of liberal paradigm for the genre, a step on from "New Frontier" idealism but still questionable on some levels; and its brand of "tough sentimentalism" stretched the limits of what network-era TV drama could achieve. At a time when the "love" sensibility of the affluent 1960s had given way to the darker sentiments associated with urban decay, to ask the question "Who loves ya?" was perhaps the most challenging enquiry of all.

Recommended Episodes

The Marcus-Nelson Murders remains an astonishing piece of TV. For a more representative snapshot of the series as it would develop, and as it would remain in the public memory, with full-on squad-room atmosphere, see: "Money Back Guarantee" (Season 3, episode 12, 1975). Co-written by Dallas L. Barnes (later of *Barnaby Jones* and *Hunter*), it concerns an insurance scam involving car theft, and the death of a cop during one of the heists. The cast is multicultural; New York is graffiti-ridden; and the car chases involve Kojak insouciantly sticking a portable red light on the roof of his speeding Buick. Poor Stavros is mercilessly bullied, given dangerous undercover jobs and called "Fatso." In the denouement, the villain hears scratching at his door, and thinking it's a cat, goes to investigate: he is greeted by a grinning Kojak, who says, simply: "Meeow, baby...."

Further Reading

The work of Paul Cobley is an excellent starting point. He has a section on *Kojak* in his *The American Thriller* (Palgrave Macmillan, 2000), and an essay about the show in Bill Osgerby and Anna Gough-Yates (eds.), *Action TV* (Routledge, 2001). A revealing Abby Mann interview, undertaken for the Archive of American Television, can be accessed at http://emmytvlegends.org/interviews/people/abby-mann. Because Savalas was such a big star, interviews with him in the media are numerous, including several in *Playboy*, but are usually not that instructive about *Kojak*; he awaits a serious biographer, though a basic TV documentary exists: *Telly Savalas: Who Loves Ya, Baby?* (A and E Home Video, 2009). Other analyses of *Kojak* use the show as a hook for discussing wider cultural theory: for example, Philip Tagg's *Kojak: 50 Seconds of Television Music (Towards the Analysis of Affect in Popular Music)* (The Mass Media Music Scholars' Press, e-book, 2009); and David C. Walker's unpublished MA thesis *The Programming of the Body: An Analysis of the Title Sequence to the Television Series Kojak* (York University, Canada, 1983) which is more about semiotics than about the show.

CHAPTER 9

Starsky & Hutch

(ABC, 1975–79)

BEN BETHELL

Producer Leonard Goldberg recalls that he and partner Aaron Spelling were still shooting *Starsky & Hutch*'s pilot episode when they knew they had a hit on their hands. The show indeed proved a triumph: as the 1970s drew to a close, Saturday evenings found ABC's primetime audience glued to the exploits of plainclothes police detectives David Starsky (Paul Michael Glaser) and Kenneth "Hutch" Hutchinson (David Soul) as they patrolled the mean streets of Bay City, the show's fictional Californian locale, in their bright red Ford Gran Torino with its signature white vector-stripe. While *Starsky & Hutch*'s winning formula can with hindsight be defined in terms of the successful transplantation to the small screen of contemporary Hollywood trends—notably, "buddy" relationships and high-octane action sequences, played out against a generalized backdrop of social breakdown and inner-city decay—there was at the time no great mystery to the show's popularity. As one English fan at the height of British "Starsky-mania" enthused, "Guys like it because it's trendy and the car, girls like it because the guys are pin-ups!"[1] By this time, re-sprayed red-and-white Ford sedans could be found cruising towns and suburbs the length and breadth of America (not to mention the UK and beyond), driven by young men sporting Glaser-style chunky cardigans. So popular was the car that in 1976 Ford even built 1,300 limited-edition *Starsky & Hutch*-brand Torinos. Soul had performed in the mid–1960s as a folk singer, making a series of bizarre masked appearances on the *Merv Griffin Show* as "The Covered Man"[2]; pursued in public by screaming female fans, he was now transformed, albeit briefly, into a genuine pop star, enjoying a number one hit on both sides of the Atlantic with the saccharine "Don't Give Up on Us."

Starsky & Hutch hit its intended demographic squarely on target; though its cross-gender appeal may have come as a pleasant surprise to Goldberg and Spelling, the show's popularity with younger viewers was exactly as they'd planned. Taking their cue from another Spelling product, *The Mod Squad* (ABC, 1968–73), a show that featured a trio of youthful undercover cops (one female and another a black male), the producers set out to capture a young audience with a pair of protagonists who, in Goldberg's words, "were this new kind of detective; they were cool, they were hip."[3] Scriptwriter William Blinn, the duo's creator, recalls that network television was at the time home to "a lot of serious, straightforward, by-the-numbers cops who we could always count on, who never made mistakes, and who pretty much went by the book."[4] Invariably, these buttoned-up heroes were middle-aged men. Even when shows such as *Hawaii Five-O* (CBS, 1968–80) or *The Streets of San Francisco* (ABC, 1972–77) featured a younger co-star, the junior sidekick was confined to a subordinate role, deferring at all times to the older man's wisdom and experience. By the middle of the 1970s, however, a generation of young people had come of age whose experience as either Vietnam combatants or anti-war student protesters (or, in some cases, both), coupled with exposure to soft drugs and anti-establishment rock music, led them to resent and mistrust their elders. As much as their collar-length hair and faded denims, Starsky and

Dynamic duo Kenneth "Hutch" Hutchinson (David Soul) and David Starsky (Paul Michael Glaser) in the famous red Ford Gran Torino (ABC TV/Photofest).

Hutch's insouciance and absence of deference placed them, in the eyes of the show's target audience, on the right side of what was by now commonly referred to as the "generation gap." Blinn was no stranger to this territory, having previously scripted *The Rookies* (ABC, 1972–76) for Goldberg and Spelling, a show that also took as its subject the "new breed" of cop (but in this case, uniformed patrolmen) whose formative experience was either military service in Vietnam or life on a college campus. He pursued the theme in his follow-up project: while the impulsive, quick-tempered Starsky is an army veteran, Hutch, the "brains" of the duo, is a college graduate.

The genealogy of the "hip" detective can be traced as far back as the late 1950s, when ABC aired a quartet of Warner-produced private-eye shows—*77 Sunset Strip* (1958–64), *Hawaiian Eye* (1959–63), *Bourbon Street Beat* (1959–60) and *Surfside Six* (1960–62)—each set (though all were in fact shot on Warner's Hollywood back-lot) in a groovy beach-side location. NBC responded with *Johnny Staccato* (1959–60), which starred John Cassavetes as a private detective-cum-jazz pianist, at home among the beatnik denizens of New York's Greenwich Village. However, with their fanciful plotlines, tongue-in-cheek humor and *Playboy* magazine–style "sophistication," these shows have little in common with *The Mod Squad*'s trio of earnest, troubled plainclothes narcs—let alone *Starsky & Hutch*'s pair of hard-nosed, battle-weary cynics. Given the seismic upheaval that occurred in American society during the intervening years, the gulf that separates the Kennedy-era bounce of *77 Sunset Strip* from *The Mod Squad*'s subdued 1968 debut is of little surprise. As well as escalating conflict in Vietnam and the rise of anti-war protest, the middle years of the 1960s witnessed both widespread rioting in American inner cities as the movement for black Civil Rights reached its apogee, and attempts by disaffected white middle-class youth to launch a full-blown, LSD-fueled cultural revolution. The assassination of President John F. Kennedy in November 1963 inaugurated this tumultuous period; less than five years later, both the president's younger brother, Robert, and Civil Rights leader Dr. Martin Luther

King, Jr., fell to the assassin's bullet—in June 1968 and April 1968 respectively. In September that year, *The Mod Squad* went to air. The show can be seen as a symbolic attempt, albeit belated and fairly clumsy, to accommodate within mainstream entertainment both Civil Rights–era black consciousness and the burgeoning hippie counterculture. By contrast, the stance taken by *The Mod Squad*'s successors—not least, *Starsky & Hutch*—was far less conciliatory. As civil disobedience gave way to insurrectionary Black Power—and the student anti-war movement sprouted its own armed, militant offshoots—primetime TV played host to a new type of TV cop, cheerfully willing to use deadly firepower and suspend due process to combat what were now routinely depicted as the forces of "anarcho-criminal barbarism."[5]

This violent turn in police procedural drama arrived partially cloaked in the mantle of diversity. Though executives balked at the prospect of a lead black police detective (*pace* Richard Roundtree's brief reprisal of private-eye John Shaft for CBS's 1973-74 season), the networks nevertheless served up cops who were female (*Police Woman*, NBC, 1974–78), disabled (*Ironside*, NBC, 1967–75) and, in the case of Telly Savalas's *Kojak* (CBS, 1973–78), a member of an (albeit somewhat marginal) ethnic minority, along with various black sidekicks, investigators and junior officers (as in *The Rookies*, *Kojak*, *Ironside*, etc.).[6] With its white, yet "different," lead characters and black supporting cast (Antonio Fargas as informant Huggy Bear and Bernie Hamilton as Captain Dobey) *Starsky & Hutch* exemplified the new paradigm. A relaxed dress code was not to be mistaken for a "soft" attitude towards crime and social ills: the "scum" pursued by the duo (in early episodes, at least) were far more likely to die in a hail of police-issue bullets than they ever were to end up facing judge and jury. In their disdain for their superiors, contempt for the rulebook and pragmatic approach to street-level law enforcement, Starsky and Hutch in fact conformed more than most to the "dirty cop" archetype epitomized by Clint Eastwood as "Dirty" Harry Callahan, the eponymous anti-hero of Don Siegel's 1971 cinema box-office smash. It was Soul's portrayal of a vigilante traffic cop in *Dirty Harry*'s sequel, *Magnum Force* (Ted Post, 1973), that first brought the actor to the attention of Goldberg and Spelling. The choice of Lalo Schifrin, who had scored both movies, as composer is a further indication of their influence on the producers (the maestro's brooding theme was replaced the following season by "Gotcha," Tom Scott's acid jazz workout, which remains a classic of the genre; the show's third season featured yet another theme, composed this time by Mark Snow, best known for his work on the *X-Files*).

Harry Callahan was, moreover, only one of several big-screen cops to whom Starsky and Hutch owed a debt. Released in 1971 and based on a true story, William Friedkin's *The French Connection* initiated the gritty, documentary-style realism that would characterize Hollywood crime movies throughout the 1970s. The movie's protagonist, New York narcotics detective Jimmy "Popeye" Doyle (Gene Hackman in an Oscar-winning performance) is, like Callahan and like Starsky and Hutch, a pragmatist who, though he breaks the rules, roughs up suspects and disobeys his superiors, gets the job done. *Starsky & Hutch*'s first season bears the clear imprint of Friedkin's movie and its 1975 sequel, *French Connection II* (John Frankenheimer), not least in Bay City's distinct Big Apple flavor, which belies its purported West Coast location. More directly, a season 1 episode entitled "The Fix" sees Hutch endure the agonies of "cold turkey," having been kidnapped and forcibly injected with heroin, a fate also suffered by Hackman's Doyle in *French Connection II*.

Far closer, however, to Starsky and Hutch than either Dirty Harry or Popeye Doyle is Frank Serpico, the "hippie" plainclothes officer portrayed by Al Pacino in Sidney Lumet's

Serpico (1973), also based on the true story of a New York police detective (a role reprised by Daniel Binney in NBC's 1976–77 flop television spin-off). There is more to this resemblance than long hair and denims: police corruption, the central theme of *Serpico* (and for that matter, *Dirty Harry*), is an underlying motif of *Starsky & Hutch*'s paranoia-tinged first season. The show's pilot episode, in which the Bay City DA covers up an extra-marital affair by employing two hit-men to commit a series of murders, establishes from the outset the rot at City Hall. Throughout the series, Starsky and Hutch confide to nobody in the Bay City police department but their chief, Captain Dobey, whom, lest operational details slip into the wrong hands, they rely on even for routine vehicle checks. The detectives' animosity towards their superiors (bar Dobey, whom they tolerate) is due simply to the fact that the higher-ups can't be *trusted*—an attitude shared, as the war in Vietnam reached its ignominious conclusion, by an entire generation of young Americans. Starsky and Hutch's scruffy, unconventional appearance, like Serpico's, served merely to underline this profound divide.

There is, equally, a clear link between *Starsky & Hutch* and blaxploitation, the subgenre of American action movies featuring black stars and aimed at black audiences spawned by Melvin Van Peebles' *Sweet Sweetback's Baadasssss Song* and Gordon Parks' *Shaft* (both 1971). Antonio Fargas, who co-starred as informant Huggy Bear, was a blaxploitation

Antonio Fargas as Huggy Bear, a character who was in some ways inspired by blaxploitation cinema, but soon one of the most popular features of the show (ABC TV/Photofest).

staple, appearing not only in *Shaft* but *Cleopatra Jones* (1973), *Foxy Brown* (1974) and *Across 110th Street* (1972)—the latter directed by Barry Shear, who would also direct the pilot episode of *Starsky & Hutch*. For his part, Bernie Hamilton (whose early career achievements included a starring role in Luis Bunuel's *The Young One* [1960]) appeared in blaxploitation turkeys such as *Scream Blacula Scream* (1973) and *Bucktown* (1975). In featuring black characters in a primetime TV drama, *Starsky & Hutch* again followed *The Mod Squad*'s progressive example (itself set by 1960s trailblazers *I Spy* [NBC, 1965–68], *Star Trek* [NBC, 1966–69] and *Mission: Impossible* [CBS, 1966–73]). Critics and scholars have, however, observed that Huggy Bear—essentially a clownish pimp (though his precise source of income is never entirely clear)—did little to challenge prevailing negative racial stereotypes. Indeed, though depicted as a community leader of sorts, America's favorite black TV character wasn't a doctor, a lawyer, a teacher or a minister of religion—a member, that is, of a profession enjoying respect and high status within the real black community. Rather, he belonged to a distinct breed (pimp/pusher/hustler) whose depredations on the community in fact ensured extremely low regard within it—a status unlikely to be enhanced by turning police informer.[7] Though no doubt repellent to many black viewers, this type of character held evident charms for ABC's script executives; witness Michael D. Roberts' performance opposite Robert Blake's eponymous lead in *Baretta*, aired by the network at the same time (1975–1978), as a pimp-cum-informer named "Rooster."

On the other hand, the gruff though ineffectual Captain Dobey, though Starsky and Hutch's nominal superior, is generally ignored, disobeyed outright, or at best treated by them as an underling. One commentator has concluded that, while it "employed many of blaxploitation's trademark codes and conventions" *Starsky & Hutch* was essentially "blaxploitation made palatable for white TV audiences … the palest of imitations."[8] It is certainly true that American viewers had never seen anything quite like Fargas's character on their TV screens. However, Huggy Bear has far less in common with blaxploitation's version of proud, beautiful, assertive black masculinity than with his network stable-mate Arthur "Fonzie" Fonzarelli, played by Henry Winkler in *Happy Days* (ABC, 1974–84). Both characters are neutered, thoroughly domesticated versions of what, twenty years earlier, had been feared and reviled subcultural archetypes: the black criminal-cum-dandy and his white counterpart, the leather-garbed "juvenile delinquent." In response to criticism of its black characters, the show's final season included an episode entitled "Black and Blue," featuring another blaxploitation regular, Vonetta McGee (*Hammer, Blacula, Shaft in Africa*, etc.) as Joan Meredith, a beautiful female detective who becomes Starsky's temporary partner while Hutch recovers from a gunshot wound. Though the reaction of the episode's black hoodlums, one of whom rebukes Meredith with an outraged "sistah!," and of Starsky himself, who indulges in some opportunistic interracial flirting, is somewhat predictable, "Black and Blue" contains refreshingly reflexive moments. "You read the papers, watch the news," explains Meredith at one point, "pressure is on the department to hire more minorities, to hire more women. So, I'm a veritable find in this one beautiful black person. I fill two quotas." "Great," replies Starsky, "why don't you sit closer to the window so everybody can see you."

No discussion of *Starsky & Hutch* would be complete without mention of the show's signature car chases, and the part played in them by Starsky's Ford Torino—nicknamed, originally by Glaser, who in reality loathed the vehicle, the "striped tomato." Driving dominated some episodes to such an extent that the English novelist J.G. Ballard (whose 1973 novel *Crash* explored the eroticism of the automobile accident) remarked that when watched with the volume turned down they "resembled instructional films on valet parking."[9] Today's TV audiences might regard a car plowing through a pile of cardboard boxes (to take a particularly well-worn example) as it hurtles up a back street a cliché so overused as to be comical. Before *Starsky & Hutch*, however, fast-paced action of the screeching-tire, kicked-in door variety had been seen only on the big screen and was experienced by the show's viewers as a genuinely exciting departure. When they're not burning rubber on the streets of Bay City, Starsky and Hutch spend much of their time careering up and down fire escapes, scrambling over chain-link fences and charging along ubiquitous back alleys in pursuit of suspects who, once apprehended, they slam with maximum force against a wall or a car roof. The fact that Glaser and Soul (unlike, say, Telly Savalas or Peter Falk) were young actors in peak physical condition allowed for a different style of procedural narrative. *Starsky & Hutch* eschewed the build-up of plot through static scenes, in which clues are puzzled over and witnesses and suspects interviewed and re-interviewed, in favor of short scenes whose principal function, story aside, is to link together a series of action sequences and choreographed car chases. Much of the detective work (such as it is) takes place inside the speeding Torino, the cerebral Hutch working out clues and moving the episode's plot forward, while Starsky grips the wheel and jams the gas pedal to the floor.

The show's car chases, filmed with multiple cameras and featuring elaborate stunt work, were the first on TV to feature a technique pioneered on the big screen by Peter Yates in *Bullitt* (1968), and refined by Friedkin in *The French Connection*, which allowed viewers to watch the spectacle from a series of prime positions while also experiencing the thrill of riding inside the participating vehicles. Though spokesmen for the era's burgeoning environmental movement were quick to criticize such "auto fetishism," questioning whether it was responsible to promote "muscle cars" during an energy crisis, theirs were voices in the wilderness. Indeed, *Starsky & Hutch*'s car chases proved so popular with TV audiences that several of the lightweight action shows that followed in its immediate wake—*CHiPS* (NBC, 1977–83), for example, and *The Dukes of Hazzard* (CBS, 1979–85)—contained little else. Few shows, however, can boast as iconic a car as the "striped tomato," which to Glaser's chagrin became something of a star in its own right. It remains to this day, along with Bruce Wayne's Batmobile and the A-Team's GMC van, one of TV's most famous vehicles.

It is, then, clear that certain key elements—a spirit of youthful rebellion, the gritty realism and high-octane pace of the Hollywood crime movie, a watered-down version of blaxploitation's funky ghetto sensibility—set *Starsky & Hutch* apart from rival cop shows and contributed to its initial success. But were it not for the principals' unique on-screen chemistry, it remains doubtful whether the show would have won the affection of TV audiences worldwide and attained enduring status as an undisputed classic of the genre. More than anything else, it was the way Glaser and Soul played off each other that convinced its producers from the outset that *Starsky & Hutch* was going to be a smash. Everybody involved in the show agrees, as do critics and its fans, that the "buddy" factor was central to its appeal. Of all the elements imported from contemporary American cinema, it was this that proved the crucial ingredient in the show's winning formula. A Hollywood staple since 1969, when Paul Newman and Robert Redford were paired in George Roy Hill's *Butch Cassidy and the Sundance Kid* (a line-up revived in 1973, when Hill again hit pay-dirt with *The Sting*), the buddy picture was by the mid–1970s fully ascendant. The year 1974 saw the release of two movies, *Freebie and the Bean* (Richard Rush, starring James Caan and Alan Arkin) and *Busting* (Peter Hyams, starring Eliott Gould and Robert Blake), which were both based around a buddy cop partnership markedly similar to the one portrayed less than a year later by Glaser and Soul. Evidently, a pacey cop drama featuring a pair of unconventional detectives was an idea whose time had arrived. It should, however, be noted that *Freebie and the Bean* (which, with its spectacular car chases and offbeat humor, bears a particularly close resemblance to *Starsky & Hutch*) wasn't released until Christmas 1974, by which time work on *Starsky & Hutch*'s pilot episode (aired the following April) was well underway.

The show marked the buddy narrative's small-screen debut. The extent to which *Starsky & Hutch* developed and explored the relationship between two male protagonists was at the time unique to TV drama of any kind, let alone a cop show. The bond shared by the detectives goes far beyond the professional: they are best friends, fiercely loyal and deeply protective of one another. And unlike their buttoned-up TV forebears, they are unafraid to physically express their mutual affection; endless shoulder-squeezing, back-patting and horseplay prompted one senior ABC executive to dub them, off record, "French-kissing prime-time homos." Echoing this assessment, critics and scholars have in turn been quick to identify *Starsky & Hutch*'s barely submerged homoeroticism,[10] attempts by its writers to emphasize the duo's robust heterosexuality notwithstanding (Starsky in particular, as a disapproving higher-up notes, "has a reputation for that sort of thing"). Girlfriends, however, come and go, often remaining unseen, and in characteristic buddy fashion are wholly peripheral to the show's core male relationship. It is no coincidence that the buddy narrative's shift towards male friendship at the expense of traditional male-female romance accompanied the rise in the U.S. of "second wave" feminism. The marginalization of female characters can be understood as a reaction to the women's movement of the 1970s, serving, in the view of one film theorist, to "punish women for their desire for equality."[11]

Goldberg acknowledges that he and Spelling had in mind the buddy template when casting *Starsky & Hutch*, though he recalls that watching Soul working with Glaser reminded him less of Redford and Newman than of Redford's partnership with Dustin Hoffman in Alan Pakula's *All the President's Men* (1976), another indication of the seriousness to which *Starsky & Hutch*'s producers initially aspired. For a show that set out to inject the TV cop genre with a healthy dose of gritty realism, there is irony in the fact that *Starsky & Hutch* ended up far closer to the lightweight, family-friendly fare with which Goldberg-Spelling enjoyed subsequent success (notably *Charlie's Angels* [ABC, 1976–81] and *Hart to Hart* [ABC, 1979–84]) than to the hard-boiled models that provided its original inspiration. While there is a widespread tendency for TV dramas to "self-destruct into ridiculous stereotypes and clichés ... achieving heights of comedy that displace their original 'serious' intentions of revealing 'social truths,'"[12] for *Starsky & Hutch* the decline was steeper and the process more rapid than for most.

The year 1977 saw the resurgence in the United States of an ongoing moral panic about the impact of TV violence on children and teenagers. Glaser, in particular, shared this concern and was unhappy with what he saw as *Starsky & Hutch*'s gratuitously violent content. As a result, the show's tone softened considerably in its third and fourth seasons, the detectives now less preoccupied with roughing up suspects than with the week's social issue or love interest. Above all, the buddy factor was pushed to the hilt, Glaser and Soul's double-act shtick complemented by the mugging Fargas in an expanded role. Goldberg and Spelling at one point even planned to give their loveable pimp his own spin-off. For the producers and for Glaser, however, hopes for the once-gritty procedural's successful transformation into anodyne family favorite were perhaps finally dashed in November 1978, when police detectives investigating the well-publicized murder of country singer Linda "Charlee" Scott, bludgeoned to death with a baseball bat in her Westchester home by a disgruntled former employee, stated that the crime's perpetrator had been inspired by a similar killing in an episode of *Starsky & Hutch*.[13] Spurious though the claim may have been, it was evident that the show remained a byword for small-screen carnage, the tough-guy aura once so assiduously cultivated proving in the end impossible to shed. A huge pay increase and a turn in the director's chair failed to mollify an increasingly disillusioned Glaser, who attempted to sue ABC for contractual release at the beginning of the third season, and whose threats to leave continued until the end of the fourth. Due principally to Glaser, a planned fifth season was abandoned before shooting even began.

The bubblegum flavor of its later seasons accounts in large part for *Starsky & Hutch*'s enduring iconic status: *Kojak* and *Columbo*, while still popular with TV audiences, do not belong to the 1970s in the way that disco, roller-skates, platform shoes, Evel Knievel and *Starsky & Hutch* all do. It was this aura of tongue-in-cheek, nostalgic camp that Todd Phillips captured in his 2004 big screen version (starring Ben Stiller as Starsky, Owen

Wilson as Hutch and Snoop Dogg as Huggy Bear), the movie less a remake than an out-and-out parody. However, before dismissing *Starsky & Hutch* as merely silly, we should bear in mind that in its early, hungrier incarnation, the show provided the TV cop genre, by then a quarter of a century old, a well-needed shot in its battle-scarred arm.

Recommended Viewing

"The Fix" is a good example of the first season's hard-boiled approach and willingness to tackle visceral subject matter. Soul's smack-addled Hutch is remarkably convincing, and, as Glaser babysits him through withdrawal, we see the duo's relationship at its most intense (banned by the BBC, British viewers didn't get to see "The Fix" until 1999!). Perhaps more representative, season 3's "I Love You, Rosey Malone," in which Starsky falls for a mobster's daughter (Tracy Brookes Swope in an Emmy-winning performance), stands out—not least for Glaser's sincere performance. For unrestrained 1970s silliness, check out season 4's "Discomania": Starsky gets to strut his undercover stuff when the duo go in search of a Travolta-inspired serial killer.

Further Reading

Very little has been written about *Starsky & Hutch*. The show is discussed in relation to blaxploitation by Elaine Pennicott in her essay on the topic in Bill Osgerby and Anna Gough-Yates (eds.), *Action TV: Tough Guys, Smooth Operators and Foxy Chicks* (Routledge, 2001); useful observations are also made in an overview by the volume's editors (writing with Marianne Wells). *Starsky & Hutch: Behind the Badge*, a documentary extra included in the first season DVD release, features interviews with David Soul, Paul Michael Glaser, Antonio Fargas, William Blinn and Leonard Goldberg.

CHAPTER 10

Hill Street Blues
(NBC, 1981–87)
RONALD WILSON

"Roll Call: 6:53 a.m." An unsettling shaky camera shows the interior of a dingy, presumably basement room in a precinct police station. Overlapping dialogue fills the room with sound. One voice makes itself heard over the rest, as we are caught in the middle of the station sergeant's early morning roll call. "All right, item 14—still got a gang of juveniles on 119th Street, hitting on old people cashing social security checks! So ... uh, how about let's give that situation a little extra effort. All right, item 15 ... ITEM 15!—At this point in time we got the same purse snatcher working...."

The emphasis of the roll call, which comprises a pre-credit sequence, is on the base realism of urban street crime. Here there is no room for romantic notions of thrilling detective-related escapades involving murder or organized criminal activity. As the sequence continues, it digresses slightly as the imposing figure of the sergeant requests, then demands, a weapons inspection from the police officers present. He wants to know if they have any unauthorized weaponry. The resulting voluntary shakedown—amusingly and horrifyingly—reveals switchblades and several handguns. Welcome to Hill Street station.

Among many critics commenting about *Hill Street Blues* when it was first broadcast in the 1980s, Steve Jenkins noted, "Anyone writing about [it] has to confront the idea that this series is 'different.' This is not simply a matter of the supposed singular nature of this cop show against others—its intersection with soap opera, its realism, its mix of drama and comedy, its more complex narrative strategies—but of the ways in which it is talked and written about, and of the image of the series which emerges."[1] This image was reinforced as scholars and literati such as Todd Gitlin, David Mamet, and Joyce Carol Oates joined the chorus of approval.[2] *Hill Street Blues* became the *cause célèbre* of what Robert J. Thompson refers to as television's "second golden age."[3] When the series premiered in the fall of 1981 it set a new aesthetic standard for commercial television as well as for the genre-driven cop show. It presented a microcosm of a police world beleaguered by organizational, social and personal conflicts and relationships, and as Joyce Carol Oates noted in her paean to the series, "the Hill Street police are figures of Sisyphus rolling their rocks up the hill and the next morning rolling them down again, and again. Human effort and intelligence, action, risk, sudden eruptions of violence, sudden death—yet very little changes. It is always the next morning, it is always roll call."[4] Few commercial television programs received such attention from the American intellectual elite; fewer still would elicit such classical allusions.

Hill Street Blues was created during a time of stylistic innovation in prime-time television programming during the early 1980s. MTM [Mary Tyler Moore] Enterprises' production strategy from 1978 to 1981 often gets the credit for creating the genre of "quality television," characterized by an emphasis on a series of hour-long episodes, marketed to a niche "blue-chip" audience. Genre hybridization, a stress on realism, and the use of an ensemble cast were also important elements. Such programming also utilized multiple story lines interwoven across several episodes, creating a kind of Dickensian narrative structure.[5] Some of these characteristics were initially apparent in the series *Lou Grant* (CBS, 1977–82) starring Ed Asner.

In 1980 NBC executive Fred Silverman wanted to create a "down-and-dirty cop show" that might appeal to a more adult constituency than *Starsky & Hutch*.[6] The result was *Hill Street Blues*, the brainchild of writer-producers Steven Bochco and Michael Kozoll, who had cut their teeth on such crime series as *Ironside, McMillan and Wife, Kojak,* and *Delvecchio*. Silverman wanted them to produce a "cop show that is not a standard cops-and-robbers show—a show that has more to do with cops' personal lives,"[7] and to this end they formulated a concept that drew from antiheroic, realistic urbanism in film and television police dramas.

Cop stories were common on American movie screens throughout the 1970s. Rather than valorize the police, they often offered a critique of law enforcement and the liberal values that pervaded its bureaucratic structure. Examples such as *Dirty Harry* (1971), *The French Connection* (1971), *Electra Glide in Blue* (1973) and *The Super Cops* (1974) showed a flawed system and cops who, as a result of their pessimism about the "over-bureaucratized" nature of their job, were prepared to operate violently. Yet the police display certain humanistic qualities that make these films unique to a 1970s zeitgeist. Film historian Carlos Clarens claims that "seventies cop films emphasized the humanity of the policeman [sic—always male], sometimes even his eccentricities.... Not quite convinced of the sacredness of his mission, the police hero was a perfect home-front surrogate for the other unsung combat fighter in Vietnam."[8] The comparison to the battlefront is an apt one, as many of these cop films featured an urban environment riven with gang warfare, corruption and street crime. This "us v. them" ambience of underlying menace recurred in 1980s movies such as *Fort Apache, the Bronx* (1981), and was reflected in several police drama series on American television prior to *Hill Street Blues*.[9]

Somebody who understood this tension very well, and one of the most important influences on television police dramas in the 1970s, was the writer Joseph Wambaugh. Often referred to as the "father of the modern police novel" Wambaugh began his prolific career with *The New Centurions* (1971). His fiction was grittily realistic and featured psychologically complex and damaged police characters, often working in the juvenile and vice departments in primarily minority districts, demonstrating "less how cops work on the job, than how the job works on cops."[10] Throughout the 1970s Wambaugh's work was adapted into films (*The New Centurions* [1972] and *The Choirboys* [1977]) or television, notably the anthology series *Police Story* (NBC, 1973–77) and *The Blue Knight* (CBS, 1975–76). Wambaugh's depiction of police in antagonistic settings emphasized the effects of urban environments on their psyches, including post-traumatic stress disorder. This sense of an urban combat zone, inflected by the experience of Vietnam, would be extremely influential on Bochco and Kozoll's concept for *Hill Street Blues*.[11]

But seriousness was not the sole intention, and it was important to have a comedic, satirical, dimension. The sub-genre of comedy-drama provided the inspiration, and cultural historian Paul Kerr includes movie influences such as Robert Altman's *M*A*S*H* (1970) and Paddy Chayefsky's *The Hospital* (1971), along with TV sitcom *Barney Miller* (ABC, 1975–82).[12] What these have in common is a single workplace environment, multiple characters, and a mixture of drama and humor. Altman, especially, was a master at finding the balance between these elements, using genre hybridity (or perhaps more accurately, genre revisionism) in the service of multi-narrative structures, visual dynamics, and satire.

As each episode of *Hill Street Blues* progresses from the opening roll call, these themes are highlighted in a variety of ways. For example, at the start of each show, several cop cars are seen leaving a police garage, sirens blaring. As they speed towards their destination in the grayness of early dawn, the musical theme (by Mike Post) does not complement the visual action; instead it provides a counterpoint. The music is lyrical and melodic, utilizing a small band playing a piano-based theme. Unlike the typical percussion-and-brass-inflected scoring for cop shows such as *Dragnet* or *The F.B.I,* or even the more contemporary funky jazz themes for *Police Story* (by Jerry Goldsmith), *S.W.A.T.,* *The Rookies,* or *Police Woman* (Henry Mancini), the *Hill Street Blues* theme belies the nature of the show itself and seems more appropriate to a soap opera than a police drama series.

Officers Bobby Hill (Michael Warren) and Andy Renko (Charles Haid) look apprehensive—"community cops" in a community that's falling apart (MTM Enterprises/The Kobal Collection).

The theme tune having hinted that this will be an unorthodox (softer?) take on macho police themes, when the plots get underway, it is clear that they will not follow any familiar generic path, instead involving cops who negotiate professional success with private failure, and vice versa. According to Jason Mittell, the genre-mixing of *Hill Street Blues* "incorporated melodramatic serial storytelling into the show's gritty vision of urban crime, humanizing both the individual officers and the system itself."[13] In other words, melodrama, a form primarily associated with a female audience, was being re-conceptualized for a broader constituency. As we've noted, the serial narrative format was similar to daytime and prime-time soap opera serials, and featured the use of "continuing storylines traversing multiple episodes, with an ongoing diegesis that demands viewers to construct a story world using information gathered from their full history of viewing."[14] Furthermore, *Hill Street Blues* utilized open-ended narratives that, in some cases, lasted over several episodes before reaching closure.

The characters in *Hill Street Blues* fall into two distinct groups: the workplace family, consisting of the police officers of Hill Street station itself; and the outsiders, existing beyond the confines of the station and peripheral to the recurring characters. There are 13 primary recurring characters in the series, and because this number was relatively large at the time, some of the characterization is sketched in broad strokes. For example, Captain Furillo is the "boss of Hill Street": clean-cut, unflappable and always trying to do the right thing. By contrast, Detective Belker looks like a homeless person because he spends a lot of time undercover (he is a kind of Serpico pastiche, always pictured with stubble, and his manner is fierce: he has some of the best put-down lines—"Right this way, kidney bag!"—and on a bad day he will growl like a dog and even bite felons).

As Robert J. Thompson notes with regard to the large ensemble casts that (for him) characterize quality television, "The variety of characters allows for a variety of viewpoints since multiple plots must usually be employed to accommodate all the characters."[15] Thus in *Hill Street Blues* the pairing of individuals (Officers Hill and Renko, Detectives LaRue and Washington, Officers Bates and Coffey) allows concurrent plot lines to develop across several episodes. Story arcs follow different character pairings throughout the series, which in turn allows personal relationships and problems to be emphasized alongside the crime-busting.

The best example of this kind of "structural engineering" comes in the second season (1982), when one of the story arcs involves the character of Captain Freedom, a citizen who is a self-styled superhero crime fighter, and who befriends Detective Belker ("I vow to give crime two black eyes and fight injustice and corruption wherever they may lurk," the Captain intones. "...And brotherhood, I want to establish universal brotherhood...."). This character was featured in four back-to-back episodes, into which were woven several other plot threads, none more prominent than the others. In the first of these, Sergeant Esterhaus sets up the storyline in his roll call address, mentioning an "intrepid masked crusader" who is pursuing purse-snatchers and rendering aid to distressed citizens. As Esterhaus advises his fellow officers, "You are invited to tip-toe through the tulips and throw a net over this guy before he hurts himself."[16] In subsequent shows, Captain Freedom continues to shadow Belker in order to "protect" him, until the final installment when he meets his demise. Specifically, in "Freedom's Last Stand," there are four plot strands, and it's worth briefly mentioning them to illustrate how complex things could become. Thus, Lt. Goldblume goes undercover in pursuit of a purse-snatching ring. Meanwhile, Captain Furillo testifies before the Sullivan Commission, which is investigating police corruption. (When he learns that he has been set up by Chief Daniels, he threatens to resign.) Then, armed robbers raid a fake saloon operation set up by the precinct in order to reveal police corruption; during the shoot-out Captain Freedom is fatally wounded and dies in Detective Belker's arms. As the multiple plots unfold, an incidental story involves the ongoing tenth annual inter-precinct poker tournament, the results of which are reported by Sergeant Esterhaus. The episode brings a tragic ending to the Captain Freedom story while extending the plot lines involving the Sullivan Commission and the fake saloon stakeout. In addition it mixes drama, pathos, tragedy, and comedy within its 50-minute time span "in a way that Aristotle would never have approved."[17]

If the structure of the show was one of its appeals, then style was another. Three aspects were important: the way that dialogue is allowed to seem "spontaneous" (in the manner of Altman's movies); the manner in which hand-held camera shots offer a sense of documentary "realism"; and how the design of the show was determinedly "grungy," in a fashion that went way beyond the dilapidated look of Kojak's squad room, in order to evoke a sense of chaos and a police force "on the edge."

Todd Gitlin has analyzed these stylistic factors, and gives much of the credit to Director Robert Butler, and his mission to "Make it look messy!"[18] In particular, Butler visualized disorder through a constantly moving camera that created a sense of a *vérité*, "you are there" style, with scenes often flowing into each other with minimal editing (Butler eschewed the typical establishing shots, preferring to create a sense of immediacy by opening a scene *in medias res*—the aforementioned morning roll call being a chief case in point). Butler also made good use of tight space, giving the sense that the Hill Street station was a cramped environment. According to Gitlin,

> The fragmentation and juxtaposition of shots and conversations would reproduce the fragmentation and simultaneity of society. Characters would brush past each other, reach over each other's shoulders, break into each other's conversations, suggesting that its people depend on each other, no man or woman is an island. The heroism of these cops would not be the swagger of loners lording it over society, or over the screen.[19]

Thus, Butler not only ensured that *Hill Street Blues* "looked messy," but that it sounded messy, too. Overlapping (Altmanesque) dialogue created a chaotic environment in the crisis-ridden police precinct, and an ambient soundtrack utilized a comedy troupe that improvised background sounds and crowd noises. (While recording, the troupe often moved toward and away from their microphones, thereby creating a sense of authenticity.) These techniques provided an atmosphere of foreground action taking place amid a cacophony of other activities within the precinct.

But it is also clear that this kind of verité style had other inspirations. For example, Bochco and Kozoll acknowledged their debt to *The Police Tapes*, a 90-minute PBS documentary broadcast in 1977. It followed the night-time activities of police officers at the 44th Precinct, South Bronx, which at that time had the highest crime rate in New York City, and utilized a hand-held camera and portable sound equipment to document various police-call responses. The focus is on street crime and some of the incidents are humorous (for example, a conflict between neighbors in a cramped apartment building) while others are tragic (including a gang-related murder). *The Police Tapes* also had its own patriarchal figure, similar to Captain Furillo, in the guise of Chief Tony Bouza, the Bronx Borough Commander, who at one point states that his station is similar to "Fort Apache—here we are surrounded by a bunch of hostiles ... we have the outside world, and the police world." Shot in three months, the documentary actually begins with a roll call, after which the presiding officer concludes by advising, "Let's be careful out in the streets." Compare this with Sgt. Esterhaus's constant concluding recommendation to his fellow officers in *Hill Street Blues*: "Let's be careful out there," delivered with various inflections.[20]

How are we to think about the politics of *Hill Street Blues*? Certainly, it had liberal pretentions, and was celebrated by a liberal-left intellectual elite at the time as being "revolutionary." But its gender politics were not always progressive. The female cop characters have to battle their way through the macho environment of the squad room, and this is demonstrated with various levels of sensitivity (anticipating some of the tropes in *Cagney & Lacey*): sometimes the culture of groping and sexist comments is hard to watch. The most prominent female character is Joyce Davenport, the public defender, who is also Captain Furillo's girlfriend. She is positioned as a sex symbol ("good enough to eat"), a love interest, and as domestic "light relief": we rarely see her at work (unlike the female public defenders in *Law & Order*), and her role seems to be to look pretty and to smarten-up Furillo's clothes. This kind of stereotyping drew flak from some feminists, and even Gloria Steinem poked gentle fun at the overall chauvinist nature of the show by suggesting in her article "If Men Could Menstruate" that the Hill Street squad room would be a better place if "the whole precinct hit the same cycle."[21]

"Race," similarly, was a controversial area, though *Hill Street Blues* was recognized as a step forward from *Kojak*. The station was multi-ethnic, and insofar as the cops were an "urban fighting unit," this reflected the situation in Vietnam when black and white troops had fought side-by-side. The pairing of officers Hill, an African American, and Renko, who is white, offered a version of the buddy trope that anticipated other such partnerships in film (e.g., the *Lethal Weapon* movies) and in TV cop dramas (Tubbs and Crockett in *Miami Vice*, Bunk and McNulty in *The Wire*, and so on). Scenarios could sometimes be contrived, in order to make a point: for example, in the series pilot, Hill and Renko break up a domestic disturbance, only to find that the neighbors who called 911 are black, but the wife who is causing the problem is white. Despite this, James Craig Holte notes, "Like earlier police series, *Hill Street Blues* employs the metaphor of the melting pot as a vehicle for dramatizing the way we wish things to be. It shows an ethnically diverse organization operating with some degree of efficiency and humanity in a world out of control. Perhaps the largest transformation is in the melting pot image. In *Hill Street Blues* it is a frame for a narrative that goes beyond propaganda."[22]

Finally, critical assessment of the show has moved on in other ways since Oates and Gitlin. Today, some scholars ask whether *Hill Street Blues* was really so different, politically speaking, to the *Dragnet* tradition. After all, here was a show that presented the cop as a hero, and which rarely asked audiences to sympathize with the felons: crime is shown as a given—an inevitable fact of the human condition. Similarly, was *Hill Street Blues* "exceptional" in terms of TV programming? Jonathan Nichols-Pethick argues, "Like most television dramas, it came to life in an intricate web of intentions, accidents, and compromises within the setting of commercial television, where creative vision runs up against industry economics, network programming strategies, and the technical challenges of production.... The producers of *Hill Street Blues* operated within familiar frameworks provided by the television industry and the conventions of police drama to expand the range of what could be represented and discussed in the genre."[23]

In terms of reception, *Hill Street Blues* was not an immediate success (at the time, it was the lowest-rated show ever to be renewed for a second season), but critical acclaim soon boosted its prospects, and led to several Emmy nominations and awards. These included technical awards in cinematography (1981), film sound mixing (1982, 1983, 1984), film editing (1983), film sound editing (1981, 1983), and writing (1982, 1983), as well as for acting and directing. Its four consecutive Emmys as Outstanding Drama Series underline its importance in American television history. Although its viewership was restricted to up-scale urban demographics, its critical reception helped keep it afloat in the unsettled waters of network TV.[24] Indeed *Hill Street Blues* helped to create the advertising concept of "must-see television" that NBC used throughout the 1980s and 1990s for its Thursday night line-up of sitcoms and dramas.

How *MAD* magazine saw the show. "Swill Street Blues," 1982: script by Tom Koch; art by Angelo Torres (from *MAD* #231. © E.C. Publications, Inc. Used with permission).

The show's impact on wider culture was reflected in the number of parodies that emerged: from *Mad* magazine's "Swill Street Blues" (1982) to SCTV's parody sketch "Benny Hill Street Blues" (1981), which transplanted the bawdy British comedian to the police precinct station, with typically ribald results. However, *Hill Street Blues* was never merchandized to any significant degree, aside from a few t-shirts and a record of the Mike Post theme music, and this was due largely to its not having any star actors or celebrity characters.[25]

The reasons for the show's cancellation were varied. Some critics pointed to a decline in quality after the death in 1983 of the actor who played the beloved Sgt. Esterhaus (Michael Conrad); others to the absence of Michael Kozoll after season 2 (he was replaced by, among others, Anthony Yerkovich, who later devised *Miami Vice*, and David Milch, who went on to co-create *NYPD Blue* with Steven Bochco). Whatever the case, the final seasons were generally agreed to be inferior, and veering more towards soap opera as the law of diminishing returns set in.

In terms of *Hill Street Blues'* longer-term legacy, it is clear that it provided a new template for prime-time drama. Its style, ensemble playing and multi-threaded construction were borrowed by cop shows (especially *Homicide: Life on the Street, NYPD Blue* and *The Wire*), as well as by hospital shows (*St. Elsewhere* and *ER*) and less classifiable kinds of drama (*Twin Peaks, The West Wing, Lost*). Indeed, Steven Bochco became a central figure in perpetuating the *Hill Street Blues* aesthetic—as well as co-creating the aforementioned *NYPD Blue*, he was responsible for the hit legal series *L.A. Law*.

As a sidebar, the show's influence was felt in other art forms, too. For example, in the world of comic books and graphic novels, the "Captain Freedom" storyline was acknowledged as an inspiration for several examples about "real superheroes" (an idea that has recently surfaced again with the success of the *Kick-Ass* comics and movies). Alan Moore, the most feted writer of comics in the modern age, has acknowledged his debt to *Hill Street Blues* for his series *Top 10*, set in a fantasy police precinct. Evidently, both comics and TV have benefitted from the creative advantages that serialization can offer.

In conclusion, whether or not *Hill Street Blues* was "expanding the range" of the cop genre, or was indeed "extraordinary," it opened up different kinds of dialogue about crime. The way it mixed comedy, soap-opera and serious drama made for a unique take on community policing, and constituted a kind of missing link between *Kojak* and *The Wire*. This was a show about a crumbling social contract in a post–Vietnam America, and a group of cops for whom humor and resignation were the only valid responses. As much as anything, it was about an existential struggle for survival—captured perfectly in Sergeant Esterhaus's understated exhortation to "Be careful out there!"

Recommended Episodes

The series pilot, "Hill Street Station," is a good introduction to the visual/aural techniques and narrative complexity that would make the series famous, and introduces all the major characters. It climaxes with officers Renko and Hill shot in the line of duty and presumed dead (not knowing if the pilot would become a regular series, Bochco and Kozoll had decided to keep things open-ended). The documentary *The Police Tapes* (available on DVD through Docurama) makes a useful complement to the pilot. Also recommended is the first season episode "Double Jeopardy" which begins in comedic fashion with several of the male police officers in drag as part of a trap set for a serial rapist. The title refers to both Sergeant Esterhaus's juggling of two women in his life and the revelation that Sergeant Macafee (Dan Hedaya) is actually married to two women and has two separate families. This twist saves Officer LaRue (Kiel Martin) from dismissal and prosecution, a plot thread that had been continuing for several previous episodes.

Further Reading

Compared to some other police dramas in this volume the critical discourse on *Hill Street Blues* is quite extensive. As noted at the beginning of this essay, this discourse began when the series originally aired and falls into two major categories: the work concerning the creation of the series, and the writings that debate the series as a primary example of "quality television." Todd Gitlin devotes a chapter to *Hill Street Blues* in his seminal work, *Inside Prime Time* (Pantheon Books, 1983), which details the building of its aesthetic. Paul Kerr's essay, "Drama at MTM: *Lou Grant* and *Hill Street Blues*" in Jane Feuer et al. (eds.), *MTM "Quality Television"* (BFI, 1984) provides an industrial context for the show's development as part of MTM's production strategy for hour-long dramatic series. Likewise, Steve Jenkins' essay in the same volume highlights some of the narrative braiding techniques that became emblems of the program's "quality" status. Robert J. Thompson's *Television's Second Golden Age: From* Hill Street Blues *to* ER (Syracuse University Press, 1996) is perhaps the definitive work on high-end television in the 1980s and 1990s. Additional contemporaneous writings concerning the series locate it within a literary discussion as a form of melodrama (e.g., Caren J. Deming's "*Hill Street Blues* as Narrative," *Critical Studies in Mass Communications* Volume 2, Number 1, March 1985: 1–25) and within a debate about issues of "race" (e.g., Larry Landrum's "Instrumental Texts and Stereotyping in *Hill Street Blues*: The Police Procedural on Television," *MELUS*, Volume 11, Number 3, *Ethnic Images in Popular Genres and Media*, Autumn 1984: 93–100). More recent scholarship includes Jonathan Nichols-Pethick's excellent *TV Cops* (Routledge, 2012), which draws on the work of Jane Feuer to interrogate the twin ideas of "exceptionalism" and progressive politics.

CHAPTER 11

Cagney & Lacey
(CBS, 1981–88)
BEN BETHELL

Set in a fictionalized version of Manhattan's midtown 14th Precinct (though filmed mainly in Los Angeles), *Cagney & Lacey* featured one of TV's all-time classic cop partnerships. Mary Beth Lacey (Tyne Daly) is a wife and working mother from Queens; a dogged, methodical detective who plays things strictly by the book. Her partner, Christine Cagney (Sharon Gless), is by contrast an impulsive hot-shot who, beneath a vivacious exterior, is troubled, vulnerable and (it transpires), like her Irish cop father, an alcoholic. Although, in terms of ratings, no match for CBS '80s smashes such as *Dallas* and *Magnum P.I.*, the show attracted a devoted, die-hard fan base and received widespread critical acclaim. It won no fewer than 14 Emmys, including four for Daly and two for Gless, who between them walked off with the award for Lead Actress in a Drama Series six years running. The show is today regarded as a landmark in television history.

Cagney & Lacey was conceived by writers Barbara Avedon and Barbara Corday as a challenge to prevailing representations of women on television. Championed by journalist and feminist leader Gloria Steinem, the show served as a primetime platform for feminist discourse, tackling issues such as rape, pornography, abortion, breast cancer, domestic violence, and sexual harassment in the workplace. A retort to such "jiggle era" fare as *Charlie's Angels* (ABC, 1976–81), its female protagonists were portrayed neither as sex objects nor "damsels in distress"—if anything, it is they who come to the rescue of male colleagues. Tough and independent, Chris and Mary Beth were not reduced to subordinate roles as wives, girlfriends, mothers and daughters, but instead represented as autonomous individuals. It was, however, to *Cagney & Lacey*'s depiction of women's friendship that, more than anything, both fans and feminist critics responded. Female viewers, in letters sent when the show faced cancellation in 1983, praised the duo's "natural and genuine chemistry" and applauded its creators for making "honest female relationships into major dramatic entertainment."[1]

Before *Cagney & Lacey*, friendship between women was virtually absent from both big- and small-screen drama: two women would, typically, share top-billing only as rivals—more often than not, for the affections of a man. Incredibly, the show was the first in the history of U.S. television drama to feature two women as lead characters. This narrative strategy allowed a far more complex depiction of women than hitherto seen on primetime TV. Far from presupposing a single "feminine" way of looking at the world, *Cagney & Lacey* examined conflicting ideas about what it meant to be a woman in Reagan-era America.

Indeed, in her study of the show, Julie D'Acci argues that it "reveal[s] the *actual terms* of cultural struggle over the meaning of femininity" that took place during the 1980s.[2] In Gless's own words, *Cagney & Lacey* "was not about two cops; it was about two women who happen to be cops."[3]

One of TV's most successful "buddy" partnerships began life in 1974 as a direct response to an observation by feminist film theorist Molly Haskell in her book *From Reverence to Rape: The Treatment of Women in Movies.* Haskell noted that, despite the current vogue for buddy pictures, Hollywood had failed to produce a female version of the genre. Writers Barbara Avedon and Barbara Corday, who had together attended women's writing workshops, took up Haskell's challenge, producing a treatment for a cop movie whose central female buddy relationship they modeled on their own as friends and writing partners. Aspiring producer Barney Rosenzweig was Corday's boyfriend at the time and, in his own words, "setting out to have his consciousness raised." He pitched the idea to Filmways (now Orion) as "the first real hit feminist film" and secured seed money to develop a full-length script. Avedon and Corday then spent a short time shadowing NYPD policewomen on the job, before writing a script entitled "Freeze," a cop spoof in which an early incarnation of Chris and Mary Beth are pitched against "The Godmother," the proprietor of a brothel whose male hookers service its female patrons. Rosenzweig, who touted "Freeze" around the major studios, recalls that the typical, disappointing response of studio executives was that "these women aren't soft enough, aren't feminine enough."

In 1980, Avedon and Corday resurrected the project, re-tooling their script as a pilot for a realistic TV series. By this time, following the mass entry of women into the American workforce during the 1970s, the major networks had embarked on a quest to capture the "working-women's market." Both *Dallas* (CBS, 1978–91) and *Dynasty* (ABC, 1981–89) were conceived with this aim, and both enjoyed huge ratings success. The networks hoped, however, that shows such as *9 to 5* (ABC, 1982–83; 1986–87) and *Remington Steele* (NBC, 1982–87), which portrayed actual working women (as opposed to scheming millionairesses), would capture a prized, yet elusive, audience of older, college-educated, female high-earners—a demographic that *Cagney & Lacey* would eventually deliver to CBS's advertisers. The show, then, resonated with viewers less as a portrayal of female cops than of women in the workplace per se. Far from "scatty" or "ditzy," Chris and Mary Beth are depicted as successful professionals working in a job traditionally dominated by men. As detectives, they are resourceful and effective, using both intellect and, where necessary, physical force to resolve cases. "Finally," recalls Steinem, "there was something that looked more or less like real life on television."

Mary Beth's relationship to work is presented as a sharp contrast to her partner's. Career-driven Cagney has her sights set on becoming the city's first female police commissioner; she makes detective-sergeant at the end of season 4, after which she serves as the precinct's second-in-command. For Mary Beth, on the other hand, career comes a firm second to her husband Harvey (Emmy-winner John Karlen), an unemployed construction worker, and their children (the third of which arrives in season 5). Though Harv's fortunes are later revived, Mary Beth is in early seasons the family breadwinner; though a dedicated police officer, her job, beyond anything else, is a means to keep her family's head above water. As Daly recalls, women were at the time "being accused of working only to fulfill their own egos and to have this wonderful time to themselves and to not be paying attention to their families." However, the actor "knew for a fact that most of the women that I knew that worked, worked because they had to work." The pressures of life as a working mother are the theme of a season 2 episode entitled "Burn Out," which sees Mary Beth walk out on both family and job (Cagney, in the meantime, goes undercover as a nun to bust a drug smuggling ring).

The 14th Precinct station house is, moreover, not just any workplace, but the ultimate *male* workplace. The ways in which women cope with casual sexism in a predominantly male work environment is one of the show's ongoing riffs. Daily life in a fast-talking, wisecracking New York station house has made both Cagney and Lacey masters of the swift comeback and devastating put-down. Mary Beth, however, remains somewhat reserved (and is treated with greater respect by male colleagues), while Chris is "one of the guys" who, when she isn't parrying their clumsy advances, engages in endless ribald banter with fellow officers. Victor Izbecki (Martin Kove), whose primary function (at least in earlier seasons) is to illustrate unreconstructed male chauvinism at its crassest, is a particular nuisance to Cagney. Removed from the show's overt feminist

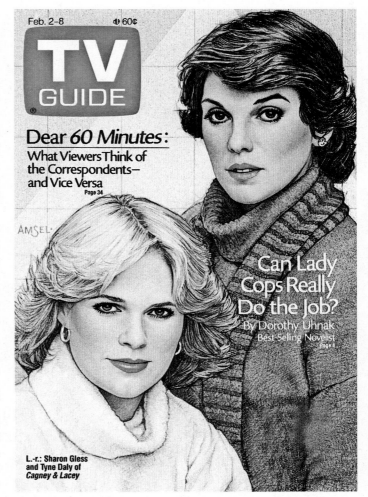

Feb. 2–8   60¢

TV GUIDE

Dear *60 Minutes*:
What Viewers Think of the Correspondents— and Vice Versa
Page 34

AMSEL

Can Lady Cops Really Do the Job?
By Dorothy Uhnak
Best-Selling Novelist
Page 6

L.-r.: Sharon Gless and Tyne Daly of *Cagney & Lacey*

TV Guide asks the question everybody wanted to know: "Can Lady Cops Really Do the Job?" This is famed illustrator Richard Amsel's impression of Christine Cagney (Sharon Gless) and Mary Beth Lacey (Tyne Daly) (courtesy TV Guide Magazine, LLC © 1985).

context, Izbecki differs little from any number of macho TV cops; indeed, in later seasons, his exploits alongside partner Marcus Petrie (Carl Lumbly) are the subject of numerous standard cop-type subplots. The difference here is that from Chris and Mary Beth's perspective, and by extension that of the show's astute female viewers, the archetypal TV cop is *ridiculous*. Indeed, Lorraine Gamman has identified as the show's most subversive element the raised eyebrows and looks of amusement the pair exchange in response to Izbecki's posturing.[4] It should also be remembered that, as well as portraying working women, *Cagney & Lacey*'s set was *itself* a place where women worked—and worked, moreover, in a male-dominated industry. The show became known as a "college" for women writers and directors, offering many the opportunity to cut their teeth for the first time on a major network production—possibly the show's most important and enduring legacy.

Though it balked at a full series, CBS committed to a one-off *Cagney & Lacey* TV movie in 1981. Although Avedon and Corday had written the part for Sharon Gless, the network stipulated that Cagney should be played by Loretta Swit (best known for her role as "Hot Lips" Houlihan in *M*A*S*H*), whom it retained on a "pay or play" contract. Tyne Daly, who had played a female cop opposite Clint Eastwood's "Dirty" Harry Callahan in *The Enforcer* (James Fargo, 1976), was cast as Lacey. Gloria Steinem, to whom Rosenzweig cannily sent an advance script, championed the project in the pages of *Ms.*, the popular and influential feminist magazine she had co-founded in 1972, and appeared with Swit on TV talk-shows to plug the forthcoming TV event—sounding, to one critic, "as if they were promoting the first woman president." CBS had yet to air the movie when Steinem and the staff of *Ms.* began lobbying the network for a series. The magazine's October issue featured Swit and Daly on its cover and a piece by leading feminist critic Marjorie Rosen, who also demanded that *Cagney & Lacey* be given a full run. The movie, in which Chris and Mary Beth appear in uniform and in the end make the grade as detectives, was broadcast that month and proved to be ratings smash. Within 48 hours, Steinem and Rosen's wish was granted when CBS called Rosenzweig to commission a series. With Swit committed to *M*A*S*H* and Gless under contract at Universal, Meg Foster, familiar to viewers as a guest star on shows such as *Hawaii Five-O* and *The Six Million Dollar Man*, was recruited to play Cagney.

Audience figures for *Cagney & Lacey*'s first season (which, from March 1982, ran head-to-head against ABC's *9 to 5*) were, however, so poor that CBS threatened to cancel the show after only two episodes. *TV Guide* reported that the network felt the show's lead characters were "too tough, too hard and not feminine," quoting an unnamed CBS executive who complained that Chris and Mary Beth were "too harshly women's lib" and "more intent on fighting the system than doing police work." The problem, according to this source, was that the network "perceived them as dykes." Just as Starsky and Hutch had been dubbed "prime-time homos" by an ABC executive, so the strength of Chris and Mary Beth's "buddy" relationship aroused network fears that the pair might be viewed as a lesbian couple. Lesbian relationships appear subsequently to have acquired something a taboo status for *Cagney & Lacey*'s scriptwriters, functioning as "the repressed of the series."[5] Despite its predilection for feminist issues, and the inclusion of gay male characters such as Cagney's neighbor, Tony, no gay woman ever appears in the show. Cagney's exploits on the singles scene and Lacey's marriage to Harv both serve (in much the same way as Starsky and Hutch's succession of bimbo girlfriends) to stress their respective heterosexual credentials. However, such is the intensity of the pair's exchanged looks and brief, understated moments of physical contact that it is nonetheless possible (as many viewers apparently did) "to read the relationship between Cagney and Lacey as structured upon desire [and] these moments of intense emotional conflict as positively erotic."[6] Gless in particular, once she took over the role of Cagney, attracted a sizeable lesbian fan base—this in spite of the fact that the National Gay Task Force, dismissing her as "kittenish," initially protested her substitution of Foster.

It seems that Cagney was viewed by network executives as particularly problematic: while Daly's role was to remain basically unchanged, CBS demanded Foster's replacement by a more "feminine" actor, along with substantial changes to the character she'd played. The network's head of audience research felt that the character should "combine competency with sensuality."[7] Avedon and Corday had initially written Chris Cagney as not only witty, single and sexually active, but a tough, working-class Irishwoman to boot—a combination that evidently gave network executives the jitters. Cagney's hard-drinking Irish cop father now suddenly acquired a wealthy ex-wife, and Cagney herself a privileged upbringing in Westchester County. In order to do justice to the character's new uptown identity, the show's budget was revised to include an additional $15,000 for wardrobe costs—most of which appears to have been spent on Gless's trademark sweaters. Daly for her part resisted attempts to give Mary Beth a makeover, retaining a dowdy look achieved by shopping with the show's wardrobe designer in the sale and basement sections of New York department stores. By season 4, Cagney had, moreover, abandoned singles bars and found a steady boyfriend— though Sergeant Dory McKenna (Barry Primus), whose cocaine addiction is the subject of season 2's "Recreational Use," proved unpopular with viewers and was eventually replaced by long-term suitor, ACLU attorney David Keeler (Stephen Macht).

Despite charges of "sugar-coating" by some critics, and though they initially felt clumsy to Rosenzweig and Corday, these changes (as far-fetched as some of them were) in the event transformed Chris Cagney into one of the all-time great TV cops. Chris's everywoman status—equally at home at a society charity event or playing pool with Dad in a downtown bar.—was a significant factor in the show's success. She was henceforth less a feminist than a rugged individualist, whose views on social issues (for instance, abortion) are often conservative. Mary Beth, on the other hand—who in a season 6 episode, while taking part in an anti-nuke demo, manages to get *herself* arrested—became the mouthpiece for *Cagney & Lacey*'s distinctly liberal brand of politics. In its concern over professional ethics, narrative focus on citizens' rights, and privileging of minority viewpoints (such as that of the Guatemalan illegal immigrant Chris and Mary Beth help in season 1's "Beyond the Golden Door"), the show can be seen as the true successor to the über-liberal *Lou Grant* (CBS, 1977–82). Indeed, in their empathy and compassion for victims—and in Mary Beth's case, sometimes even perpetrators—the duo at times seem less like cops than social workers. Though those involved with the show tended, in later years, to distance themselves from the overt feminism of its early seasons, *Cagney & Lacey* remained a paradigm of liberal TV drama. Disavowing the "feminist" tag as "limiting," Gless in a 1987 interview instead chose to describe the show as "humanist."

Cagney & Lacey's second season, and Gless's performance as the new Cagney, were well received by critics. Ratings, however, continued to disappoint, leading to renewed cancellation threats from CBS. A letter campaign followed, supported by Steinem, *Ms.*, and the National Organization for Women (NOW). The campaign was orchestrated by Rosenzweig, who, on the principle that this way their letters might actually be read by CBS executives, urged fans to write not directly to the network but instead to the *New York Times* and the *Los Angeles Times*. Its producer's smarts notwithstanding, *Cagney & Lacey* was finally axed by CBS in May 1983. However, the network was left red-faced when the show received four posthumous Emmy nominations and Daly went on to land the first of her Lead Actress wins. Letters continued to flood in and ratings for re-runs were high. In spring 1984, though its sets had been destroyed and the cast's contracts cancelled, CBS granted *Cagney & Lacey* a second stay of execution. The show would run for five more seasons— and a decade later, for the 1994-95 season, Gless and Daly would return once again, reprising in four full-length TV movies the roles that made them famous.

As time went on, *Cagney & Lacey* evolved into a hybrid: part cop show, part soap opera. The show's later seasons devoted increasing attention to the exploration of its characters' personal and professional problems, and less to the business of catching crooks. Its primary focus was now, on the one hand, Lacey's family life: Harv's efforts to start his own

Hardworking cops Christine Cagney (Sharon Gless) and Mary Beth Lacey (Tyne Daly) prove that they can indeed, "do the job" (CBS TV/The Kobal Collection).

business; the couple's growing children (the eldest of whom, Harvey Junior, eventually enlists in the Marines), and the family's eventual move to the suburbs. On the other hand, there was Cagney's tempestuous personal life, her relationship with her alcoholic father (Dick O'Neil) and her own descent into alcoholism. As *Cagney & Lacey* grew soapier, its male supporting characters, and their various struggles as "new men," also came into sharper focus. An episode might, for example, feature a subplot about Lieutenant Bert Samuels' (Al Waxman) problematic relationship with his estranged son, or Detective Petrie's devotion to his daughter. By the final season, even the Neanderthal Izbecki was given the opportunity to display his sensitive side, via a subplot dealing with the death of his mother and love for an older woman (he also discovers that he's Jewish).

As early as season 3, in two episodes written by Terry Louise Fisher (who went on to create *L.A. Law* with Steve Bochco), crime-fighting is entirely relegated to subplot status. In "Choices," Cagney, following a phantom pregnancy, faces the fact that she may never have children, while in "The Baby Broker," Lacey becomes emotionally attached to an abandoned infant. It may be noted here that while the cop show is traditionally a masculine genre (and one, moreover, which "function[s] ideologically to reproduce notions of male social authority"), soap, with its emphasis on dialogue and problem-solving, has been defined as primarily feminine.[8] Whereas the cop genre is centered around the workplace (sometimes exclusively—viewers are, for instance, never vouchsafed even a glimpse of

Kojak or Columbo's living quarters), soap's focus, like that of sitcom, is the home. Up until the mid–1980s, subjects of the kind tackled by *Cagney & Lacey*'s writers, if addressed at all on primetime television, were dealt with in the domestic setting of the soap or the sitcom, and "resolved" through family interaction. It is significant, then, that key scenes between Chris and Mary Beth normally take place in either their car or the "jane" (the stationhouse's female restroom). While nominally part of the workplace, these spaces serve as a private (female) domain beyond the (male) station-house; at their desks, the duo will often speak guardedly about the true course of an investigation. Moreover, as Mary Beth tends to use husband Harv (a staunch liberal) as her sounding board, discussion and debate of a particular case's finer ethical points often occurs in the couple's home—typically, during their regular bedtime scene together (Rosenzweig jokes that actor John Karlen had a great job, turning up at the studio "once a week in his pajamas").

Writers such as Fisher who pioneered the cop/soap hybrid successfully interweaved its twin elements into a new kind of TV show. For example, a season 6 episode entitled "The Zealot," in which the duo track down the murderer of a colleague who has been working on a child pornography case, also features a subplot in which Mary Beth discovers her teenage son's own porn stash. Similarly, in season 5's "The Clinic," an episode about the bombing of an abortion clinic, Mary Beth reveals to Chris that, as a teenager, her own unwanted pregnancy was terminated. This narrative approach allowed not only greater depth of characterization, but a far more nuanced account of crime itself. Rather than the feared "Other"—taking place "out there," beyond the domestic sanctuary of the middle-class American home—crime was resituated as part of a broad behavioral spectrum. By introducing soap's multiple viewpoints and narratives to the cop show, writers were able to move beyond the simplistic universe of "good guys and bad guys" and begin to tackle social subjects in their true complexity. In this way, *Cagney & Lacey* (along with *Hill Street Blues*, its exact contemporary) not only rewrote the rules of the cop show, but paved the way for TV dramas such as *L.A. Law, The West Wing* and *The Wire.*

Among feminist critics, however, the show's later soapy trajectory was viewed by some as a betrayal of first principles. Discussing Cagney's descent into alcoholism at the end of season 6, Beverly Alcock and Jocelyn Robson label *Cagney & Lacey* "fundamentally reactionary" and point to the convention, common in Hollywood melodramas of the 1940s, whereby "independent women who transgress against the heteropatriarchal order must be punished and face rehabilitation (or death)." Cagney's "humiliation," they argue, "can be seen as the price she must pay for her independence and her rejection of traditional family and sexual roles." The show's final season—in which Cagney is raped, turns down her ACLU lawyer's proposal of marriage, affirms her single, independent status, and then takes up with a plumber she meets in an AA meeting—Alcock and Robson brand "a disaster." "In breaking Cagney," they conclude, "the series destroyed itself."[9] Gamman, however, to whom their comments are directed, while she draws a distinction between its "progressive" early episodes and "conservative" denouement, defends *Cagney & Lacey* against the "reactionary" charge: "How many pregnant and working women have you seen on [TV] defending a woman's right to abortion?"[10] This is a reference to "The Clinic," an episode that anti-abortion groups tried to force CBS to pull prior to broadcast in 1985, lobbying affiliates for a black-out when the network rejected their demands. The campaign was fierce: one anti-abortion spokesperson declared publicly that "any further violence at abortion clinics would be on CBS's conscience." In response, Daly and Rosenzweig attended pro-choice events in Washington, D.C., and Rozenzweig debated the issue with the president of the National

Right to Life Committee live on *The McNeil/Lehrer News Hour*. A child of the women's movement of the 1970s, *Cagney & Lacey* stuck—often bravely—to its liberal guns. Before we dismiss the show as little more than a reflection of Reagan-era conservatism, its fighting spirit should be recalled.

Recommended Viewing

From its opening scene, in which Lacey criticizes her partner for joining officers who hire a stripper to celebrate a colleague's birthday, season 2's "Date Rape" (written by Terry Louise Fisher) is an essay in feminist TV. Startling even today, the episode is a reminder of the degree to which *Cagney & Lacey* represented a radical departure from primetime norms. As usual, the eponymous topic's grey areas are explored: when Lacey doubts the crime's promiscuous victim, both Cagney and husband Harvey must remind her that "no" always means "no." Male attitudes are caricatured by the pair's colleagues—one of whom even refers to them dismissively as "Gloria Steinem types."

Further Reading

Several feminist critics and academics (some, evidently, aficionados of the show) have written about *Cagney & Lacey*; containing not only valuable insight, but a wealth of information, these texts will be of interest to students and fans alike. A good place to start is Danae Clark's "*Cagney & Lacey*: Feminist Strategies of Detection" in Mary Ellen Brown (ed.), *Television and Women's Culture* (Sage, 1990). Lorraine Gamman's seminal "Watching the Detectives: The Enigma of the Female Gaze" can be found in Lorraine Gamman and Margaret Marshment (eds.), *The Female Gaze: Women as Viewers of Popular Culture* (The Women's Press, 1988). Gamman is critiqued in Beverley Alcock and Jocelyn Robson's essay, "Cagney and Lacey Revisited," *Feminist Review*, 35 (Summer 1990), and responds in "Response: More Cagney and Lacey," *Feminist Review*, 37 (Spring 1991). Julie D'Acci's source material for *Defining Women: Television and the Case of Cagney and Lacey* (University of North Carolina Press, 1994) includes viewers' letters, network files, and interviews with the show's creators; an earlier essay of the same title can be found in Lynn Spigel and Denise Mann (eds.), *Private Screenings: Television and the Female Consumer* (University of Minnesota Press, 1992). Somewhat frothier, Barney Rosenzweig's *Cagney & Lacey ... and Me: An Inside Hollywood Story or How I Learned to Stop Worrying and Love the Blonde* (iUniverse, 2007) is available as an e-book. Rosenzweig, Corday, Gless, Daly, Gloria Steinem, Terry Louise Fisher and Julie D'Acci all appear in *Breaking the Laws of TV*, a documentary feature included in the show's season 2 DVD release.

CHAPTER 12

Miami Vice
(NBC, 1984–89)
BRIAN FAUCETTE

Originally conceptualized as "MTV Cops," NBC's *Miami Vice* introduced American audiences to a new type of police drama, one that replaced the gritty urban realism of cop series of recent years with the tropical feel of South Florida and the glossy aesthetic of high-end fashion magazines and music videos. With its emphasis on conspicuous consumption, as well as on law and order, this was a show for the Reagan era. It was a product of a time when many Americans had embraced the Reagan administration's model of limited government that, his campaign argued, was responsible for rebuilding the American economy. While at first *Miami Vice* was not a ratings hit, it became a cultural emblem of the decade, worthy to stand alongside Pac-Man, the Rubik's Cube, *E.T.*, and Michael Jackson. The show's leading characters, officers Crockett (Don Johnson) and Tubbs (Philip Michael Thomas) influenced the direction of men's fashion, as their look—typified by Ray-Ban sunglasses, pastel suits, and facial stubble—became a marker of American masculinity. In 1985, *Miami Vice* appeared on the cover of *Time* magazine with the headline "Cool Cops, Hot Show," which just about summed things up.[1]

The pilot episode "Brother's Keeper" aired as a TV movie in 1984, part of NBC's *Sunday Night at the Movies*, with a trailer proclaiming, "The cop show has just graduated to the 1980s."[2] At the time NBC was seeking to capture the attention of younger audiences; the company's president, Brandon Tartikoff, believed that one way to do this would be to create a series catering to the same market as MTV, a demographic that was attractive to advertisers. Industry lore has it that Tartikoff scribbled the words "MTV cops" on a napkin to describe the sort of program he was looking for.[3] When Anthony Yerkovich, a writer on the successful NBC series *St. Elsewhere* and *Hill Street Blues,* shared an idea for a movie about two vice cops in Miami, Tartikoff, along with NBC-Universal executive Kerry McCluggage, immediately endorsed the project.[4]

Yerkovich had conceived *Miami Vice* in response to a news story which suggested that "nearly one third of unreported income in the United States originated in or was funneled through South Florida."[5] In an interview he said, "I wanted a city [Miami] in which the American Dream had been distilled into something perverse."[6] Miami had been used to such an effect before, most recently in Brian De Palma's movie *Scarface* (1983). Yerkovich wanted to go further, saying, "It seemed to be an interesting socio-economic tide pool: the incredible number of refugees from Central America and Cuba, the already extensive

Shades, suits and nice cars were hallmarks of *Miami Vice*. Tubbs (Philip Michael Thomas) and Crockett (Don Johnson) bring some 1980s flash to the buddy trope (Universal TV/The Kobal Collection).

Cuban-American community, and on top of all that the drug trade. There is a fascinating amount of service industries that revolve around the drug trade: money laundering, bail bondsmen, attorneys who service drug smugglers. Miami has become a sort of Barbary Coast of free enterprise gone berserk."[7] It was this connection between free enterprise, money, and luxury that Yerkovich emphasized when he wrote the pilot.[8]

For the pilot and the series, Michael Mann was hired as executive producer: his previous television experience included writing for *Starsky & Hutch* (1975–79) and *Police Story* (1973–77) and then creating the series *Vega$* (1978–81). Mann joined after directing several unsuccessful feature films, including *Thief* (1981), and, indeed, he had wanted to turn the pilot script into a feature film rather than a made-for-TV movie.[9] Politically, he was left-liberal leaning and was taken with Yerkovich's critique of Reagan's America, although it was his fascination with cinematic style that most influenced the early *Miami Vice*. From the start, he aimed to "pump a contemporary rock and roll sensibility into [the] policier genre."[10] NBC turned over control of the series to Mann and his production company, and Yerkovich was pushed aside: he left after the first seven episodes.[11] Mann went on to oversee 111 episodes and, as Steven Sanders argues, it was his voice "that would come to have a predominating influence."[12]

Along with Yerkovich and Mann, the other individual who would establish the style of *Miami Vice* was the Czech composer Jan Hammer, former keyboardist with the Mahavishnu Orchestra, who created the soundtrack and the opening music. Hammer's pulsating theme played over a montage of women in bikinis, luxurious yachts, high-rise penthouses, Florida wildlife and exotic sports cars. Together they made the most glamorous opening sequence since *Hawaii Five-O*, propelling the theme to the number one spot on the Billboard Hot 100. Hammer had no real experience working in television, but he had worked in feature films, and his "cinematic" musical sense was allowed full reign.[13] For each episode he composed 20 minutes of music using a Fairlight CMI synthesizer in combination with a Memory Moog and Yamaha DX7. The results, embracing a diverse range of musical styles from rock, to reggae, to jazz,[14] often functioned as a form of meta-narration, commenting on or interpreting the images.

The soundtrack also featured three pop songs per episode, thus connecting with Tartikoff's vision of "MTV Cops" and Mann's concept of a "rock and roll sensibility." The series was given $10,000 per episode to acquire original songs from artists such as Phil Collins, ZZ Top, The Rolling Stones, Kate Bush, Tina Turner and Glenn Frey.[15] (Musicians who made guest appearances in the show included Collins, Ted Nugent, Miles Davis, Frank Zappa, Little Richard, James Brown and Willie Nelson—not to mention Jan Hammer himself.) Mann told *Rolling Stone*, "We're … contemporary. And if we're different from the rest of TV, it's because the rest of TV isn't even contemporary."[16] Yerkovich, echoing Mann, stated that the music was not "gratuitous or extraneous to the storyline but [is] designed to contribute to the dramatic narrative."[17] To this end, the songs were used in both diegetic and non-diegetic contexts.

Academic James Lyons suggests that *Miami Vice*'s emphasis on music was also important for its position within NBC, who wanted to take advantage of new sound technologies. He writes, "Right from its inception *Miami Vice* was conceived with one eye on the fundamental shift in the media industries in the 1980s, which was to think of television programs and movies as content that could be repurposed in different formats."[18] In 1984 the Federal Communication Commission approved the use of Multichannel Television Sound (MTS) as the industry standard, a technological shift that allowed for more complex stereo sound. *Miami Vice* exploited MTS skillfully and was the first primetime series to be broadcast using the technology. (Tartikoff suggested that it was the ideal format to "showcase the new cop show [because] music plays such a strong part in the action," and therefore put his full weight behind the initiative.[19])

Miami Vice's main characters were the white cop Sonny Crockett (Don Johnson) and the black cop Ricardo Tubbs (Philip Michael Thomas), a biracial buddy pairing in the fashion of the time: Hollywood movie examples were evident in *48 Hrs.* (1982), *Beverly Hills Cop* (1984), and *Lethal Weapon* (1987). Yerkovich created the pair as a deliberate contrast to the relationship between the characters Renko and Hill in NBC's *Hill Street Blues* (1981–87), in which the racist, wisecracking farm-boy Renko was paired with the earnest, responsible African American patrolman Hill. To this end, Yerkovich downplayed any racial tension: as Lyons points out, *Miami Vice* avoids any direct discussion of "race," and instead focuses on the friendship between the two men, which, he argues, erases any sense of racial consciousness from the series.[20] Furthermore, when interviewed by the media, Mann's comments on the pairing typically diverted discussion onto aesthetics, for example: "We loved the way a dark star and a blond star played off against each other—visually it's very exciting."[21] For academic Douglas Kellner, "[*Miami Vice*] presents one of the most striking images of interracial friendship in the history of television."[22]

Another inspiration for Crockett and Tubbs was *Starsky & Hutch* (1975–79), a series that both Yerkovich and Mann had worked on, and which offered a groundbreaking model of fast cars and gunplay. However, Don Johnson and Philip Michael Thomas were not known stars, and it was thought unlikely that they would generate the same sort of fan interest as Paul Michael Glaser and David Soul. Johnson had studied drama in San Francisco at the American Conservatory Theater. He struggled to find steady work in television, where he was cast in bit parts, in pilots that were never picked up, and in several forgettable made-for-TV movies, including *Revenge of the Stepford Wives* (1980). Thomas began his career acting in blaxploitation films and the black-themed musical *Sparkle* (1976); his break into television came in *Roots: The Next Generation* (1979). Like Johnson, Thomas struggled to find steady work until he was cast in *Miami Vice.*

The pilot established Crockett and Tubbs' back-stories and identities. We learn that Crockett is not only a former star football player for the University of Florida, but also an ex-husband, father, and Vietnam veteran. Crockett's military past is thus used to masculinize his glamorous playboy image, in an attempt to offset the series' competing and often contradictory depictions of masculinity. James Lyons argues that the producers modeled him on the character of Thomas Magnum from CBS's *Magnum P.I.*, also a Vietnam veteran, and that the connection to Vietnam works as a moment of "ideological rehabilitation" of the veteran in 1980s popular culture, "overturning earlier portrayals of them as complicit in wartime atrocities or returning home traumatized."[23]

Tubbs is a less well delineated character, at least at first, but still macho and willing to bend the rules. The pilot episode opens in New York, where Tubbs is a plainclothes New York beat cop who packs a decidedly non-official sawn-off shotgun. When he sees his brother killed in the line of duty, he disobeys orders and uses forged NYPD papers to pursue the killer to Miami. Naturally, he gets his man, but refuses to shoot him with the shotgun, preferring instead to take him to jail: Tubbs may be unorthodox, but he's not that unorthodox. At the end of the show, he resolves to stay in Miami.

Crockett and Tubbs bond in the pilot, if hesitantly at first: "Well, I don't know how this is gonna work, Tubbs. I mean, uh, you're not exactly up my alley—style and persona-wise. Heaven knows I'm no box of candy. But with all things considered, I think we may have to consider some type of ... temporary working relationship." Much of the narrative is built around Florida native Crockett showing outsider Tubbs the delights of the city, and also how to deal with its underbelly—a protective scenario, in the manner of most buddy stories.[24]

Of course, the "temporary relationship" was never intended to be temporary, and the duo would go on to be the show's central characters through its five seasons. Their under-cover work would see them infiltrating drugs rings, but also dealing with serial killers, cor-rupt attorneys, white supremacists, bikers, prostitutes, arms dealers and vigilante cops. In each story, they would take on different guises, "becoming" like the villains they were after, with the concomitant necessity to avoid "blowing their cover." This trope was only subverted in seasons 4 and 5, when Crockett suffers from amnesia and seriously believes he is a drug dealer, thereby setting up an inevitable showdown and reconciliation with Tubbs.

The cast of supporting characters included two undercover policewomen, one African American (Trudy Joplin, played by Olivia Browne); one white (Gina Calabrese, played by Saundra Santiago); two comical detectives, Switek (Michael Talbot) and Zito (John Diehl); and the commanding officer Lt. Castillo (Edward James Olmos). Although the private lives of these characters were often brought to the fore, the kind of soap opera-inflected narrative threading that had been seen in *Hill Street Blues* was not initially a priority.

Thus, *Miami Vice* was certainly a "masculine" show, but the image of masculinity it offered was not orthodox. The focus on style became a way to market products, and a lifestyle. As the concept of the "new man" entered popular parlance, so aspects of consumer culture began to fashion masculinity more along the lines of femininity: in the words of Lynne Joyrich, "[Men] must attend to self-image, and their value of exchange, similarly losing the distinction between subject and object that has characterized the proto-typical 'female consumer.'"[25] The need to consume "the story" and images of masculinity thus became a vital element of *Miami Vice*, and represents the changing dynamic of gender roles in the 1980s. Indeed, Joyrich and others have argued that, as a show about "male excess and display," it can be analyzed "as a hysterical response to a feminine conta-gion."[26]

In terms of fashion per se, Benjamin King has pointed out how the series treated Crockett as a "mannequin" for designer fashion labels like Versace and Armani. Fashion became his "underworld disguise" and a means of directing viewers to enjoy gazing at Don Johnson.[27] In this way, Johnson became a sartorial icon, associated with a particular look: epitomized by "Italo-casual" jackets in pastel colors with rolled-up sleeves, often worn over a t-shirt, and obligatory sunglasses. He thus joined a tradition of cop show stars who were similarly feted: think of the Telly (Kojak) Savalas menswear line or the craze for "Starsky cardigans." How far Crockett/Johnson was "feminized" is debatable, but fan fiction based on *Miami Vice* has taken up this idea with gusto.

As the show evolved, so there was an increasing emphasis on story arcs, thereby antic-ipating the 21st century preoccupation with "novelistic" scripting. By seasons 3 and 4, new writers were joining the series, taking the plots into more topical territory, in the time-honored cop show tradition of stories "ripped from the headlines." One of these writers was Dick Wolf, who had worked on *Hill Street Blues* (and who cited *Dragnet* as his creative inspiration), and who eventually became *Miami Vice*'s co-executive producer with Mann. (In 1988, Wolf left the show to begin work on his own crime drama, *Law & Order*.)

As part of this new direction, supporting characters were made more prominent. There were also gaps to fill: for example, Don Johnson was by now starring in movies, and was spending less time on *Miami Vice*. Thus, female characters received greater emphasis, especially the aforementioned Gina Calebrese, who had at first featured in somewhat clichéd scenarios (for example, going undercover as a hooker), but who now developed more dra-matic agency. For example, in a 1986 episode, notable for its topicality, the character becomes romantically involved with a former IRA man, who tries to convince her he's abandoned

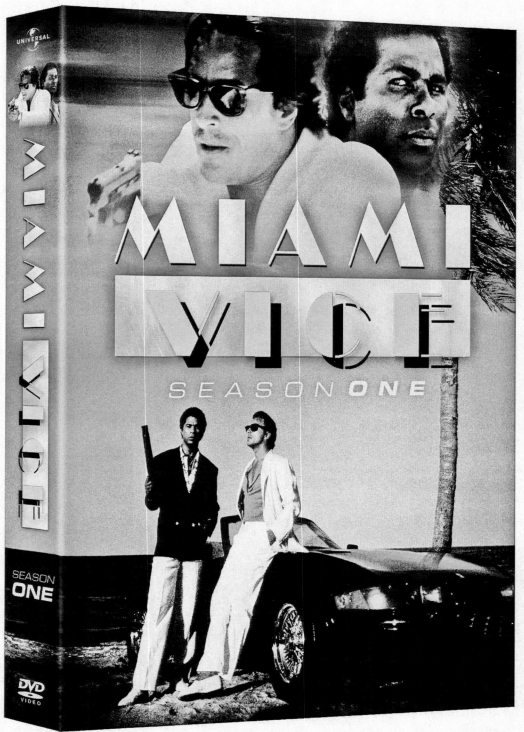

Not Rated

UNIVERSAL

FULL SCREEN

his violent past, but who is in fact plotting to destroy a Concorde jet mid-flight. Instead, it is Gina who has to bring him down.

The story arcs also increasingly emphasized the "sunshine noir" elements of the show. This term, as explained by Steven Sanders, reflects how the series managed to morph film noir's "dark portent, enveloping paranoia, and sense of doomed fatefulness, into the South Florida sunshine."[28] He goes on to suggest how the series "preserves many of classic noir's narrative elements and themes: crime, featuring a contrast between good and evil in which the protagonists, as often as not, are seen as antiheroes; betrayal and violence, plot twists and reversals, and a cinematic style."[29] Another critic, Jeremy Butler, focuses on the use of noirish cinematic style, and how the show rejects standard "three-point lighting" in favor of unconventional blocking (positioning of figures in the frame), extreme low and high camera angles, and strong contrasts of black and white.[30] Butler also notes how Miami itself becomes a character in the series, and despite its Art Deco beauty can be thought of as noir because of the city's pervasive atmosphere of paranoia.[31]

Arguably the most remarkable story arc was left till last. By the late 1980s, the show's ratings were sliding, and cancellation was becoming inevitable. However, this situation allowed the writers the freedom to come up with something darker and more political than anything seen previously (by now, Michael Mann was very much taking a back seat). Specifically, the final season (1988–89) saw Crockett and Tubbs become involved in a "suicide mission" to get a corrupt dictator, Manuel Borbon (played by Ian McShane), out of a riot-torn Central American country ("Costa Morada"). Relative to previous seasons, there is a lot more gunplay, rougher language, less synthesizer music—and, perhaps symbolically, Crockett is seen wearing leather. The storyline involves government collusion with drug cartels, and the two leads are in a state of existential crisis, burned out by the responsibilities thrust upon them, ever more cynical about their role. In a still-shocking finale, the season ends with them quitting the force.[32]

Here is a sample of the dialogue:

COLONEL ANDREW BAKER [OF THE DRUG ENFORCEMENT TASK FORCE]: Hey, what the hell have you done?
TUBBS: Just swatted an insect. You got a problem with it?
BAKER: Yeah, I got a problem. Borbon was working for us. He was gonna give us names.
CROCKETT: But not *the* name, right, Baker? This whole damn mess was a setup from the get.
BAKER: What a couple of lightweights. What do you think this is, cops-and-robbers? It's not about your personal sense of justice.
CROCKETT: What's it about, Baker? Is it about protecting dictators and letting drug dealers go free? Is that it?
BAKER: Take a look at the map, Crockett. Real estate's turning red all over this hemisphere. Your brand of law and order went out with Wyatt Earp. There's only two things that count, American interests and anything that's counter to 'em…. I got carte blanche, babe. I could shoot you right now, easy. Pin it on Borbon. No one's ever gonna ask any questions.
CROCKETT: Do it. If you got the stones.
[Guns are cocked. Crockett and Tubbs start to leave]
BAKER: Hey, punk! Cowboy! I'm gonna have your badges for this. That's a promise!
[Crockett and Tubbs throw their badges to the ground in disgust.]

Opposite: A DVD cover, featuring distinctive art deco–style typography (Universal TV/Photofest).

Such a politically-loaded exposure of police corruption on primetime TV was unusual, to say the least, and examples in the history of TV cop shows are rare (this went beyond the clichéd *Kojak*-style unveiling of "a few rotten apples"). Crockett, a Vietnam veteran who fought for his country in a losing war against a foreign enemy, was now again on the losing side in the war against drugs. The fact that the corruption highlighted in the storyline goes up to the very top—to a government that's in league with the cartels—can also be seen as a metaphor for the way that some commentators viewed Vietnam as a war that "the grunts won but the government lost." Furthermore, as a general commentary on the drug trade, nothing of this pessimistic fury would be seen again until *The Wire*. Thus, the *Miami Vice* finale was spectacular in its own way, and a fine sign-off to a season that had been, until that point, disappointing.

Or was the big finale just one more sensationalist flourish in tune with the overall superficial aura of the show? For ultimately, *Miami Vice*'s reputation as a "style show" was both a strength and a weakness, and there was ample negative commentary. For example Lawrence Grossberg noted that "*Miami Vice* ... is all on the surface. And the surface is nothing but a collection of quotations from our own collective historical debris, a mobile game of trivia.... The narrative is less important than the images."[33] Jane Feuer argued that the show was "often unreadable at the level of narrative or, worse, readable as a mainstream sexist cop show whose premise was unbelievable."[34] John Thornton Caldwell argued that series like *Miami Vice* represented how "television moved from a framework that approached broadcasting primarily as a form of word-based rhetoric and transmission, with all the issues that such terms suggest, to a visually based mythology, framework, and aesthetic based on an extreme self-consciousness of style."[35] Caldwell labeled this new framework of television "televisuality," because, he suggested, "style itself became the subject, the signified" of 1980s television as the networks sought to compete with the increasing number of cable channels, including MTV.[36]

Thus, *Miami Vice* became associated with "postmodernism," a strain of philosophical thinking about society that progressively took hold of academia through the 1980s and 90s. In Fredric Jameson's words, postmodernism was "the cultural logic of late capitalism," and although it was defined in different ways by different thinkers, it tended to involve themes that could easily be mapped onto the show, such as confusions of identity (the cops' undercover work), a bricolage of influences (for example, noir and a "rock and roll sensibility"), and, above all, an emphasis on spectacle and style.[37] Miami itself was typically listed in such accounts as one of the world's great "postmodern cities" (along with New York, Las Vegas, Tokyo, Berlin and Vancouver).

The series was eventually cancelled in 1989, but Mann and Yerkovich returned to *Miami Vice* when they transformed it into a feature length film in 2006. The movie starred Colin Farrell as Crockett and Jamie Foxx as Tubbs; and by now, Mann had become one of the most respected directors in Hollywood, where his films included *Manhunter* and *The Last of the Mohicans*. The *Miami Vice* film gave greater prominence to female characterization and attempted to retain a hip musical soundtrack (which meant excluding Jan Hammer). But by now the stylistic tropes activated by the original series had been standard on TV and in movies for over two decades, and the film received lukewarm reviews.

Fan interest in the original series, however, remained intense for many years—constituting one of the most vibrant fandoms around any TV drama. It existed at the time of broadcast in the form of fanzines that made the most of new desktop publishing technology, and which took the idea of the zine away from a predominantly musical/punk orientation (though some showed a fascination with the show's rock 'n' roll aesthetic). Examples included *This Guy I Gotta Wait For, Vice Line, Crockett Dial* and *Gold Coast*. In the 1990s, fandom started to extend onto the Internet, where dozens of sites blossomed. The kinds of content could include interviews and news reports as well as fan fiction, illustrations, and poetry, with slash material becoming an increasing feature (usually involving a relationship between Crockett and Tubbs, but occasionally involving other characters such as Lt. Castillo). Today, traces of fandom are still active: there are regular conventions, and homages to the show on YouTube are plentiful.

In conclusion, *Miami Vice* represents both the epitome of 1980s cool, and a symbol of postmodern vacuousness. Style was indeed a crucial aspect of the series, and the pleasures afforded by the clothes, locations, people, and the city should not be underestimated. But what scholars such as Grossberg and Caldwell overlook in their analysis is how *Miami Vice* changed the narrative models of primetime television, partly—indeed—through stylizing genre conventions, and how it presented a new form of American masculinity. Add to this a subtext about the futility of ridding America of drugs and drug-related crime, and you have a show that was more sophisticated than is commonly imagined. Beyond the gloss, *Miami Vice* is ripe for rehabilitation.

Recommended Episodes

The pilot episode "Brother's Keeper" (1984) puts all the elements in place: rapid editing, rock music, fast cars, speedboats, glamorous women, gunfights, and snappy banter. The movie-level production values were a revelation at the time. "Smuggler's Blues" (1985) sees Crockett and Tubbs travel to Colombia to help the Drug Enforcement Administration investigate who is murdering dealers and their families. It was directed by Paul Michael Glaser (who had played Starsky in *Starsky & Hutch*) and provided something of a model for the 2006 movie. "Freefall" (1989) is the final episode of the final season, and brings things to a controversial, and moving, end (Crockett: "I'm gonna miss you, man." Tubbs: "I'm gonna miss you, too...").

Further Reading

James Lyons' *Miami Vice* (Wiley-Blackwell, 2010) examines the series' connection to changes in the economic, political, cultural, and gender landscape in the U.S. along with the shifts in the American broadcasting model. Steven Sanders' *Miami Vice* (Wayne State University Press, 2010) explores the program's debt to noir, and its philosophical outlook in relation to crime and the city of Miami. (His previous book, co-written with Aeon Scoble, *The Philosophy of TV Noir* [University Press of Kentucky, 2008], looks at these themes in a broader context.) Jean-Paul Trutnau's *Miami Vice: A One-Man Show?* (Trafford Publishing, 2006) offers trenchant political critiques of particular story arcs, and was the first book to challenge the "all flash, no substance" thesis. For discussions of the show's aesthetic see Jeremy Butler's *Television Style* (Routledge, 2010) and John Thornton Caldwell's *Televisuality* (Rutgers University Press, 1995). For a useful general overview see Douglas Snauffer's *Crime Television* (Praeger, 2006). The most extensive fan site can be found at http://www.miami viceonline.com/content.php.

CHAPTER 13

Law & Order

(NBC, 1990–2010)

BRIAN FAUCETTE

One of the most influential police series of the 1990s, *Law & Order* was framed by its opening statement, delivered by a disembodied voice: "In the criminal justice system the people are represented by two separate and equally important groups: the police who investigate the crimes and the district attorneys who prosecute the offenders. These are their stories." The combination of routine police work and the dedication of legal professionals offered a formulaic, and somewhat controversial, vision of how democracy and "the rule of law" worked. Over the course of 20 seasons the show would become so popular and profitable that it would create a new mode of television production, the franchise series, which to this day dominates the production of contemporary cop dramas like *C.S.I.* Along with winning multiple Emmys, including Outstanding Drama Series for 1996–97, *Law & Order* developed a cult-like fan base, to the extent that in 2010 an exhibition of fan art and reviews took place in Los Angeles.[1]

The show, developed and created by Dick Wolf, premiered on NBC in 1990. Wolf, who had worked as a writer/producer on *Hill Street Blues*, had offered a prototype of the idea to Universal Television president Kerry McCluggage in 1988. McCluggage liked it but felt that a series called *Arrest and Trial* (1963–64) had already combined the genres of police drama and legal show. Wolf investigated *Arrest and Trial* and concluded that it focused on cops and defense counsel but not the prosecutors. This was his opportunity: *Law & Order* would spotlight the prosecutors, who incidentally worked for less money than the defense attorneys.

Wolf's other inspiration was *Dragnet,* to which he paid homage by using actual police cases and an opening voiceover, and focusing on the procedural elements of police work. Still, *Law & Order* differed from *Dragnet* in that it did not always offer a vision of the system that was wholly supportive of the political status quo. Notably, for example, in the program's fifth season the new Assistant District Attorney Jack McCoy is depicted as an old-fashioned liberal who has lived through the hippie era, and whose often anti-establishment values exert a strong influence on the way the lawyers operate.

The show was designed as twin half hours, one focusing on the police, the other on the lawyers. The two halves could potentially be broken apart in syndication: in the late 1980s the networks were not interested in hour-long primetime dramas due to their expensive production costs; in any case, 30-minute series were more profitable in the syndication market.[2] Even so, Wolf was able to convince NBC president of entertainment, Warren Littlefield, to take a risk. (The back-story was complex: Wolf had first sold the show to Fox, who then backtracked and rejected it as they felt it did not fit their brand. He then took it to CBS, who ordered a pilot to be produced, but then passed because the series lacked big-name stars.)

One of the most important writers Wolf hired was René Balcer, who worked on *Law & Order* throughout its entire run (and who also became a producer). Balcer liked Wolf's concept because it was "a great vehicle for every week, just addressing any kind of topic you can imagine and not having to service these personal stories that end up overtaking most series."[3] (His comment was undoubtedly a dig at soap opera-inflected shows such as *Hill Street Blues*.) He also approved of the look and feel of the series noting that "it seemed to hark back to those cop movies of the early 70s (*Across 110th Street* [1972], *Dog Day Afternoon* [1975], *The French Connection* [1971])."[4] The show may have had the look of 1970s cop movies, but its politics were in stark contrast to the conservative image of law and order that was often in evidence in Nixon-era cinema. There, the relationship between cops, lawyers and politicians was far from harmonious; a good example is *Dirty Harry* (1971), in which the cop gets his man only to see the suspect released due to a legal technicality. (This then served Harry as a cue for vigilante justice.) The Wolf vision of "heroism" was instead tied to a romantic image of cops as "working stiffs"—out in the streets in all weathers, questioning witnesses and suspects, using their own kind of slang and morbid humor—and lawyers as dedicated professionals, albeit working from contrastingly cozy offices. Thus the downbeat action of 1970s and 80s TV police procedurals was combined with the glamour of the legal drama.

The focus on the two halves of the criminal justice system allowed Wolf greater freedom to explore mature themes than other cop shows. The format also provided scope to focus on the stories rather than on the characters and their problems—almost the opposite of the *Hill Street Blues* model. As Jonathan Nichols-Pethick has remarked, "The detectives of *Law & Order* are ruthless in their movement from point to point during their investigation. And the lawyers are equally focused and efficient in their potentially ponderous discussions of legal ethics and the nature of justice."[5] Thus, the structuring had to be spare: an episode typically comprised an average of between 11 and 13 scenes, broken up over four acts. René Balcer noted that "we're trying to cram 20 pounds of show into a ten-pound bag, so there isn't room for anything else."[6]

Critics have argued that, unlike other cop programs, the stars of *Law & Order* are not the actors but the writers and their words. As Dick Wolf noted, "There's a whole litany of the best writers in the business who've been with the show. And they have been vastly underappreciated.... It's incredibly difficult to write. It requires unbelievable discipline and talent ... to give what is essentially a very dry procedural so much intellectual spin and so much character spin every week is really a testament to the written word."[7] The work of the best writers for the series, including Balcer, Joe Stern, Robert Nathan, Michael Chernuchin, Walon Green, and David Black, confirmed that, in the words of Nathan, "this was a writer's show because it featured wall-to-wall dialogue. This was a writer's dream because it was all about words."[8] David Black echoed Nathan's praise: "I was happy to be writing quality. I was working with Dick Wolf. He creates a safe place for writers to be able to do the best they can do."[9]

If words were at the heart of *Law & Order*, location was the other major element. Wolf and his team wanted to transform the city of New York into more than a backdrop; they wanted to make it an integral part of the storytelling. Thus the city became a character that could not be replaced, unlike the detectives and the lawyers, who came and went. Wolf wanted to use his hometown rather than Los Angeles because "the light in California is different": unlike California, New York offered a variety of weather conditions, not to mention the image of vertical thrusting skyscrapers that created dynamism and illustrated the scale of the city, its citizens, the system, and its challenges.[10] By shooting on location, *Law & Order* also fulfilled Wolf's desire to capture a sense of (*Dragnet*-style) realism, with the police working in run-down precinct houses and lawyers arguing in the large galleries of the courts. "We get city buildings and city offices for free," location manager Moe Barduch noted approvingly as he explained the ease with which Wolf's production team functioned within the city.[11]

The other elements of *Law & Order* that allowed it to stand out were the lack of star-power and a refusal to focus on individual characters. Nichols-Pethick points out that the "lack of attention given to the private lives of the show's characters" allowed Wolf and his team to create a format where the cast could be regularly changed.[12] This mode of production was demonstrated in the first season when Sgt. Max Greevey, played by George Dzunda, was dropped after the actor complained about his character's development and importance. Dzunda was replaced in season two by Brooklyn native Paul Sorvino, who played Det. Paul Cerreta. However, like Dzunda, Sorvino felt that the series constrained his opportunities and in 1992 he told the *Los Angeles Times* "the cops have no arias. All the drama is in the "Order" section."[13] Sorvino then left, to be replaced by veteran New York stage actor Jerry Orbach, who played Det. Lennie Briscoe.

The character of Briscoe first appeared at the end of season two. The irony was that Dick Wolf had considered Orbach for a key role twice before, only to pass him over for Dzunda and Sorvino. Briscoe was given some of the snappiest, grimmest lines, and Orbach played him as a sardonic, by-the-book, working-class cop. The character became one of the most popular in TV cop show history, and stayed with the show until Orbach's death in 2004. By contrast, Chris Noth played Det. Logan as a mixture of urbane rebel and New York conformist. Noth took the role from 1990 until 1995, when his bickering with Wolf and the writers caused his removal from the series. As a result, Det. Logan was written out of the series in an episode in which he punches a corrupt city official on the steps of the courthouse. The fan reaction to Noth's removal was long-lasting and led to constant questioning of casting decisions, especially when Wolf hired Benjamin Bratt to replace him.

The other major shake-up on the "Law" side of the series came when NBC urged Wolf to increase the program's diversity. NBC President Warren Littlefield told Wolf in no uncertain terms, "The show's too testosterone-driven. There aren't any women watching it. I love *Law & Order* but it's over next year without women."[14] Wolf responded and in 1993 replaced the character of Capt. Donald Cragen (Dann Florek) with Lt. Anita Van Buren, played by S. Epatha Merkerson, an African American actress. For the rest of the series' run Van Buren managed the detectives and the homicide unit in laconic style. Mindful that she could be seen as simply a 1990s variant of Captain Dobey (in *Starsky & Hutch*), the scriptwriters invested her character with increasing depth, and she became a favorite with fans.

For example, in the final season Van Buren's battle with cancer had audiences gripped by moments of intense grief, as well as by frustration and worry that Wolf and company might kill her off (which would have been in keeping with the established attitude of not concentrating on individual characters). As critic Mike Hale noted in a review, "It didn't look good when Van Buren was lying under the scanner while what sounded like Pavarotti

The 1999–2004 team of detectives Ed Green (Jesse L. Martin) and Lennie Briscoe (Jerry Orbach) investigate New York's watering holes for clues (Universal TV/Wolf Film/The Kobal Collection).

singing 'Nessun Dorma' boomed on the soundtrack. But then came the show's final minutes, and the phone call from the doctor. The lieutenant's shoulders heaved and we were left in awful suspense until she whispered 'thank you' and walked back in to her colleagues in the bar." Hale then explains that "the camera pulled away through the crowd, and while the show ended, life went on...."[15]

For the "Order" section of the series, Wolf needed to cast actors who could make the legal scenes seem electric while convincing the audience that these lawyers were indeed some of the best minds in the city. To head the District Attorney's office in season one, Wolf cast Steven Hill to play D.A. Adam Schiff. Hill, who was a founder of the Actor's Studio, played the character as the witty, impatient, and intelligent voice and mind behind the city's judicial system; he remained in the cast until 2000. Hill explained his development of the character thus: "I throw in the practical wisdom of Robert Morgenthau, who is the real New York City D.A. I sort of figure out what he would say."[16]

The role of Assistant District Attorney Paul Robinette fell to African American actor Richard Brooks. Robinette acts as investigator for the D.A.'s office and liaison with the police officers and detectives. To argue the city's cases Wolf cast Michael Moriarty as Executive A.D.A. Ben Stone, a workaholic public servant who sought to ensure that justice was carried out for both the victims and, when necessary, the defendants. Stone served as the conscience of the series until Moriarty was fired by Wolf in 1994 for his awkward behavior. The problems began in 1993 when Moriarty denounced Attorney General Janet Reno at an event in Washington, D.C. What upset Moriarty was Reno's suggestion that the federal government might have to take a more active role in monitoring and regulating violent content on television. Moriarty felt that Reno was singling him out and, like his character Ben Stone, gave voice to his self-righteous indignation. He began to challenge Reno and the federal government's authority, a move that caused problems for Wolf and NBC. Moriarty eventually moved to Canada.

Lieutenant Anita Van Buren (S. Epatha Merkerson), as she appeared (in pixilated form) in the credits to Season 17. The character was originally introduced after cries for "more diversity" from series producers.

In 1994 Wolf brought Sam Waterston into the cast; he played Executive A.D.A. Jack McCoy who, like Stone, was a workaholic. What made his character different was that McCoy was a throwback to 1960s liberalism, in that he believed that government could indeed help people in their daily lives. Waterston noted of his character, "He's aggressive, confrontational, and a little bit of a know-it-all" because "he loves his work, is absolutely convinced he's doing the right job and that job is an honorable thing."[17] Waterston would become a fixture, playing McCoy until the series' finale in 2010.

Thus, the "Order" half of the show was where the mental chess games tended to be played. It wasn't just a question of whether the cops had enough evidence to prosecute, but whether other factors could be controlled, for example, pressure from a baying mob on the courthouse steps, seeking "justice," and stoked-up by the callous media. Such scenarios called for levels of diplomacy that would not have been out of place in *The West Wing*, and when Schiff tells McCoy to stop struggling and "take the deal," the anguish in the legal office is palpable.

The casting of S. Epatha Merkerson as Van Buren had set a precedent and later additions to the cast reflected changes in American society, with women and characters from different ethnic backgrounds having greater prominence. Notable cast members included Diane Wiest (2000–02), Fred Thompson (2002–07), Angie Harmon (1998–2001), Carolyn McCormick (1991–2009), Jesse L. Martin (1999–2008), Jeremy Sisto (2007–10), and Dennis Farina (2004–06).

Another factor which set *Law & Order* apart from similar programs was its minimalist style, championed by Wolf and established with the pilot episode, shot on 16 mm film and using mostly hand-held cameras. Joe Stern, a producer on the series, called it "unsentimental" while actor Dann Florek observed, "I had never seen anything quite like this—the sense of, almost, *News at Eleven* … the immediacy of it. The visceral quality."[18] To encourage this look Stern showed the classic semi-documentary film *Battle of Algiers* (1966) to the pilot director John Patterson. As a result the visual style of *Law & Order* was unique among television series of the era, while also reflecting Wolf's time working on *Hill Street Blues,* which had been filmed like PBS documentaries. Another stylistic feature was the use of de-saturated color. As Wolf noted, "There are a lot of people who think *Law & Order* is in black and white. You tend to remember it [that way], not in color."[19]

The visual style, the staging of short scenes and the use of music to help orient viewers, were key to the series' longevity and eventual popularity. As producer Lew Gould said, "We very rarely start a scene with a greeting.... You come into the scene, you're in the middle of it. And very often, when we close a scene and there's no end to it ... we're on to the next thing."[20] To help viewers with the transition from scene to scene the producers and composer Mike Post developed a style of minimalist music to match the show's abbreviated aesthetic. The series used two mysterious notes between scenes, characterized by a journalist from the Associated Press as "a pungent little hiccupping sound": "'BEE-bing!' Or is it 'BAH-bong!' Or maybe 'BEEB-ong?'"[21] In an interview with *Entertainment Weekly,* Mike Post labeled the signature sounds "the clang."[22]

Together, these qualities were quickly celebrated by the critics. The program aired relatively late (10 p.m.) which tended to emphasize its "adult" nature, and the opening episode was important for setting the tone, announcing to audiences that no topic or political issue was too sacred or controversial for the series to explore. In the episode, the health care system becomes a target for scrutiny. Sgt. Max Greevey and Det. Logan investigate the hospital emergency room death of a young woman who dies from cardiac arrest, and come up against a system which focuses on secrecy and the protection of the doctors. Their investigation leads them to the hospital's chief of medicine, an eminent cardiologist who turns out to be an alcoholic. In the "Order" section of the show, Assistant D.A. Ben Stone duly proves the medic guilty of malpractice. For all its stylistic contrivances, the story was hailed as a powerful indictment of the medical profession and its outdated hierarchy.

Throughout the first season *Law & Order* tackled the hot-button topics of the year: child abuse (Episode 9: "Indifference"), abortion rights (Episode 12: "Life Choice"), racism (Episode 11: "Out of the Half Light"), AIDS (Episode 3: "The Reaper's Helper"), vigilante justice (Episode 2: "Subterranean Homeboy Blues"), rape (Episode 14: "The Violence of Summer"), police corruption (Episode 8: "Poison Ivy"), and underworld crime (Episodes 15–16: "The Torrents of Greed"). Many of these same issues would be the subject of future episodes, with post–9/11 shows often taking on stories about Homeland Security (which sometimes involved putting Muslim characters in the dock and a full-on debate about the "true meaning of Islam") and about veterans of the Iraq War (commonly involving post-traumatic stress disorder, and allowing McCoy to draw parallels with the tragedy of Vietnam). Thus, throughout its 20-year run the show was unwavering in its commitment to a *Dragnet*-style "ripped from the headlines" approach.

Whether this made the show "realistic" was another question. A sociological/criminological study in 2001 looked at three entertainment-based "justice" programs (*Law & Order, The Practice,* and *NYPD Blue*), and one reality-based show (*COPS*). The study argued that "depictions of crime in the entertainment justice programs revealed an over-representation of officially less common violent crime, especially murder, and an under-representation of officially more common property crime, corporate crime and drug crime. As well, the entertainment justice programs presented offenders as predominantly white, middle-aged and relatively affluent and victims as primarily white and female, countering official offender and victim portraits."[23]

Notwithstanding this, the program's "realism" did make enemies. As Wolf noted, "We had $800,000 in advertiser pull-outs on the abortion clinic bombing episode ['Life Choice'] ... half a million dollars in pull-outs on the assisted suicide for AIDS victims episode ['The Reaper's Helper']."[24] But NBC's support remained steadfast; every attack by right-wing critics seemed to strengthen the creative team's resolve. Indeed, sometimes they spoke of *Law & Order* in terms of a moral crusade: writer/producer David Black noted, "My dream for every show is that it presents issues the country is trying to deal with, moral issues, [and that] it presents both sides equally strongly and when the show goes off the air, people start arguing with each other."[25] In this sense, *Law & Order* was a kind of "cultural forum" unto itself.

This willingness to tackle controversial content was carried over into the *Law & Order* spin-offs, *Law & Order: Trial by Jury*, *Law & Order: LA*, and the more successful *Law & Order: Criminal Intent*, and *Law & Order: Special Victims Unit*. The last-named was particularly "dark and gritty" (albeit in a glamorous, prime-time TV way) due to its emphasis on crimes of a sexual nature. It consistently out-performed its progenitor in the Nielsen ratings. Crossover episodes between these series became commonplace, and the franchise also extended to include international TV adaptations, video games, and merchandising. Thus, a "universe" was created, with each aspect being mutually supportive: an economic model that would be much-imitated.

The franchise aspect of the show has also been the subject for criticism, however, for "flattening out" the content and for turning the initial concept into a McDonalds-style production line—a kind of TV comfort food. It has also contributed to the perception among some younger viewers that this is a blandly voracious variety of programming primarily aimed at an older demographic ("mom and pop drama"). In the words of one youth-oriented satirical video, "like the mythological Hydra, when one *Law & Order* meets its demise, two more sprout in its place," and the show's longevity lies in its "awe-inspiring resilience to harsh predatory factors such as changing tastes, aging actors, much better shows, and Benjamin Bratt. As the mother pod reaches maturity, and begins to sense its impending extinction, its outer membrane sends out a series of rerun seedlings … assimilating the entire ecosystem into one homogenous blob."[26] This idea of the enervating nature of "patterned sameness" has been explored (and critiqued) in more scholarly fashion by Derek Johnson in his book *Media Franchising* (see below).

In conclusion, *Law & Order* raised the bar in terms of "adult content"; its style of grappling with difficult social and criminological issues at a breakneck pace would become an industry standard. Admittedly, this formula could look contrived, congested, and often painfully didactic: by the end, it was appearing decidedly dated against the new wave of "story arc" shows like *The Wire*. But, despite criticisms that *Law & Order* was merely a "Mc-cop show," it can be said to have succeeded in Dick Wolf's aim of transforming the police genre in a more political direction, and of bringing *Dragnet*-style morality plays into the franchise era.

Recommended Episodes

The unofficial pilot "Prescription for Death" not only remains relevant today but is also a compelling hour of television that demonstrates the broad goals of the series. For a show that ran for 20 seasons it is difficult to single out one or two episodes that are representative, but "Reaper's Helper" (season 1, episode 2, 1990), written by Thomas Francis McElroy, illustrated the series' social conscience by examining issues of LGBT rights, the AIDS epidemic, and assisted suicide. A more "pulpy" episode is "American Dream" (season 4, episode 74, 1993), in which Ben Stone is forced to revisit an old case when a newly discovered skeleton turns out to be the body of someone killed by a man whom Stone had helped convict. New evidence enables the convicted man to convince the appeals court of his innocence, but the episode ends with the "innocent" defendant back in custody for another murder: turns out, he is a criminal mastermind brought down by his own arrogance. In "Thin Ice" (season 11, episode 8, 2000) sports rage is offered as a defense in the murder of a hockey coach—based on a true case.

Further Reading

The best scholarly analysis is Jonathan Nichols-Pethick's chapter on *Law & Order* in his *TV Cops: The Contemporary American Television Police Drama* (Routledge, 2012). For more general discussions, see Kevin Courrier and Susan Green's *Law & Order: The Unofficial Companion* (Renaissance Books, 1998), which contains a catalogue of episodes, and Douglas Snauffer's *Crime Television* (Praeger, 2006). Wulf Kansteiner's essay "Migrants, Foreigners, Jews and the Cultural Structure of Prejudice: The Nation as Performative Event in US and German TV Dramas" in S. Berger, C. Lorenz, and B. Melman (eds.), *Popularizing National Pasts: 1800 to the Present* (Routledge, 2012), offers a view of *Law & Order* as part of a conservative renaissance in U.S. culture. Dawn Keetley's "Law and Order" in Robert Jarvis and Paul Joseph (eds.), *Prime Time Law: Fictional Television as Legal Narrative* (Carolina Academia Press, 1998), is mainly interested in the "law" side of things, but is still useful: likewise, Elayne Rapping's book *Law and Justice as Seen on TV* (New York University Press, 2003). On the news stories that influenced the show, see K. Dwyer and J. Fiorillo, *True Stories of Law & Order: The Real Crimes Behind the Best Episodes of the Hit TV Show* (Penguin/Berkley Trade, 2006). There are also some interesting higher degree dissertations. Danielle Marie Soulliere's *Prime Time Criminal Justice: If All We Know Is What We Saw on Television* (unpublished PhD dissertation, Wayne State University, 2001) argues that shows like *Law & Order* distort viewers' knowledge of the criminal justice system. Melanie A. Cattrell's *Gendered Crimes, Gendered Fans: Intersections of Gender, Sexuality, and Fandom in the Contemporary American Television Crime Drama* (unpublished PhD dissertation, University of New Mexico, 2011) analyzes the changing representation of gender and sexuality in series like *Law & Order*, and the way in which Internet fan communities respond. On the franchising dimension, see Derek Johnson, *Media Franchising: Creative License and Collaboration in the Culture Industries* (New York University Press, 2013).

CHAPTER 14

Homicide: Life on the Street
(NBC, 1993–99)
LINDA SPEIDEL

Once described in *TV Guide* as "the best show you're not watching,"[1] *Homicide: Life on the Street* had a relatively long life (seven seasons) but had to constantly battle to get renewed. NBC's nervousness is reflected in the staccato nature of the early seasons (13 episodes in the first, four in the second and 22 in the third), prompted in part by the fact that rival show *NYPD Blue* (ABC), launched in the same year, was garnering more of the limelight, and more of the ratings. *Homicide* came to an end in 1999, although a one-off television movie in 2000 reunited the cast.

Both *Homicide* and *NYPD Blue* feature in Robert Thompson's book, *Television's Second Golden Age*, as examples of "Quality TV." Thompson argues that in the 1980s and 1990s a number of American television series emerged which could be categorized as "quality television." There appeared to be a growing consensus among viewers, scholars and the industry that television drama was worth watching and Thompson outlines twelve characteristics which define "quality." These include the notion of "not regular TV"; directors/writers/creators from "other classier media"; "desirable" audiences (affluent, well-educated, urban, youngish); a large ensemble cast; a "memory," with continuing storylines and references to previous episodes; the creation of a new genre by mixing old ones; a literary and writer-based approach; self-referentiality; controversial subject matter; a drive for "realism"; awards and critical acclaim, and, of course, a struggle in the ratings (especially initially) which could be seen as a battle between "Art and Commerce."[2]

Homicide therefore fits exactly with many of Thompson's descriptors. Set and filmed in Baltimore, and depicting the cases and lives of the detectives in the Homicide Unit, it was produced by Baltimore filmmaker Barry Levinson, along with established television producer Tom Fontana.[3] The series is based on former crime reporter David Simon's non-fiction book *Homicide: A Year on the Killing Streets* (which supplies much material for HBO's *The Wire* also), and Simon began writing for the series from the end of season 2 onwards. It follows an episodic structure but has ongoing narrative strands, and several cases run for more than one episode. It is also at the vanguard of a trend towards "crossover" episodes with other series (*Law & Order*) and makes frequent references to other TV shows: "Partners" (3:11), for example, begins with bar owner Detective John Munch bemoaning the lack of customers on a Friday night because they are home watching the *X-Files* and *Picket Fences* (scheduled against *Homicide*). The first few seasons are also particularly notable for their aesthetic, as the series makes use of lightweight handheld cameras associated with documentary and is filmed on 16 mm film, a medium more common in independent filmmaking. In early seasons, the color is bleached out, a visual technique again more often associated with cinema than television. As Tod Hoffman notes in *Homicide: Life on the Screen*, producers, reviewers and fans made much of the series' realism: "we want to see absolutely *real* police TV."[4] Hoffman stresses that *Homicide* is based on true stories, with technical advice from a former lieutenant with the Baltimore PD (who also makes occasional appearances on the show),[5] that the main characters are based on some of the detectives in David Simon's non-fiction book (controversially in some cases[6]) and much is made of the location shooting and the re-creation of the police headquarters in Fells Point.[7]

Homicide aired at a time when "quality" was almost mainstream, as Thompson comments: "At the start of the 1994-95 season, quality dramas could be seen on prime time six nights a week, occasionally scheduled against each other."[8] Jancovich and Lyons point out that quality TV, and what they term "must see" TV (referring to NBC's tagline), evolved at a time when network audiences seemed to be declining.[9] It arises therefore out of a highly commercial aim to keep audiences interested in network television. The priority had been to generate advertising revenue by attracting large audiences, but by the 1990s, with multi-channel television becoming well-established, large audience numbers could no longer be guaranteed and the emphasis shifted to keeping viewers engaged with a show (and often its merchandise). There is a trade-off between attracting a wider audience where viewers can dip in and out of a series and establishing a smaller but loyal viewer base which invests in the program.[10] The shift therefore was from episodic drama—a continual return to the beginning—which viewers could pick up at any point without needing to know much about what had previously occurred, towards ongoing narrative strands which encouraged them to watch every week to find out what happens next. As Henry Jenkins states: "Serialization rewards the competency and mastery of loyals."[11]

As Hoffman and Kalat note, *Homicide* fulfilled the brief of creating a loyal audience and ran for seven seasons in spite of the constant threat of cancellation. But the ongoing struggle to gain consistently high ratings illustrates the tension in the shift to "loyals" and the difficulties for producers in fully committing to this. As Bernard Weinraub comments: "NBC executives, while obviously pleased with the critical reception, never quite knew what to make of the show."[12] The critical acclaim was welcome, but viewing figures could not be entirely ignored, and *Homicide* was therefore pushed around the schedules in the hope of maximizing audience numbers (while potentially alienating regular viewers). The DVD release subsequently made much of the fact that for the first time the series could be watched in the order intended by its creators. While Weinraub notes that continuing storylines were problematic for NBC when showing repeats, the success of *Homicide* on DVD nicely illustrates the possible financial rewards of the new model, and sales of *Homicide* DVDs received a renewed boost in the wake of the critical success of *The Wire*.

In terms of the crime genre, and specifically the police procedural, *Homicide* continues an apparent shift towards an ensemble cast and the police team. This can be seen in the programs' titles which change from an emphasis on individuals' names in the 1970s and early 1980s, such as *Starsky & Hutch*, *Kojak*, *Cagney & Lacey*, to the ensemble or team in the mid–1980s and 1990s: *Hill Street Blues*, *NYPD Blue*, *Homicide: Life on the Street* ("Homicide" referring to the unit as well as to the crime). *Homicide* is arguably a more truly ensemble show than *NYPD Blue*, where Sipowicz and his partners became the principal focus.

Although over time the character of Frank Pembleton becomes particularly noteworthy, the early episodes in particular give almost equal screen time to the various partnerships within the unit, which include (in seasons 1 and 2) John Munch (Richard Belzer) and veteran Stan Bolander (Ned Beatty—bringing a big screen name to television); Steve Crosetti (Jon Polito) and Meldrick Lewis (Clark Johnson); Beau Felton (Daniel Baldwin) and Kay Howard (Melissa Leo); Frank Pembleton (Andre Braugher) and Tim Bayliss (Kyle Secor), as well as shift lieutenant Al "G" Giardello (Yaphet Kotto). In later seasons, individual episodes focus on different characters, such as "The Last of the Watermen" (3:5), when Kay Howard returns to her childhood home, and "Full Moon" (4:10), in which the only regular characters to appear are Meldrick Lewis, Mike Kellerman (Reed Diamond) and (briefly) John Munch. Two episodes also present a view "other" than that of the police: "Bop Gun" (2:4), which focuses on the bereaved husband of a shooting victim (guest starring Robin Williams) and "The Gas Man" (3:22), where the detectives are observed by a former criminal hoping for revenge.

Yet in spite of the ensemble cast, the individual skills of the detective continue to be foregrounded. Crime is solved in the interrogation room—in spite of the program's title, the detectives in *Homicide* spend more time there than on the street.[13] Individuals must find the "truth," even if not always successfully, and detective Frank Pembleton appears especially gifted in this area. The most desirable outcome is a confession, or at least a verbal slip on the part of the suspect. The interrogation room is appropriately named "the box" and detectives perform in front of the "screen" of the two-way mirror. The focus on the interrogation room and the prevalence of the handheld camera serve to reinforce both the particular insight of the detective and individual performance. Here, the television police detective has retreated to the interior: crime is solved *inside* and the individual with considerable autonomy remains in play.[14]

Homicide's aesthetic is particularly noteworthy, with its use of a single handheld camera, 16 mm film and unusual color palette. This would seem to support Jonathan Bignell's claim that "contemporary U.S. police/investigation series have been one of the locations where television style has in fact become a key component of their textual form and their appeal to audiences."[15] Bignell provides a useful analysis of the pilot episode of *Homicide* noting that "the long take privileges verbal performance."[16] Even now, the first few episodes of the series, and in particular the pilot, are startling in their use of color—a pale brown/green palette—and in the unusual dialogue, such as Crosetti's discussion of the shooting of Abraham Lincoln, and Kay Howard's laconic reply to Tim Bayliss's enquiry after the homicide unit's boss: "We work for God." *Homicide* extends the brief of *Hill Street*

Detective Bolander (Ned Beatty), Lieutenant Giardello (Yaphet Kotto) and Detective Lewis (Clark Johnson) debate tactics in the "box" (interrogation room).

Blues to "make it messy" as the camera swirls and pans, breaking with conventions such as the 180-degree line, following characters up stairs, along corridors, into cars and out into the street. There is the sense of a real physical space, as the viewer moves with the police. Scenes occur in cramped spaces such as the bathrooms (very effectively, for example in a confrontation between Meldrick Lewis and Felton in "See No Evil" [2:1]) but also in the "real" city, now a specific place, Baltimore, rather than the indeterminate "every city" of *Hill Street Blues*.

The aesthetic is important for three reasons: it is a signifier of quality; there is a clear link between the camera and the detective,[17] and there is a particular insistence on the "real." The handheld camera both suggests the police view and a sense of "not TVness": this is "real" police work and the physical proximity of the handheld camera reinforces the police view of the world.[18] The image is grainy ("gritty") and therefore "not TV" in two senses—it is more like film, which could be fictional but at the same time uses documentary conventions more like "real" life. The aesthetics of "reality" programs and the predominance of "real" narratives in the 1990s influenced what constituted "realism" in fictional portrayals of police: as Gareth Palmer for example notes, the handheld camera had enabled "real" police work to be filmed and became a marker of "realistic" shows such as *Homicide: Life on the Street*.[19] The move into the interrogation room also denotes a striving for ever greater realism, as it contrasts to some extent with the earlier more action oriented series of the 1970s and 1980s. The emphasis is now on "real" police work, which does not involve car chases or gun battles and which is supposedly more mundane (although over the course of its run, the series saw its fair share of shootings and chases).

The 1990s saw the proliferation of both non-fiction cop books and reality crime programs, suggesting a convergence of trends in the depiction of the police in the written form and on television. Both the police and the police point of view became a very common feature of television and as Leroy Panek points out, police writers and ethnographic work gave the public a sense of fully understanding police work.[20] Fishman and Cavender similarly note that reality TV became a way of promoting certain types of policing and a particular view of crime: the police are portrayed positively and at the same time there is a sense that their job is impossible.[21] Television series serve as an apology for the police, who are portrayed as frontline workers fighting both crime and organizational incompetence, and police work is normalized and justified. However, Pamela Donovan suggests that the fictional representations in 1990s dramas provide more context and nuance than much reality TV,[22] and although the handheld camera signifies the "real," *Homicide* also makes much use of the jump-cut and the repetition of scenes. As Bignell notes, this is unusual in both fictional and documentary television where cuts are made to seem invisible. The deliberate use of these techniques not only lends *Homicide* a very particular visual style but also draws attention to the instability and constructed nature of the police view.[23]

As Martin Priestman has noted, part of the appeal of police fictions is "the genre's increasingly confident probing of the dynamics of day-to-day workplace relationships."[24] The workplace as a key site where interpersonal relationships are enacted is made explicit in *Homicide*, in an exchange between detectives Tim Bayliss and Frank Pembleton. When Bayliss complains that the homicide unit is less of a family than other departments he has worked in, because homicide detectives do not socialize outside work hours, Pembleton responds:

> We are like a *real* family—opinionated, argumentative, holding grudges, challenging each
> other. We challenge each other to be better than we are—kind of thing doesn't happen at

barbecues and ball games. Happens on the job where it's supposed to, on a case, putting down a murder. The work itself is the most important thing.... We speak for those who can no longer speak for themselves ["Stakeout" (4:16)].

Here, work stands in for family, and it is the workplace which facilitates "real" relationships. The familial set-up is reflected in the aesthetics of the squad room, a highly distinctive and relatively confined space, the Broadway Pier building in Fells Point. The workplace family is evident in many police dramas, even those such as the *CSI* and *Law & Order* franchises which, although emphasizing procedure rather than character, continue to focus on a tight-knit group, often with a hint of romantic undercurrents, and cases which involve people personally known to the investigators. But the cop show has tended to function as "one big masculine home," a familial space from which women are excluded.[25] In the workplace family, it is not so much that the feminine enters the masculine sphere, as that women are excluded from "every narrative sphere."[26] While *Homicide* appears to offer a less conventional representation of womanhood in characters such as Kay Howard and Teri Stivers (Toni Lewis), they exist in a largely male environment and two other women, Megan Russert (Isabella Hofmann) and Julianna Cox (Michelle Forbes) are also romantically linked with male detectives, Beau Felton and Mike Kellerman. It is therefore unclear that the representation of women in the homicide unit is wholly progressive, and indeed Kalat suggests that both on and off screen, women are marginalized.[27] Joyrich contends that there has been a tradition of programs which serve the construction of a "hypermasculinity" in reaction against the feminine: "By aiming for the status of 'quality' television (producing texts that can function under the name of an author), creating 'proper' spectator distance by mimicking cinematic conventions, or obsessively re-marking the masculinity of their thematics, some programs attempt to evade TV's 'unmanly' connotations,"[28] and *Homicide* could be seen to fit exactly this description.

Jane Gibb and Roger Sabin note, however, that *Homicide* is unusual in the diversity of its cast: "Here we see a re-constituted squad room in which African-Americans are represented as one ethnic group among others (and so are 'whites'). The program's strength lies not only in the way it articulates differences of race and ethnicity but also in how it invokes a dispersed notion of subjectivity by incorporating gender and generational differences as the basis of tension within and between ethnic characters."[29] Hoffman, Kalat and Hilmes[30] also note the number of African American actors, and the unusualness of this for mainstream network television is illustrated in an anecdote recounted by Andre Braugher about a scene from the episode "From Cradle to Grave" (3:23), featuring Detective Frank Pembleton, Lieutenant Giardello and Captain Barnfather: "I realized it was the first time I'd ever been in a room with three other African-American actors and the scene wasn't about us."[31] But Kalat also suggests that the relatively high proportion of black actors may have been a reason for lower than expected viewing figures.

The significance of *Homicide* for subsequent crime dramas should not be underestimated as many of the cast and crew went on to work on *The Wire*. In particular, it provided the training ground for former journalist David Simon to go on and write and produce both *The Corner* and *The Wire*. David Simon also wrote a season 3 episode of *NYPD Blue*, which features a police informer played by actor Giancarlo Esposito, who appears as Detective Mike Giardello in season 7 of *Homicide*. Actor/director Clark Johnson (Meldrick Lewis) went on to direct the pilot and final episodes of both *The Wire* and *The Shield*, as well as several other episodes during the course of each series. He is a cast regular in season 5 of

Detectives Frank Pembleton (Andre Braugher), Rey Curtis (Benjamin Bratt) and Megan Russert (Isabella Hofmann) and Tim Bayliss (Kyle Secor) get on with the mundane work of policing (NBC TV/The Kobal Collection).

The Wire and makes a cameo appearance in the last episode of *The Shield*, and he also directed an episode of *NYPD Blue*.

Recommended Episodes

It is always difficult to isolate episodes in a long-running television series, and *Homicide* delivered many great stories. "Three Men and Adena" (1:6) is often cited as a classic episode and won an Emmy. Almost the entire episode is devoted to the interrogation of a murder suspect and ends with the case no nearer to being resolved. Another unusual episode is "The Night of the Dead Living" (1:3) which takes place entirely in the squad room, on a very hot night. A memorable season 3 episode is "Crosetti" (3:4), which features the suicide of Detective Steve, which is hard for his colleagues and particularly his partner Meldrick Lewis to accept, because they are never offered any concrete reasons for his death. "In Search of Crimes Past" (3:18) concerns a death row prisoner who has been wrongly convicted and Detective Stan Bolander is forced to re-visit the case. These episodes serve to confound the expectation that the detective is all knowing (although many cases in *Homicide* of course are closed). "The City That Bleeds" (3:13) perhaps marks a gear change for

Homicide, in that it concerns the shooting of three of the detectives. The opening of the episode is shocking and unexpected, as previous episodes had noted the unlikelihood of police drawing their guns in "reality," and the storyline reflects the pressures on any long running series to keep viewers engaged. While this shift has often been attributed to the vagaries of network television, it is also true that a series based on nothing happening and routine work would be difficult to sustain.[32] Nonetheless, the seventh and final season of *Homicide*, in which the squad room has been renovated after a previous end-of-season shootout, seems to have moved a long way from the series' origins. The color palette is much glossier, and newer cast members are generally younger and easy on the eye. However, there are notable episodes throughout the series, such as, to name but a few, "Stakeout" (4:16), "Prison Riot" (5:3), "The Documentary" (5:11), and "The Subway" (6:7).

Further Reading

Michele Hilmes, in *Only Connect: A Cultural History of Broadcasting in the United States* (Wadsworth, 2002), provides an excellent background to the industrial and production context of *Homicide: Life on the Street*, and Jonathan Bignell offers a detailed textual analysis in "The Police Series," in J. Gibbs and D. Pye (eds.), *Close-Up 03* (Wallflower, 2009). Peter Billingham's *Sensing the City through Television* (Intellect, 2000) considers the social issues which are articulated through characterization and dialogue, and Bambi L. Haggins' essay "*Homicide*: Realism" in Ethan Thompson and Jason Mittell (eds.), *How to Watch Television* (New York University Press, 2013), explores the show's "RealFeel" effect. Although included in a collection about *The Wire*, Jane Gibb and Roger Sabin offer a very useful overview of the racial dynamics of TV crime dramas in their essay "Who loves ya, David Simon," *darkmatter*: The Wire Files [4] (29 May 2009), http://www.darkmatter101.org/site/2009/05/29/who-loves-ya-david-simon/. And while both Tod Hoffman's *Homicide: Life on the Screen* (ECW Press, 1998) and David Kalat's *Homicide: Life on the Street: The Unofficial Companion* (Renaissance, 1998) must be recognized as fan texts, they nevertheless include some interesting background information. Jason Vest, in *The Wire, Deadwood, Homicide and NYPD Blue: Violence is Power* (Praeger, 2011), also offers a useful analysis of the series, although his interest is primarily in the author figure of David Simon.

CHAPTER 15

NYPD Blue
(ABC, 1993–2005)
LINDA SPEIDEL

With its twelve seasons, beginning in 1993 and concluding in 2005, *NYPD Blue* is one of the longest-running police series in this collection. It initially aired in September 1993, the same year as *Homicide: Life on the Street*, which began its run in January. The series was co-created by David Milch and Steven Bochco, Bochco being already well-known for earlier series such as *Hill Street Blues* (NBC, 1981–87) and *LA Law* (NBC, 1986–94). As Jonathan Bignell notes, the first episode of *NYPD Blue*, with its near-fatal wounding of a protagonist and a long sex scene (explicit for network television at that point in time), serves to "make clear the program's ambition to innovate in the police series genre while also connecting it to the heritage of 'quality' work associated particularly with Bochco."[1] From the outset, *NYPD Blue* set out to push the boundaries of network television, particularly in regard to nudity and language, and in its portrayal of sympathetic yet flawed characters.

While often paired with its contemporary, *Homicide: Life on the Street*, the two series are more distinct than frequently acknowledged, and there is a marked difference in their aesthetic. *NYPD Blue*, although set in New York, was filmed in LA using a fluid head camera which simulated the jerky appearance of the handheld camera. *NYPD Blue* has a richer color palette than *Homicide* and fewer outdoor scenes. The series merely uses establishing shots filmed in New York in order to convey a sense of the city and much of the action in fact takes place in the precinct building.[2] *NYPD Blue* places even greater emphasis than *Homicide* on scenes in the interior space of the squad room. This is a cramped space, divided into small interconnecting offices and reflects the focus on the emotional and private lives of the protagonists. Indeed, nearly all the detectives, and office staff, are involved with each other at some point, and a high proportion of cases concern people personally known or connected to the detectives.

Yet while *Homicide* and *NYPD Blue* each have a distinct look, invariably the contemporaneousness of the two series invites comparisons. David Kalat cites a comment by *Homicide* producer Tom Fontana: "A very good friend of mine said that *NYPD Blue* is the television version of *Homicide*."[3] Kalat notes the greater audience figures for *NYPD Blue* and attributes this to the fact that the series "pushed out the boundaries of network TV in a more lurid and crowd-pleasing fashion."[4] Since Kalat's writing is in effect a fan text for *Homicide*, it is not surprising that he compares *NYPD Blue* somewhat unfavorably, but

Fontana's comment chimes with the assumption in Robert Thompson's analysis of "quality" television—that it is defined by being "not TV."[5] While *NYPD Blue* is included in Thompson's examples of "quality" television, there is a sense in which it seems to conform more to the expectations of television than its contemporary, even as it pushes the limits of what is permissible. For example, the opening credits showcase each actor/character individually (unlike *Homicide, The Shield* and *The Wire*, where only the actors' names appear, and the images bear no particular relation to the protagonists). Bignell notes the use of "prominent music to underscore emotional tone."[6] Each episode, like the earlier *Hill Street Blues*, ends with a return to the domestic setting, usually that of either Andy Sipowicz (Dennis Franz) or his partner. Moreover, while narrative strands span more than one episode, these tend to relate to characters' personal lives rather than police investigations (although the corruption case involving John Kelly (David Caruso) and Janice Licalsi (Amy Brenneman), runs through the whole of the first season and the beginning of the second). Generally, each case is resolved within one episode, few cases are left open, and very rarely is a suspect wrongly brought in for questioning. Although there is ambiguity in the portrayal of some of the characters, most notably Sipowicz, and his partner in the first season, John Kelly, very few episodes leave cases unexplained. While policing in New York may be challenging, the viewer is left with little doubt that wrongdoing will be put right, and Jason Vest suggests that *NYPD Blue*, more than Bochco's previous *Hill Street Blues*, is a cop series which functions as an apology for the police rather than interrogating the social causes of crime.[7]

It is tempting to conclude that *NYPD Blue* is more "soap-like" than *Homicide: Life on the Street*, but the influence of soap narratives on all cop dramas should not be underacknowledged. Later series such as *The Shield* and *The Wire* rely heavily on ongoing narrative strands, characters who become familiar over time, and the intertwining of personal and professional lives, and although *Hill Street Blues* has generally been credited as being a pioneer in mixing the narrative structures of soaps and episodic drama, Jane Feuer also notes the significance of serials such as *Dallas* in establishing the series/serial hybrid as a staple of prime time U.S. television.[8] Michael Z. Newman notes too that the depth and development of characterization in long format television are as important as plot in engaging viewers,[9] and comments (in a later article): "As much as any narrative medium, television affords intense engagement with characters. We get to know the people on the screen so intimately that they become our 'TV friends.'"[10]

There is therefore a distinct emphasis on the personal lives of the detectives in *NYPD Blue*, and this is reflected in the camera work. Robin Nelson points to the panning between speakers rather than shot/reverse shot editing and suggests that this is "so strictly controlled in its movement, however, that the result has more the feel of a breathless, excited immediacy than the slightly leaden conviction of the handheld documentary camera."[11] He also notes how the camera focuses on the faces of individual characters and the touching of hands, suggesting that this "serves to bring out thematic links between the various narrative strands and the series' ethos of mutual support, of people being there for each other amidst a street-wise cynicism."[12] Frequently the camera in *NYPD Blue* catches looks which pass between the detectives, and these looks often open up an ambiguity for the viewer, as they are not always explained by dialogue. The emphasis, as Nelson suggests, is on the detectives' emotional reaction to and involvement with their cases, as much as any concern with crime itself. Bignell too comments on "richly detailed facial expressiveness and physical gesture to convey moral and emotional turmoil."[13] Nelson suggests, "This sense of general human concern and mutual respect, transcending particular interpersonal or sexual relationships, is the underlying communitarian ethic of Bochco's productions."[14] Like many other police dramas, *NYPD Blue* is about a "work family," but this focus avoids setting either crime or police work against a broader social background. The wider sociological conditions in which crime occurs are obscured, and in the foregrounding of characters' emotions and reactions, each case becomes a matter of personal pursuit, or even vengeance.[15]

Detectives Sipowicz (Dennis Franz) and Simone (Jimmy Smits) meet for the first time.

The emphasis on the personal and the interior, along with the lack of location filming, generates a particular sense of the city of New York. Bignell notes that even the lighting serves to convey the "spatial confinement that would match the characters' embattled relationships with their jobs and each other."[16] Those scenes that take place outside the precinct building convey a sense of the city as grimy, graffiti-ridden and claustrophobic. Typically, the city is experienced through an establishing shot of an external facade, moving rapidly into the interior space of a crime scene within a building. Outside scenes frequently take place in anonymous alleyways, and move quickly to corridors and hallways, and characters are rarely seen in external spaces. Unlike *Homicide*, where the camera follows the characters as they move through space, in *NYPD Blue* the transition from one space to another is experienced as a cut from one scene to the next (an inevitable consequence, of course, of the series not being filmed on location). The focus on the interior—both in the crime scenes and in the squad room, and the frequent close-ups of facial expressions serve to reinforce the notion of the "embattled" detectives contending with a dangerous and threatening urban environment "out there." The city is experienced quite differently from *Homicide*, and later series such as *The Shield* and *The Wire*, which make extensive use of location filming. While both *Homicide* and *The Shield* also incline towards a depiction of the city as alien, the camera nevertheless moves through space and picks up both the urban geography and the (seemingly) incidental details of the city's inhabitants.[17]

NYPD Blue, in a similar vein to *Homicide*, puts the interrogation room at the center of police work, and neither series places much emphasis on technology or forensics. While ballistics and autopsies sometimes serve as an aide to the detectives, other technologies such as voice analyzers are derided or seen as a hindrance. Interrogation is once again the key to closing a case, and as in both *Homicide* and *The Shield*, it is the verbal dexterity and the intuitiveness of the detective which is showcased. For example, both *NYPD Blue* and *Homicide* are distinct from *CSI* in their emphasis on traditional methods. In *CSI*, technology and science have become the key tools in "solving" crime—a reflection perhaps of a wider societal shift in which "proof" is demanded and scientific knowledge is expected to be able to explain everything. In *NYPD Blue* and *Homicide*, the priority is human interaction, and indeed technology is often flawed, unreliable or misleading. The messiness and unpredictability of human behavior not only informs the nature of detective work, but also manifests itself in the depiction of institutional work. *NYPD Blue*, like *Homicide*, gestures towards both the institutional dysfunction that becomes a key focus of *The Wire*, where "the bosses" frequently undermine good police work, and also the solidarity among street cops in *The Shield*, who unite against Internal Affairs.

While ostensibly an ensemble show, *NYPD Blue* tends to focus on the main cop duo of Andy Sipowicz and his partners. Sipowicz provides the continuity through all twelve seasons and is undoubtedly the series' central character. Steven Rubio notes the shift from season 1, which focuses more on John Kelly, to season 2 when Andy Sipowicz takes center stage.[18] At the beginning of season 1, Sipowicz is an alcoholic divorcee and across the lifetime of the show has much to contend with: a continual struggle with alcoholism; the death of his first son, Andy Jr. (from whom he had previously been estranged); the death of his partner, Bobby Simone (Jimmy Smits); the death of his second wife, Sylvia Costas (Sharon Lawrence); raising his and Sylvia's son, Theo, alone; and beating prostate cancer. Not to mention numerous other incidents, such as the death of his sponsor, Dan Breen, in "Don We Now Our Gay Apparel" (2:9). The dominance of Sipowicz is suggested even in the title of Glenn Yeffeth's collection of essays on *NYPD Blue*: *What Would Sipowicz Do?* Several commentators in that anthology note that Sipowicz is undergoing a learning process across the twelve seasons. He is certainly a formidable character, a solid, old-fashioned work-a-day cop. The threat of physical violence is never far away, and in this he foreshadows the brutality of Vic Mackey in *The Shield*. Indeed Rubio notes the comparison made between Andy Sipowicz and Vic Mackey in advance publicity for *The Shield*, although he suggests that in fact Andy is "mild" compared to Vic.[19]

Where Sipowicz does somewhat foreshadow Vic is in the ambiguity surrounding his character. He is allowed by the writers to espouse all manner of racist, homophobic and sexist views, and although these are challenged in the narrative by those around him, such as his colleagues Bobby Simone (played by Jimmy Smits), a Latino character, and Lieutenant Arthur Fancy (played by James McDaniel), a black officer, Sipowicz nevertheless gives expression to uncomfortable opinions. These views are all the more troubling because Sipowicz is by and large a sympathetic central character. While it can be argued that the airing of these sentiments allows difficult subject matter to be discussed in the open, there is a fine line between exposing and endorsing prejudice, and it is not always clear whether *NYPD Blue* fully succeeds in the former. As Jason Vest comments: "Bochco and Milch, by choosing this narrative focus, ensure that *NYPD Blue* presents a white homicide detective's jaded law enforcement perspective on crime, punishment, injustice, and poverty."[20] There is no doubt that Andy Sipowicz, as an experienced "everyman" cop, lends legitimacy to some objectionable views, and while others speak back, they are narratively marginalized, with even Bobby Simone playing a secondary role to Sipowicz. Kenneth Meeks, while acknowledging that Sipowicz grows as a character and is challenged on his views, feels moved to comment: "It's extremely offensive that Hollywood has made a hero out of someone who is racist by nature."[21] While across its twelve seasons *NYPD Blue* attempts to address many difficult and sensitive issues, and much of this occurs through the character of Sipowicz, it remains troubling that his prejudices are allowed so much airtime. It is not the case that he is articulating the unheard voice of a minority: rather, in allowing these views to be expressed through the series' central white male protagonist, the unfortunate impression is created that "after all, this is what (white) people really think." Certainly, there is nothing particularly progressive in the amount of screen time occupied by black or gay characters:

Fancy may be a lieutenant, but narratively he is a secondary character.[22] And as nearly every episode ends with a criminal apparently brought to justice, *NYPD Blue* does not fully succeed in generating the moral nuances which are so much a feature in *The Shield*. The ambiguity of Sipowicz's character sits somewhat uncomfortably in a series where generally transgressors are quickly brought to justice.

Jason Vest dwells at length on the racial dynamics of *NYPD Blue*, and notes the involvement of David Mills in seasons 2–4, who also wrote for *The Wire* and collaborated with David Simon on *The Corner*.[23] Vest sees the involvement of Mills, a black writer, as not entirely unproblematic, partly because of the fact that so much was made of this. Vest suggests that in fact co-creator David Milch views himself as giving a black writer a chance, rather than fully acknowledging the power imbalances embedded in the television industry in the hiring of writers: "Milch, like Sipowicz, seems incapable of facing the structural barriers that keep minority workers from succeeding as much as their white counterparts, ascribing the constricted opportunities faced by African American television writers to the vagaries of white-audience prejudice rather than acknowledging the significant influence that a producer as powerful as he is has on the industry."[24] While Vest notes that *NYPD Blue* advanced David Mills' writing career, he also re-iterates the argument put forward by Herman Gray, that ultimately television remains a "white" medium: white writers, directors, producers and actors dominate, and it is the white audience which counts and is taken into account.[25]

The representation of women in the series is also problematic. Although *NYPD Blue* features more women than *Homicide: Life on the Street*, arguably *Homicide's* Kay Howard, whose femininity is unconventional (for television) and who is allowed simply to be another cop, is a far more progressive character than those in *NYPD Blue*. As Nelson notes of the series: "It simultaneously reaffirms traditional representations: all the women featured are conventionally attractive, if not actually glamorous, and the male Caucasian leads remain ultimately tough-minded and independent."[26] Many of the women detectives are themselves victims, such as Detective Diane Russell (Kim Delaney), who has suffered sexual abuse as a child, and nearly all are involved in relationships with their male counterparts. Although the women detectives are supposedly equal to the men around them, they often have to be protected or "saved" by their male colleagues—as for example in the relationship between Bobby Simone and Diane. In spite of the presence of a number of women characters, particularly in later seasons, there remains an underlying maleness about the series—the men have far more screen time, and in "Don We Now Our Gay Apparel" (2:9) it is taken for granted that Lieutenant Fancy really wants a son—he has two daughters already (this is an assumption also apparent in *The Shield*, when male colleagues congratulate Danny Sofer on learning she is expecting a boy). This assumption is left unchallenged, and once again reinforces a male view of the world.

Not surprisingly for a series which ran for so long, *NYPD Blue* has many links to other critically acclaimed crime dramas. Steven Bochco also created *Hill Street Blues* and Mike Post composed the music for both series. Directors on *NYPD Blue* include Charles Haid (Andrew Renko in *Hill Street*) and Clark Johnson. As mentioned elsewhere, David Simon also wrote a season 3 episode of *NYPD Blue*, which features a police informer not unlike Bubbles in *The Wire*.[27] The character is played by actor Giancarlo Esposito, who appears as Detective Mike Giardello in season 7 of *Homicide: Life on the Street*. Jon Seda, a *Homicide* regular from season 6 onwards, appears in "You Bet Your Life"(2:8), as does Paul Ben-Victor (Vandos in *The Wire*).

Sipowicz quizzes a suspect. His interviewing technique could often leave much to be desired in the sensitivity department (Steven Bochco Productions/The Kobal Collection).

There is no doubt therefore that *NYPD Blue* is a police series of some significance, not least because it ran for so long, and had greater viewing figures than some of its contemporaries. For a generation of television viewers, it is *the* cop show. It is therefore surprising that its availability on DVD was so limited and stalled for many years after the release of season 4.[28] This has perhaps had an implication for *NYPD Blue's* legacy: the delayed availability of the collected series has meant that it has not been fully part of the DVD box set phenomenon, and later episodes/series have remained, until very recently, relatively inaccessible for television scholarship. This lack of DVD legacy has perhaps consigned the series, unfortunately and unjustifiably, to a more traditional view of television, that it is ephemeral and does not merit re-watching. Although DVDs may be in the process of being superseded by downloads, James Walters argues that DVD in particular turns TV into "an artifact that can be held, purchased, collected, displayed, replayed and revisited."[29] Sean O'Sullivan, noting the coincidence of HBO's serial format and the growth in DVD sales, comments: "The thirteen-episode uninterrupted complete season provided, for the first time in American television history, a distinct narrative form, one that was large enough to occupy significant time and space but not so large as to turn into vague sprawl."[30] While perhaps not necessarily "vague," *NYPD Blue's* twelve seasons might certainly constitute a "sprawl." The belated availability of the complete series may finally allow a new audience of scholars to reassess that sprawl.

Recommended Episodes

As always, it is difficult to extract single episodes from a long-running series. *NYPD Blue* certainly has a number of dramatic episodes, such as the death of Bobby Simone in season 6 and the shooting of Sylvia Costas. An episode which is less emotionally highly charged, but which underscores the human relationships in the series, is "Simone Says" (2:5). At the time, this marked a potentially difficult transition for the series, as former lead David Caruso made way for newcomer Jimmy Smits (and the shift in focus to Andy Sipowicz). Jimmy Smits was already relatively well known from *LA Law* (another Bochco series), but his arrival is remarkably low-key. Sipowicz (like the viewer) is resistant to a new partner, and his initial dislike of Simone is instinctive, immediate—and ridiculous. He complains to (an incredulous) Lieutenant Fancy that the new partnership cannot work because Simone asked him, "How's it going?" By the end of the episode, already a mutual respect is developing between the two detectives, and while the trajectory of their working relationship is somewhat predictable (deepening into trust and friendship) it is nevertheless humorous and a pleasure to watch: in a great moment in "Large-Mouth Bass" (2:12) they argue over radio stations during a surveillance operation, find a classic tune they both enjoy, and are then interrupted in their singing by amused colleagues. The replacement of one lead character with another is therefore effected fairly smoothly, a hurdle which would have to be overcome more frequently as time and the series progressed.

Further Reading

For an excellent textual analysis of an early *NYPD Blue* episode, see Jonathan Bignell's essay, "The Police Series" in J. Gibbs and D. Pye (eds.), *Close-Up 03* (Wallflower, 2009). There are useful sections placing the series in its televisual and industrial context in Robin Nelson's *TV Drama in Transition: Forms, Values and Cultural Change* (Macmillan, 1997) and Robert Thompson's *Television's Second Golden Age: From Hill Street Blues to ER* (Syracuse University Press, 1997). Jason Vest's *The Wire, Deadwood, Homicide and NYPD Blue: Violence Is Power* (Praeger, 2011) focuses on the author figure of David Milch. C.P. Wilson, *Cop Knowledge: Police Power and Cultural Narrative in Twentieth-Century America* (University of Chicago Press, 2000) is a very useful background text for situating 1990s police crime dramas in their cultural context and Glenn Yeffeth's collection of essays *What Would Sipowicz Do? Race, Rights and Redemption in NYPD Blue* (Benbella, 2004) includes contributors from a variety of backgrounds. Finally, Jennifer Holt's essay "*NYPD Blue*: Content Regulation" in Ethan Thompson and Jason Mittell (eds.), *How to Watch Television* (New York University Press, 2013) explores a landmark case in TV regulation, involving nudity in a 2003 episode.

CHAPTER 16

CSI: Crime Scene Investigation

(CBS, 2000–)

ROGER SABIN

From its very first season, *CSI* broke new ground. At that time, there weren't too many other prime-time television dramas that dared to discuss—and depict—topics such as how a victim's entrails got smeared across a road after being hit by a car, or how semen spattered over a hotel room wall as a result of the rough removal of a condom.[1] Here was a show that redefined the boundaries of taste in mainstream entertainment, while doing so in a tasteful neo-noir style. The series' achievement was to re-invigorate the crime genre by offering a hip twist on the procedural, in this case, procedures relating to forensic science. The blend of lurid detail, elaborate killings, and frankness about sex did not make it a favorite with the Parents Television Council, but did make it a top–25 network show for all of its 15 seasons (so far) and one of the most successful TV dramas of all time.

The idea of *CSI* was simple enough. Each week, a team of crime scene investigators working for the Las Vegas Police Department takes on the task of solving two or three cases. The team, in its "classic" incarnation, is led by the introverted but brilliant Gil Grissom (William Petersen). His colleagues include no-nonsense former stripper Catherine Willows (Marg Helgenberger), workaholic Sara Sidle (Jorja Fox), anxious-to-please Nick Stokes (George Eads), problem gambler Warrick Brown (Gary Dourdan) and rookie Greg Sanders (Eric Szmanda). Among the supporting cast are Detective Jim Brass (Paul Guilfoyle) and medical examiner Al Robbins (Robert David Hall). These characters work in various combinations, allowing space for the requisite personality clashes and simmering desires.[2]

The premise for the work they perform is also straightforward: to collect forensics and follow the evidence. Thus, the mundane toil of collecting samples, dusting for fingerprints, swabbing for DNA, taking molds of footprints, snapping photos of the scene, and measuring blood spatter, is at the very center of the show. (As Grissom explains in characteristically deadpan style, "My only real purpose is to be smarter than the bad guys: to find the evidence they did not know they'd left behind, and make sense of it all."[3]) As such, *CSI* did for forensics what *Dragnet* did for police procedure: it re-conceptualized a profession in "entertainment" terms, as producing and possessing its own body of expert knowledge and language. Instead of "APBs" and "radiograms," it was now "trace," "transfer," and "tox screens."

Language was one way of glamorizing the unglamorous, but there were other tricks. For example, the CSI team itself just happens to be telegenic, and the program-makers obviously recognized that a sexy CSI with a pipette is still a sexy CSI. Similarly, the lab they work in is formidably high-tech, with enough gadgets, both scientific and science-fictional, to put a James Bond movie to shame. At times the elaborate gadgetry took credit for things it couldn't achieve in real life: for example, it's not actually possible to take fuzzy surveillance camera footage of a man in a car and blow up the pixels to the point where you can make out the design of his earring.

The aesthetic of the show is carefully considered. The color scheme offers cool blues in the lab to contrast with both the bright yellows of the Nevada desert, and the Vegas neon reds and greens at night. Fast-paced editing, including energetic use of jump cuts, keeps things lively, while the music, often a variety of ambient techno, is non-diegetic. Finally, in what became known as "the *CSI* shot," the reconstructions of the crimes themselves involve the camera following a bullet or knife as it makes its way through the victim's innards. This now legendary technique required a mix of CGI, prosthetics and "accelerated zooms" (unusual for TV); its typical accompaniment was a sickening sound effect: "schlooop!"[4]

The show's creator was Anthony E. Zuiker, a formerly untested writer, who was swiftly teamed up with more experienced hands, while the executive producer was Jerry Bruckheimer, previously responsible for such glossy movie fare as *Top Gun* and *Con Air*. After ABC had turned down the show, Bruckheimer took it to CBS, which snapped it up. At the time, CBS had ambitions to dominate the mid-evening drama schedules over NBC, and to fight back against the critically-lauded dramatic product of the newcomer (cable) channels of the neo-network era.[5] As such, *CSI* was sold on the basis that it would be high-end, in the Bruckheimer manner, but that it would also have within it the DNA of previous crime shows. So, for example, influences included *Quincy ME* (NBC, 1976–83), which had starred Jack Klugman as a forensic pathologist, and which featured many of the plotlines and themes that would become *CSI* staples: evidence that contradicts a confession, detailed post-mortems, disreputable surgeons, and so on. Other precursors included *Dragnet*, for its emphasis on mundane work; *Hill Street Blues*, which had a similar ensemble cast set-up; and *Homicide: Life on the Street*, which offered a mixed-race paradigm. Finally, *CSI* would have a central character who was an old-style sleuth: Grissom as Columbo (he even owns a dog).

But there were more contemporary influences that set it apart. Foremost was the horror/crime aesthetic pioneered by author Thomas Harris in his "Hannibal Lecter" novels, and their subsequent movie adaptations. The emphasis on serial killers, body horror, "deviance," forensic science and criminal profiling were especially important. As it happened, William Petersen had played a cop in the best of the Lecter movies, *Manhunter* (1986), directed by Michael Mann, who had executive produced *Miami Vice*. In *CSI*, Petersen riffed on the persona he had created in the movie, making Grissom a character who was both empathetic and deeply methodical. Michael Mann's use of music in *Manhunter* was unusual in that it was non-diegetic and rock-based, and he favored lighting that was often suffused with cool blues. Later, when Harris's *The Silence of the Lambs* became a hit movie in 1991 (according to many critics, it was the defining horror film of the decade), it popularized a whole range of horror tropes which were equally significant for *CSI*,[6] not least a "realistic" post-mortem scene.[7]

The fact that the Harris novels focus on serial killers has been a notable influence on the many serial killer plots in *CSI*. In particular, Harris makes Lecter a kind of supernatural figure, a Dracula for the modern age, who has an ongoing rapport with his pursuers. This

Catherine Willows (Marg Helgenberger) and Gil Grissom (William Petersen) discover a bunker in the Nevada desert (CBS TV/The Kobal Collection/Ron Jaffe).

is reflected in *CSI* episodes featuring the "miniature killer," who builds meticulous scale models of crime scenes, and those about Paul Millander, who is portrayed as Grissom's arch-enemy, and who, in a scene apparently lifted from a Lecter story, waves at him via a surveillance camera. All these killers seem to be evil geniuses: as Grissom says of Millander, "He never slips up." In reality, of course, serial killers tend to be rather banal individuals, not much interested in psychological game-playing.[8]

Beyond the specifics of the Harris influence, *CSI* drew from a wider cultural pool and a new appetite for "transgressive culture," a term that came to prominence in the 1990s to describe an incoherent cocktail of "taboo" and "weird" topics, typically celebrated in sections of post-punk underground culture. Magazines like *Answer Me!* and *Headpress*, and book lists from Re/Search and Feral House, reveled in such diverse phenomena as body modification, extreme horror films, serial killers, circus "freaks," the occult, sexual fetishes, mystical cults, conspiracy theories, "modern primitivism," and extreme subcultures. The idea of transgressive culture soon went overground; before long what was once transgressive became (relatively) mainstream, the popularity of the Lecter stories being a case in point.[9]

CSI can be seen as part of this mainstreaming process. Thus, episodes include routinely outlandish tales about, for example: a fetishist who likes being treated as a baby, and who has a gigantic nursery built to the scale of an adult; a UFO cult that commits mass suicide; themed wedding chapels where "priests" perform services dressed as Elvis or aliens; a vampire subculture, complete with a body drained of blood; David Icke–style lizard-people; "freak" characters, such as a young girl who has hair on her face like a werewolf; and a mad artist who, in a manner reminiscent of the Gunther von Hagens displays, poses corpses in an effort to "cross art's final frontier."

These stories were sensationalist and great fun, but they also attempted to convey a moral about "normalcy," and specifically about tolerance towards social and sexual nonconformity. For example, "Ch-Ch-Changes" (season 5, 2004) concerns sex-change operations undertaken by somebody who isn't a surgeon. It therefore has the requisite "ugh!" factor, but incorporates enough gender politics to show that it is up-to-date with debates within the academy. As Grissom explains, "There are two types of male oysters, and one of them can change genders at will. And before man crawled out of the muck, maybe he had the same option. Maybe originally we were supposed to be able to switch genders, and being born with just one sex ... is a mutation."

The figure of Grissom is therefore an important intermediary in this process of mainstreaming the "nonconformist" and the "transgressive." He considers himself an outsider, a freak of sorts, and his efforts to empathize reveal his tolerant attitude to difference. In fact, it's only when he is in the company of fellow outsiders that he truly becomes human: in other scenarios, as he himself admits, he is "not good with people." Grissom may raise an eyebrow, but, unlike some of his colleagues, he does not judge. Indeed, it's clear that on a personal level he enjoys some aspects of the less orthodox sexual practices he comes across: at one point he has a brief affair with dominatrix Lady Heather.[10] As he explains to her: "I find all deviant behavior fascinating, in that to understand human nature we have to understand our aberrations."[11] For many viewers, this makes Grissom "the sexiest man in the morgue" (in the words of *Slate* magazine).[12]

Las Vegas is thus the perfect setting for the show (despite the fact that, in actuality, most of it is shot in Los Angeles). Otherwise known as "Sin City," and defined in the popular imagination by the saying "what happens in Vegas, stays in Vegas," it is a place where tourists let their hair down, and things happen that could happen nowhere else in the United States. It is the ideal location for stag parties, hen parties, and any other kind of party as well as for conventions for "unorthodox" interests and visits from every kind of celebrity and wannabe celebrity. With its reputation for gambling, gangsterism, vice and "good times," Vegas thus has the atmosphere of "the world turned upside down." It has become a site of Bakhtinian carnival that is almost out of control,[13] where even the most bizarre of *CSI* cases is met by the refrain, "It's Vegas...."

But at the same time "Vegas" can mean other things. *CSI* was never slow to depict, for example, the sprawling suburban metropolis of Clark County, and the city's surrounding landscape, in particular the desert and Lake Mead. This allowed space for other stories to be told, about, for example, "everyday" domestic violence or strange goings-on in the desert. As an example of the latter, "Scuba Doobie-Doo" (season 2, 2001) opens with the discovery of a dead scuba diver in a burned-out tree after a bush fire in the desert, as if in realization of an urban myth in which a Fire Service helicopter accidentally scoops up a diver from Lake Mead and then dumps him as part of the effort to quench the fire.

CSI thus hit on a winning formula early; by season 2, it was routinely appearing in the number 1 spot in the Nielsen ratings. Yet the show did not stand still. Like every successful serial, it developed over time. This was particularly evident in the way it took on elements of soap opera, with the CSIs functioning as a kind of family. In one sense, they are "the normals" around whom the craziness happens; but at the same time they are flawed. Thus, we learn about Catherine's fraught relationship with her father, a man with gangster connections and a symbol of "old Vegas"; Warrick's inner-city upbringing; Sara's childhood

The death of Warrick in season 9 marked a watershed, and highlighted the CSI team as "family" (CBS TV/Photofest).

within an abusive family; and Grissom's hearing problems, and his unrequited love for Sara. When Nick gets buried alive ("Grave Danger" parts 1 and 2, season 5, 2005, guest directed by Quentin Tarantino), it's up to the team to rescue him, and protective family feelings come to the fore. That two-parter was watched by a staggering 35 million people.

Such supportive behavior is the norm, but sometimes the characters' back-stories are shown to endanger cases, as when Catherine uses DNA sampling to find out if her "dear old dad" really is her father; or when Sara becomes so enraged by a case involving spousal abuse that she temporarily quits. At these moments, the veneer of "clinical detachment" begins to crack, and we see the characters as "real" people who are not unaffected by their work. In these circumstances "the evidence" may no longer be the sole route to the truth. In the words of academic Steven Cohan, "Catherine takes into account the subjective basis of truth but without disqualifying scientific objectivity, just as Grissom always finds most intriguing the crimes that push beyond the limits of normalcy."[14]

Fandom played a significant part in *CSI*'s evolution. The 2000s saw TV fandom reinventing itself on the internet, and, among crime shows, *CSI* became a focal point, rivaled only by the *Law & Order* spin-off *Special Victims Unit*. In recognition of this, significant financial investment went into the *CSI* website to the point where it became one of the most sophisticated in the business. On the official site, and more often on unofficial ones, fans re-imagined the show and speculated about where plotlines might end up, especially with regard to the relationships between the characters. And, perhaps inevitably, the show adapted some of these speculations to its own ends. Other aspects of fandom were not so easy to co-opt, such as the many "slash fiction" sites that postulated homosexual pairings of key characters, notably Greg and Nick, and Catherine and Sara. CBS was in no position to stop counter-readings, even if it wanted to.[15]

CSI thus blossomed into a fully-fledged TV phenomenon. Yet controversy was never far away. The most obvious bone of contention was the level of sex and violence, and, predictably, right wing groups, led by parents' associations, went on the offensive. Their arguments, re-hashed from previous protests about cinema, centered on "gratuitousness" and the idea that such content would lead to imitative behavior. The aforementioned "King Baby" episode saw the Parents Television Council lodging 13,000 complaints. But liberal-left groups were also worried about the sex and violence, for different reasons. They argued that audiences were invited to enjoy violence predominantly directed against women, and that on many occasions the LGBT community was misrepresented as being deviant or driven to kill because of sexual orientation.

All these complaints were vigorously contested, the show's defenders arguing that the case for imitative behavior has never been proved. They pointed to academic research within the "effects theory" tradition suggesting that "violence" is an impossible category to define, and that therefore more attention should be paid to how social factors and background make some people consume media in a specific way.[16] They added that, in any case, *CSI* merely represented TV catching up with levels of sex and violence in the cinema. As for violence against women, defenders pointed out that many *CSI* shows took a feminist perspective, while others shone a light on domestic violence, including the episode mentioned above, in which Sara quits her job. Against LGBT objections, it was pointed out that *CSI* frequently offered progressive representations and had done its best to distance itself from the "queer killer" stereotypes that had become popular in much horror and crime fiction (e.g., *The Silence of the Lambs*).

Another major issue was the possible effect of the representation of science. It was argued that the series gave the wrong impression of the way police do things. It might be entertaining to see telegenic CSIs striding through state-of-the-art labs and getting convictions on the basis of a strand of hair left in the wrong place, but it was far from the truth. TV writers more invested in "real crime" and "real policing" (based on depictions of underfunded public institutions and the social causes of law-breaking) started to make their feelings known. In one of the most celebrated examples of one crime show attacking another, *The Wire* introduced a story about a serial killer which mercilessly lampooned the scientific rationale behind *CSI*.[17]

Then there was the problem of what has become known as "the *CSI* effect": the perceived impact that the series had on real-life juries.[18] Jurors, it was argued, now expected conclusive scientific proof of guilt before they convicted; the underlying assumption being that they believed the science in *CSI* to be real rather than science fictional, which it often was. The result of this unrealistic expectation was that guilty defendants were often acquitted because of a lack of forensic evidence. How much of this theory was a media invention is open to debate, and, indeed, some commentators have argued that it is equally likely that a "reverse *CSI* effect" has come into play as jurors increase their tendency to convict.[19]

Finally, science was said to be depicted as "morally authoritative," which in turn reinforced the "moral authority" of the police. As one academic puts it: "*CSI*'s mantra—that physical evidence cannot lie, that evidence is a truth that science will reveal—suggests that the police have harnessed science."[20] Yet, as many real-life miscarriages of justice have shown, the scientific evidence is not always reliable and truthful. Moreover, some argue that *CSI* helped to normalize some very intrusive surveillance techniques, especially the collection of DNA samples. Thus, critics suggest that despite the show's outwardly liberal stance on such issues as sexuality and lifestyle choices, it is actually a deeply conservative show that facilitated the state's mission to "govern through crime."[21]

To date, *CSI* has lasted for 15 seasons, and its glory days are over. William Petersen left in 2008, and subsequently, familiar cast members have made their exit either freely or by force (the death of the character they played). Grissom's place as the show's mainstay was taken first by Laurence Fishburne, as the furrow-browed and rather stern Dr. Raymond Langston. This was a rare instance of a minority lead actor cast in a TV drama (a study from 2005 had concluded that *CSI* was one of the ten most popular programs among African American viewers[22]), but Fishburne is widely regarded as never having fully found his feet with the role. In 2011 he was followed by Ted Danson, as Supervisor D.B. Russell, a more upbeat contrast who brought with him a talent for comedy that took time to be comfortably harnessed to the established rhythm of the show, mellowing into a more emotional take on the character.

Meanwhile, *CSI* had become one of the most formidable franchises in entertainment history.[23] The original show spawned two immensely popular spin-offs: *CSI: Miami* (2002–12) and *CSI: New York* (2004–13). Both featured central characters who were the opposite of Grissom in that they were more traditionally "heroic": namely, Lieutenant Horatio Caine, played by David Caruso (formerly of *NYPD Blue*); and Detective Mac Taylor, a Gulf War veteran who lost his wife in the 9/11 attacks, played by Gary Sinise. The new shows were carefully branded, each with the same basic structure, each with a theme tune by the Who; and offered possibilities for crossovers, for example the episode in which Catherine and Warrick join forces with Horatio to hunt a serial killer who has fled to Miami (*CSI: Miami*, "Cross Jurisdictions," 2002).[24] There are plans to launch a further spin-off series *CSI: Cyber*. How far this strategy has led to a homogenizing of a once-interesting concept, and a contribution to the era of the "Mc-cop show," is open to debate.[25]

The franchise spread onto other platforms, as franchises do, the original show becoming the inspiration for comics, novels, computer games, toys, and large-scale elaborate exhibits where "you can become a CSI and test your inner crime-solver."[26] Occasionally, these extra-diegetic accounts offered deeper portraits of the characters, often pulling in ideas from fandom. A movie version of *CSI: Vegas*, with Grissom once more at the helm, has been mooted.

CSI's impact on wider TV culture has been similarly seismic. Crime shows in a similar mold include examples from CBS itself: *Without a Trace* (2002–09), *NCIS* (2003–), *Cold Case* (2003–), and *Numb3rs* (2005–). In fact, there were so many CBS examples, often with Jerry Bruckheimer's imprimatur, that critics joshed that "CBS" stood for "Crime Broadcasting System." These series have been joined by NBC's *Crossing Jordan* (2001–07), Fox's *Bones* (2005–), and ABC's *Body of Proof* (ABC, 2011–), while international TV companies have added their own contributions to the list. The influence of *CSI* worked in other directions, too, as documentary makers produced a slew of "Real *CSI*" shows.[27]

In conclusion, *CSI* offered the crime show genre a new paradigm. As well as its stylistic sheen and emphasis on "the forensic gaze," it allowed viewers to vicariously enjoy fringe culture. This was "transgression done tastefully," and the mix of titillation and the show's ability to maintain a cool distance was compelling. On a deeper level, *CSI* could often encompass nothing less than an arch distillation of the kind of cultural theory that had been fashionable in the academy for the last 15 years. Thus, although the show might be in the same tradition as 19th century dime novel "shock literature," its postmodern knowingness made it very much a 21st century phenomenon. This layered appeal helped it achieve what many thought would never again be possible: to create a mass audience for a major network drama at a time when the networks were perceived to be in decline.

Recommended Episodes

"Fur and Loathing" (season 4, 2003) sees *CSI* in its pomp, going places no other TV drama will go. In it, the team investigates the Vegas "furry" scene, in which "fans" dress up as fictional animals, in fluffy ("plush") suits, and engage in mass orgies at PAFCon, the "Plushies and Furries Convention." As the other CSIs outwardly show their distaste ("we're gonna need samples of your ... uh ... fur"), Grissom observes dispassionately that "the only unnatural sexual behavior is none at all." "Unfriendly Skies" (season 1, 2000) is an earlier offering involving the in-flight murder of a passenger, who turns out to have been kicked to death by multiple assailants as he tried to open the emergency door. The show is interesting for sorting out the moral perspectives of cast members, as they gather to debate what they would have done. It aired less than a year before 9/11.

Further Reading

CSI has been the subject of several book-length studies, many PhD dissertations, and dozens of academic essays. Unlike some shows in this book, it benefits from an abundance of research material. The best place to start is Steven Cohan's concise but very thoughtful *CSI: Crime Scene Investigation* (BFI TV Classics, BFI Publishing, 2008). Derek Kompare's *CSI* (Wiley-Blackwell Studies in Film and Television, 2010) expands on many of Cohan's themes and is particularly good on the meaning of Las Vegas. Michael Allen (ed.), *Reading CSI: Crime TV Under the Microscope* (I.B. Tauris, 2007), is an excellent collection, and includes chapters about the use of sound, and fandom. For some non-academic background, the *CSI* DVD extras are expansive, and Anthony Zuiker's autobiography *Mr. CSI: How a Vegas Dreamer Made a Killing in Hollywood, One Body at a Time* (Harper, 2011) is as lively as its title would suggest. At the other end of the spectrum, one of the best PhDs is Elke Weissmann's *Crime, the Body and the Truth: Understanding the Shift Towards Forensic Science in Television Crime Drama with the CSI-franchise* (unpublished thesis, University of Glasgow, 2006), which has much to say about bodies and their destruction. On the topic of "the CSI effect," Michele Byers and Val Marie Johnson (eds.), *The CSI Effect: Television, Crime and Governance* (Lexington Books, 2009) is a politically astute anthology that emphasizes *CSI*'s relationship to "the war on terror," while the website for NCSTL.org, a forensic science organization run out of Stetson University, lists dozens of further sources.

CHAPTER 17

The Shield

(FX, 2002–08)

LINDA SPEIDEL

The Shield burst onto television screens with perhaps one of the most shocking pilot episodes in the history of all cop shows. The Emmy-nominated episode ends with the central character, detective Vic Mackey (Michael Chiklis), shooting a fellow cop, Terry Crowley (Reed Diamond). The final moment of the scene is framed from the POV of the downed officer, and the image of Vic standing over the body is one which haunts the entire seven seasons which follow, and sets the tone for a police series where the two sides of the law have finally become indistinguishable from each other.

The Shield is set in Farmington, a fictional district of Los Angeles, and follows the fortunes of an embattled police unit, located in a squad room known as "The Barn," led (initially) by a newly appointed captain, David Aceveda (Benito Martinez). The protagonists are the four members of the Strike Team, an elite but aggressive and controversial unit set up to combat gang crime. The lead detective is Vic Mackey and the three other members are Shane Vendrell (Walton Goggins), Curtis Lemansky (Kenneth Johnson) and Ronnie Gardocki (David Rees Snell). Also working in the Barn is Claudette Wyms (CCH Pounder), a veteran homicide detective, who is partnered with Dutch Wagenbach (Jay Karnes), who has an unhealthy obsession with serial killers. The series also focuses on two uniformed officers, Danny Sofer (Catherine Dent) and Julian Lowe (Michael Jace), a rookie officer who, as season 1 opens, has only been on the beat for three weeks.

The Shield initially aired to some controversy, as the portrayal of the Strike Team appeared to echo real-life events in LA, a city long associated with aggressive police tactics and corruption.[1] In 1985 Chief Daryl Gates authorized an armored vehicle to smash into a suspected drug house, only to find that it was occupied by children eating ice cream.[2] In 1992 four police officers were acquitted of the Rodney King beating, leading to wide-scale demonstrations and rioting. Further scandal erupted in the 1990s, when it became apparent that the much reduced gang-related crime rate in the Rampart Division was the result of the police themselves using similar tactics to the criminals they were pursuing. The Strike Team in *The Shield* resembles the CRASH (Community Resources Against Street Hoodlums) unit of the Rampart Division, and as Ben Marshall notes, Vic Mackey has been perceived to be a "composite" of three of the most prominent officers leading the CRASH unit.[3]

In terms of television scheduling, *The Shield* can be seen as a response by cable channels such as FX and AMC to compete with the high-end serial dramas produced by subscription channel HBO. Like so many of the crime dramas in this anthology, it fits Thompson's descriptors of "quality" television, particularly in its aesthetic and narrative structure.[4] While many episodes focus on a single case which is "closed," the series has a "memory" and there are ongoing narrative strands and story arcs which span several seasons. Vic's shooting of Terry Crowley, seemingly forgotten for many episodes, resurfaces periodically during the course of the

The final moment of the pilot episode of *The Shield* shows Vic Mackey (Michael Chicklis) looking down at the body of fellow detective Terry Crowley, whom Mackey shot.

series, and the robbery of the money train at the end of season 2 is an ongoing narrative strand for all subsequent seasons. *The Shield* is also notable for its high-profile cast members, particularly in later seasons, with the inclusion of actors such as Glenn Close, Forrest Whitaker and Franka Potente, better known for their film roles. While the main cast are "unglamorous," nevertheless the attraction of big names from cinema marks the increasing acceptance of television as a "quality" medium.

The Shield is also more or less contemporaneous with *The Wire*, as both aired for the first time in 2002 in the U.S. and both screened their final seasons in 2008 (although *The Shield* has seven seasons to *The Wire's* five). Both the pilot and final episodes of the two series were directed by Clark Johnson (who had risen to prominence as an actor in *Homicide: Life on the Street* and makes a cameo appearance in the final episode of *The Shield*). The two series therefore seem to invite comparisons (indeed critic Chris Petit explicitly sets out to compare them, in an article prefaced with the heading "*The Wire* vs. *The Shield*"[5]) and as both are cable productions they necessarily position themselves as "different" from network fare such as *CSI* or *Law & Order*. While (in the U.S.), *The Shield* initially aired to much greater publicity and controversy than *The Wire*,[6] this was later eclipsed by the critical attention given to *The Wire*. *The Shield* nevertheless stands as a useful counterpoint to any notion that *The Wire* is the only or inevitable endpoint of a linear trajectory in the evolution of the police series. Whereas *The Wire* slows the pace of the cop series to one case per season (or even longer) and broadens its scope to include in-depth studies of institutional life and (as argued elsewhere) attempts to offer a sociological understanding of crime and the drug trade, *The Shield* remains focused on a very small group of police detectives and officers. Although *The Shield* continues many of the formal conventions of earlier series, it moves to a morally ambiguous depiction of the police. The police were not always portrayed entirely sympathetically in *Homicide* and *NYPD Blue*, but by and large they were on the side of "good." In *The Shield*, this is no longer the case. Vic Mackey and his Strike Team are openly corrupt. As Vic comments in "Pilot" (1:1): "Good cop's gone for the day. So's the bad cop. I'm a different kind of cop."[7] The notion that the police can be bad is itself not new, but *The Shield's* Vic Mackey perhaps offers the logical endpoint of an aggressive law and order policy, where the distinction between crime and crime prevention/reduction has not only become blurred but has been erased. As Sheehan and Sweeney argue:

The gap between law and justice has widened in TV drama as it has widened in social consciousness. Cops such as Andy Sipowicz [*NYPD Blue*], Frank Pembleton [*Homicide: Life on the Street*], Vic Mackey [*The Shield*] and Olivia Benson [*Law & Order: SVU*] are a different species from Joe Friday [*Dragnet*]. They are no longer untainted and uncomplicated agents of righteousness, but morally conflicted, psychologically complex men and women struggling with difficult personal lives as well as a crumbling social contract.[8]

Vic Mackey embodies the "morally conflicted" cop in the extreme.

Yet in spite of his formidable presence, the choice of title, in both *The Shield* and *The Wire,* can be seen to continue a trend (noted in regard to *Homicide*) within the crime genre, and in particular the police series, of moving away from a focus on individuals. In the 1990s, this shift was towards an interest in the unit or team. In the 2000s, a further shift occurs, as the series' main words, "shield" and "wire," are even more abstract and barely refer at all to the human agents. While there are two significant 1990s crime dramas, the *Law & Order* and *CSI* franchises, which also refer to the abstract, they continue to connote either a certainty about transgression and justice, as in "law and order," or the ability to find answers, "crime scene investigation." The titles of *The Shield* and *The Wire*[9] open up a far greater ambiguity. A "shield" implies both the institution and the police badge: the protection offered *by* the police (badge) and *to* the police, and suggests that the police occupy a position of power which is often abused, since they can hide behind their "shield." Indeed "the shield" connotes the idea of a battle or war, although it is no longer a question of morality. While "the shield" implies a continuing division between the police and others (as ever, the police are set apart from ordinary people) this is no longer necessarily between those on either side of the law. The image in the very brief title music is of a broken police shield—the ideal "to protect and serve" is now shattered as the police are fully implicated in the systems they are supposed to uncover and the superior insight of the detective is now fractured.

Filmed on location on LA, but set in the fictional district of Farmington, *The Shield* continues and extends the aesthetic of *Homicide: Life on the Street* and *Hill Street Blues*. This is thoroughly in keeping with the series' narrow focus on the police—the handheld camera signifies the police view of the world. The camera movement is even more extreme than in *Homicide*, frequently moving in to close-ups of the characters, but often offering only a partial shot of their bodies or faces. The camera is rarely stationary. Frequently the camera is positioned so as to suggest the point of view of an onlooker. As Michael Chiklis notes in the season 1 DVD featurette "Making of *The Shield*," the camera itself appears to be a character in its own right. This in part reflects the extent to which the police themselves are constantly watched in the over-heated urban environment of LA/Farmington—at every crime scene, the detectives and uniformed officers are acutely aware of how their actions are judged by civilian bystanders (although this does not prevent the Strike Team from acting with impunity!). And as Vic and his crew stray further and further into murky territory, the overt presence of the camera also increases the sense of their paranoia, particularly apparent in the scenes in season 7 when Shane is on the run. The frenetic camera work accentuates the chaos, urgency and speed with which incidents occur and are dealt with at the Barn, and is particularly striking in the foot chase scenes, where the camera moves at the pace of the chase in close proximity to the police and their quarry. At times the image even appears speeded up, almost cartoon-like, echoing the larger-than-life tactics of Vic and his crew. Occasionally as the camera swirls, it picks out the skyscrapers of downtown LA, hazy in the distance, or the street activity close by. There are particularly striking city scenes in the pilot episode—the meeting in Echo Park between Terry Crowley, David Aceveda and the FBI agent, and the floodlit basketball court at night where Vic Mackey gives his informant, prostitute Connie, money for soup and a heroin fix. But in general, LA remains an indistinct chaotic environment "out there," a patchwork of unconnected crime scenes.

As in *Homicide*, the HQ building—the Barn—is the central location in *The Shield*. The work space here is cramped and inadequate—the men's toilets are sealed off in the first episode, and remain so until the arrival of Captain Monica Rawling in season 4. The constant activity in the work space is very reminiscent of the squad room in *Homicide*, as is the distinctive building, although in *The Shield*, the exterior is rarely shown, since of course unlike the real Broadway Pier building in the real city of Baltimore, Farmington District is a fictional construct.[10] The shabby nature of the Barn reflects both the "down and dirty" tactics of the cops as well as the brutal nature of the neighborhood, and the fact that it is a former church (a fact frequently alluded to by many of the characters) perhaps emphasizes a loss of faith in the system and of stable core values. As in *Homicide*, the handheld camera accentuates the cramped physical spaces such as the bathrooms and the interrogation room. The interrogation room remains a key tool for the police, but here it is a very stark room indeed, with basic prison-like furniture, no two-way mirror, and only a camera which can be conveniently unplugged. The brutal tactics of Detective Vic Mackey and his colleagues in the Strike Team are contrasted with the more cerebral approach of detectives Dutch Wagenbach and Claudette Wyms, although all interrogations rely on trickery and deception to elicit confessions from suspects.

Yet Vic Mackey "knows" the street and his unconventional tactics reap results. In "Dawg Days" (1:4) he settles a turf war by locking two feuding rappers in a container overnight to settle their differences: only one emerges the next morning. Vic's knowledge of the underbelly of LA echoes that of the hardboiled private investigator, but as an agent he is, at least officially, sanctioned by the state. In spite of his corruption, the viewer is drawn to him and the narrative endorses the view expressed by Claudette Wyms in "Pilot" (1:1) that people need and want a cop like Vic Mackey who will make the streets safer. Over the course of the seven seasons even Claudette (possibly the only character with any sort of functioning moral compass) becomes more and more critical of Vic. And unlike both the PI and the police detectives of the 1990s, Vic's corruption suggests that his ability to operate autonomously has been compromised. His ability to control events diminishes considerably over the course of the last two seasons. He no longer occupies a position of "romantic alienation," bucking the system from within, but remaining on the side of good. Instead he becomes fully implicated in the very crimes he is supposed to prevent.

The Shield perhaps strains the limits of credibility in its depiction of Vic Mackey. But it is also this larger than life character, and the tension between the viewer's credulity and disbelief, which lend *The Shield* a mark of distinction. All those who try to bring Vic to justice fail, and one of the most troubling characters is Jon Kavanaugh (Forest Whitaker), who conducts an investigation into the Strike Team which spans season 5 (and the beginning of season 6), but who himself is revealed to be increasingly unstable, with a problematic, even abusive, attitude towards women (specifically, his wife, and Vic's estranged wife Corrine Mackey [Cathy Cahlin Ryan]). At the end of season 2, the Strike Team successfully robs the Armenian mob's "Money Train," and from then on is engaged in sequences of ever-more corrupt activities to avoid being caught (such as stealing Captain Aceveda's safe in order to find the serial numbers of notes which have been marked by the Treasury). This

Mackey threatens to "necklace" a foe on an LA hillside. *The Shield* **drew flak for its level of violence (in Mackey's inimitable words: "Money and pussy make men do evil shit") (Fox TV/The Kobal Collection).**

plotline in particular pushes the bounds of believability, but it is precisely Vic's continued if somewhat unlikely success in outwitting those who try to contain him that emphasizes the central tension on which *The Shield* hinges, and which arguably lends it a streak of brilliance. The viewer is constantly forced to negotiate highly ambivalent moral territory, where there is never an easy division between right and wrong, and is drawn into engaging with characters who are not only flawed, but are in fact wholly corrupt. Indeed all characters in *The Shield* are morally dubious, including Dutch, and even Claudette on occasion. It is difficult to like any of the characters unequivocally, and yet the viewer is invited at some point to sympathize with each. The series continually flirts with taboos, such as David Aceveda's highly troubling reaction to the assault he suffers in season 3, and, in the same season, Dutch's strangling of a cat (in order, apparently, better to understand the psyche of a serial killer), without offering the comfort of resolution, explanation or redemption— the cat strangling incident, for example, is never revisited (although Dutch later contemplates adopting a kitten). It is this aspect of *The Shield* which marks it out even from its contemporary *The Wire*, which in comparison takes a clearer moral line. *The Shield* leaves forever in doubt what is right and wrong, and even *if* there is such a distinction.

The moral ambiguity of *The Shield* is also apparent in its portrayal of the multi-ethnic neighborhood of LA, where police officers are expected to have at least a working knowledge of Spanish (Dutch Wagenbach is hampered in his work when he does not). The detectives and police officers at the Barn to some extent reflect the diverse ethnic mix of the area they police. The tensions between the police and Hispanic residents are made apparent in the political aspirations of Captain David Aceveda who has been promoted because he is the "right color," and who frequently has to deal with complaints of police brutality and prejudice from fellow Latino politicians and officials. Officer Julian Lowe also breaks new ground in embodying the problems for a black and gay police officer. A conversation with Claudette makes explicit the very real hurdles that both have had to overcome, when she tells him: "Don't talk to me about the struggle. I am the struggle" ("Insurgents," 4:6). There is also a nod to racial tensions in the aftermath of 9/11, when Officer Danny Sofer shoots an innocent Asian man (2:2). Season 4 deals with the controversial policy of assets seizures. The new captain, Monica Rawling (Glenn Close) pursues local gangster Antwon Mitchell (Anthony Anderson) and here, once again, the series straddles an uncomfortable line between personal vendettas and social and political tensions. Both Captain Rawling as a white woman, and Antwon Mitchell, a black man, are from the outset constrained and contained by their mutual prejudices and those of people around them. It is perhaps surprising that Vic allies himself to Monica Rawling, a partnership which both strengthens her tactical position—she is able to count on the support of him and his team—and weakens her morally, as she too is implicated in the brutality which is completely at odds with supporting the community she polices.

But for all its admirable ambiguity, ultimately it is difficult to avoid the conclusion that *The Shield* upholds and endorses the notion of people of color needing to be contained and controlled by white (male) police—there is no black equivalent of Vic Mackey. The key members of Vic Mackey's Strike Team are male and white and this inner circle is exclusive and hyper masculine, as Pamela Hill Nettleton also notes.[11] It is a brotherhood which does not welcome outsiders (they even get shot!) and which metes out an aggressive form of street justice which, like the real life CRASH unit, not only emulates the tactics of the "criminal" world, but is fully implicated in it. Claudette and Julian are marginalized, both narratively and in terms of their gender and sexuality: from the point at which Claudette becomes captain she in fact occupies less screen time and is furthermore compromised and weakened by a serious medical condition, lupus. She is never really allowed to equal Vic Mackey, in spite of promising beginnings.

However, notwithstanding the somewhat regressive aspects of *The Shield*, the characters are compelling, perhaps in particular Dutch Wagenbach, Claudette Wyms, Danny Sofer and Julian Lowe. Dutch invites both the viewer's sympathy and scorn—he breaks down after a particularly intense interrogation "Dragonchasers" (1:10), but the viewer cannot help laughing with the Strike Team at his frequent social ineptness (the hidden camera in his car, in "Tar Baby" [4:1], records the cringe-worthy blind date with Claudette's friend, followed by his singing along to "Hungry Like the Wolf"). He is apparently the antithesis of the über-macho Vic, yet they are attracted to the same women (Danny and Corinne), and Dutch is prepared to take on Vic physically at the end of season 4. Claudette is rarely impressed by the posturing of the men around her, unintimidated by Vic and the Strike Team or her superiors and while she works well with Dutch, she frequently has little patience with him. Although the Strike Team is hyper-masculine, *The Shield* presents in Claudette, Danny, Corrine and Monica Rawling a number of strong women characters, who often offer an explicit critique of Vic, and in this respect the series, perhaps surprisingly, compares favorably to its contemporary *The Wire*, which has a much larger cast, but fewer women protagonists.

After the initial controversy surrounding its portrayal of the LAPD, *The Shield's* critical and popular reception has been somewhat muted in the long term. This perhaps marks the point at which the police series has so long been positioned as "not TV" that it (like quality TV) has become institutionalized. The police series has a literary and televisual history which is intertwined and has always sought to act as counterpoint to crime "fiction." There has constantly been the drive to make the police drama seem "not TV," as in not fictional, a tradition inherited from the literary form, where police detectives constantly make references to their "fictional" counterparts to flag up what the work is "really" like.[12] Even as *The Shield* marks the point at which the cops can no longer be assumed to be the "good guys," the causes and nature of "crime" remain relatively un-interrogated and unlike *The Wire*, which broadens its scope, *The Shield* continues to present a narrow view of crime which focuses on the street level police.

Recommended Episodes

The Shield has many memorable episodes, the standout perhaps being the pilot, as already noted. Similarly, the finale of season 5 continues the tendency of *The Shield* to continually shock the viewer, as do the last two episodes of season 7, with the murder/suicide of Shane and his family. In contrast, Vic's fate is very low key, although the ending is apt—what could be worse for Vic than being tied to a desk? There are also some moments of great comedy, particularly as Vic and the Strike Team tie themselves in ever greater knots, such as the attempt on Aceveda's safe in season 3.

Further Reading

There is something of a dearth of writing on *The Shield*, perhaps due to the critical attention given to *The Wire*. However, useful sources include: Lucy Fife Donaldson, "Camera and Performer: Energetic Engagement with *The Shield*," in Steven Peacock and Jason Jacobs (eds.), *Television Aesthetics and Style* (Bloomsbury, 2013); Ben Marshall, "Badge of Dishonour," *Guardian Guide* (26 June–2 July 2004), pp. 8–10; Pamela Hill Nettleton, "Rescuing Men: The New Television Masculinity in *Rescue Me, Nip/Tuck, The Shield, Boston Legal,* & *Dexter*," PhD dissertation, University of Minnesota, 2009, 307 pages, http://conservancy. umn.edu/bitstream/57963/1/Nettleton_umn_0130E_10769.pdf; Chris Petit, "Non-fiction Boy," *Guardian Review* (Saturday, 27 December 2008), pp. 13–14; and David Stubbs, "LAPD Blues," *Guardian Guide* (22–28 November 2008), pp. 10–12. Mike Davis's *City of Quartz: Excavating the Future in Los Angeles* (Pimlico, 1998; Verso, 1990) and Christopher Wilson's *Cop Knowledge: Police Power and Cultural Narrative in Twentieth-Century America* (University of Chicago Press, 2000) provide an excellent background to the cultural and political context of television crime dramas.

CHAPTER 18

The Wire
(HBO, 2002–08)
LINDA SPEIDEL

Produced by cable company Home Box Office (HBO), and running for five seasons, *The Wire* has been heralded as television of exceptionally high quality. Typical of claims made for the show are "The best American cop show and greatest programme of all time"[1] and "The best show on television."[2] Set in Baltimore, the series begins with a police investigation into a drug organization based in the city's housing projects. Unusually, it depicts the work of both police and drug dealers, as well as the politics which inform the police operation. From its second season onwards, while the drug investigation remains a central thread, the series expands to include the port, the politics of City Hall, the school system and the newspaper industry.

Helena Sheehan and Sheamus Sweeney in their essay "*The Wire* and The World: Narrative and Metanarrative" suggest that "*The Wire* represents a leap in the evolution of the genre" and highlight those aspects of *The Wire* which for many commentators, both popular and scholarly, have marked it as different from crime drama and unusual for television.[3] The breadth and depth of *The Wire's* depiction of crime far exceeds previous police series, as the focus is not only on the police, but on other public institutions and on criminal organizations as well. Crime is not solved, the social causes are analyzed, and there is a wealth of detail about the bureaucracy of law enforcement and comment on the nature of policing. Whereas crime narratives often simply involve locating and detaining perpetrators, *The Wire* contextualizes crime, particularly in relation to the drug trade, and suggests that many contemporary policing strategies in the "war on drugs" are ineffective. The police detectives in *The Wire* are not all-knowing and all-powerful individuals who quickly bring criminals to justice but employees, contending with institutional constraints and social conditions beyond their control. In terms of its narrative structure, *The Wire* is unusual in that cases span a whole season or more and the series takes its time over exposition, introducing a wide range of characters. The cast is generally not glamorous, nor are the locations, and *The Wire* has very little extra-diegetic music. Its soundtrack and dialogue are at times difficult to follow. The series is considered to be "complex" television both in terms of its thematic content and the demands it makes of its viewers and for Sheehan and Sweeney this "has opened narrative up" by allowing television drama to grapple with contemporary social issues and problems.

HBO is a premium subscription channel which, as is well documented, has developed a reputation for high-end productions targeted at a niche audience (Leverette, Ott and Buckley; Edgerton and Jones). It has produced a number of critically acclaimed TV dramas over the last decade and a half, such as *The Sopranos* (1999–2007), *Deadwood* (2004–06), and *Sex and the City* (1998–2004). In spite of the similar critical praise awarded to the series, *The Wire* never achieved particularly high ratings but the funding model of HBO allowed for a less obviously popular drama to survive, and creator David Simon (2004) has documented the apparent artistic freedom granted by HBO. It must be remembered, however, that much of HBO's marketing strategy *depends* on cultivating content perceived as challenging and on perpetuating the notion of artistic freedom—and indeed on flattering the audience that it is particularly discerning.[4] In this respect *The Wire* could be seen as typical of HBO's programming rather than a departure from it.

Yet at the same time, there is no doubt that *The Wire* has generated almost unprecedented academic interest in a television show. As Eve Ng has noted, *The Wire* is seen as "the epitome of quality TV,"[5] but interest in the series reaches far beyond the expected academic disciplines of television, media and cultural studies.[6] Its broad subject matter and narrative structure have gripped audiences, and while the serial form is by no means new or uncommon in television, Sean O'Sullivan points out that "*The Wire* exemplifies the consequences of the thirteen-episode uninterrupted season."[7] It abandons episodic closure in favor of one main plotline (the case) and several parallel story strands, and marks the distinct shift in the last decade towards the serial as a finite entity. Whereas previously a series would last indefinitely, there is now an expectation of an *ending*, a reward for watching the show. The newness of the serial form in television should not be over-stated,[8] but O'Sullivan is right to emphasize the significance of the 13 (or 12) episode season, which has become a unit picked up by other cable channels. Changes in the way in which television is commissioned, created and consumed, and in particular the popularity of the DVD box set, seem to have tapped into a hunger for serials.

Whereas in the series/serial hybrid the ending is either immediate or forever deferred, the 13-episode serial offers the viewer the pleasures of both long-format television as well as the promise of a resolution. Mittell argues that *The Wire* offers "a new model of serial procedurality," that the "pay-off" for the viewer is in the "procedural journey,"[9] but the expectation of an ending is just as significant and indeed Mittell has suggested elsewhere that viewers of long-format television "trust in the payoff that we will eventually arrive at a moment of complex but coherent comprehension, not the ambiguity and questioned causality typical of many art films."[10] Mittell also accounts for *The Wire's* particular success on DVD: "Even more than its narrative techniques, *The Wire's* internal storyworld is arguably the most complex ever to appear on American television, providing a rich experience that encourages—or even demands—multiple viewings."[11] Here he refines what is meant by "narrative complexity," that the program not only withstands, but in fact demands, repeated viewings.[12] Ted Nannicelli similarly notes: "David Simon and the other creators are forthright about the pleasure they take in making episodes so dense that viewers may not absorb all of the pertinent information in a single viewing."[13]

The Wire like many police series before it has been praised for its realism and fits many of Robert Thompson's descriptors of "quality TV."[14] Like the early seasons of *Homicide: Life on the Street*, *The Wire* concentrates on the mundane aspects of policing and particularly notable is the painstaking attention to detail. In season 1, screen time is devoted to explaining the necessary paperwork to clone a pager (a "wiretap affidavit"), or to police detectives simply observing drug dealers. In "The Pager" (1:3), scenes of street arrests (standard TV police fare) are juxtaposed with detective McNulty reading, and this "slow painstaking work" is ultimately more effective in tackling the illegal operations of the Barksdale crew.

The Wire, unlike its contemporary *The Shield*, marks a break with the handheld camera aesthetic. Brian G. Rose suggests that the camera work in *The Wire* uses "a more filmic strategy, emphasizing clarity, spatial depth, and the relationship of characters to their environments."[15] This can be seen partly as a continuation of the drive to be "not TV" ("filmic" being an important feature of the HBO brand), but also denotes a departure from the police point of view. It also allows the cityscape to feature more prominently: the long shot and long take situate characters within their surroundings, suggesting that individual action is limited and constrained by external circumstances. There is a shift away from the domestic and the interior to a focus on the outside world. There are many scenes without dialogue, accentuating the tele*visual*, and as has been frequently noted, the city is a central feature within the series. *The Wire* moves the police series and the viewer into the city and ceases to configure the urban merely as a dangerous place "out there," inhabited by "others." Indeed, as Brian G. Rose suggests: "*The Wire* has, in many ways, helped to re-invent the wheel, transforming the police drama from its emphasis on investigative heroics into one of the few places in television willing to argue passionately about the world outside the boundaries of the small screen."[16]

D'Angelo Barksdale (Larry Gilliard, Jr.) explains drug dealing as "the game." In *The Wire*, everybody's a pawn in one way or another (HBO/Blown Deadline/The Kobal Collection/David Lee).

Most obviously, *The Wire* marks a break with a focus on the police and the traditional authority of the lone detective is thoroughly compromised. While in season 1, Detective Jimmy McNulty is apparently the lead character and impetus behind the drug investigation, in seasons 2, 3 and 4 he occupies much less screen time. Whereas the television workplace frequently continues an illusion of individual autonomy (in the standard police procedural the detective follows a case, has complete control, and success depends on individual flair and tenacity),

The Wire depicts more accurately the alienation of the postmodern workplace where the worker is removed from the outcome. As David Simon notes in the DVD commentary to "The Target" (1:1), there was a conscious decision to locate the police headquarters in a modern unremarkable office block rather than the "mythologized" old-fashioned squad room. The contemporary police headquarters occupies a bland and corporate space, echoed by the newsroom in season 5. The focus moves from the lone individual flaunting the rules to a more nuanced position: the tension for the individual worker between holding on to the vision of what it is right and acting within institutional constraints. Not only is the impossibility of the detective's overview signaled, but also the outdated notion of the maverick cop within the postmodern workplace: the institution can no longer simply be conveniently ignored or overcome by the unorthodox police detective.

The full enactment of this shift is achieved in part by *The Wire's* careful depiction across each of its five seasons of a different institution, as Rose comments:

> Parallels are drawn between the various worlds … to connect the strains of organizational life and the price that individuals who work for them, in whatever capacity, must pay. With only a few scenes detailing domestic concerns, the focus remains firmly on the rigours of work and survival, whether for a regular paycheck, untaxed cash, or a dope vial.[17]

These shifts in focus across working environments allow similarities in structures and hierarchies to become apparent, probing the dynamics of institutional (dys)function as well as drawing parallels between the legitimate and illegitimate world of work. The long-format narrative structure of *The Wire* enables it to offer a more detailed and nuanced account of work than that of many episodic dramas, which deal with a particular event or situation that is quickly resolved. Because each season of *The Wire* builds on what has gone before, introducing new characters and institutions, while allowing those from previous seasons to remain in play, it is possible to show connections between them and their interdependence. What is merely alluded to in many police dramas (such as political influence) can be drawn out in more detail here, and the long-term consequences of a decision in one episode are played out in a subsequent episode or season. Moreover, characters such as Lieutenant Daniels, Rhonda Pearlman, Ellis Carver and Pryzbylewski are able not only to have jobs, but whole careers, or career changes.

The Wire also probes the concept of work itself, and suggests a void at the heart of "work" in postmodernity. Season 2 depicts the decline of the shipping industry and the loss of opportunities which has created a vacuum in which the drug trade flourishes. Season 3 tackles the dynamics of policing, often only touched on in many dramas, and attempts to depict the "out-and-out mundanity of police work (filing, report writing, etc.)" identified by Paul Cobley as lacking in most police dramas.[18] Throughout the series, the loss of "real" work occurs in tandem with the "work" of the media in both constituting and reflecting conceptions of work: fictional representations, marketization, media awareness and government policy have combined to make the nature of "real" police work ever more elusive.

However, the possibility of collectivist and collaborative work is offered in the form of the police "Detail."[19] The episode "Old Cases" (1:4) opens with Detective Herc, Detective Carver, Lieutenant Daniels, Detective Sydnor and McNulty attempting to move a desk. After much effort it becomes apparent that the detectives are pushing against each other— watched sardonically by Detective Lester Freamon. However, this metaphor for a disparate and ineffective group signals a turning point for the Detail: in the course of the episode Kima supports McNulty in requesting a wiretap; Lester Freamon provides D'Angelo Barksdale's

A crime scene from the final season. Left to right: Lester Freamon (Clarke Peters), Kima Greggs (Sonja Sohn), Jimmy McNulty (Dominic West) and Bunk Moreland (Wendell Pierce) (HBO/Blown Deadline/The Kobal Collection).

cell phone number; and Herc spends time "talking" to drug dealer Bodie's grandmother. The Detail now acquires the insights previously assigned to the individual detective. The group includes Herc, who is "fighting the war on drugs one brutality case at a time"; Pryzbylewski who had previously shot up his patrol car, and Lester Freamon, who has had an office job for over 13 years and is more interested in constructing intricate doll's house furniture. Each detective is apparently a misfit, but over the course of the first season the team coalesces as they each find a niche. This is painstaking collective work, and when Herc expresses impatience in "The Wire" (1:6), Lester responds with his much-quoted line: "We're building something here and all the pieces matter." This statement refers not only to the Barksdale case but also to *The Wire* itself, where the viewer is presented with snippets of information, episode by episode, as the series (and the case) develops, and the connections extend into other parts of the city and its institutions. Lester Freamon suggests also that "real" detective/police work is a collective endeavor amounting to far more than the instincts and singular abilities of one person.

   The Wire has been much commented on for its large African American cast,[20] unusual in the context of the wider landscape of U.S. television.[21] In *The Wire*, there are more black characters than white characters; both black and white characters appear across the social spectrum and are not easily stereotyped as "good" or "evil." There is a move away from a one-dimensional portrayal of race, as Todd Fraley for example notes: "*The Wire* offers a blend of the contested meanings of race, and recognizes that racial experience is not singular. Black is no longer code for violence, poverty, crime, deviance, and drug abuse."[22] *The*

Wire allows its characters, black and white, rich and poor to speak. In "Sentencing" (1:13), D'Angelo Barksdale describes to Bunk and McNulty his lack of options, not just growing up in the projects, but as part of a family embedded in the drugs trade: "You just live this shit until you can't breathe no more.... I was freer in jail than I was at home." In season 4, Namond Brice struggles as D'Angelo did, with the role he is expected to assume and is only able to leave the corner through the intervention of a police officer (Bunny Colvin). Here the intersection of race and class is made explicit: it is not *only* being black or white nor *only* being rich or poor which shapes life.

However there has not been universal praise for the representation of African Americans in *The Wire*, and some commentators have felt that the series continues to reinforce stereotypes—Elijah Anderson for example laments the absence of "the decent people"[23] and Ben Walters suggests that *The Wire* exoticizes black poverty for white "tourists."[24] Jane Gibb and Roger Sabin note "the diminishing depth of characterization" and a "flattening-out of character" of those in "the higher echelons of power" and suggest that characters such as Clay Davis reinforce the stereotype or caricature of black people as entertainers.[25] Furthermore, although *The Wire* attracted early scholarly interest from the online post-colonial studies journal *darkmatter*, editor Ash Sharma commented on "the strange 'absence presence' of race in the critical dialogues" noting that "race is either assumed as given and not commented upon, or that it is not race but class that is the important dynamic in the series." He suggests that while *The Wire* is progressive in that it "normalizes" blackness and marks whiteness, the relative silence on race in commentary on the series "makes race either marginal or invisible to the politics of the show."[26]

Also somewhat troubling is the representation of women in *The Wire*. Although Andrea Press finds that *The Wire* offers a "diversity" among the women characters seldom seen elsewhere on U.S. television,[27] Sophie Jones points to well-established stereotypes of "the gold digging girlfriend," "the tyrannical dragon-lady mother" and "the idealized angelic woman-savior." While acknowledging the depth and breadth of the series, she also notes the sheer paucity of female characters: "In *The Wire*, it is boys who are at stake. Women and girls are bit parts in a compelling drama played out by men." And in a similar vein to Sharma, Jones suggests that above all it is the silence on gender, in this case within the text as well as surrounding it, which is particularly troubling: "That one of the most progressive TV shows in the medium's history consistently demonstrates its ignorance of and disinterest in gender politics is utterly depressing."[28] In this sense, *The Wire* seems to both re-assert the hyper-masculinity of the police series and to engage in a masculinization (and legitimization?) of television, a medium which in the past has frequently been theorized as feminine.

Recommended "Episodes"

The narrative structure of *The Wire*, where there is little episodic narrative closure, makes it almost impossible to isolate notable episodes, and any attempt do so seems as pointless as identifying a "best" chapter in a novel. It is even difficult to pinpoint a "best" season, although many fans and reviewers particularly praised season 4, and season 5 was less well received. However, there are many great characters and moments. Perhaps particularly memorable are the montage sequences at the end of each season, each with its accompanying song (a rare instance of extra-diegetic music in *The Wire*): Jesse Winchester,

"Step by Step" (season 1); Steve Earle, "I Feel Alright" (season 2); Solomon Burke, "Fast Train" (season 3), and Paul Weller, "I Walk on Gilded Splinters" (season 4). The montage scene at the end of season 5 is set to the Tom Waits song "Way Down in the Hole," cover versions of which are used as the theme of all five seasons, but here the Blind Boys of Alabama's recording used in season 1 is repeated, signaling the cyclical nature of *The Wire's* stories. Other notable scenes include gangster Omar accidentally sticking up a stash house while popping out to buy Cheerios in blue silk pajamas; drug lord Stringer Bell attending an economics evening class; mid-level dealer D'Angelo Barksdale explaining the rules of chess (and the drug trade) to his "hoppers"; all of Prop Joe's (very eloquent) speeches; the ending of season 2, in which the case is so nearly but not quite closed; and finally Slim Charles's shooting of fellow (but incompetent and treacherous) drug dealer Cheese.

Further Reading

There is an ever-expanding breadth of critical analysis in the field of "*Wire* Studies," but good overviews of the series are provided by Brian G. Rose, "The Wire," in G.R. Edgerton and Jeffrey P. Jones (eds.), *The Essential HBO Reader* (University Press of Kentucky, 2008), pp. 82–91, and Blake D. Etheridge, "Baltimore on *The Wire*: The Tragic Moralism of David Simon," in M. Leverette, B.L. Ott, and C.L. Buckley (eds.), *It's Not TV: Watching HBO in the Post-television Era* (Routledge, 2008), pp. 123–164. Two wide-ranging and oft-cited analyses of *The Wire* are Helena Sheehan and Sheamus Sweeney, "*The Wire* and the World: Narrative and Metanarrative," *Jump Cut* 51 (Spring 2009), http://www.ejumpcut.org/archive/jc51.2009/Wire/index.html, and J. Kraniauskas, "Elasticity of Demand: Reflections on *The Wire*," *Radical Philosophy* 154 (2009), pp. 25–34. For a consideration of the racial dynamics of *The Wire*, see *darkmatter*: "The Wire Files" [4], 29 May 2009, http://www.darkmatter101.org/; and for an analysis of gender, see S. Jones, "Women and *The Wire*," *Popmatters*, 25 August 2008, http://www.popmatters.com/pm/feature/women-and-the-wire/. Jason Mittell considers *The Wire* and seriality in "*The Wire* in the Context of American Television," 9 February 2010, http://mediacommons.futureofthebook.org/content/wire-context-american-television and "All in the Game: *The Wire*, Serial Storytelling and Procedural Logic," in P. Harrison and N. Wardrip-Fruin (eds.), *Third Person: Authoring and Exploring Vast Narratives* (MIT Press, 2009), pp. 429–438. Three more recent collections of essays are T. Potter and C.W. Marshall (eds.), *The Wire: Urban Decay and American Television* (Continuum, 2009); L. Kennedy and S. Shapiro (eds.), *The Wire: Race, Class, and Genre* (University of Michigan Press, 2012); and D. Bzdak, J. Crosby, and S. Vannatta (eds.), *The Wire and Philosophy: This America, Man* (Open Court, 2013); while the latest additions to the "*Wire* shelf" include Sherryl Vint's *The Wire* (Wayne State University Press, 2013), Frank Kelleter's *Serial Agencies: The Wire and Its Readers* (Zero Books, 2014), and Linda Williams' *On The Wire* (Duke University Press, 2014).

CHAPTER 19

Justified

(FX, 2010–15)

BRIAN FAUCETTE

Justified was built around three elements: the bad boy charm of its star Timothy Olyphant; the unique and often poetic language of crime novelist Elmore Leonard; and a vision of the American South in Kentucky that recalls television Westerns of the 1950s and 60s. The series was a different kind of cop show at a time when most television crime dramas focused on medical forensics and high tech surveillance, and were predominantly structured as police procedurals. "Hillbilly noir" is probably as good a description as any.

The blending of the Western with the cop show was not new per se; *Justified* continued a tradition that included *Sheriff of Cochise* (Syndicated, 1956–58), *McCloud* (NBC, 1970–77), *Cade's County* (CBS, 1971–72), and *Walker Texas Ranger* (CBS, 1993–2001). Indeed, *Justified* has inspired other crime Westerns, including *Longmire* (A&E, 2012–14), which like *Justified* was adapted from a literary source (in this case the fiction of Craig Johnson). Where *Justified* took the merging of the genres into new territory was in its emphasis on character and morality, even if that meant veering into controversy when it came to "justifying" gun violence, an issue that is often top of the political agenda for the American public.

The show was developed and written by showrunner Graham Yost, and premiered in 2010 with the pilot "Fire in the Hole" on the cable network FX (Fox Extended). Yost developed the series around the recurring character of Raylan Givens, who appears in Elmore Leonard's short story "Fire in the Hole" (2001), and his earlier novels *Pronto* (1993) and *Riding the Rap* (1995). The working title for the series was "Lawman," later changed to "Justified"[1] for reasons that Yost explained: "['Lawman' was confusing because] Steven Seagal's reality show [of the same name] came on and we felt we had to come up with something else. My rationalization for ['Justified'] goes back to one of my favorite Sam Peckinpah films, *Ride the High Country*. I think it's Joel McCrea who says, 'A man wants to enter his father's home justified.'"[2] Yost continues: "I think that Raylan, like the cowboy heroes of the past, and even private detectives of pulp fiction, has a very strong moral code and he lives by that."[3]

Yost, who is Canadian, first found success working in Hollywood when he wrote the screenplay for the movie *Speed* (1994). He also wrote screenplays for the HBO mini-series *Band of Brothers* (2001), for which he won a Golden Globe Award, and *The Pacific* (2010), both World War II dramas. Yost's reputation as a showrunner was established with the crime series *Boomtown* (2002–03), which attracted the attention of the executives at FX and allowed him the chance to develop *Justified*. *Band of Brothers*, *Pacific*, and, to a lesser extent, *Boomtown* celebrated a certain kind of uncomplicated masculinity, sometimes framed as old-fashioned heroism; Yost wanted *Justified* to follow in the same vein. He told the *Los Angeles Times*, "Raylan is a kind of no-nonsense hero, he's got some stuff in his past, he shoots people and gets into trouble. But he's not—as we're getting a lot on TV on these days—a tortured anti-hero. He's a hero. He walks the walk."[4]

The tension with the tradition of the Western was therefore a productive one. While the inspiration for the series came from Elmore Leonard's fiction, it also corresponded with a resurgence of interest in the Western genre in Hollywood with films like *Appaloosa* (2008), *The Assassination of Jesse James by the Coward Robert Ford* (2007), and *True Grit* (2010); and with television series such as *Deadwood* (HBO, 2004–06).[5] However, it's interesting to note that both Leonard and Yost initially tried to distance themselves from contextualizing the show as a Western. Yost said, "When we were developing the series and shooting the pilot, and even after, we never used the W word."[6] The media were not so squeamish: *The San Francisco Chronicle* review of the pilot noted that "Givens recalls every badass good guy in Western lore."[7] Yost eventually relented, explaining that he understood the show's aesthetic in terms of "a chance to meld the two halves of Elmore's career, starting with Westerns and then going into crime fiction."[8]

Elmore Leonard was born in New Orleans and worked in advertising in the 1950s when he began his career writing fiction for magazines such as *Dime Western* where his story "3:10 to Yuma" first appeared.[9] Leonard also published Western novels including *Hombre* (1961) and during the classical Hollywood era several of his stories were made into films. Like Ernest Hemingway, whose style he emulated, Leonard employed a spare prose technique that appealed to readers of the pulp magazines. It was a style that could be repurposed for different genres, as became necessary when interest in Westerns began to wane in the 1960s. Though he continued to write within the genre, Leonard chose to focus on contemporary subject matter, in part using the

U.S. Marshal Raylan Givens (Timothy Olyphant) pulls his sidearm. Old-style western shoot-outs are a trademark of the show (FX Network/The Kobal Collection/Prashant Gupta).

work of George V. Higgins as a model (especially Higgins' 1970 novel, *The Friends of Eddie Coyle*).[10]

Reinventing himself as a crime writer with books such as *The Big Bounce* (1969) and *Swag* (1976), Leonard began to write in a style more akin to screenplays, placing emphasis on the dialogue: "The line of dialogue belongs to the character," he explained, "the verb is the writer sticking his nose in."[11] As his ear for everyday speech became more attuned, so his reputation for characterization spread, eventually bringing him critical acclaim with such books as *Get Shorty* (1990) and *Rum Punch* (1992). As one commentator put it, "What his writing always showed was a sense of how notions of law and order are in abeyance when men get desperate; and desperation, albeit infused with gallows humor, was the atmosphere Leonard's characters breathed."[12]

Thus, in Leonard's work dialogue becomes the key means of understanding the characters and their situations. As Leonard put it, "From the very beginning, my purpose was [to let the characters talk]. To first of all establish the characters, as many as possible in the first 100 pages, and audition them. [To see] if they can talk. If they can't talk, they're liable to slip from view or get shot early on."[13] And perhaps no character of Leonard's is a more interesting talker than Deputy U.S. Marshal Raylan Givens.

Justified wasn't the first TV show to be based on the work of a crime novelist—notably, in the 1970s, *Police Story* had drawn upon the novels of Joseph Wambaugh—but it was arguably the most faithful adaptation. Leonard embraced Yost's idea for the series and Yost made him an executive producer, but Leonard was not involved in much of the writing, though he did feed ideas for potential themes to the writing team. At the beginning, he went along with Yost's alterations to the source material, the aforementioned short story, "Fire in the Hole." For example, Yost decided to keep the character of Boyd Crowder alive (he is killed in the story) and resurrect Raylan's father (who is dead in the story). Yost explained that Raylan's father was useful as a villain to add a new dynamic to the series: "that's what Raylan rebelled against, and that's why he became a U.S. Marshal."[14] This in turn amplified Raylan's sense of unease. In his fiction Leonard makes Raylan's purpose more about his job and less about personal motivation. However, Yost said, "When you have to do a television series, week in and week out … [you] need to have something that [you] could explore further." Thus Raylan's anger towards his father becomes an important aspect of the show.[15]

As Raylan, Yost cast Timothy Olyphant, who had previously made his name as a sheriff in HBO's *Deadwood*, and whose sex appeal was not lost on critics. *The Washington Post* called him "tightly wound [and] casually handsome," and noted that "Givens does look darn good in his jeans and his spotless cocky cowboy hat."[16] *The New York Times* concurred that "[Olyphant is] an actor of rangy grace and wolfish good looks—his easy grin seems designed to induce swoons and suspicion in equal measure."[17] But Olyphant also brought intelligence to the role. Leonard said, "He played Raylan exactly like I heard him when I was writing him,"[18] while Yost applauded the fact that he instinctively "gets the combination of the good-guy, bad-guy thing."[19] Olyphant, for his part, saw the show as an attempt "to do Elmore Leonard right: and Elmore Leonard is always about some sort of moral code amongst cops and thieves … [and] about which ones are the assholes and which ones aren't."[20]

The Leonard/Yost/Olyphant take on Givens involved taking the character of the stereotypical "rural cop" and giving it a 21st century twist. The prototype had been officer Sam McCloud back in the 1970s, and Givens is similar in some respects: both men possess "country sense," and both are unflappable in the cowboy mode. The difference is that McCloud was a guileless hick who believed in "the good in everyone," and thus was positioned as a contrast to the cynical cops in his adopted home of New York. Givens, on the other hand, is anything but wide-eyed, and embodies the idea that cynicism isn't just the preserve of the metropolises.

When it came to casting the bad guys, Walton Goggins was chosen to play Boyd Crowder, an all-round troublemaker from Raylan's past in Kentucky; Boyd's family, like Raylan's, is connected to the criminal underworld. Goggins brought a recognizable persona to the series, having played the character of Shane Vendrell in *The Shield* (also broadcast on FX). Like Shane, Boyd is a Southerner with a history of criminal leanings, racist tendencies, and an inflated ego; he uses his rhetorical skills to manipulate people and situations.

To round out the cast, Yost chose Nick Searcy as Chief Art Mullins, who manages the Lexington U.S. Marshal field office and serves as Raylan's friend, mentor, and surrogate father. Jacob Pitts played Tim Gutterson, a former Army Ranger who has done a tour of duty in Afghanistan as a sharpshooter/sniper and now suffers from post-traumatic stress disorder; he is also a comic foil to Raylan. Erica Tazel was cast as Officer Rachel Brooks, an African American who struggles with personal demons even as she tries to show that she is capable of performing the job. To play Raylan's father, Yost cast industry veteran Raymond J. Barry.

Hardly less important is the place where the action unfolds. Yost wanted to portray a locale not normally seen on television. Kentucky, especially Harlan County, is here a region down on its luck that is made up of seedy bars and run-down trailer parks. Its economy is fueled by the dangerous labor of working in the coal mines, and trading in illegal drugs. As the series depicts it, the area is a mélange of churches, brothels, and long-standing family homes and traditions that together resist the prying eyes and influence of outsiders. It is Raylan Givens' return to this world that provides the series with its drama and its argument for law and order as "justified" and necessary.[21]

Walton Goggins as Boyd Crowder (Boyd: "What brings you to my house?" Raylan Givens: "Oh, this is your house now?" Boyd: "Why, yes, prison is my home"). Goggins has become a favorite in TV cop shows—he can in fact be glimpsed in the background of the second image in the Shield chapter.

The pilot episode got things off to a stylish start, and the first few scenes are set in Miami. Givens in his cowboy hat is a fish-out-of-water in such a metropolitan setting, a situation that echoed *McCloud*. Raylan gives a smartly dressed villain an ultimatum to leave Miami or face a showdown, but the villain merely laughs. As the two men discuss what has led them to this moment, the staging and editing resembles the classic Western gunfight. The men's faces are then shown in extreme close-up, recalling the style of Sergio Leone's spaghetti films. When the shooting starts, there's only one winner. Afterwards, the police chief in Miami explains to Raylan, "We're not allowed to shoot people on sight any more, and have not been, I don't know, for maybe 100 years." Raylan replies, "He pulled first...."

The pilot continues with Raylan being re-assigned to Kentucky, where he comes up against Boyd Crowder, who we see blowing up an African American church, shouting, "Fire in the hole!" as he does so. During the investigation Raylan is also reunited with Ava Crowder (Joelle Carter), Boyd's sister-in-law, who killed her husband after suffering years of abuse. The pilot episode ends with more gunplay, including Raylan shooting Boyd in the chest (not fatally). "I guess I just never thought of myself as an angry man," Raylan tells Winona, his ex-wife (Natalie Zea), who replies: "Honestly you're the angriest man I have ever known." The last scene, with Raylan staring dolefully into the night sky, sets up the dynamics of the series. He is a character struggling with his anger, a marker of traditional masculinity, and with his own feelings of confusion and insecurity.

Having established the basic premise for the show, the subsequent six seasons continued in a similar semi-ironic vein. Subsequent plots have involved another Kentucky family clan (the Bennetts), a child abductor, and the Detroit mafia. There have been fine performances from new characters: for example, tough matriarch Mags Bennett (Margo Martindale) was widely regarded to have stolen season 2. Meanwhile, the main changes in tone have entailed upping the "gallows humor," an amplification of the female roles (especially those of Ava and Winona), and the deepening relationship between Raylan and Boyd. Thanks to the unexpected popularity of Boyd, this last relationship became the engine of the show.

Raylan, for his part, is increasingly portrayed as somebody who "knows." In the same way that Kojak was a New Yorker who knew his locale, Raylan is a Harlan boy, and empathizes with "folks' ways." This is a form of "cop knowledge," as described in Christopher Wilson's book of that title, which is about police authority and how "the working cop" maintains "an intimate, interstitial, nearly mystical understanding of crime ... neighborhoods, working-class identity ... and more."[22] Thus, Raylan's hunches are not just hunches: he "knows" who shot whom, who's lying and who isn't, and his "justifications" rely on this knowledge.

Above all, he knows Boyd. After a stint in jail, and surviving being shot, Boyd becomes a born-again preacher. This allows him to become another Leonard-esque "talker," able to parry Raylan's verbal assaults with biblical hyperbole. But Raylan isn't fooled by Boyd's turn to religion; a game of cat and mouse ensues, always tempered by the two men's pasts. So, for example, Raylan despises Boyd's racism, and some of his best lines involve undermining it. At the same time, Raylan shows affection towards him, and when Boyd attempts to become Harlan's criminal kingpin, Raylan does his best to keep him alive. Boyd, for his part, refrains from metaphorically stabbing Raylan in the back, as he would anybody else, preferring to fight him face-to-face. The two men are, in effect, "the best of frenemies," and by season 4, viewers are strongly encouraged to believe that they are different sides of the same coin: Raylan could easily have become Boyd, if he hadn't moved away from Harlan and chosen law enforcement—and he knows it.

This kind of character play could only work over an extended period, and by utilizing the creative possibilities that serialization offers. In this case, it has also clearly been influenced by audience feedback, as Boyd's name increasingly racked up the hits on discussion websites and in the Twitterverse. Partly as a consequence, Boyd's part has expanded and Goggins' performance has grown in stature and confidence. As one critic noted, "Goggins is unlike any other actor I know in his ability to alternate between deadly, hypnotic stillness and sudden, galvanizing expression. His words become weapons, tools, instruments with which he stimulates the responses required in the spaces he dominates while speaking."[23]

Justified's six seasons have featured story arcs, in the manner of *The Sopranos* or *The Wire*, but at the same time the shows are episodic in the old-fashioned way, with plenty of room for digressions. Thus the structure is a kind of hybrid, leading to a staccato rhythm, with the scriptwriters attempting to "channel Leonard" as much as possible. As the critic for the *New Yorker* observed, "Many of the show's elegant, oddball tales work just as well in 40 minutes [as they would over the length of a season]. These stories also more closely resemble the twisty little noirs that Leonard writes, or those by Flannery O'Connor; knotty and compressed, they're tiny tales with philosophical depth."[24]

The show's visual aesthetic also developed over time. The first two seasons were shot using film, but for season 3 the production shifted to high-definition digital cameras. As Francis Kenny, the director of photography explained, "We persuaded Sony Entertainment that by shooting with Epic Cameras … it would look spectacular."[25] Also, the series adopted a new technology called Image Interchange Framework, which allowed the producers to enhance the amount of information captured during filming and to ensure that the series had a consistent look in terms of color, tone, and image resolution.[26]

What of the politics of the show? As it has gone on, so negative critical voices have grown louder, and two elements in particular have caused concern: the image of Kentucky, and the attitude to guns. In the same way that other cop shows have drawn attention to the portrayal of their setting (notably *The Wire* and Baltimore), so *Justified* has offered a florid depiction of Kentucky as essentially locked in the 19th century: backward, racist, and ruled by gun law. This has upset a minority of commentators. For example, a member of a civic improvement group in Harlan County was quoted in one newspaper as saying, "Please don't leave the audience thinking we are dumb, uneducated and alcoholics,"[27] while one web reviewer complained, "[It is] an insult to the people of my state. I am from the same area that this show is 'based.' It only furthers the stereotypes that we face from the rest of the country."[28] The fact that the majority of *Justified* was shot in California doubtless only added insult to injury.

The racism depicted in the show has also caused controversy in terms of stereotyping the South. Walton Goggins, himself born in Alabama, was initially dubious about taking the role of Boyd: "I've been in quite a few Southern films. And initially, when this was sent to me, I wasn't interested in playing another Southern guy labeled as a racist. You know, I think racism is a problem throughout our country, and it's not confined to those states below the Mason-Dixon line."[29] Inevitably, perhaps, some critics have been angered by the way in which Boyd's character has become more sympathetic over the seasons, and that audiences might be led to applaud him "for the wrong reasons." Thus far, however, the majority of opinion is that the scripters of the show have walked a fine line with some skill.

These worries about stereotyping tap into wider concerns about classism and "redneck-bashing" on American TV. For example, a slew of reality shows have focused on the rural poor with an unremittingly prejudiced eye, and the hit comedy drama *Orange Is the New Black* (Netflix, 2013–) features a character ("Pennsatucky") who is a hate figure and object of ridicule. The cop show *True Detective* (HBO, 2014–), set in Louisiana and featuring a bayou-dwelling underclass, has also drawn fire. Complaints about such depictions stretch back to the movie *Deliverance* (1972) and were occasionally heard about regarding *McCloud*.

But they have grown to such a pitch today that critics argue that the rural poor (especially "white trash") have become the only sector of U.S. society that it's socially acceptable to denigrate. However, to get the issue in proportion, the majority of critical opinion about *Justified* has been united in judging that it has avoided the worst excesses of this kind of thinking.

More saliently, perhaps, there have been criticisms about the political position that *Justified* takes on firearms. Those cavils grew louder every time there was a real-life mass shooting (for example, those in Aurora, Colorado, and Sandy Hook, Connecticut, both 2012), and every time statistics were published about the real victims of police shootings, who happen to be disproportionately black.[30] (The national average is about 400 shootings per year.) Thus, one academic essay has argued that, despite the way in which *Justified* explicitly interrogates the rhetoric of self-defense, and the justifications for homicide (often couched in "southern" biblical language), the show ends up "championing the resolution of conflicts at the end of a gun."[31] The essay concludes that "this show … is inherently conservative, deeply continuous of the traditional, triumphalist Western's glorification of private gun violence and resonant with a paradigmatic shift in the popular understanding of justifiable gun violence."[32]

It is possible to extend these criticisms into a broader critique of post–9/11 America. Another academic commentator has argued that *Justified* sets up a philosophical premise that has to be assessed on its own terms, rather than by imagined larger "political solutions." Therefore "any such justification [of America] will have to account for the distinctly American legacy of racism, the radical form of American capitalism with its structural poverty, and also the gamut of distinctly American socio-political stances like radical libertarianism, gun possession, and the saturation of the American public space by religion. Justifications must occur in response to such American specifics."[33] From this point of view, the fact that the show did not question the bigger picture, and was specifically not critiquing the validity of modern capitalism (in the way that, say, *The Wire* arguably did), is a symbol of America as an "unachieved hope."[34]

Justified was cancelled in 2014, with a final season debuting in 2015: Yost told the press he wanted it to end before the formula went stale. By then, along with a Peabody award for the first season, it has been nominated for eight Primetime Emmy awards. As for Elmore Leonard, it was something of a surprise when, in 2012, he announced that his next novel would be entitled *Raylan*, and would feature not only the title character but other figures from *Justified*; which is to say, characters invented and developed by other writers. It would be Leonard's final book; he died in 2013, receiving eulogistic obituaries that questioned why he had been underrated for so long. The final season of *Justified* then fed upon the book's ideas, underlining the unique symbiosis between the two mediums that had always underpinned the storytelling.

In conclusion, *Justified* has joined that elite group of shows that are not just admired but loved by audiences. Along with series such as *The Shield, Rescue Me, Damages,* and *Sons of Anarchy* it demonstrated that FX could compete with HBO on the level of "quality drama." Its "literariness" was of a different quality to the novelistic aspirations of a show like *The Wire*, but by emphasizing the role of the writer it reinforced the trend in the TV drama business towards spending more of the budget on this aspect. While competitor police shows went for gravitas, *Justified* steadfastly pursued a lighter, wittier path; this made its moral ambiguity all the more intriguing. Raylan Givens may wear a white hat, but that doesn't necessarily signify what it used to.

Recommended Episodes

The pilot "Fire in the Hole" (2010) acts as a good introduction to the series' themes, characters, and use of Leonard's unique language (Art Mullen: "Tell me about the shooting." Raylan: "It was justified.") In "The Lord of War and Thunder" (season 1, 2010), written by Gary Lennon, Raylan confronts his father Arlo when he is called to bail him out of jail (Art Mullen: "He's probably not a candidate for father of the year. He shot a cop, among other things..."). Finally, in "Bloody Harlan," the closing episode of season 2 (2011), Raylan faces off with Mags Bennett ("bad things are fixin' ta happen...") after becoming involved in a mess of Boyd's making. The episode climaxes in oddly moving fashion when Mags sips from a glass of her own poison moonshine.

Further Reading

William Rothman's essay about *Justified* in S. Peacock and J. Jacobs (eds.), *Television Aesthetics and Style* (Bloomsbury, 2013) is excellent on "the poetry of the ordinary." Justin A. Joyce's essay "The Warp, Woof, and Weave of This Story's Tapestry Would Foster the Illusion of Further Progress: *Justified* and the Evolution of Western Violence," in *Western American Literature* 47, Number 2 (Summer 2012), pp. 174–199, explores the legal discourse around "justifiable homicide." Martin Shuster's essay "'Boyd and I Dug Coal Together': Norms, Persons and Being Justified in *Justified*" is a useful philosophical discussion of agency and invokes Kant, Arendt and Wittgenstein (in *Modern Language Notes*, available at http://www.academia.edu/3248940/_Boyd_and_I_Dug_Coal_Together_Norms_Persons_and_Being_Justified_in_Justified). The post-mortem season interviews that creator Graham Yost has conducted with television critic Alan Sepinwall for the website *HitFix* are usefully detailed. In his essay for his blog *Remotely Interesting,* Jamiesen Tyler Borak's "Is Raylan Givens Justified? The Ethics of Fictional Harlan County" (available at https://remotelyinterestingtv.wordpress.com/2012/04/23/is-raylan-givens-justified-the-ethics-of-fictional-harlan-county/) asks if any of the characters are ever truly justified in their actions. For a well-considered meditation on Walton Goggins' performance as Boyd, see Jason Jacobs' essay "Preacher Man" at http://cstonline.tv/preacher-man.

CHAPTER 20

They also served…

A Roll Call of Other Notable Cop Shows

BEN BETHELL

Treasury Men in Action (ABC/NBC, 1950–55)

Of numerous future Hollywood stars appearing on *Treasury Men in Action*, none were bigger than James Dean, Charles Bronson and Lee Marvin, all three of whom received an early TV break on the show. Introduced by a character known only as "The Chief," played, case file in hand, by veteran character actor Walter Greaza, episodes in which forgers, smugglers, fraudsters and tax evaders are run to ground by tenacious Federal agents carried a single emphatic message: crime—specifically, withholding revenue from Uncle Sam—simply does not pay. Though later seasons were pre-recorded, *Treasury Men* (aired in syndication as *Federal Men*) was originally broadcast live from Hollywood, first by ABC and then by NBC in the network's pre–*Dragnet* Thursday night slot (the show returned to ABC for its final season). Like *Dragnet* (1951–59), it belongs to a liminal period in American entertainment history. William Beaudine, who directed *Treasury Men* at NBC, served as D.W. Griffith's assistant on *The Birth of a Nation* (1915) and went on to work with such silent era legends as Mary Pickford and Clara Bow. His extraordinarily prolific career concluded with a mid–1960s stint at ABC, directing Bruce Lee in *The Green Hornet*. By contrast, John Stephenson, who as a young actor was among the show's rotating line-up of Treasury agents, went on to become a renowned voice artist: the last surviving member of *The Flintstones*' original cast, he continued to provide characters for TV movies and video games until his death in 2012.

The Lawless Years (NBC, 1959–61)

Dismissed by some as a cut-price version of *The Untouchables* (ABC, 1959–63), *The Lawless Years* was in fact the first "Roaring Twenties" period cop drama to hit network television, predating the rival network's adaptation of Federal Prohibition agent Eliot Ness's bestselling memoir by several months. Of the two shows, NBC's offering, based on former NYPD detective Barney Ruditsky's unpublished memoir, was if anything the more authentic: as part of his job as technical advisor, the ex-cop recruited former underworld associates to act in it as gangsters. Due to involvement in numerous high-profile organized crime cases, Ruditsky, who had joined the NYPD in 1921, enjoyed fame as a detective in the 1920s and '30s. In 1940, he played a key role in bringing down Louis "Lepke" Buchalter's "Murder Incorporated" and retired a year later. A reputation for sleazy dirt-digging and his continued association with leading mob figures, among them Benjamin "Bugsy" Siegel, murdered in Beverly Hills in 1947, tainted Ruditsky's subsequent career as a Hollywood nightclub owner and private investigator. He was played in the show by the gravel-voiced James Gregory, soon to feature in John Frankenheimer's *The Manchurian Candidate* (1962) and later to play the fascistic General Ursus in *Beneath the Planet of the Apes* (1970). Gregory is, however, best known as the exasperating Inspector Frank Luger in *Barney Miller* (ABC, 1975–82), a character directly inspired, according to his creator Danny Arnold, by the actor's earlier portrayal of the mob-busting celebrity cop.

This Man Dawson (Syndicated, 1959–60)

A major radio syndicator since the late 1930s, broadcasting pioneer Frederick W. Ziv started Ziv Television Productions in 1949, producing a string of hit shows, notably *Highway Patrol* (1955–59), *Science Fiction Theatre* (1955–57) and *Sea Hunt* (1958–61). The company sold its products directly to regional sponsors, who in turn supplied them to local affiliates. The networks' lucrative discovery that their own re-runs could be licensed for syndicated broadcast brought first-run syndication's golden era to an abrupt close. *This Man Dawson* was among Ziv Television's final productions as an independent; its founder sold the outfit in 1960 to United Artists. The show was inspired by *Damn Citizen*, a 1958 movie starring the brooding Keith Andes as Francis Grevemberg, a real-life crusading cop who, appointed police superintendent in 1952, waged a three-year war against police corruption and rampant mob activity in the state of Louisiana. It too starred Andes, whose previous credits included an appearance as Marilyn Monroe's possessive boyfriend in Fritz Lang's 1952 noir classic *Clash by Night*. The actor was now cast as Chief Frank Dawson, a former U.S. Marine colonel hired to clean up police corruption in an unnamed American city. William Woodson played veteran sidekick Sergeant Ed Blankey, while director and co-producer William Conrad, who starred at the time in the radio version of *Gunsmoke* (1952–61), provided narration—his voice as familiar to late '50s audiences as his corpulent frame would be a generation later to viewers of *Cannon* (CBS, 1971–76) and *Jake and the Fatman* (CBS, 1987–92).

87th Precinct (NBC, 1961–62)

Author and screenwriter Evan Hunter first achieved literary success in 1954 with *The Blackboard Jungle*, a novel based on his brief experience teaching high school in the Bronx. Two years later, under the pen-name Ed McBain, he published *Cop Hater*, the first of over fifty gritty police novels in the 87th Precinct series—the last, *Fiddlers*, appeared just before his death in 2005. Early volumes were strongly influenced by Jack Webb's *Dragnet* (name-checked, for instance, in 1959's *Killer's Wedge*), their main character, Detective Steve Carella, modeled on Hunter himself. By 1961, when producer Hubell Robinson commissioned their network adaptation, over a dozen titles in the bestselling series were already in print. Set, like the novels, in the fictional city of Isola, a thinly disguised version of Manhattan, *87th Precinct* starred Robert Lansing as Carella and the equally prolific Norman Fell (Mr. Roper in the ABC comedy *Three's Company*) as the eccentric Detective Meyer Meyer. The show's supporting cast included Ron Harper as rookie detective Bert Kling and Geoffrey Walcott (remembered today for his 1959 starring role in Ed Wood's outlandish *Plan 9 from Outer*

Space) as his veteran colleague, Detective Roger Havilland. A youthful Gena Rowlands, later an Oscar nominee for acclaimed performances in husband John Cassavetes' *A Woman Under the Influence* (1974) and *Gloria* (1980), featured as Carella's deaf-mute wife, Teddy. Guest spots included early TV appearances from *Columbo*'s Peter Falk (who would himself become a Cassavetes regular) and *Star Trek*'s Leonard Nimoy.

Ironside (NBC, 1967–75)

Having starred for ten years as the nation's favorite defense attorney on CBS's *Perry Mason* (1957–66), Raymond Burr then spent almost another decade on NBC as Robert T. Ironside, once the San Francisco Police Department's chief of detectives, now paralyzed by a sniper's bullet, confined to a wheelchair and operating informally as "special departmental consultant." Created by screenwriter Collier Young, *Ironside* co-starred Don Galloway as Detective Sergeant Ed Brown and Barbara Anderson as socialite-turned-SFPD detective Eve Whitfield (replaced from the fifth season onwards by Elizabeth Baur playing Officer Fran Belding). As Mark Sanger, a parolee recruited by Ironside to work as his personal assistant, Don Mitchell completed the ex-chief's close-knit team. The inclusion among its supporting cast of a policewoman (still at the time a small-screen rarity) *and* one of prime-time TV's first regular black characters was a measure of the show's progressive inclinations. In an attempt to reflect post–Civil Rights era black aspiration, Sanger, an ex-con originally employed as the disabled hero's home-help, soon becomes Ironside's trusted bodyguard and indispensable right-hand man, later enlisting as an SFPD officer and eventually qualifying as an attorney. Quincy Jones's jazz fusion theme tune made musical history as the first on American TV to use a synthesizer; its insistent intro was later employed by Quentin Tarantino in *Kill Bill: Volume 1* (2003). In 1993, the show's cast transferred en masse to Denver, Colorado, for a TV movie, *The Return of Ironside*; a 2013 TV movie sees *L.A. Law*'s Blair Underwood reimagine Burr's original.

N.Y.P.D. (ABC, 1967–69)

Familiar to TV audiences as the urbane host of late-night talk-show *Open End* (Syndicated, 1961–87), producer David Susskind's reputation as an industry maverick was cemented by the drama *East Side/West Side* (CBS, 1963–64), an heroic attempt at small-screen social realism, featuring George C. Scott as a New York City social worker. Scott's secretary, played by Cicely Tyson, was among the first recurring black female characters on American television. With a pair of Emmys under his belt for 1966 CBS broadcasts of John Gielgud's *Ages of Man* and Arthur Miller's *Death of a Salesman*, Susskind then turned his hand to the cop genre, teaming up with screenwriter Arnold Perl to create *N.Y.P.D.* The show starred Jack Warden, best known at the time for his 1957 performance in Sidney Lumet's *12 Angry Men*, as Lt. Mike Haines. Frank Converse co-starred as Detective Johnny Corso and Robert Hooks, the recent founder of New York's Negro Ensemble theatre company and a noted Civil Rights activist, as Detective Jeff Ward. As guest stars, Al Pacino, Harvey Keitel, Roy Scheider and James Earl Jones all made early TV appearances. Filmed using a hand-held camera in a variety of NYC locations, *N.Y.P.D.*'s *vérité* approach to the police procedural anticipated the documentary feel of *Hill Street Blues* (NBC, 1981–87), *Homicide: Life on the Streets* (NBC, 1993–99), *NYPD Blue* (ABC, 1993–2005) and many others. The show's progressive social attitudes were of equal note: for example, its pilot

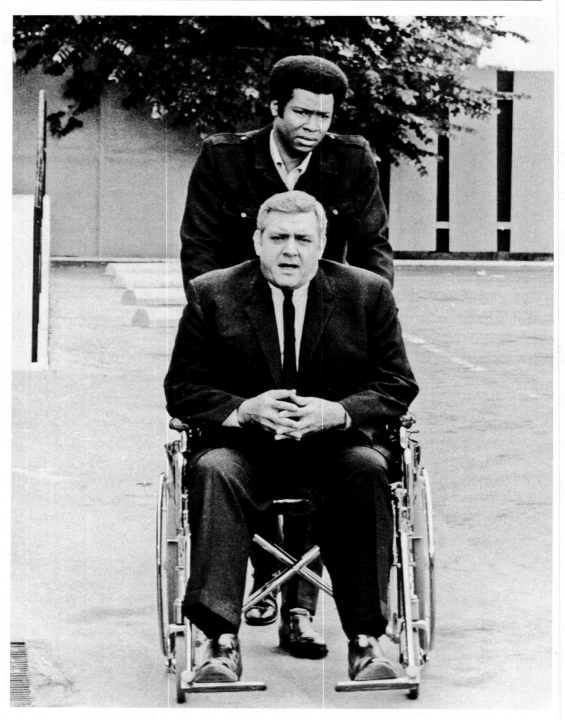

Chief of Detectives Robert T. Ironside (Raymond Burr) is wheeled by delinquent-turned-bodyguard Mark Sanger (Don Mitchell) in a scene that some would find "politically incorrect" today. (In the 2013 remake, Ironside is black.) Sanger was often dissed by "the brothers" for "living with the fuzz" (NBC TV/The Kobal Collection).

episode, "Shakedown," included the first depiction of male homosexuality in an American TV drama.

Adam-12 (NBC, 1968–75)

Faced by a career dip and an emergent "flower power" generation with which he was perceived to be deeply out of touch, *Dragnet* creator and star Jack Webb's response was twin-pronged. First, Webb produced a re-tooled color version of the show that made him famous (1967–70); then he created a spin-off, *Adam-12*. Though the revival (now titled *Dragnet 1967*, *Dragnet 1968*, etc.) enjoyed respectable ratings, Webb decided eventually to pull the plug on it and devote himself fully to the new project, collaborating with screenwriter Robert A. Cinader, with whom he had first worked on *Dragnet 1967*. The show starred Martin Milner (who in the early 1950s had appeared in *Dragnet* on both radio and TV) as veteran patrolman Pete Malloy, paired with Kent McCord as rookie partner Jim Reed. With the obsessive attention to mundane detail for which Webb was renowned, it depicted the typical daily routine of two uniformed LAPD officers whose patrol car's call sign is "1-Adam-12." Regarded by some critics as the buttoned-up cop show's "last gasp," *Adam-12* swam successfully against the era's permissive tide, a dependable bastion of square-jawed conservatism for a nation battered by social upheaval, political scandal, economic recession and the tragedy of Vietnam. Though hugely popular, its success was dwarfed by Webb and Cinader's next project, the paramedic drama *Emergency!* (NBC, 1972–79), a ratings smash that even spawned a cartoon spin-off. The new show saw *Adam-12*'s cops swapped for a pair of paramedics: the appetite of TV audiences for uncomplicated, unreconstructed action drama evidently remained substantial.

The Mod Squad (ABC, 1968–73)

An early hit for TV mogul Aaron Spelling, *The Mod Squad* was among the entertainment industry's less risible attempts to accommodate the burgeoning youth "counterculture" of the late 1960s, represented here by a trio of young detectives, "one white, one black, one blonde." "The times are changing," explains the squad's LAPD handler, channeling ABC executives; "they can get into places we can't." Spelling hoped that ex-cop turned screenwriter Buddy Ruskin's pilot script, based on his experience as a plainclothes narc and rejected by the networks a decade earlier, would appeal to a generation suckled on TV from *Dragnet*-era infancy, but now as wary of law and order's fictional representatives as they were the real thing. Tige Andrews played Captain Adam Greer, an LAPD detective who cuts a deal with three disaffected, delinquent youngsters, sparing them jail if they agree to work for him as unarmed, undercover investigators. Michael Cole starred as Pete Cochran, a car thief disowned by his wealthy Beverly Hills parents, alongside Peggy Lipton in a Golden Globe–winning performance as flower-child runaway Julia Barnes, and Clarence Williams III, in one of American TV drama's first black lead roles, sporting shades and a 'fro as ghetto progeny Linc Hayes. *The Mod Squad* is today seen as a landmark cop show, breaking decisively with its middle-aged, buttoned-up forbears, and tackling such topical issues as student protest, racial discrimination, drug addiction and abortion. Despite a strong cast that included *Homeland*'s Claire Danes in Lipton's role, MGM's 1999 big-screen adaptation was resoundingly panned by critics.

The Mod Squad. **Publicity shot of the grooviest cops in TV history, against a suitably psyche-delic backdrop. Left to right: Clarence Williams III, Peggy Lipton and Michael Cole (Thomas/Spelling/The Kobal Collection).**

McCloud (NBC, 1970–77)

Sam McCloud's DNA can be traced to an earlier Stetson-wearing law enforcement officer, Walt Coogan, played by Clint Eastwood in Don Siegel's 1968 movie *Coogan's Bluff*. Like McCloud, Coogan, an Arizona deputy sheriff, pursues a fugitive to New York, where, to the astonishment of the natives and irritation of his NYPD handlers, he proves a law unto himself, striding around the city in his cowboy boots, utterly unfazed by anything it can throw at him. The story, credited to *McCloud*'s creator Herman Miller, who co-wrote Siegel's screenplay, was evidently one too good to waste. Re-tooled for television, the character became a deputy marshal from Taos, New Mexico, on semi-permanent NYPD special assignment. Dennis Weaver (awarded an Emmy in 1959 for his portrayal of *Gunsmoke*'s bumpkin deputy Chester Goode) starred as the wily McCloud, riding Manhattan's streets on horseback and solving cases with a mix of diligent detective work and old-fashioned country smarts. J.D. Cannon featured as irascible superior Chief Peter Clifford, with Terry Carter as the reliable Sergeant Joe Broadhurst and Diana Malduar as the show's love interest, reporter Chris Coughlin. The cast reprised their roles in a 1989 TV movie, *The Return of Sam McCloud*, Weaver's character now a U.S. senator. During *McCloud*'s early seasons, both its lead actor and its creator were each involved in two more iconic 1970s television productions, Weaver as the star of Steven Spielberg's TV movie *Duel* (ABC, 1971), and Miller as co-creator of the martial arts-western hybrid *Kung Fu* (ABC, 1972–75).

The Rookies (ABC, 1972–76)

The first show produced jointly by Aaron Spelling and Leonard Goldberg, the partnership later responsible for such hits as *Starsky & Hutch* (ABC, 1975–79) and *Charlie's Angels* (ABC, 1976–81), *The Rookies*, like Jack Webb's *Adam-12* (see above), depicted the working lives of uniformed officers—in this case, a trio of young recruits to the fictional South California Police Department. The show's creator Rita Lakin (as a female screenwriter at the time an industry rarity) had worked for Spelling on *The Mod Squad* (see above), whose popularity with young audiences she now aimed to replicate (as would co-writer William Blinn a few years later with *Starsky & Hutch*). Michael Ontkean (later Sheriff Harry S. Truman in David Lynch's *Twin Peaks*) starred as college graduate Willie Gillis, alongside Georg Stanford Brown as minority recruit Terry Webster and Sam Melville as ex–Marine Mike Danko. Their mentor, Lt. Ed Ryker, was played by Gerald S. O'Loughlin, and Kate Jackson, soon to achieve fame in *Charlie's Angels*, co-starred as Danko's wife, Jill. Ontkean was replaced in the show's third season by Bruce Fairburn as Officer Chris Owens; among its guests, John Travolta, Sissy Spacek and *Cagney & Lacey*'s Tyne Daly (married to Stanford Brown since 1966) all made early TV appearances. The show's theme, composed by maestro Elmer Bernstein, accompanied a title sequence that remains one of American TV's most stylish. A spin-off, *S.W.A.T.* (ABC, 1975–76), cancelled after its second season, was resurrected as a 2003 Columbia motion picture starring Samuel L. Jackson and Colin Farrell.

The Streets of San Francisco (ABC, 1972–77)

Based on characters in Carolyn Weston's 1971 novel *Poor, Poor Ophelia*, *The Streets of San Francisco* was filmed on location in San Francisco in close cooperation with the city's police department. The show was developed for television by screenwriter Edward Hume and producer Quinn Martin, who had together scored a recent hit with *Cannon* (CBS,

Assistant Inspector Steve Keller (Michael Douglas) and Lt. Mike Stone (Karl Malden) share a laugh against a famous backdrop; the bridge was useful for its "postcard effect" in the credits, and was the focus for several notable stories, for example when Keller hunts down a bankrobber, played by Martin Sheen, in Golden Gate Park (Quinn Martin/Warner Bros. TV/The Kobal Collection).

1971–76). The lead role of veteran homicide detective Lt. Mike Stone provided a late-career fillip for Karl Malden, an Oscar-winner in 1951 for his supporting role in Elia Kazan's screen adaptation of Tennessee Williams' *A Streetcar Named Desire*, but by 1971 reduced to starring in Dario Argento's bizarre *giallo* shocker *The Cat O' Nine Tails*. In his first major role—and the one that made him a household name—a young Michael Douglas co-starred as Inspector Steve Keller, Stone's college-graduate rookie sidekick, while guest appearances included early small-screen outings for James Woods, Nick Nolte, Martin Sheen and Arnold Schwarzenegger. The show's popularity was due not least to the intelligence and commitment of its lead performances, the protagonists' mentor/protégé relationship mirroring the close friendship enjoyed off-screen by Malden and Douglas. As co-producer of *One Flew Over the Cuckoo's Nest*, Douglas cleaned up at the 1976 Oscars and quit *Streets* after only two episodes of the show's fifth season to pursue a successful career as a Hollywood producer and leading man. His replacement Richard Hatch, as Inspector Dan Robbins, proved unpopular with viewers, leading ABC to axe the show from its schedule.

Police Story (NBC, 1973–78)

The creation of author and former LAPD detective Joseph Wambaugh, *Police Story* set a new benchmark for accuracy in police procedural drama, to which shows such as *Hill Street Blues* (NBC, 1981–87), *Law & Order* (NBC, 1990–2010) and *NYPD Blue* (ABC, 1992–2005) would later aspire. It followed an anthology format, with episodes ranging in tenor from dark comedy to gritty drama, each based around an officer serving in one of the LAPD's various branches. Continuity was provided by recurring characters, including Tony Lo Bianco and former NFL star Don Meredith as robbery–homicide detectives Tony Calabrese and Bert Jameson, and Scott Brady as Vinnie, a retired cop-turned-bar owner. In what proved to be a vintage year for Wambaugh, 1973 also saw the publication of his true-crime bestseller *The Onion Field* (which he would successfully adapt for cinema in 1979) and a CBS TV adaptation of his 1972 novel *The Blue Knight*, starring William Holden as veteran LAPD beat officer Bumper Morgan (a role reprised by George Kennedy when CBS aired *The Blue Knight* as a series in 1975–76). *Police Story* won a 1976 Emmy for outstanding drama series and generated no fewer than three spin-offs: the hit show *Police Woman* (see below) and, somewhat less successfully, *Joe Forrester* (NBC, 1975–76), which starred Lloyd Bridges as its eponymous veteran detective, and *David Cassidy: Man Undercover* (NBC, 1978–79), in which the former *Partridge Family* heartthrob played Dan Shay, a plainclothes detective whose youthful looks allow him to pose as a troubled LA teenager.

Get Christie Love! (ABC, 1974–75)

Taking his cue from assertive black heroines played by Tamara Dobson in *Cleopatra Jones* (1973) and Pam Grier in both *Coffy* (1973) and *Foxy Brown* (1974), screenwriter George Kirgo transformed Christie Opara, the white NYPD detective heroine of a 1970 novel by Dorothy Uhnak, into Christie Love, an LAPD detective in the blaxploitation mold. Love's killer catchphrase, "You're under arrest, *Shugah!*" is delivered with brio to apprehended suspects. Following the success of a one-off TV movie aired by ABC in 1974, the character was then developed for a full network series by screenwriter and producer Glen Larson (whose later creations would include *Knight Rider*, *Battlestar Galactica* and *Magnum P.I.*). Starring Teresa Graves in the title role, alongside Charles Cioffi as her boss Lt. Matt Reardon and *Maverick*'s Jack Kelly as veteran detective Lt. Arthur Ryan, the show's one and only season was a disappointing flop. Its success was perhaps hampered by Graves' recruitment, shortly after shooting commenced, by the Jehovah's Witnesses; her contractual obligations fulfilled, the actor, who had demanded sanitized script re-writes and refused to engage in on-screen kissing, then retired permanently from the profession. A black female cop might also have proved an innovation too far for mid-'70s primetime audiences only just getting to grips with Sergeant "Pepper" Anderson in NBC's *Police Woman* (see below). *Get Christie Love!* was without doubt truly ahead of its time, Graves the first female black actor to star in an hour-long U.S. television drama. The second, Kerry Washington, appeared as political fixer Olivia Pope in ABC's thriller series *Scandal* only in 2012.

Police Woman (NBC, 1974–78)

Angie Dickinson first appeared as an undercover LAPD police officer named Lisa Beaumont in an episode of *Police Story* (see above) entitled "The Gamble." Renamed Sergeant Suzanne "Pepper" Anderson by creator Robert L. Collins, the character proved a huge hit in a spin-off series of her own. Though Pepper wasn't TV's first lead female cop—that distinction belongs to undercover NYPD officer Patricia "Casey" Jones (Beverley Garland) in *Decoy* (syndicated, 1957–59)—*Police Woman* was the first successful U.S. television drama of any description based around a female lead character. Already in her early 40s,

Dickinson's career highlights included co-starring with Ronald Reagan in Don Siegel's *The Killers* (1964) and with Lee Marvin in John Boorman's 1967 cult classic *Point Blank* (1967). It was, however, as Pepper that the actor became a household name, winning a Golden Globe in 1975 (followed by three further nominations) and securing an enduring place in the pantheon of TV cops. Each episode saw Dickinson adopt a different undercover guise— nurse, hooker, schoolteacher, prison inmate and air hostess, among many others. Though often cited as forerunner to Tyne Daly and Sharon Gless's detective partnership in *Cagney & Lacey* (CBS, 1981–88), the appeal of Dickinson's character, in contrast to theirs, was overtly sexual. Particularly popular with young male viewers, the show ushered in prime-time TV's "jiggle era": *Wonder Woman* (ABC/CBS, 1975–79), *Charlie's Angels* (ABC, 1976–81) and *The Bionic Woman* (ABC/NBC, 1976–78) were all aired in its immediate wake.

Serpico (NBC, 1976–77)

Frank Serpico was a NYPD undercover vice cop, the first officer in the department's history to testify publicly about widespread systemic corruption in its ranks. In 1970, the detective's contribution to a *New York Times* front page exposé prompted the city's mayor to establish a special commission to investigate its police force. By this time the victim of a near-fatal shooting widely believed to have been set up by his colleagues, Serpico appeared before the commission and subsequently received the NYPD's Medal of Honor before retiring in 1972. A year later his biography, authored by journalist Peter Maas, topped the *New York Times'* bestseller list, followed closely by Sidney Lumet's movie adaptation, its title role filled by a hirsute Al Pacino, fresh from his breakthrough in Francis Ford Coppola's *The Godfather*. TV screenwriter Robert L. Collins, who had scored a recent hit for NBC with *Police Woman* (see above), developed the character for the small screen, and a network series followed his full-length TV movie, *Serpico: The Deadly Game*. Both starred David Birney, a respected stage actor whose TV appearances included *Police Story* and *Police Woman*. Though he brought considerable subtlety to his portrayal of the principled, unorthodox NYPD loner, who in pursuit of justice battles not only crooks but corrupt fellow officers and indifferent superiors, Birney struggled to fill Pacino's shoes. Disappointingly, *Serpico* was never much more than a run-of-the-mill cop drama, poor ratings leading NBC to cancel the show midway through its first season.

CHiPs (NBC, 1977–83)

Created by NBC executive Rick Rosner, *CHiPs* starred Larry Wilcox and Erik Estrada as California Highway Patrolmen Jonathan Baker and Frank Poncherello, better known as "Jon" and "Ponch," a pair of motorcycle cops whose loyalty and affection for one another— Ponch forever getting the duo into scrapes from which the level-headed Jon must then extricate them—was in marked contrast to the actors' mutual off-screen animosity. Adopting a lightweight formula concocted in the wake of *Starsky & Hutch*'s primetime success (during this period CBS aimed for something similar with *The Dukes of Hazzard*), the show delivered family-friendly drama built around set-piece car chases that usually culminated in one of its signature multi-vehicle freeway pile-ups. Riding C-Series Kawasaki Police Specials, the actors performed many of their own stunts; Estrada, who only admitted many years later that he hadn't at the time held a motorcycle license, was frequently injured, seriously so when he broke both wrists in 1979. Wilcox finally walked for good before shooting began on a sixth, final season. Ponch's new partner, Officer Bobby "Hot Dog" Nelson, was played by Tom Reilly, whose arrest during filming on an LAPD drug charge somewhat tarnished the show's squeaky-clean image. By 1998, Wilcox and Estrada's differences had been patched up sufficiently for them to reunite in a full-length TV movie, *CHiPs '99*; a big-screen adaptation, first announced by MGM in 2005 and rumored to star Wilmer Valderrama (*That 70s Show*) as Ponch, remains in development.

T.J. Hooker (ABC/CBS, 1982–86)

The swansong of Spelling-Goldberg Productions (the partnership that delivered *Starsky & Hutch*, *Charlie's Angels* and *Hart to Hart*), *T.J. Hooker* was the creation of screenwriter Rick Husky, who'd first worked for Aaron Spelling on *The Mod Squad* (see above) and later as a regular on Goldberg-Spelling's *The Rookies* (see above), before going on to develop the show's flop spin-off, *S.W.A.T.* (ABC, 1975–76). By 1982, the writer no doubt believed he was due a hit, and though his show *The Renegades*, starring Patrick Swayze as a street-gang leader turned undercover cop, bombed when it premiered on ABC the same year, Husky scored with *Hooker*, which he'd first conceived as an updated version of *The Rookies*. Thomas Jefferson "T.J." Hooker is a veteran detective in the show's fictional Lake City Police Department who, when his partner is murdered, returns to the beat as a uniformed sergeant, acting as mentor to his younger colleagues. The role consolidated William Shatner's comeback after over a decade in the wilderness following NBC's cancellation of *Star Trek*. Support included Adrian Zmed as rookie partner Vince Romano and Heather Locklear (next cast by Spelling in *Melrose Place*) as Officer Stacy Sheridan, who in turn was partnered by another uniformed veteran, Jim Corrigan, played by James Darren. Following its cancellation by ABC in 1985, CBS picked up the show's final season, which was marked by grittier plot-lines and a location shift to Chicago, Shatner now partnered by streetwise detective Lt. Pete O'Brien (Hugh Farrington). The changes proved deeply unpopular with fans.

Hunter (NBC, 1984–91)

Fred Dryer just missed out on playing Sam Malone in *Cheers*; two years later, the 6'6" former NFL star hit the big-time with an altogether different kind of role, maverick LAPD homicide detective Sergeant Rick Hunter, a thuggish cop cast in the "Dirty Harry" mold. Its creators, screenwriter Frank Lupo and producer Stephen J. Cannell, who had enjoyed a recent smash with *The A-Team* (NBC, 1983–87), conceived the show as a tough, violent antidote to the era's increasingly anodyne primetime fare. However, when first season ratings proved poor, Cannell drafted veteran producer Roy Huggins (with whom, a decade earlier, he had created *The Rockford Files*) to re-tool the show. Huggins played up the relationship between Dryer's character and partner Sergeant Dee Dee McCall (Stephanie Kramer) and turned the violence down a couple of notches—though gun-play remained a motif, with Dryer normally managing to pile up at least a few corpses by the end of any given episode. Driven by Dryer and Kramer's on-screen chemistry, *Hunter* evolved into a sort of cross between *Moonlighting* and *Magnum Force*, its writers resisting pressure from both fans and the network for the partnership to blossom into full-blown romance. Kramer stood down for what turned out to be the show's final season and for a 1995 TV movie, but returned for two further TV movies in 2002 and 2003. Following a dispute with Dryer,

NBC then cancelled an eighth season after only three episodes; a big-screen adaptation is rumored, starring John Travolta and Jessica Alba.

Crime Story (NBC, 1986–88)

With *Miami Vice* (NBC, 1984–89) under his belt, producer Michael Mann turned his attention to criminal history, commissioning screenwriter Gustave Reininger and ex-cop Chuck Adamson to script *Crime Story*. The show was initially conceived as the decade-spanning saga of a mafia crew's rise to power, beginning in Chicago in the early 1960s and concluding in Las Vegas in 1980. In an attempt to control the cost of recreating period Chicago, Mann ended up shifting the plot action to Vegas far earlier than planned, though this failed to dissuade NBC from reneging on its commitment to the project, which it axed after only two seasons. Left suspended on a cliff-hanger, the narrative at this point reached only as far as 1964, its lead protagonists locked with one another in an escalating spiral of obsessive enmity. Tony Denison (seen more recently playing Detective Andy Flynn in *The Closer* [see below] and its spin-off, *Major Crimes*) starred as rising mobster Ray Luca. His implacable adversary, Lt. Mike Torello, a Chicago detective transferred to a Federal Strike Force set up to combat mob activity in Vegas, was played by Dennis Farina, who in films including *Midnight Run* (1988) and *Get Shorty* (1995) later specialized in mafia grotesques. Guest appearances from up-and-coming actors included the TV debuts of both Julia Roberts and Kevin Spacey. The acknowledged inspiration for *Casino*, Martin Scorsese's 1995 mafia epic, *Crime Story* pioneered the long story arc in TV crime drama, anticipating such ground-breaking series as *The Sopranos* (HBO, 1999–2007) and *The Wire* (HBO, 2002–08).

21 Jump Street (Fox, 1987–91)

21 Jump Street was the Fox Network's first hit and, though he would later distance himself from it, the show that made Johnny Depp a household name. Depp played Tom Hanson, an LAPD officer whose youthful appearance results in his assignment to a special squad of undercover detectives, headquartered at the show's eponymous address, all of whom look young enough to pass as high school students. Though less of a resounding hit than either *The A-Team* (NBC, 1983–87) or *Hunter* (see above), the show was another in a run of 1980s successes for producer Stephen J. Cannell (collaborating on this occasion with screenwriter Patrick Hasburgh). Aimed squarely at a teenage audience, episodes tackled such issues as drug addiction, bullying, homophobia and child abuse, and often concluded with a public service-style announcement by a cast member. By the time Fox cancelled the show in 1990, Depp had departed, his next cinema roles—in John Water's *Cry-Baby* and Tim Burton's *Edward Scissorhands*—calculated to subvert the teen idol persona he had now come to despise. A fifth and final season aired in first-run syndication without the star. A spin-off, *Booker*, starring Richard Grieco as Dennis Booker, now ex–LAPD and working as a renegade insurance investigator, was dropped by Fox after a single season. *21 Jump Street* was resurrected for the big screen in 2012 as a comedy feature starring Jonah Hill and Channing Tatum; the movie included cameos from Depp and original co-stars Holly Robinson and Peter DeLuise.

In the Heat of the Night (NBC/CBS, 1988–95)

Conceived as a vehicle for Carroll O'Connor (*All in the Family*'s Archie Bunker), *In the Heat of the Night* saw the roles made famous by Sidney Poitier and Rod Steiger in Norman

Jewison's 1967 Oscar-winning movie (itself adapted from a novel by John Ball) reprised by Howard Rollins as Virgil Tibbs, a Philadelphia detective who returns on a visit to his hometown of Sparta, Mississippi, and O'Connor as the town's police chief, Bill Gillespie. Though updated to accommodate such late–80s themes as HIV, homophobia and crack cocaine, the series followed the original's premise, its protagonists forced into an uneasy partnership when Tibbs is persuaded to stay in the town and help its police force overcome a reputation for racism and incompetence. Cancelled by NBC after its fifth season, CBS picked up the show for three further seasons. Rollins was dropped at the end of season 6, his off-screen struggle with drug and alcohol addiction having led to four arrests during his time in the series, culminating in a month in jail for driving under the influence. Following a spell in rehab, the troubled actor made sporadic guest appearances in the show's final seasons; his tragic early death a year later was from lymphoma. With Gillespie put out to pasture as a county sheriff, Carl Weathers (best known for his role as Apollo Creed in *Rocky*) was introduced as Rollins' replacement, Inspector Hampton Forbes, Sparta's new black police chief. Two decades earlier, the storyline would have been inconceivable.

Walker, Texas Ranger (CBS, 1993–2001)

The early '90s saw the career of Chuck Norris, once Cannon Films' biggest box-office draw, on the wane, and the budget action studio responsible for such hits as *Missing in Action* (1984) and *The Delta Force* (1986) on the verge of bankruptcy. Taking inspiration from *Lone Wolf McQuade* (1983), a spaghetti-flavored martial arts/western hybrid that had starred Norris a decade earlier, screenwriter J. Michael Straczynski (creator of *Babylon 5*) developed *Walker* for Cannon during its brief, last-gasp foray into small-screen production, CBS picking up the project when the studio finally hit the skids in 1993. Norris plays Dallas-Fort Worth–based Texas Ranger Cordell Walker—like the actor, a martial arts expert and military veteran—supported by Clarence Gilyard as his young partner, Jimmy Trivette, by contrast a tech-savvy, college-educated, black East-coaster. Sheree J. Wilson featured as love interest DA Alex Cahill, whom Walker eventually marries in the show's final season, while Sioux activist Floyd Red Crow Westerman (whose big-screen credits included 1990's Oscar-winning *Dances with Wolves*) made regular appearances as Walker's uncle, Ray Firewalker. The show's eclectic blend of Old West conservatism and martial arts action, seasoned with a New Age dash of Native American spirituality, proved hugely popular with audiences. A spin-off, *Sons of Thunder* (CBS, 1998–2001), in which former Dallas PD detective Carlos Sandoval (Marco Sanchez) and Walker's black-belt ex–Army protégé, Trent Malloy (Jimmy Wleck) team up as private investigators, enjoyed equally healthy ratings. CBS aired a full-length TV movie, *Trial by Fire*, in 2005.

New York Undercover (Fox, 1994–98)

A collaboration between *Law & Order* creator Dick Wolf (its characters inhabit *Law & Order*'s fictional universe) and screenwriter Kevin Arkadie (who went on to write and produce *The Shield*), *New York Undercover* was the first police drama to feature a lead partnership of two non-white officers. Malik Yoba starred as undercover NYPD detective James "J.C." Williams and Michael DeLorenzo as his partner, Detective Eddie Torres. Ice T and Naomi Campbell both took recurrent roles in the show's early seasons (both of them on the wrong side of the law), while soul icon Gladys Knight played the eponymous proprietor of Nathalie's, a nightclub at which each episode's featured musical guest would perform. Soul, rap and Latin legends booked to appear on the show by its musical director, Grammy-winner and former Miles Davis sideman James Mtume, included Mary J. Blige, Erykah Badu, the Notorious B.I.G., George Clinton, Tito Puente, Celia Cruz, the Temptations, the O'Jays, and Knight herself. The presence of former Warhol Factory scenester Patti D'Arbanville as superior officer Lt. Virginia Cooper underscored *New York Undercover*'s authentic NYC credentials. Lauren Vélez also co-starred as Detective Nina Moreno, Torres's love interest, whom he marries in the third season finale, only to die shortly afterwards attempting to foil a bank heist. As the show's popularity depended largely on Yoba and DeLorenzo's on-screen buddy chemistry, ratings nosedived in its fourth, final season (now also minus D'Arbanville). Yoba recently announced plans to revive the series.

Martial Law (CBS, 1998–2000)

Long-time collaborator of childhood friend Jackie Chan, and pivotal figure in the Hong Kong movie industry since first employed by Raymond Chow at Golden Harvest in 1970 (where early roles included a brief appearance with Bruce Lee in *Enter the Dragon*), revered actor, director, choreographer and martial artist Sammo Hung Kam-bo enjoyed a surprise crossover hit late in his career with *Martial Law*. Hung played Sammo Law, a Shanghai detective and hand-to-hand combat specialist who, having pursued his Triad-boss arch-nemesis to Los Angeles, remains there on assignment to the LAPD. The result of a collaboration between screenwriter Carlton Cuse (who later attained cult status as the creator of *Lost*) and Hong Kong producer/director Stanley Tong, responsible in 1995 for Chan's U.S. breakthrough in *Rumble in the Bronx*, the show was unique among its U.S. primetime peers in featuring Asian lead characters—Kelly Hu co-starring alongside Hung as undercover officer Grace "Pei Pei" Chen. Comedian and talk-show host Arsenio Hall joined the cast midway through the show's first season as the loquacious Terrell Parker, an LAPD press liaison officer reassigned to work as Law's handler. In an East/West culture-clash buddy partnership distinctly similar to Chan and Chris Tucker's in *Rush Hour* (which hit cinemas at the same time), Hall proved the perfect foil, his wisecracks offsetting Hung's awkward English (it was reported that the Chinese star recited dialogue phonetically if ever required to deliver lines) and providing light relief between martial arts set-pieces.

Third Watch (NBC, 1999–2005)

Before teaming up with Chicago police officer-turned-screenwriter Edward Allen Bernero to write a script based on the ex-cop's own experiences, John Wells, as executive producer of NBC's long-running medical drama *ER*, had wanted to create a show that dealt specifically with the experience of Chicago paramedics. The eventual result, *Third Watch*, set instead in New York City, revolved around members of all three branches of the city's emergency services—NYPD officers, FDNY firefighters and NYC paramedics. The show thus succeeded where Dick Wolf had failed with *H.E.L.P.* (ABC, 1990), the *Law & Order* creator's own attempt at a "three-services" drama. Noted (and criticized by some) for its realistic violence and profanity, it featured among an ensemble cast Jason Wiles and Coby Bell as police officers Maurice "Bosco" Boscorelli and Tyrone Davis, Eddie Cibrian as firefighter Jimmy Doherty, and Kim Raver and Bobby Cannavale as paramedics Kim Zambrano and Bobby Caffey. The characters all work the eponymous 3 p.m. to 11 p.m. "third watch" in Manhattan's fictional 55th Precinct; their stationhouse, due to its location on the corner of "King Blvd." and "Arthur Street" is nicknamed "Camelot." *Third Watch*'s third season was delayed in the immediate wake of 9/11, eventually premiering only a few weeks later with an episode entitled "In Their Own Words," in which real emergency services personnel recounted their experiences of responding to the attack. The season's original opener aired the following week, its topical poignancy underscored by a new title: "September Tenth."

Without a Trace (CBS, 2002–09)

Screenwriter Hank Steinberg's first hit series, *Without a Trace* took as its subject the New York City branch of the (fictional) FBI Missing Persons Unit, whose agents use psychological profiling to piece together the lives of missing individuals and reconstruct their "day of disappearance." Each episode followed a single case during the crucial 72-hour period that followed a report being filed, often concluding with a brief appeal for information about a real missing person. Long story arcs explored the principals' personal lives, with Anthony La Paglia, in a Golden Globe–winning performance, leading a strong cast as unit head Special Agent Jack Malone, alongside fellow–Australian Poppy Montgomery as Special Agent Samantha Spade. Britosh actor Marianne Jean-Baptiste, a 1997 Oscar nominee for her role in Mike Leigh's *Secrets & Lies*, co-starred as Special Agent Viv Johnson, with Enrique Murciano—offered the part by Jerry Bruckheimer following a big-screen appearance in the producer's *Black Hawk Down* (2001)—playing Special Agent Danny Taylor. Though belonging nominally to *CSI*'s fictional universe, there was in fact only a single crossover episode: season 6's "Where and Why," which sees Malone join forces with *CSI*'s Las Vegas forensics expert Dr. Gil Grissom, played by William Petersen. *Without a Trace* encountered controversy in 2004 when a campaign by a conservative pressure group, the Parents Television Council, resulted in CBS incurring a record $3.6 million fine for indecency, "Our Sons and Daughters," an episode involving a teenage sex orgy, having aired pre-watershed on West Coast affiliates.

Cold Case (CBS, 2003–10)

Cold Case creator, screenwriter and producer Meredith Stiehm, a recent Golden Globe– and Emmy-winner for her work on *Homeland* (Showtime 2011–), received her first Emmy in 1998 for an episode of *NYPD Blue*. *Cold Case* starred Kathryn Morris as Detective Lilly Rush, assigned to a fictional division of the Philadelphia Police Department devoted to cases that, though unsolved, are no longer actively pursued. Each episode was based around a single investigation, normally a murder, some cases only a few years old, others dating as far back as the early decades of the twentieth century. Scenes in which Rush tracks down and re-interviews surviving witnesses alternated with period flashback sequences, a format that allowed the show's writers to explore from an historical perspective themes such as racism, homophobia, domestic abuse, and police corruption and brutality. Episodes often concluded with the dead victim, now finally at peace, looking on as the crime's perpetrator is at last brought to book. Like *Without a Trace* (see above), *Cold Case* was nominally linked via a single crossover episode to Jerry Bruckheimer's *CSI* universe; Danny Pino, as Rush's partner Detective Scotty Valens, appearing in a 2007 *CSI:NY* episode entitled "Cold Reveal." Pino currently stars on NBC as Detective Nick Amoro in *Law & Order: Special Victims Unit* (NBC, 1999–), while veteran character actor John Finn, who played superior officer Lt. John Stillman, has made recent appearances in *Blue Bloods* (see below) and *Homeland*. Stiehm's latest work was on the U.S. adaptation of Scandinavian noir thriller, *The Bridge* (FX, 2013–14).

NCIS (CBS, 2003–)

As its protagonists work for the Naval Criminal Investigative Service (the law enforcement division of the U.S. Navy and Marines), *NCIS* is not, according to the terms of this volume, strictly speaking a police procedural. The show's characters are, however, engaged in police work, and since premiering in 2003 its combination of wry humor and pacey post–9/11 storylines have made *NCIS* a firm favorite with TV audiences. As Special Agent Leroy Jethro Gibbs, head of the Service's DC-based Major Case Response Team, Mark Harmon leads a tight ensemble cast, with Mike Weatherly playing Special Agent Tony DiNozzo (ex–Baltimore Police Department) and Cote de Pablo as former Mossad operative Special Agent Ziva David. The team's forensic support comes in the unconventional shape of specialist Abby Sciuto, conceived by the show's creators as an energy drink–quaffing "alternafreak" and played by poet, activist and rock musician Pauley Perrette. David McCallum, who in NBC's *The Man from U.N.C.L.E.* (1964–68) first achieved TV fame some four decades earlier, is Chief Medical Examiner Donald "Ducky" Mallard, and another small-screen heavyweight, Robert Wagner, makes regular appearances as Agent DiNozzo's father, Anthony senior. The show's creators, writer/producer Don McGill and veteran Donald P. Bellisario (the latter responsible for '80s hits including *Magnum, P.I.* and *Quantum Leap*) first collaborated on the long-running CBS military-legal drama *JAG* (1995–2005), of which *NCIS* was an even more successful spin-off. The show in turn spawned its own hit spin-off, *NCIS: Los Angeles* (CBS 2009–), starring Chris O'Donnell and LL Cool J.

The Closer (TNT, 2005–2012)

In a career-making role for which she received a Golden Globe in 2007 and an Emmy three years later, Kyra Sedgwick played Deputy Chief Brenda Leigh Johnson, a former CIA interrogator assigned to the LAPD's Major Crimes Division, her determination to secure confessions (and broad interpretation of suspects' rights) gaining her a reputation as a "closer." Located at the sophisticated end of the police procedural spectrum, *The Closer* tackled police work's ethical, moral and existential dimensions. Though the debt remains unacknowledged, it is widely assumed that James Duff, the show's creator, based Sedgwick's character on Inspector Jane Tennison, the tenacious Metropolitan Police detective played by Helen Mirren in the UK crime drama *Prime Suspect* (the U.S. version of which bombed on NBC in 2011). Like Tennison, Johnson finds her seniority resented and her authority undermined by male colleagues, chief among them G.W. Bailey and *Crime Story*'s Tony Denison as detectives Louie Provenza and Andy Flynn. A strong ensemble cast also included J.K. Simmons as Johnson's superior, Assistant Chief Will Pope, and Corey Reynolds as right-hand man Detective Sergeant David Gabriel. Two-time Oscar nominee Mary McDonnell joined the show in its fifth season as Captain Sharon Raydor of the LAPD's Force Investigation Division, her relationship with Johnson, though initially adversarial, gradually evolving into one of wary mutual respect. According to TNT, the decision in 2012 to end *The Closer* was Sedgwick's; the show's success on the network is currently replicated by a spin-off, *Major Crimes*, starring McDonnell and featuring most of its original cast.

Criminal Minds (CBS, 2005–)

Criminal Minds focuses less on conventional detective work than the tracking of unknown perpetrators, primarily serial killers and other sadistic violent criminals. The show is based around a close-knit team of criminal profilers located at the FBI's Behavioral Analysis Unit in Quantico, Virginia, its creator, screenwriter Jeff Davis, taking his cue from novelist Thomas Harris, whose Hannibal Lecter novels and their equally successful movie adaptations explored the application of the profiler's science to the darkest regions of the criminal psyche. Structured around the return to work following a nervous breakdown of veteran profiler Jason Gideon, the show's first two seasons starred veteran stage and screen actor Mandy Patinkin who, unhappy with its preoccupation with sexual violence, then quit the series, describing his decision to play Gideon as "the biggest public mistake I ever made." (Best loved for his 1987 role in Rob Reiner's *The Princess Bride*, Patinkin currently stars as *Homeland*'s CIA Chief, Saul Berenson.) Following the actor's departure, *Criminal Minds* enjoyed continued success, ensured not least by a strong ensemble cast that includes Thomas Gibson (still remembered as Greg in *Dharma and Greg*) as unit chief Aaron "Hotch" Hotchner, along with Shemar Moore as hot-headed Special Agent Derek Morgan and Matthew Gray Gubler as his colleague, the hyper-intelligent Dr. Spencer Reid. The show's producer, ex–Chicago cop and *Third Watch* creator Edward Allen Bernero, scored a turkey in 2011 with *Criminal Minds: Suspect Behavior*, a spin-off based (somewhat unimaginatively) on a rival team of profilers working in the same department.

Saving Grace (TNT, 2007–10)

Saving Grace's creator Nancy Miller began her screenwriting career with a 1990 episode of *Law & Order*, and later explored female friendship against the backdrop of recent American history in *Any Day Now* (Lifetime, 1998–2002). Turning her attention to her native Oklahoma City, she then wrote this offbeat magic realist/police procedural hybrid, structured (as, by this time, much American TV drama was) around a novelistic story arc. In her first role in a TV series, Holly Hunter, a 1994 Oscar-winner for her performance in Jane Campion's *The Piano*, starred as Oklahoma City police detective Grace Hanadarko, a chain-smoking, hard drinking, sexually promiscuous addict who is also an industrious, dedicated police officer and kind, warm, generous human being. In what is essentially an extended meditation on the necessity and impossibility of faith, Hanadarko is visited throughout the series by Earl (Leon Rippy) a forthright, tobacco-chewing angel, who offers her the prospect of salvation in return for her acceptance of God and renunciation of worldly temptation. Among the show's corporeal characters were Hanadarko's partner, Detective Hamilton "Ham" Dewey, with whom she is engaged in an extra-marital affair, her superior, Captain Kate Perry (Lorraine Toussaint, star of *Any Day Now*), and her best friend, forensics expert and devout Catholic Rhetta Rodriguez (Laura San Giacomo). Another of Miller's narrative refrains was the long-term impact of the 1995 Oklahoma bombing, whose victims, it emerges, included Hanadarko's sister, the mother of beloved teenage nephew Clay (played by Dylan Minnette).

In Plain Sight (USA Network, 2008–12)

Following a trend in police drama towards strong female lead characters (notably Kyra Sedgwick as Brenda Leigh Johnson in *The Closer* [see above]), screenwriter David Maples based *In Plain Sight* around Mary Shannon (Mary McCormack), a deputy U.S. marshal attached to the Albuquerque, New Mexico, office of the Federal Witness Security Program. Maples' narrative followed twin trajectories. One strand explored Shannon's turbulent personal life and the family from whom she must conceal the true nature of her job, the other her work in witness protection and professional relationship with partner Marshal Marshall Mann (Fred Weller), their role often placing them at odds with fellow law enforcement officers. Like AMC's *Breaking Bad*, which also premiered in 2008, Albuquerque's sterile suburbs provided an incongruous, sun-bleached backdrop to a saga of addiction, emotional trauma and violent crime. Shannon's mother, Jinx (Lesley Anne Warren), is a recovering alcoholic, her sister Brandi (Nicole Hiltz) becomes enmeshed via a meth-slinging ex-boyfriend with a gang of drug traffickers, and her father (Steven Lang), a bank-robber and chronic gambler, is eventually shot dead protecting Shannon from his business partner, her ne'er-do-well half-brother Scott (Aaron Ashmore). It becomes clear that Shannon's

Officer Ben Sherman (Benjamin McKenzie) keeps his finger away from the trigger ("accidental shootings" were a feature of several *Southland* tales). The show gave audiences a post–Rodney King take on the LAPD (NBC TV/The Kobal Collection).

warped sense of responsibility towards her clients, whose protection she treats as a fiercely personal matter, can be traced directly to her own abandonment issues. However, USA Network decided to rein in Maples' long story arc from season 3 onwards. *In Plain Sight* then became less a study in psychic turmoil than an upbeat and fairly conventional police procedural.

Southland (NBC/TNT, 2009–13)

Like *Cold Case* creator Meredith Stiehm, screenwriter and producer Ann Biderman began her career on *NYPD Blue*, winning an Emmy in 1994, as Steihm would four years later, for her work on the ground-breaking show. On the back of the cinema release in 2009 of Michael Mann's *Dillinger*, whose original screenplay she authored, Biderman conceived *Southland* as a dark, sprawling saga of life and law enforcement in twenty-first century Los Angeles. Unflinching in its depiction of the city's seamy underbelly, the show was cancelled by jittery NBC execs just two weeks before its scheduled second season premiere, then picked up by TNT who, having completed the season's shoot, then added the series to its permanent schedule. However, a reduced production budget resulted in a considerable narrowing of Biderman's original vision, the show's large ensemble cast now pruned and elements of its long story arc abandoned. Retooled as a conventional, albeit unusually gritty, police procedural, *Southland*'s primary focus became veteran uniformed LAPD officer John Cooper (Michael Cudlitz), secretly addicted to painkilling medication and, unbeknownst to his colleagues, gay. Though cropping up in shows such as *NYPD Blue* (ABC, 1993–2005) since the mid–1990s, gay TV cops remain to this day notably thin on the ground; Cudlitz's was the first lead gay male character in an American police drama. The show's cast also included Regina King as Detective Lydia Adams, struggling to balance work with care for her elderly mother (played by L. Scott Caldwell) and *The O.C.*'s Ben McKenzie as rookie officer Ben Sherman.

Blue Bloods (CBS, 2010–)

Whimsical Alaskan comedy-drama *Northern Exposure* (CBS, 1990–95), the show that husband-and-wife screenwriting team Mitchell Burgess and Robin Green first worked on together, couldn't be further from their most recent creation, *Blue Bloods*. The hard-boiled New York police saga does, however, bear a certain resemblance to *The Sopranos* (HBO, 1999–2007), for which the couple, as writers and producers, won a trio of Emmys. Where David Chase served up an Italian-American family of New Jersey mobsters, Burgess and Green give us the Irish-American equivalent: three generations of NYPD cops. Tom Selleck makes a welcome return to small-screen crime drama as Police Commissioner Frank Reagan, while Donnie Wahlberg co-stars as his son, Danny, an archetypally hard-nosed New York police detective. Having served respectively in Vietnam and Iraq, both father and son are U.S. Marine veterans, as is Frank's father, grizzled family patriarch Henry Reagan (Len Cariou), a retired NYPD police commissioner who saw military action in both World War II and Korea. Danny's sister, Erin (Bridget Moynahan), attending assiduously to her duties as an assistant DA, represents a more progressive approach to law enforcement, as does her equally conscientious younger brother, Harvard Law grad Jamie (Will Estes) who, having himself enlisted in the NYPD, now serves as a uniformed rookie. Each episode of *Blue Bloods* features a scene in which the characters discuss various cases as the whole family eats together; as much as a cop drama, the show is an intimate study of a close-knit Irish-American clan.

Mob City (TNT, 2013–14)

With *Mob City*, the cop show came full circle. Over 50 years before, ABC's *The Untouchables* (1959–63) and NBC's *The Lawless Years* (1959–61; see above) entertained audiences with stories based on the exploits of Prohibition era mob-busting cops. In 2013, TNT brought viewers a fictionalized account of the fight against organized crime in 1950s Los Angeles, the very era and locale in which those pioneering shows were themselves produced. Based on journalist John Buntin's non-fiction *L.A. Noir*, the show was set in a world already familiar to readers of James Ellroy's L.A. Quartet crime novels, not to mention players of *L.A. Noire*, the videogame whose publisher, Rockstar, cowed producers into changing its name first from *LA Noir* to *Lost Angels* and then again to *Mob City*. The show was created by Frank Darabont, director of *The Shawshank Redemption* (1994) and *The Green Mile* (1999), and a scriptwriter, director and producer on AMC's *The Walking Dead* (2010–). It featured Jon Bernthal and Jeffrey DeMunn, both of whom starred in the zombie apocalypse drama, as ex–Marine turned LAPD officer Joe Teague and freshly appointed mob-squad boss, Detective Hal Morrison. The narrative's backdrop was provided by the decades-long conflict between LAPD chief William H. Parker (Neal McDonough) and Mickey Cohen (Jeremy Luke), the Chicago street thug sent by the mob to Los Angeles in 1939, who rose to become its leading underworld figure, flaunting his celebrity and reveling in notoriety until finally imprisoned for tax evasion in 1961. Though bold, lavish and ambitious, the show was axed by TNT after only six episodes.

Fargo (FX, 2014–)

Taking as its departure point Joel and Ethan Coen's 1996 Oscar-winning movie of the same name, *Fargo* shares its namesake's pitch-black sense of humor and small-town Minnesota locale—the action now transferred from Brainerd in 1987 to the equally remote Bemidji, nineteen years later. Creator Noah Hawley cut his screenwriting teeth on Fox's popular forensic-anthropology comedy-drama, *Bones* (2005–), before writing a pair of off-beat flops for ABC: NYPD comedy-drama *The Unusuals* (2009) and the Generation Y mockumentary *My Generation* (2010). Like HBO's *True Detective*, the other ground-breaking cop show to receive a network debut in 2014, *Fargo* is notable for its narrative sophistication. Following the Coens' lead, Hawley's story is tightly wound around twin plot-lines, its protagonists' fates converging with the delicious inevitability of a Jacobean tragedy. Harried insurance salesman Lester Nygaard (Martin Freeman, best known for his portrayal of Bilbo Baggins in Peter Jackson's *The Hobbit* trilogy) is sucked into the orbit of psychopathic drifter Lorne Malvo (Billy Bob Thornton), while Bemidji's deputy sheriff, Molly Solverson (newcomer Allison Tolman) enlists Gus Grimley (Colin Hanks), a law enforcement officer from neighboring Duluth, to help her crack a string of unsolved murders. The characters inhabit the original's fictional universe: a season 1 subplot, for instance, concerns ransom money buried in a snow-drift back in 1987 by the luckless Carl Showalter (played in the movie by Steve Buscemi). A second season, currently in production, rewinds the narrative back to 1979: set in Sioux Falls, South Dakota, it will feature an entirely new cast of characters.

True Detective (HBO, 2014–)

Hardboiled noir seasoned with a liberal dash of Southern Gothic and an added pinch of neo-nihilist philosophy: *True Detective*'s creator, Nic Pizzalotto, a native of New Orleans, honed his distinctive literary vision writing short stories and a novel (2010's *Galveston*) before switching to the small screen as a writer on AMC's remake of Scandi-noir crime drama, *The Killing* (2011–2014). Like *Fargo*'s Noah Hawley, Pizzalotto extends the possibilities of the novelistic story arc in TV drama and, in doing so, redefines the cop genre's parameters. His narrative is cinematic in ambition: seventeen years after their 1995 investigation into a series of satanic ritual murders, a pair of Louisiana State Police homicide detectives find themselves under scrutiny when the case is reopened. The project attracted two of Hollywood's edgier leading men, Woody Harrelson as Detective Martin "Marty" Hart, and Matthew McConaughey, fresh from an Oscar triumph in Jean-Marc Vallée's *Dallas Buyers Club*, as Hart's colleague, Rustin "Rust" Cohle. An instant smash, *True Detective* clocked the highest viewing figures ever recorded for a rookie network TV drama, its

Detectives Martin Hart and Rustin Cohle (played by Woody Harrelson and Matthew McConaughey, two of the biggest stars in Hollywood at the time) ponder a serial killing in the bayou (HBO/Photofest).

finale crashing HBO's streaming service. It received no fewer than 12 Emmy nominations, with McConaughey and Harrelson going head-to-head for Lead Actor in a Drama Series (though in the event, the show lost out to *Breaking Bad*'s swansong season). Season 2, currently in production, will feature what promises to be an equally watchable double-act: Colin Farrell and Taylor Kitsch are California detectives pitted against a professional hoodlum played by Vince Vaughn.

Appendix:
The Tommy Westphall Hypothesis
Or: Why *Homicide: Life on the Street*, *Law & Order*, *The Wire* and *CSI* Don't Exist

The Tommy Westphall Hypothesis is a classic of fan creativity, and has become a "web meme." The basic idea is that certain TV dramas are connected by a series of crossovers, which trace back to a scenario which brings into question their having "existed" in the first place. This takes some explaining.

From the point of view of the cop show genre, the character John Munch is the key figure. Sergeant Munch, played by Richard Belzer, made his first appearance on *Homicide: Life on the Street*. He is honest, fastidious, amicably divorced, left-wing, Jewish and a mentor to younger cops. He's also co-owner of "The Waterfront," a bar located across the street from their Baltimore police station. In the *Homicide*/*Law & Order* crossover shows, Munch featured prominently. Upon the cancellation of *Homicide*, Munch transplanted to *Law & Order: Special Victims Unit*, the first spin-off of the *Law & Order* franchise. Here, his politics are more pronounced, as he buffers up against the homophobic/racist views of villains, witnesses and fellow officers; his paranoia about right-wing conspiracy theories and "black

Detective Munch (Richard Belzer), who appeared in several shows (notably, *Homicide: Life on the Street, Law & Order: SVU*, and *The Wire*), and who was himself a conspiracy theorist, is a key link in the chain that forms the Tommy Westphall Hypothesis (NBC TV/The Kobal Collection/Chris Haston).

ops" is also played up, sometimes to comedic effect. Finally, Munch had a cameo in *The Wire*: late in the final season, there is a very brief scene set in a bar. It's the cop bar, "Kavanagh's," and there's an unidentified, lanky, white-haired customer with spectacles (Munch) telling the barman that he used to run a bar in Baltimore.

So far, so good, so trivial. However, Munch's appearance has a much greater significance, because in connecting *The Wire* to the fictional worlds of *Homicide* and *Law & Order*, it also connects the show with other programs in which characters have crossed-over. Thus, *Law & Order* crosses over with prison drama *Oz*, which crosses over with *CSI*, and *CSI* crosses over with *Criminal Minds*, and so on. Similarly, *Homicide* crosses over with hospital show *St. Elsewhere*, sci-fi cop drama *The X-Files*, and so on. (In some versions of the hypothesis, the grid extends almost endlessly: other shows from the cop genre can include *NYPD Blue*, *Hill Street Blues*, *Martial Law*, *NCIS*, and *Walker: Texas Ranger*; while shows from other genres include *Buffy the Vampire Slayer*, *Seinfeld*, *Fresh Prince of Bel Air* and dozens of others.)

The *St. Elsewhere* connection is the one that is key to the hypothesis. Once that show is brought into the discussion, then the argument that all the connected shows are "fantasies" can be made. Here's how: in the final episode of *St. Elsewhere*, the autistic 11-year-old son of one of the medics is seen gazing into a snow dome. His father laments: "I don't even know if he can hear me, because he sits there, all day long, in his own world, staring at that toy. What's he thinkin' about?" Then, as the camera zooms in, we see that inside the snow dome is a tiny model of the hospital in which his dad works, and in which the show is set.

The fans' interpretation of this scene is that all the events in *St. Elsewhere* are the product of the boy's imagination. And so, by extension, must be the events in other shows that are connected to *St. Elsewhere* via character crossovers. This is the "Tommy Westphall Universe"—dozens of shows all sharing the same fictional storyworld. The logical extension of this is that *The Wire*, *Law & Order*, *Homicide*, etc., are all illusions.

Chapter Notes

Introduction

1. This most famous phrase in cop TV history was never actually uttered. The nearest *Dragnet*'s Joe Friday came to it was "All we want are the facts, ma'am."

2. "Race" is a difficult word. All the terms in this list—class, gender, race and sexuality—are constructed, but it has become customary to place "race" in quote marks to emphasize this fact. Baldly, this is because there is a perceived need to distance the idea from Victorian-era prejudices based on essentialism, i.e., that race is biologically determined, and therefore can be stratified.

3. The chapters don't include detailed listings of production crews, casts, and so on because this information is easily available on the web—see, particularly, IMDB (Internet Movie Database).

4. We'd like to thank staff at the Paley Center, New York; the British Film Institute, London; and the various university archives in the U.S. and Europe that have been referenced.

5. And not just arts courses—these shows are studied as part of criminology and sociology degrees (one recent academic conference was entitled "*The Wire* as Social Science Fiction").

6. "A Cop (and a Raincoat) for All Seasons," *Time*, 26 November 1973.

7. James Poniewozik, "Television: New Cops on the Beat," *Time*, 10 June 2002.

8. For example: Jonathan Bernstein, "US Networks Ditch Police Shows for High-Concept Drama," *The Guardian*, 24 September 2011.

9. C. P. Wilson, *Cop Knowledge: Police Power and Cultural Narrative in Twentieth-Century America* (Chicago: University of Chicago Press, 2000), p. 6.

10. For more context, see A. Bodroghkozy, *Groove Tube: Sixties Television and Youth Rebellion* (Durham: Duke University Press, 2001).

11. Sometimes the term "post-network" is used in preference to "neo-network," though this can give the impression that the older networks died out. Other studies prefer to use the categorization: TV1, TV2 and TV3 to denote the network, cable and digital eras.

12. The essay by Bill Osgerby, Anna Gough-Yates and Marianne Wells, "The Business of Action: Television History and the Development of the Action TV Series" in Osgerby and Gough-Yates (eds.), *Action TV* (Routledge, 2001) is a good introduction to the industry context.

13. The obvious models would be Hulu and Netflix, but illegal downloads need to be factored into this picture. There are no reliable statistics, but this is obviously significant (for example, many critics speculated that the success of *The Wire* was partly down to illegal viewing—going against the received wisdom that the show was watched almost solely by a connoisseur viewership on cable and DVD).

14. Alessandra Stanley, "You Are What You Watch," *New York Times*, 23 September 2007. (Note: audiences, as we shall see, are never as passive as some theorists believe.) The same kind of trajectory was simultaneously being witnessed in other areas of the arts: for example, comic books were now marketed as "graphic novels."

15. As the chapters on individual shows will demonstrate, there were occasional exceptions when it came to high audience figures. However, because (for example) *CSI* could record high numbers for discrete episodes does not necessarily compare with the sustained success of something like *Dragnet* (though the former show's international reach was much more impressive).

16. Spoof news article, *Dodgem Logic* magazine (Knockabout, UK), November 2009.

17. "Mainstream" is a relative term: HBO, for example, has been owned by Time Warner since 1990. We should also note that the picture is further complicated by the phenomenon of cable channels purchasing old (network era) cop shows and re-running them; and of "old model" networks diversifying into the "new model" sector—indeed, two of our featured shows, *Justified* and *The Shield* are made by FX, an offshoot of Fox.

18. The discussion about valuing TV shows is inevitably invested with notions of "cultural capital" and "taste distinctions," in the tradition of French sociologist Pierre Bourdieu. *Distinction* (Harvard University Press, 1984) is his most relevant work, but readers are advised to consider it in conjunction with Richard Shusterman (ed.), *Bourdieu: A Critical Reader* (Wiley-Blackwell, 1999).

19. See Amanda Lotz, *The Television Will Be Revolutionized* (New York: New York University Press, 2007), p. 62. The idea of the cultural forum is most closely associated with Horace Newcomb and Paul Hirsch's essay "Television as a Cultural Forum" in H. Newcomb (ed.), *Television: The Critical View* (Oxford: Oxford University Press, 1983, updated 2007).

20. Which in turn might be seen as a sub-genre of "fiction drama," and on and on. We should also note that as a shorthand classificatory system, genre can be defined any number of ways—as Brian McNair points out with regard to movies: "There are various types dependent on subject matter (the western, the war film), the narrative arc (film noir...), the intended audience (the women's film, the teen film), the production context (independent film, blockbusters, auteur film) or the presence of a particular aesthetic (French New Wave, Dogme 95," *(Journalists in Film* [Edinburgh University Press, 2010], pp. 28–29). With regard to TV studies, some commentators have tried to classify shows according to who made them: "an HBO drama," "a ZIV production," etc. However, this tactic can unravel when shows imitate each other and become very similar. As a final point, it's as well to be aware of the fact that the idea of genre itself has a history, and struggles over "naming" often reveal prejudices: see Rick Altman's *Film/Genre* (BFI, 1999).

21. Similarly, the first interracial kiss in a TV drama happened in a genre noted for its "un-realism," namely science fiction, in *Star Trek* (1968).

22. Paul Cobley, *The American Thriller* (Palgrave, 2000), p. 3. This idea has been taken further by other theorists, who argue that by legitimating police powers and playing on fears of crime, cops shows naturalize a set of assumptions and contribute to the pernicious idea of "governing through crime" (see Jonathan Simon, *Governing Through Crime*, Oxford University Press, 2007).

23. With this evolution has come the elevation of the role of the writer. Critics increasingly see film as a "director's medium" and TV as a "writer's medium," with the corollary that sometimes the writer gets promoted to auteur status as a "showrunner." All this is questionable, bearing in mind that these mediums are, by their nature, collaborative.

24. A subsidiary question might be: are they "political" or "performing politics"? On that score, the work of Jacques Rancière is a useful starting point. He argues, for example, that the "politics of aesthetics" involves deciding whether "Dix's paintings in the 1920s, 'populist' films by Renoir, Duvivier or Carne in the 1930s, or films by Cimino and Scorsese in the 1980s appear to harbor a political critique or appear, on the contrary, to be suited to an apolitical outlook on the irreducible chaos of human affairs or the picturesque poetry of social differences" (*The Politics of Aesthetics*, Continuum, 2006, p. 62).

25. The best-known director to be enticed to work in TV is Martin Scorsese on *Boardwalk Empire*.

26. Stephan Packard, "Why Are Story Arcs Dark and Gritty?," talk delivered at Giessen University,

Germany, 14 November 2010, available at http://blip.tv/dancetechtvbliptv/stephan-packard-why-are-story-arcs-dark-and-gritty-ethics-and-the-political-in-serial-tv-and-video-aesthetics-4639218. The talk takes its cue from *Dexter* rather than cop shows, but is recommended for its theoretical insights.

27. Jonathan Nichols-Pethick in *TV Cops: The Contemporary American Television Police Drama* (Routledge, 2012), pp. 22–23 says of the post–1981 shows: "[They] cannot be explained away by romantic tales of ... maverick writers and producers flying in the face of network demands. Nor can critical attention to this period be divided so neatly along aesthetic lines, as if production values equate with political or cultural values. Such views make the mistake of characterizing the police genre as a singular phenomenon: one that consistently reproduces a conspicuously uniform ideology, while a few anomalous rogues find a way to work round the system."

28. This kind of research tends to be scattered throughout the specialist journals, such as *American Communication Journal* and *Participations* (both of which contain essays specifically about cop TV drama).

29. Nichols-Pethick, 14.

30. Further, there is a recurring tradition in the media of comparing cop shows to "real life": The 1973 *Time* magazine article mentioned above enlisted real cops to comment, while a special issue of *Saturday Review* did the same in 1977 ("How TV Cops Flout the Law," 19 March). Similarly, Peter Moskos' book *Cop in the Hood* (Princeton University Press, 2009) was about his time as a Baltimore cop, and directly referenced *The Wire*.

31. Gérard Genette, *Paratexts* (Cambridge University Press, 1997), p. xix.

32. A quick sidebar about fans. Without them, cop shows would be much harder to research. Fans have often performed an almost academic role in tracking down lost episodes, monitoring cast changes, and providing detailed listings, not to mention suggesting sophisticated ways to think about the topic. The "further reading" sections at the end of each chapter in this book often attest to the value of this work—which can possibly be interpreted in theoretical terms as a "first level of consecration" for the genre (bringing us back to Bourdieu).

Chapter 1

1. A recording of the *Dragnet* theme by Ray Anthony and His Orchestra reached No. 3 on the *Billboard* chart in 1953.

2. The "tyranny of statistics" was something that would be commented upon by subsequent TV dramas, most eloquently in *The Wire* (HBO, 2002–2008).

3. The psychiatrist who had been at the center of the comic book panic, Fredric Wertham, also wrote about the dangers of TV programming (see chapter on *The Untouchables*).

4. Though, strictly speaking, the genre was undergoing a process of critical definition when *Dragnet* was being conceived—see Jason Mittell, *Genre*

and Television: From Cop Shows to Cartoons in American Culture (Routledge, 2004), p. 129.

5. This was an innovation later picked up by medical and legal dramas as well as cop shows.

6. "Jack, Be Nimble!," *Time*, 15 March 1954.

7. More recent (fictional) takes on the LAPD as it existed at (roughly) the same time have not been so kind—see, for example, the movies *Mulholland Falls* (1996) and *LA Confidential* (1997), the video game *LA Noire* (2011), and the TV series *Mob City* (2013).

8. Mittell, p. 139.

9. His anti-racism was relative, of course. From a leftist viewpoint, it could be argued that by supporting the police force he was endorsing a racist political system.

10. Wolf, quoted in Michael J. Hayde, *My Name's Friday: The Unauthorized but True Story of Dragnet and the Films of Jack Webb* (Nashville: Cumberland House, 2001), p. 245.

Chapter 2

1. Kathleen Battles, *Calling All Cars: Radio Dragnets and the Technology of Policing* (Minneapolis: University of Minnesota Press, 2010), p. 233.

2. "Frequently Asked Questions," http://www.highwaypatroltv.com. The California Highway Patrol (CHP) specifically would be a focus for many subsequent cop shows, notably *CHiPs* (1977–83). (In the opening episode of CHiPs, the cops pull over a car with an old guy driving, who turns out to be Broderick Crawford—and they proceed to chat about a TV show he made "before the cops were born.")

3. Largely on the back of the success of *Highway Patrol*, Ziv was bought by United Artists in 1960, which later became a subsidiary of MGM.

4. "General Information for Writers on *Highway Patrol*." Document viewable at http://www.highwaypatroltv.com/ZIV1955b/.

5. Ibid.

6. Ibid.

7. Ibid.

8. It's also worth mentioning an episode called "The Sniper" (1957), about somebody taking potshots at passing cars—a story later borrowed for Peter Bogdanovich's acclaimed movie *Targets* (1968).

9. Other cameos by future stars included ones by Leonard Nimoy and Barbara Eden.

10. "General Information for Writers."

11. Ibid.

12. Ibid.

13. Morleen Getz Rouse, *The History of the F.W. Ziv Radio and Television Syndication Companies: 1930–1960* (unpublished PhD dissertation, University of Michigan, 1976), p. 205.

14. "General Information for Writers."

15. Battles, p. 149.

16. Ibid., p. 154.

17. Hal Erickson, *Syndicated Television: The First 40 Years: 1947–1987* (Jefferson, NC: McFarland, 1989), p. 30.

18. John L. Hawkins, "Highway Patrol Rolls Again—10–4!," available at: http://www.advisor.com/story/highway-patrol-rolls-again-10-4.

19. Ibid.

Chapter 3

1. David Boroff, "Television and the Problem Play," in Patrick D. Hazard (ed.), *TV as Art* (Champaign, IL: National Council of Teachers of English, 1966), p. 107.

2. Mark Alvey, *Series Drama and the "Semi-Anthology": Sixties Television in Transition* (unpublished PhD dissertation, University of Texas–Austin, 1995), p. 100.

3. Alvey, pp. 100–101.

4. Ibid., p. 116.

5. Ibid.

6. Ibid., p. 115.

7. See, in particular, William Sadler and Ekaterina Haskins, "Metonymy and the Metropolis: Television Show Settings and the Image of New York City," *Journal of Communication Inquiry*, vol. 29, no. 3, July 2005, Sage. *Naked City*'s resistance to the postcard effect was echoed by *Kojak* and *The Wire*.

8. Alvey, p. 107.

9. Ibid., p. 108.

10. Alvey.

11. Ibid.

12. The complete boxed set of *Naked City* was released in 2013—before that, the half hour shows had been unavailable, bar a few on the web.

13. Ibid., p. 110.

14. Mary Ann Watson, *The Expanding Vista: American Television in the Kennedy Years* (Durham: Duke University Press, 1994; original edition: Oxford University Press, 1990).

15. Horace Newcomb and Paul Hirsch, "Television as a Cultural Forum," in H. Newcomb (ed.), *Television: The Cultural View* (Oxford: Oxford University Press, 1994), pp. 503–515.

16. Alvey, p. 130.

17. Ibid.

18. For David Boroff, a more apt comparison was with *The Untouchables*: "Eliot Ness and his cohorts were men of stone, absolutely implacable. In fact, they played the gangsters' own game of graceful, stylized violence from the other side of the fence. The police in *Naked City*, however, were gentle creatures, almost disabled by pity—with an infinite capacity for being pained. As much social workers as cops, they bore witness to man's folly and anguish." Boroff, p. 107.

19. David Bushman, *Dragnet v. Naked City: A Great Debate,* The Paley Center for Media, http://paleycenter.org/dragnet-v-naked-city-another-great-debate.

20. Alvey, p. 129.

Chapter 4

1. *TV Guide*, October 22–28, 1960.

2. Both the Wertham article and Senator Dodd's

remarks can be found in U.S. Senate, Committee on the Judiciary, Subcommittee to Investigate Juvenile Delinquency, *Investigation of Juvenile Delinquency in the United States, Part 10: Effect on Young People of Violence and Crime Portrayed on Television*, Hearings, 87th Congress, 1st and 2nd sessions, 1961–62, 1925, 2586.

3. When the show was first broadcast on CBS in 1959 as part of the *Desilu-Westinghouse Playhouse* it captured a large audience share, the largest, in fact, for the anthology series. Trendex (a television ratings system based on phone calls) gave ratings for the program of 31.8 percent (of the total phone callers surveyed) for the first installment and 37.5 percent for the second. Note: there were three television ratings systems in the late 1950s and early 1960s: Trendex, Arbitron, and Nielsen. Trendex and Arbitron were what were known in the industry as "telephone coincidentals." According to Hugh Malcom Beville, Jr., "Trendex throve because it was fast, flexible, and relatively inexpensive." For more information concerning TV audience ratings see Hugh Malcolm Beville, Jr., *Audience Ratings: Radio, Television, and Cable* (Hillsdale, NJ: Lawrence Erlbaum Associates, 1988), pp. 62–82.

4. In reality, Ness had little, if anything, to do with bringing down Capone. Indeed, he rarely met any of the villains in the series.

5. The definitive source of information concerning ABC's programming strategy in the 1950s remains Christopher Anderson's *Hollywood TV: The Studio System in the Fifties* (Austin: University of Texas Press, 1994). See also James L. Baughman, "The Weakest Chain and the Strongest Link: The American Broadcasting Company and the Motion Picture Industry, 1952–60" in Tino Balio (ed.), *Hollywood and the Age of Television* (Boston: Unwin Hyman, 1990) and James L. Baughman, *Same Time, Same Station: Creating American Television, 1948–1961* (Baltimore: Johns Hopkins University Press, 2007).

6. *TV Guide*, October 10–16, 1959, p. A-41.

7. For more on the crime genre more generally in this period see Douglas Snauffer, *Crime Television* (Westport, CT: Praeger, 2006).

8. Quote from a young admirer in "The Vincent 'Mad Dog' Coll Story" (1959).

9. The Miranda decision required that the police advise suspects of their rights to remain silent and to consult a lawyer before being questioned about a crime.

10. Strictly speaking, *The Untouchables* was predated by six months by the much less popular *The Lawless Years* (NBC, 1959–61). See chapter "They also served...."

11. Neal Gabler, *Winchell: Gossip, Power, and the Culture of Celebrity* (New York: Vintage, 1994), p. 508.

12. *Newsweek*, "The New 'Untouchables'" (8 August 1960), p. 73.

13. Gabler, p. 16.

14. Kenneth Tucker, *Eliot Ness and the Untouchables: The Historical Reality and the Film and Televi-*

sion *Depictions* (Jefferson, NC: McFarland, 2000), p. 63.

15. Ayn Rand, novelist, philosopher and founder of "Objectivism," was a fan of the show for this reason—and wrote in praise of Ness's "ethical egoism."

16. Robert Stack with Mark Evans, *Straight Shooting* (New York: Macmillan, 1980), p. 209.

17. U.S. Senate Hearings, 2354.

18. Quoted in Vahimagi, p. 35.

19. For an introduction to the contours of this debate, see Martin Barker and Julian Petley (eds.), *Ill Effects* (Routledge, 2001 edition).

20. One of the most vocal celebrity supporters of these organizations was Frank Sinatra.

21. Information concerning Hoover's investigation of the series is documented at the following: Federal Bureau of Investigation. Freedom of Information Act, Desi Arnaz files, 1959–1979. http://foia.fbi.gov/arnaz/arnez_desi_pt01-pt06.pdf. The Bureau of Prisons protests are documented in the U.S. Senate, Committee on the Judiciary, Subcommittee to Investigate Juvenile Delinquency, *Investigation of Juvenile Delinquency in the United States, Part 10: Effect on Young People of Violence and Crime Portrayed on Television*, Hearings, 87th Cong. 1st and 2nd sess., 1926–28.

22. Currently the only book-length study of Quinn Martin is Jonathan Etter, *Quinn Martin, Producer* (Jefferson, NC: McFarland, 2003). This provides a comprehensive overview of Martin's career and includes interviews with QM production personnel.

Chapter 5

1. While the White House stands for the authority of individual presidents, the Washington Monument represents the executive as an institution.

2. Richard Gid Powers, *G-Men: Hoover's FBI in American Popular Culture* (Carbondale: Southern Illinois University Press, 1983), p. 244.

3. David Marc and Robert J. Thompson, *Prime Time, Prime Movers* (Boston: Little, Brown, 1992), p. 157.

4. Interview with Paul Mavis, *DVD Talk*, 2011, available at: http://www.dvdtalk.com/interviews/dvd_talks_inter.html.

5. Its basic format was later retooled for an hour-long show, the phenomenally successful *Law & Order* (NBC, 1990–2010).

6. Other shows that riffed on Cold War themes included the comedy *Get Smart* (NBC/CBS, 1965–70) and the proto-steampunk western-spy hybrid *The Wild, Wild West* (CBS, 1965–69).

7. After the show was finally axed, Zimbalist maintained his connection with the Bureau, lending his voice to recruitment videos and his support to fund-raising activities.

8. For example, it was claimed that one such appeal led to the arrest of James Earl Ray, Martin Luther King, Jr.'s, assassin. If true, this would have been ironic: not only was King among the FBI's

harshest critics, but the Bureau was censured for failing to guard him adequately on the day of his death.

9. Quoted in Jonathan Etter, *Quinn Martin, Producer* (Jefferson, NC: McFarland, 2003), p. 65.

10. Quoted in ibid.

11. Powers, p. 242.

12. Quoted in ibid.

13. Hoover had in fact been responsible for introducing several key innovations to American law enforcement, a centralized fingerprinting system and up-to-the-minute forensic labs among them.

14. Powers, p. 248.

15. Quoted in John Morton Blum, *Years of Discord: American Politics and Society, 1961–1974* (New York: Norton, 1991), p. 372.

16. *The F.B.I* was consistently among the top 30 programs in Nielsen ratings from 1966 to 1973, and rose to the number 10 position in its sixth season, 1970–71.

17. Speech to students from the University of Oklahoma, April 29, 1971. The transcript of the speech forms part of the file on Hoffman kept by the FBI itself, and recently made public under Freedom of Information legislation: see http://vault.fbi.gov/abbie-hoffman/abbie-hoffman-part-33-of-65.

18. Marc & Thompson, p. 157.

19. Michel Foucault, *Power / Knowledge: Selected Interviews and Other Writings, 1972–1977*, ed. Colin Gordon (Hemel Hempstead: Harvester Press, 1980), pp. 104–105; Michel Foucault, *Discipline and Punish: The Birth of the Prison* (Harmondsworth: Penguin, 1979), pp. 25–26.

20. Foucault, *Discipline and Punish*, p. 195.

21. David Edwards, "Rove: NSA Surveillance Is OK Because Fictional Cops Do It on TV Shows," *The Raw Story*, 16 June 2013.

22. David Martindale, *Television Detective Shows of the 1970s* (Jefferson, NC: McFarland, 1991), p. 154.

Chapter 6

1. The appellation "mystery" is not straightforward: for many years, *Dragnet* was categorized as such (see Mittell, p. 127).

2. The 1973 episode "Requiem for a Falling Star" made a wry comment on formula cop shows, when Columbo, in the course of his investigation, wanders onto a TV production set where we see a stereotyped cop giving a suspect the third degree.

3. It was a phrase borrowed by the late Steve Jobs to conclude his keynote presentations.

4. The one exception to the "no overt politics" rule was the final episode of the series, "The Conspirators" (1978), about an IRA man.

5. Alvin H. Marill, "Films on TV," *Films in Review*, vol. 26, 1 January 1975, p. 41.

6. They claimed to have originated the character themselves, and in interviews and their memoirs would invoke Sayers, Christie and Queen, and sometimes others, e.g.: "When we created Columbo, we were influenced by the bureaucratic Petrovitch in *Crime and Punishment* and by G.K. Chesterton's marvellous little cleric, Father Brown." *Stay Tuned: An Inside Look at the Making of Prime Time Television* (New York: St. Martin's Press, 1981), p. 93.

7. An excerpt from Levinson and Link's *Stay Tuned* in *American Film* magazine (March 1981, American Film Institute).

8. Levinson and Link, *Stay Tuned*, pp. 90–91.

9. Michael Leahy, "Peter Falk Celebrates 20 Years of TV Acclaim as Schlump Sleuth Columbo," *TV Guide*, 14 December 1991.

10. This is not to mention stellar cameos from George C. Scott, Edith Head and even Robby the Robot.

11. CBS Vice President of Programming Fred Silverman, quoted in "A Cop (And a Raincoat) for All Seasons," *Time*, 26 November 1973, p. 117.

12. Michael Wood, "Seasons of the Private Eye," in *Channels of Communications*, December 1981/January 1982.

13. In addition, *Diagnosis: Murder* would often use the "inverted mystery" formula—and the same was also true of *Monk*.

Chapter 7

1. The others were *Bourbon Street Beat* (ABC, 1959–60), set in New Orleans, and *Surfside 6* (ABC, 1960–62), set in Miami.

2. Quoted in Peter Britos, "Symbols, Myth and TV in Hawaii: 'Hawaiian Eye,' 'Five-O,' and 'Magnum P.I.': The First Cycle" (unpublished doctoral dissertation, University of Southern California), p. 48.

3. Ibid., p. 53.

4. Quoted in Karen Rhodes, *Booking* Hawaii Five-O: *An Episode Guide and Critical History of the 1968–1980 Television Detective Series* (Jefferson, NC: McFarland, 1997), p. 26.

5. Ibid., p. 19.

6. Peter Britos, "Symbols, Myth and TV in Hawaii, The First Cycle: An Overview," *Oceania in the Age of Global Media*, Special Issue of *Spectator* 23:1 (Spring 2003), p. 104.

7. Rhodes, p. 18.

8. Dwight Whitney, "Jack Lord, Superstar," *TV Guide*, 4 September 1971.

9. Quoted in Rhodes, p. 75.

10. Britos, "The First Cycle: An Overview," p. 104.

11. Rhodes, p. 261.

12. Ibid., p. 33.

13. Quoted in Britos, "'Hawaiian Eye,' 'Five-O,' and 'Magnum P.I.,'" p. 69.

14. Quoted in Elizabeth Withey, "TV Gets Jazzed: The Evolution of Action TV Theme Music," *Action TV: Tough Guys, Smooth Operators and Foxy Chicks* (New York: Routledge, 2001), p. 200.

15. Rhodes, p. 258.

16. Cleveland Amory, "Review: Hawaii Five-O," *TV Guide*, 7 December 1968.

17. Quoted in Rhodes, p. 12.

18. Britos, "The First Cycle: An Overview," p. 104.

19. Ibid., p. 106, 104.

20. Quoted in Rhodes, p. 14.

21. Quoted in ibid., p. 15.

22. Ibid.
23. Ibid., p. 222.

Chapter 8

1. *Kojak Detective Game* (Arrow Games- Milton Bradley, 1975) and the Corgi *Kojak Buick,* still in production; The Clash "I'm So Bored with the USA," on *The Clash* (CBS, 1977); *The Benny Hill Show* (Thames Television, December 1975); *MAD* (no. 173, March 1975).
2. In the original 1966 case, the false confession of the suspect was cited by the United States Supreme Court in its Miranda decision, which required that the police advise suspects of their rights to remain silent and to consult a lawyer before being questioned about a crime.
3. Abby Mann obituary, *Los Angeles Times,* 28 March 2008, by Susan King, quoting David Bushman, television curator at the Paley Center for Media in New York.
4. Mann, interviewed for "The Archive of American Television" at: http://emmytvlegends.org/interviews/people/abby-mann.
5. Ibid.
6. President Ford never actually spoke these words, and later released funding. But the headline captured what was going on.
7. Press release, CBS TV, 1973.
8. C. P. Wilson, *Cop Knowledge: Police Power and Cultural Narrative in Twentieth-Century America* (Chicago: University of Chicago Press, 2000).
9. See, in particular, William Sadler and Ekaterina Haskins, "Metonymy and the Metropolis: Television Show Settings and the Image of New York City," *Journal of Communication Inquiry,* vol. 29, no. 3, July 2005, Sage.
10. A possible predecessor in this respect was *N.Y.P.D.* (ABC, 1967–69)—an unjustly forgotten show, again about the underbelly of New York, noted for its black actors and "realistic" dialogue.
11. Paul Cobley, "Who Loves Ya, Baby?" in Bill Osgerby and Anna Gough-Yates (eds.), *Action TV* (Routledge, 2001), p. 65. "Kojak liberalism" was a phrase that briefly became fashionable in 1990s political reportage in relation to a perceived "crisis in policing" at the local government level; see, for example, E.J. Dionne Jr.'s op ed piece in *The Washington Post,* "Saving Cities: Is Kojak Liberalism the Answer?" (15 June 1993), http://www.highbeam.com/doc/1P2-951224.html.
12. "Comment" by George W.S. Trow, 28 February 1977.
13. Cynthia Fuchs, "Kojak," *Popmatters,* 28 March 2005, available at: http://www.popmatters.com/pm/review/kojak-2005. At the time of writing, Universal Pictures is planning a *Kojak* movie, with Vin Diesel in the title role.

Chapter 9

1. Unnamed fan, from the Channee 4 documentary Word on the Street (UK, 1999, not currently available).

2. "I want to be known for my music," the young Soul explained.
3. *Starsky & Hutch:* Behind the Badge, documentary extra included in the first season DVD release (Sony Pictures, 2004).
4. Ibid.
5. Todd Gitlin, "Prime Time Ideology: The Hegemonic Process in Television Entertainment," *Social Problems* 26:3 (Feb. 1979), p. 257.
6. Henry Taylor and Carol Dozier, "Television Violence, African-Americans, and Social Control 1950–1976," *Journal of Black Studies,* 14:2 (Dec. 1983), p. 125.
7. Taylor and Dozier, pp. 128–129.
8. Elaine Pennicott, "'Who's the cat that won't cop out?' Black Masculinity in American Action Series of the Sixties and Seventies," in Bill Ogersby and Anna Gough-Yates (eds.), *Action TV: Tough Guys, Smooth Operators and Foxy Chicks* (London: Routledge, 2001), p. 110.
9. J.G. Ballard, "In Cold Blood," guardian.co.uk, 25 July 2005.
10. E.g., John Fiske, *Television Culture* (London: Routledge, 1987), p. 174.
11. Ed Guerrero, discussed by Phillipa Gates, "Always a Partner in Crime: Black Masculinity in the Hollywood Detective Film," *Journal of Popular Film and Television* 32:1 (Spring 2004), p. 22.
12. David Marc, *Demographic Vistas: Television in American Culture* (Philadelphia: University of Pennsylvania Press, 1996), p. 8.
13. Martin Barker, *The New Racism: Conservatives and the Ideology of the Tribe* (London: Junction Books, 1981), p. 135.

Chapter 10

1. Steve Jenkins, "Hill Street Blues," in Jane Feuer, Paul Kerr and Tise Vahimagi (eds.), *MTM "Quality Television"* (London: BFI Publishing, 1984), p. 183.
2. The notable exception was *New Republic* magazine, in which critic Mark Crispin Miller excoriated the show for promoting liberal propaganda (18 July 1981).
3. Robert J. Thompson, *From Hill Street Blues to ER: Television's Second Golden Age* (Syracuse University Press, 1996).
4. Joyce Carol Oates, "For Its Audacity, Its Defiantly Bad Taste and Its Superb Character Studies," *TV Guide,* vol. 33, no. 22, Issue 1679 (1 June 1985), pp. 4–7.
5. Robert J. Thompson elaborates: "It was not uncommon for a single episode to follow threads from over a dozen stories. Eventually some of the threads would be tied up, but some of them would lead nowhere, or would finally be picked up many episodes or even many seasons later. This narrative method provided a way of finally breaking free of one of episodic television's greatest constraints: the need to tell a story from beginning to end in each episode, returning everything back to where it came from by the final credits"(p. 70).

6. Todd Gitlin, *Inside Prime Time* (New York: Pantheon, 1983), p. 274.

7. Ibid., p. 274.

8. Carlos Clarens, *Crime Movies: An Illustrated History* (New York: W.W. Norton, 1980), p. 315.

9. Mention should also be made of the 1976 cult movie *Assault on Precinct 13*, which took the cops-under-siege trope to hyperreal extremes.

10. www.josephwambaugh.net/Joseph_Wambaughs_Rancho_M.

11. Another novelist who was undoubtedly important was Ed McBain, especially for his series of "87th Precinct" police procedurals. As he put it when interviewed by the website *Crime Time*, "I really don't think *Hill Street Blues* was an homage to Ed McBain, I think it was a rip off. Without even a tip of the hat." See http://www.crimetime.co.uk/interviews/edmcbain.html.

12. Paul Kerr, "Drama at MTM: *Lou Grant* and *Hill Street Blues*," in Jane Feuer et al., *MTM "Quality Television*," p. 148.

13. Ibid., p. 230.

14. Thompson, p. 70.

15. Ibid., p. 14.

16. Thus the roll call effectively became a means to identify key story arcs either being introduced or continuing within the episode. In addition, from season 3, the series utilized a "Previously on…" montage that would recap important narrative threads from past episodes, reminding audiences where they were.

17. Thompson, p. 15.

18. Gitlin, pp. 274–275.

19. Ibid., p. 292.

20. Documentary historians Jack Ellis and Betsy McLane claim that *The Police Tapes* "resulted in a chilling view of criminal activity in the city, and of public servants trying to do an impossible job." This attitude would become part of the ideological viewpoint of *Hill Street Blues*. Jack C. Ellis and Betsy A. McLane, *A New History of Documentary Film* (New York: Continuum, 2008), p. 235.

21. Gloria Steinem, *Outrageous Acts and Everyday Rebellions* (New York: NAL, 1986). Available at http://www.haverford.edu/psych/ddavis/p109g/steinem.menstruate.html.

22. James Craig Holte, "Unmelting Images: Film, Television and Ethnic Stereotyping," *MELUS*, Oxford University Press, vol. 11, no 3 (1984), p. 107.

23. J. Nichols-Pethick, *TV Cops: The Contemporary American Television Police Drama* (New York: Routledge, 2012), p. 3.

24. For more on this, see Robert Sabal's essay "Television Executives Speak about Fan Letters to the Networks" in Lisa A. Lewis (ed.), *The Adoring Audience* (New York: Routledge, 1992), which discusses the party that NBC threw for the critics to thank them for "saving" the network.

25. The most notable bit of merchandising came posthumously, in 1991, in the form of a computer game (Digitek Software). The game attempted to stay faithful to the show's structure by allowing players to "interact with up to nine crime incidents simultaneously."

Chapter 11

1. Quoted in Julie D'Acci, "Defining Women: The Case of *Cagney and Lacey*," in Lynn Spigel and Denise Mann (eds.), *Private Screenings: Television and the Female Consumer* (Minneapolis: University of Minnesota Press, 1992), p. 188.

2. Ibid., p. 170.

3. Interviewed in *Breaking the Laws of TV*, a documentary feature included in *Cagney & Lacey*'s season 2 DVD realease. Quotes in this chapter from Barney Rozenweig, Tyne Daley and Gloria Steinem are also taken from this source.

4. Lorraine Gamman, "Watching the Detectives: The Enigma of the Female Gaze," in Lorraine Gamman and Margaret Marshment (eds.), *The Female Gaze: Women as Viewers of Popular Culture* (London: The Women's Press, 1988), pp. 15–16.

5. Ibid., pp. 21–22.

6. Beverley Alcock and Jocelyn Robson, "Cagney and Lacey Revisited," *Feminist Review*, 35 (Summer 1990), p. 52.

7. Quoted in D'Acci, p. 184.

8. Gamman, p. 184; Debra Baker Beck, "The 'F' Word: How the Media Frame Feminism," *NWSA Journal*, 10:1 (Spring 1998), p. 147.

9. Alcock and Robson, p. 43; p. 45; p. 52.

10. Lorraine Gamman, "Response: More Cagney and Lacey," *Feminist Review*, 37 (Spring 1991), p. 120.

Chapter 12

1. Richard Zoglin, "Cool Cops, Hot Show: With Flashy Visuals and a Rock Score, *Miami Vice* Sets a New TV Beat," *Time*, 16 September 1985.

2. James Lyons, *Miami Vice* (Malden, MA: Wiley Blackwell, 2010), p. 2.

3. Ibid., pp. 20–21.

4. Steven Sanders, *Miami Vice* (Detroit: Wayne State University Press, 2010), p. 8.

5. Ibid..

6. Ibid.

7. Zoglin, 60.

8. He knew that audiences would have been familiar with the city's history of racial unrest; the Liberty City Riots of May 1980 were the country's first "race riots" since the 1960s. Miami was, according to the F.B.I., one of the most crime-ridden cities in America, though this did not discourage regeneration, and indeed fueled aspects of it. Sanders notes that "*Miami Vice* used South Beach as the site for many of its early episodes, at a moment when the area's small, postwar Art Deco apartments, houses and residential hotels were being renovated or prepared for demolition, eventually to be replaced by upscale retail shops, trendy clubs, and open air cafes" (p. 23).

9. David Marc and Robert J. Thompson, *Prime Time Prime Movers* (Syracuse: Syracuse University Press, 1992), p. 235.

10. Sanders, p. 9.

11. Lyons, p. 13.

12. Sanders, p. 9.

13. Hammer had composed the music for the 1983 teen film *A Night in Heaven* using a synthesizer, and had been an early adopter of the instrument during his time with The Mahavishnu Orchestra in the early 1970s.

14. Lyons, p. 37.

15. Sanders, p. 25.

16. Lyons, p. 38.

17. Sally Bedell Smith, "Miami Vice: Action TV with Some New Twists," *New York Times,* 3 January 1985.

18. Lyons, p. 20.

19. Ibid., p. 22.

20. Ibid., p. 9.

21. Sanders, p. 27.

22. Douglas Kellner, *Media Culture: Cultural Studies, Identity, and Politics between the Modern and Postmodern* (London: Routledge, 1995), p. 244.

23. Lyons, p. 9. Lyons also locates other possible inspirations for the character, notably the fiction of Florida mystery novelist John D. MacDonald and his character Travis McGee, who first appeared in the novel *The Deep Blue Goodbye* (1964). McGee is a former college football player and Korean War veteran who lives on a houseboat in Ft. Lauderdale and drives a sports car.

24. This dynamic is reversed in season 2, when the pair visit New York. "The Prodigal Son" (1985) features a now-famous shoot-out at the World Trade Center.

25. Lynne Joyrich, *Re-Viewing Reception: Television, Gender and Postmodern Culture* (Bloomington: Indiana University Press, 1996), p. 78.

26. Ibid., p. 85.

27. Benjamin Scott King, "Sonny's Virtues: The Gender Negotiations of *Miami Vice*," *Screen* 31, no. 3 (Autumn 1990), p. 283.

28. Sanders, p. 31.

29. Ibid.

30. Jeremy Butler, "Miami Vice: The Legacy of Film Noir," *Journal of Popular Film and Television* 13, no. 3 (1985), pp. 127–38. The noir elements could also carry over into the hardboiled dialogue: Yerkovich had imagined his Miami as a version of Casablanca in the eponymous 1942 (noir-influenced) movie, and some of Crockett's lines in the pilot are a direct reference (e.g., "five thousand street corners in Greater Miami and gumbo here's gotta pick ours…").

31. Jeremy Butler, *Television Style* (New York: Routledge, 2010), p. 88.

32. Fans disagree about which episode should be considered "the last." There was a strike by the Screenwriters Guild in 1989, which upset scheduling and meant that a few episodes were broadcast after the "Freefall" finale to the final season. Plus, one example premiered in 1990 on USA network because NBC had deemed it to be too controversial to broadcast first time around: "Too Much, Too Late" had a plotline about pedophilia.

33. Lawrence Grossberg, "The In-difference of Television," *Screen* 28, no. 2, pp. 28–45.

34. Jane Feuer, *Seeing Through the Eighties* (Durham: Duke University Press, 1995), p. 103.

35. John Thornton Caldwell, *Televisuality: Style, Crisis and Authority in American Television* (New Brunswick: Rutgers University Press, 1995), p. 4.

36. Caldwell, p. 5.

37. Fredric Jameson, *Postmodernism, or, The Cultural Logic of Late Capitalism* (Durham: Duke University Press, 1990). On links with *Miami Vice*, see Dominic Strinati, *An Introduction to Theories of Popular Culture* (London: Routledge, 2005), pp. 231–232.

Chapter 13

1. See http://brandonbird.com/stories.html. On the site there is a listing of the episode summaries from which the fans drew inspiration, as well as electronic copies of the drawings and paintings created by those who participated in the project. However, also note that, in terms of popularity, even in its most successful season, 2001–02, the show only reached number 7 in the Nielsen ratings.

2. Jonathan Nichols-Pethick, *TV Cops: The Contemporary American Television Police Drama* (New York: Routledge, 2012), p. 129.

3. Kevin Courrier and Susan Green, *Law & Order: The Unofficial Companion* (Los Angeles: Renaissance Books, 1998), p. 22.

4. Ibid.

5. Nichols-Pethick, p. 137.

6. Ibid.

7. Courrier and Green, p. 45.

8. Ibid., p. 46.

9. Ibid.

10. Ibid., pp. 59–60.

11. Ibid., p. 84.

12. Nichols-Pethick, p. 129.

13. Courrier and Green, p. 124.

14. Ibid., p. 33.

15. Mike Hale, "A Law & Order Farewell: These Were Their Stories," *New York Times Arts Beat,* 25 May 2010. Artsbeat.blogs.nytimes.com/2010/05/25/a-law-order-farewell-these-were-their-stories/?.

16. Courrier and Green, p. 131.

17. Ibid., p. 141.

18. Ibid., p. 68.

19. Ibid., p. 68.

20. Ibid.

21. Frazier Moore, *Savannah Morning News*, 25 November 1992. archives.savannahnow.com/sav_pdf_archive/text/fr286/D_2351421.pdf.

22. Courrier and Green, p. 69.

23. Abstract, Danielle Marie Soulliere's unpublished PhD dissertation *Prime Time Criminal Justice: If All We Know Is What We Saw on Television* (Wayne State University, 2001).

24. Courrier and Green, p. 51.

25. Ibid., p. 52.

26. Mock-educational video *The Science Behind Law & Order*, CollegeHumor.com, 2010, viewable at: http://www.youtube.com/watch?v=ZUHN64wzM9k. The video goes on to explain that "*Law & Order* obtains the energy it needs by feeding off, and metabolizing, a unique electro-magnetic force of de-

pression, given off by sad old people sitting in front of a television."

Chapter 14

1. *TV Guide Book of Lists* (Running Press, 2007), p. 212.

2. R. J. Thompson, *Television's Second Golden Age: From Hill Street Blues to ER* (New York: Syracuse University Press, 1997), pp. 13–16.

3. Jonathan Bignell, Tod Hoffman and David Kalat all note the filmic style of Levinson and the "quality television" pedigree of Fontana. Bignell, "The Police Series," in J. Gibbs and D. Pye (eds.), *Close-Up 03* (London: Wallflower, 2009); Hoffman, *Homicide: Life on the Screen* (Toronto: ECW Press, 1998); Kalat, *Homicide: Life on the Street: The Unofficial Companion* (Los Angeles: Renaissance, 1998).

4. Hoffman, p. 13.

5. Gary D'Addario, who appears as Lieutenant Jasper, the head of the Quick Response Team (QRT) in *Homicide: Life on the Street* and the corrupt court clerk Gary Di Pasquale in *The Wire*.

6. Hoffman, pp. 42–82.

7. Ibid., p. 84.

8. Thompson, p. 184.

9. M. Jancovich and J. Lyons (eds.), *Quality Popular Television* (London: British Film Institute, 2003).

10. J. Mittell, "Narrative Complexity in Contemporary American Television," *Velvet Light Trap*, 58 (Fall 2006), p. 31.

11. H. Jenkins, *Convergence Culture: Where Old and New Media Collide* (New York: New York University Press, 2008), p. 78.

12. B. Weinraub, "A Gritty Portrayal of Police Life Gets a Kind of Closure," *New York Times*, 6 February 2000, http://query.nytimes.com/gst/fullpage.html?res+9E0CE0DC143FF935A35751C0A96…

13. See also Thompson, p. 186.

14. P. Messent (ed.), *Criminal Proceedings: The Contemporary American Crime Novel* (London: Pluto Press, 1997), p. 12.

15. J. Bignell, "Seeing and Knowing: Reflexivity and Quality" in J. McCabe and K. Akass (eds.), *Quality TV: Contemporary American Television and Beyond* (London: I.B. Tauris, 2007), p. 159.

16. Bignell, "The Police Series," p. 38.

17. As indeed Bignell comments, "Seeing and Knowing," p. 163.

18. Although as Bignell also notes, because the proximity of the camera to the detectives in *Homicide* denies the viewer any knowledge beyond that of the police, this serves to somewhat de-stabilize the "mastery" of the detective ("The Police Series," p. 40). Similarly, the link between seeing and knowing in *CSI* is problematic because "there are things that cannot be seen and can be only partially known" ("The Police Series," p. 62).

19. G. Palmer, *Discipline and Liberty: Television and Governance* (Manchester: Manchester University Press, 2003), pp. 32–50.

20. L. Panek, *The American Police Novel: A History* (Jefferson, NC: McFarland, 2003), pp. 267–275.

21. M. Fishman and G. Cavender (eds.), *Entertaining Crime: Television Reality Programs* (New York: Walter de Gruyter, 1998), pp. 7–13.

22. P. Donovan, "Armed with the Power of Television: Reality Crime Programming and the Reconstruction of Law and Order in the United States," in M. Fishman and G. Cavender (eds.), *Entertaining Crime: Television Reality Programs* (New York: Walter de Gruyter, 1998), p. 123.

23. Bignell, "The Police Series," p. 40.

24. Priestman, M. (ed.), *The Cambridge Companion to Crime Fiction* (Cambridge: Cambridge University Press, 2006), p. 178.

25. L. Joyrich, *Re-Viewing Reception: Television, Gender and Postmodern Culture* (Bloomington: Indiana University Press, 1996). Gerardine Meaney also comments on the "sub-genre of amoral crime drama aimed at a predominantly male audience such as *Prison Breakout* (aka *Prison Break*) (2005), *The Shield* (2002–) and *24* (2001–)" in "Not Irish Enough? Masculinity and Ethnicity in *The Wire* and *Rescue Me*," in W. Balzono, A. Marshall, and M. Sullivan (eds.), *Irish Postmodernisms and Popular Culture* (London: Palgrave Macmillan, 2007), pp. 3–14.

26. Joyrich, pp. 102–104.

27. Not only did Kay Howard occupy less and less screen time as the series progressed, being joined in season 3 by the more "feminine" Megan Russert, but seemingly actor Melissa Leo was also not invited to join football games on the set. Kalat, pp. 20–21.

28. Joyrich, p. 79.

29. J. Gibb and R. Sabin, "Who loves ya, David Simon," *darkmatter*: The Wire Files [4] (29 May 2009), http://www.darkmatter101.org/site/2009/05/29/who-loves-ya-david-simon/.

30. M. Hilmes, *Only Connect: A Cultural History of Broadcasting in the United States* (London: Wadsworth, 2002).

31. Kalat, p. 157. This anecdote is echoed in a much later article about actors Andre Royo and Lance Reddick, in relation to appearing in *The Wire* (Saner, 2010), as are some of the discussions regarding the relatively low initial viewing figures for *The Wire*, suggesting perhaps that not much has changed in the intervening decade.

32. Although see the comments regarding "work" in the chapter on *The Wire*.

Chapter 15

1. J. Bignell, "The Police Series," in J. Gibbs and D. Pye (eds.), *Close-Up 03* (London: Wallflower, 2009), p. 41.

2. Whereas of course *Homicide* was filmed on location in Baltimore.

3. D.P. Kalat, *Homicide: Life on the Street: The Unofficial Companion* (Los Angeles: Renaissance, 1998), p. 129.

4. Ibid.

5. R.J. Thompson, *Television's Second Golden*

Age: From Hill Street Blues *to* ER (New York: Syracuse University Press, 1997), p. 13.

6. Bignell, p. 41.

7. J.P. Vest, *The Wire, Deadwood, Homicide and NYPD Blue: Violence Is Power* (Oxford: Praeger, 2011), p. 40.

8. J. Feuer, "Melodrama, Serial Form and Television Today," *Screen* 25 (Jan.-Feb. 1984), p. 4.

9. M.Z. Newman, "TV Binge," FlowTV, 23 January 2009, http://flowtv.org/2009/01/tv-binge-mich ael-z-newman-university-of-wisconsin-milwaukee/, p. 23.

10. M.Z. Newman, "From Beats to Arcs: Towards a Poetics of Television," *Velvet Light Trap* 58 (Fall 2006), pp. 16–28.

11. R. Nelson, *TV Drama in Transition: Forms, Values and Cultural Change* (Basingstoke: Macmillan, 1997), p. 186.

12. Ibid., p. 187.

13. Bignell, p. 41.

14. Nelson, p. 185.

15. Robin Nelson contends, however, that focusing on characters, the personal, is not necessarily depoliticizing: in looking at the face, the viewer has to actively engage with working out "the implications of internal drama" (Nelson, p. 147).

16. Bignell, p. 42.

17. An interesting comparison in its representation of New York's cityscape is *Gossip Girl*. While its subject matter is very different and the series is located among "Manhattan's elite" in the Upper East Side, nevertheless the characters spend much more time actually moving through the city, and the establishing shots are frequently (very striking) aerial shots of Manhattan. There is a much greater sense of physically being in the city, in spite of the affluence on display. And, as an aside, the location of Rufus (and sometime Dan's) Humphrey's Brooklyn apartment, just under the bridge, bears some resemblance to Bobby Simone's domestic environment.

18. S. Rubio, "From Sisyphus to Junior, Or How Andy Sipowicz made *NYPD Blue* Safe for Syndication," in G. Yeffeth (ed.), *What Would Sipowicz Do? Race, Rights and Redemption in NYPD Blue* (Dallas: Benbella, 2004), pp. 1–8.

19. Rubio, p. 7.

20. Vest, p. 44.

21. K. Meeks, "Racism and Reality in *NYPD Blue*" in G. Yeffeth (ed.), *What Would Sipowicz Do? Race, Rights and Redemption in NYPD Blue* (Dallas: Benbella, 2004), p. 49.

22. Although there are a few episodes which explicitly confront racism, such as 2:11.

23. Vest, pp. 63–66.

24. Ibid., p. 66.

25. H. Gray, *Cultural Moves: African Americans and the Politics of Representation* (Berkeley: University of California Press, 2005).

26. Nelson, p. 187.

27. And, as Jason Vest notes, also foreshadows Omar (p. 73).

28. An old discussion thread about the (non)release of season 5 on DVD suggests that sales figures were disappointing for the then rights holders, Fox: http://www.hometheaterforum.com/t/241010/nypd-blue-season-5.

29. J. Walters, "Repeat Viewings: Television Analysis in the DVD Age," in J. Bennett and T. Brown T. (eds.), *Film and Television after DVD* (London: Routledge, 2008), p. 69.

30. S. O'Sullivan, "Broken on Purpose: Poetry, Serial Television and the Season," *Storyworlds* 2 (2010), p. 68.

Chapter 16

1. These incidents happened in, respectively, "Blood Lust" (season 3, 2002) and "Room Service" (season 6, 2005).

2. Steven Cohan emphasizes that the CSIs are not technically police officers (*CSI: Crime Scene Investigation*, BFI TV Classics [London: BFI Publishing, 2008]). However, for the purposes of this book, they are included under the rubric of "cops": they work for the police, they wear vests that say "LVPD," they carry guns, they have badges, they solve cases (like detectives), and they are occasionally referred to as "law enforcement officers." Note that in the *CSI* spin-offs, the lead characters (Horatio Caine and Mac Taylor) have full police powers. This is also true of many real-life CSIs.

3. "The Execution of Catherine Willows" (season 3, 2002).

4. The technique was not unusual elsewhere, e.g., in documentaries and in the movies. Anthony Zuiker has pointed to the film *Three Kings* (1999) as an inspiration.

5. Along with Zuiker and Bruckheimer, there was a large team of creatives who made the show a success, and who should be taken into account for any in-depth study: obvious names to mention are writers Carol Mendelsohn, Ann Donahue and Jerry Stahl, and director Danny Cannon. In addition, there were "real life" CSI consultants, and so forth. As ever, TV is a collaborative medium.

6. As noted film scholar Linda Ruth Williams explains, "contemporary horror has specialized in making the inside visible, opening it up and bringing it out and pushing the spectacle of interiority to the limit to find out what that limit is." Linda Ruth Williams, "The Inside-Out of Masculinity: David Cronenberg's Visceral Pleasures," in Michael Aaron (ed.), *The Body's Perilous Pleasures: Dangerous Desires and Contemporary Culture* (Edinburgh: Edinburgh University Press, 1999), p. 34.

7. Which is not to say that *Silence of the Lambs* was "first" to emphasize the autopsy scene: other frequently cited precedents include the novels of Patricia Cornwell and the BBC series *Silent Witness*, about forensic pathologists, which dates from 1996.

8. Other popular CSI examples included the "Blue Paint Killer," the "Strip Strangler" and the "Mannekiller."

9. Co-option was swift: it was not long before "modern primitives" were being seen on daytime TV

chat shows. For more background, see the academic journal *Transgressive Culture* (Gylphi 2012–).

10. In one way, Lady Heather can be seen as a variant on the classic film noir femme fatale (a point made in Sanders, S. and Skoble, A. (eds.), *The Philosophy of TV Noir* [University Press of Kentucky, 2008]), but at the same time she harkened back to some of the "fetishistic" horror movie characters that had been rediscovered by the transgressive magazines (e.g., as played by Barbara Steele).

11. "Slaves of Las Vegas," season 2, 2001.

12. Dana Stevens, "The Sexiest Man in the Morgue," *Slate*, 11 February 2005.

13. See in particular Bakhtin's *Rabelais and His World* (Bloomington: Indiana University Press, 1984).

14. Cohan, *CSI*, p. 22.

15. When in 2007 Jorja Fox was rumoured to be leaving the show, fans lobbied CBS to "save her." It was the most impressive show of "fan power" in the context of crime TV since *Cagney & Lacey* (see chapter on same).

16. For a good introduction to this position, see Martin Barker (ed.), *Ill Effects* (London: Routledge, 2001).

17. *The Wire* episode was entitled "Clarifications" (2008).

18. This phrase has also been used to describe the phenomenon of the huge rise in applications to forensic science courses in higher education. The *National Geographic* estimated that at least 90 forensic science programs existed across universities in the United States in 2004.

19. See, for example, T. Tyler, "Viewing *CSI* and the Threshold of Guilt: Managing Truth and Justice, Reality and Fiction," *Yale Law Journal*, 115 (2006), pp. 1050–1085.

20. Gray Cavender and Sarah Deutsch, "CSI and Moral Authority: The Police and Science," *Crime, Media, Culture*, Sage, 2007, p. 78.

21. See Jonathan Simon, *Governing Through Crime* (New York: Oxford University Press, 2007).

22. D. Hunt (ed.), *Channeling Blackness: Studies on Television and Race in America* (New York: Oxford University Press, 2005).

23. For general background, see Derek Johnson, *Media Franchising: Creative License and Collaboration in the Culture Industries* (New York: New York University Press, 2013).

24. In this show, Grissom doesn't appear in any scenes with the Miami team because Petersen had voiced his objections to any *CSI* spin-offs.

25. There are at present so many hours of *CSI* programming in existence that it is a frequent occurrence for CBS and the other networks that have bought the show to schedule entire days of re-runs, or themed evenings (see also chapter on *Law & Order*).

26. Publicity for *CSI: The Experience* at MGM Hotel and Casino, Las Vegas.

27. As a sidebar, Zuiker has said that his initial inspiration was a documentary about forensic science on the Discovery Channel.

Chapter 17

1. Mike Davis documents the development of the LAPD in the twentieth century and also its long-time association with the military in *City of Quartz: Excavating the Future in Los Angeles* (London: Pimlico, 1998; Verso, 1990), pp. 251–306.

2. D. Stubbs, "LAPD Blues," *Guardian Guide* (22–28 November 2008), pp. 10–12.

3. B. Marshall, "Badge of Dishonour," *Guardian Guide* (26 June–2 July 2004), pp. 8–10.

4. R.J. Thompson, *Television's Second Golden Age: From* Hill Street Blues *to* ER (New York: Syracuse University Press, 1997).

5. C. Petit, "Non-fiction Boy," *Guardian Review* (Saturday, 27 December 2008), pp. 13–14.

6. Marshall, "Badge of Dishonour."

7. Cited also by Stubbs.

8. H. Sheehan and S. Sweeney, "*The Wire* and the World: Narrative and Metanarrative," *Jump Cut* 51 (Spring 2009), http://www.ejumpcut.org/archive/jc51.2009/Wire/index.html.

9. "The Wire" refers in the first instance to the wiretap, the surveillance which enables the police to watch and listen to others: here, the detective's superior vision is simply a matter of access to technology (which is often flawed) and seeing is at arm's length. But whereas "The Shield" signifies separation, "The Wire" implies connection (as do the visuals for the opening credits, where the camera follows the cables). "The Wire" suggests both the detective's limited and distorted vision (seeing is only possible with the help of technology, which may not deliver the "full" picture), but also, again, the detective's implication within a wider system, outside which no one may operate independently.

10. Although it should be noted that the Broadway Pier Building in Fells Point was never a police HQ!

11. Pamela Hill Nettleton, "Rescuing Men: The New Television Masculinity in *Rescue Me, Nip/Tuck, The Shield, Boston Legal, & Dexter*" Ph.D., University of Minnesota, 2009, 307 pages; 3387291 http://conservancy.umn.edu/bitstream/57963/1/Nettleton_umn_0130E_10769.pdf.

12. G.N. Dove, *The Police Procedural* (Bowling Green, OH: Bowling Green University Popular Press, 1982), p. 141.

Chapter 18

1. Jim Shelley, *Guardian Guide*, 1 April 2006.

2. J. Weisberg, *Slate.com*, 13 September 2006.

3. H. Sheehan and S. Sweeney, "*The Wire* and the World: Narrative and Metanarrative," *Jump Cut* 51 (Spring 2009), http://www.ejumpcut.org/archive/jc51.2009/Wire/index.html.

4. Deborah Jaramillo points out that HBO's parent company, AOL Time Warner, has been instrumental in popularizing the ratings discourse and perpetuating the notion that network television is concerned with ratings at the expense of quality, while obscuring HBO's own dependence on product place-

ment. "The Family Racket: AOL Time Warner, HBO, *The Sopranos*, and the Construction of a Quality Brand," in H. Newcomb (ed.), *Television: The Critical View* (Oxford: Oxford University Press, 2007), p. 592.

5. E. Ng, "Telling Tastes: (Re)producing Distinction in Popular Media Studies," *Flow* 13:5 (17 December 2010), http://flowtv.org/2010/12/telling-tastes.

6. See for example Drake Bennett in "This Will Be on the Midterm. You Feel Me?: Why So Many Colleges Are Teaching *The Wire*," www.slate.com, 24 March 2011, and Ruth Penfold-Mounce, David Beer and Roger Burrows, "The Wire as Social Science-fiction?" *Sociology,* 45:1 (February 2011), pp. 152–167.

7. S. O'Sullivan, "Broken on Purpose: Poetry, Serial Television and the Season," *Storyworlds* 2 (2010), p. 69.

8. Jane Feuer for example commented over 20 years ago on "the pervasive influence of serial form and multiple plot structure upon *all* American television." J. Feuer, "Melodrama, Serial Form and Television Today," *Screen* 25 (Jan.-Feb. 1984), p. 5.

9. J. Mittell, "All in the Game: *The Wire*, Serial Storytelling and Procedural Logic," in P. Harrison and N. Wardrip-Fruin (eds.), *Third Person: Authoring and Exploring Vast Narratives* (Cambridge: MIT Press, 2009), p. 437.

10. J. Mittell, "Narrative Complexity in Contemporary American Television," *Velvet Light Trap* 58 (Fall 2006), p. 38.

11. J. Mittell, "*The Wire* in the Context of American Television," 9 February 2010, http://mediacommons.futureofthebook.org/content/wire-context-american-television.

12. "Saptarshi Ray," a contributor to the *Guardian* Blog, comments on the experience of re-watching: "As has been noted many times here, D is a far more influential character in this season on second viewing." S. Busfield and P. Owen (eds.), *The Wire: Re-up* (London: Guardian Books, 2009), p. 57.

13. T. Nannicelli, "It's All Connected: Televisual Narrative Complexity," in T. Potter and C.W. Marshall (eds.), *The Wire: Urban Decay and American Television* (London: Continuum, 2009), p. 196.

14. R.J. Thompson, *Television's Second Golden Age: From* Hill Street Blues *to* ER (Syracuse: Syracuse University Press, 1997).

15. B.G. Rose, "The Wire," in G.R. Edgerton and Jeffrey P. Jones (eds.), *The Essential HBO Reader* (Lexington: University Press of Kentucky, 2008), p. 88.

16. Ibid., p. 90.

17. Ibid., p. 85.

18. P. Cobley, "'Who loves ya, baby?': Kojak, Action and the Great Society," in B. Osgersby and A. Gough-Yates (eds.), *Action TV: Tough Guys, Smooth Operators and Foxy Chicks* (London: Routledge, 2001), p. 64.

19. The special team formed, initially, to investigate the Barksdales' drug-dealing organization.

20. See for example Jones; Kinder; Kelly; Sharma.

21. Highlighted by an *Entertainment Weekly* article from 2008 entitled "Diversity in Entertainment: Why Is TV So White?," and Lisa Kelly similarly notes

that HBO's programming is also predominantly white. L. Kelly, "Casting *The Wire*: Complicating Notions of Performance, Authenticity, and 'Otherness,'" *darkmatter*: The Wire Files [4], 29 May 2009, http://www.darkmatter101.org/site/2009/05/29/casting-the-wire-complicating-notions-of-performance-authenticity-and-otherness/.

22. T. Fraley, "A man's Gotta Have a Code: Identity, Racial Codes and HBO's *The Wire*," *darkmatter*: The Wire Files [4], 29 May 2009, http://www.darkmatter101.org/site/2009/05/29/a-mans-gotta-have-a-code-identity-racial-codes-and-hbos-the-wire/.

23. Cited in M. Bowden, "The Angriest Man in Television," *Atlantic Magazine,* January/February 2008, http://www.theatlantic.com/magazine/archive/2008/01/the-angriest-man-in-television/6581/1/.

24. B. Walters, "*The Wire* for Tourists?" *Film Quarterly* 62: 2 (Winter 2008/2009), pp. 64–65.

25. J. Gibb and R. Sabin, "Who loves ya, David Simon," *darkmatter*: The Wire Files [4], 29 May 2009, http://www.darkmatter101.org/site/2009/05/29/who-loves-ya-david-simon/.

26. A. Sharma, Editorial: "'All the pieces matter'—Introductory Notes on *The Wire*," *darkmatter*: The Wire Files [4], 29 May 2009, http://www.darkmatter101.org/site/2009/05/29/editorial-all-the-pieces-matter-introductory-notes-on-the-wire/.

27. A. Press, "Gender and Family in Television's Golden Age and Beyond," *The ANNALS of the American Academy of Political and Social Science,* 625:1 (September 2009), pp. 139–150.

28. S. Jones, "Women and *The Wire*," *Popmatters*, 25 August 2008, http://www.popmatters.com/pm/feature/women-and-the-wire/.

Chapter 19

1. Robert Seidman, "FX's Original Series *Justified* Already a Lock to be Renewed," *TV by the Numbers,* 14 March 2010, http://tvbythenumbers.zap2it.com/2010/03/14/fxs-original-series-justified-already-a-lock-to-be-renewed/44880/.

2. "Interview: Graham Yost and Elmore Leonard Talk *Justified*," Elmoreleonard.com, 3 May 2010, http://www.elmoreleonard.com/index.php?/weblog/more/interview_graham_yost_elmore_leonard_talk_justified#.UVDwfnBhVUQ.

3. Ibid.

4. Sarah Hughes, "Return of the TV Western," *The Independent,* 15 November 2011, http:// www.independent.co.uk/arts-entertainment/tv/features/return-of-the-western.

5. TV horror drama *The Walking Dead* (AMC), which premiered in the same year as *Justified* (2010), was also hailed as a Western hybrid.

6. "Interview: Graham Yost and Elmore Leonard."

7. Tim Goodman, "*Justified* Scores with Hot Star, Smart Scripts," *San Francisco Chronicle,* 15 March 2010, p. E1.

8. "Interview: Graham Yost and Elmore Leonard."

9. Itself filmed for a second time in 2007.

10. See the biography on ElmoreLeonard.com.

11. Elmore Leonard, "Writers on Writing: Easy on the Adverbs, Exclamation Points, and Especially Hooptedoodle," *The New York Times,* 16 July 2001, http://www.nytimes.com/2001/07/16/arts/writers-writing-easy-adverbs-exclamation-points-espe cially-hooptedoodle.html.

12. Nick Kimberley, Obituary for Elmore Leonard, *The Guardian,* 20 August 2013.

13. Brian Naylor, "Elmore Leonard's Characters Talk or Die: Writer Says Dialogue Is Key to Survival in His Novels," *NPR Weekend Edition,* 8 February 2004, http://www.npr.org/templates/story/story.php?storyId=1651959.

14. "Interview: Graham Yost and Elmore Leonard."

15. Ibid.

16. Tom Shales, "Reviews FX's *Justified,*" *The Washington Post,* 16 March 2010, p. C5.

17. Jeremy Egner, "Defined by a Smile and a Drawl," *The New York Times,* 5 January 2012, http://www.nytimes.com/2012/01/08/arts/television/tim othy-olyphant-in-elmore-leonards-justified-on-fx.html.

18. Ibid.

19. Ibid.

20. Sarah Dobbs, "Timothy Olyphant Interview: *Justified, Deadwood* and More," *Den of Geek,* 8 January 2013, http://www.denofgeek.com/tv/timothy-olyphant/23996/timothy-olyphant-interview-justi fied-deadwood-more.

21. The importance of an unusual locale was mirrored in shows like *Longmire* (the flatlands of Wyoming) and, later, *Fargo* (snowy North Dakota) but also in documentary shows like *Alaska State Troopers* (National Geographic Channel, 2009–present). All make much of the idea of "cops who know the territory." (*Fargo*—another FX series—was based on the eponymous Coen brothers film of 1996, and it is interesting to note that the brothers cite Elmore Leonard as one of their chief inspirations.)

22. Wilson, *Cop Knowledge,* p. 215.

23. Jason Jacobs, "Preacher Man," http://cston line.tv/preacher-man.

24. Emily Nussbaum, "Trigger Happy," *New Yorker,* 1 January 2013.

25. Beth Marchant, "Francis Kenny, ASC: Shooting *Justified* on Epics Will Increase Production Tenfold," *Studio Daily,* 20 October 2011, http://www.studiodaily.com/2011/10/francis-kenny-asc-shoot ing-justified-on-epics-will-increase-production-ten fold/.

26. Stephanie Argy, "*Justified* Adopts Academy's New Workflow," *American Cinematographer,* March 2011, pp. 16–18.

27. Bobbie Gothard quoted in "'Justified' may exaggerate, but many in Harlan like the TV show" by Bill Estep, *Lexington Herald-Leader,* 15 January 2012.

28. "Ashton-Weaver," from Morehead, Kentucky, commenting on IMDB, 23 February 2011, http://www.imdb.com/title/tt1489428/reviews?start=70.

29. "Fresh Air" interview, National Public Radio, 13 January 2012, http://www.npr.org/templates/run downs/rundown.php?prgId=13&prgDate=1-13-2012.

30. See, for example, Cynthia Lee, "'But I thought he had a gun'—Race and Police Use of Deadly Force," *Hastings Race and Poverty Law Journal,* 2004, http://papers.ssrn.com/sol3/papers.cfm?abstract_id=6087 81.

31. Abstract, Justin A. Joyce, "The Warp, Woof, and Weave of This Story's Tapestry Would Foster the Illusion of Further Progress: *Justified* and the Evolution of Western Violence," *Western American Literature* 47, no. 2 (Summer 2012), pp. 174–199.

32. Ibid. The essay draws upon the landmark Supreme Court case District of Columbia v. Heller, 2008, in which it was decided that the Second Amendment protects an individual's right to possess a firearm for traditionally lawful purposes, such as self-defense within the home and within Federal enclaves.

33. Martin Shuster, "'Boyd and I Dug Coal Together': Norms, Persons and Being Justified in *Justified,*" Modern Language Notes (MLN), p. 1041, http://www.academia.edu/3248940/_Boyd_and_I_Dug_ Coal_Together_Norms_Persons_and_Being_Justi fied_in_Justified.

34. Ibid.

Bibliography

The following is a selected list of useful books and academic journals. When researching TV cop dramas, it goes without saying please to start with the shows themselves, which are mostly downloadable. Beyond that, Google Scholar and JSTOR are indispensable (especially for tracking down individual essays) and many unpublished dissertations are also available online, or can be ordered via an inter-library loan system. (The "open access" movement is increasingly making secondary sources more available.) A final tip: DVD "extras" often contain a wealth of information.

Books

Aaker, E. *Encyclopedia of Early Television Crime Fighters: All Regular Cast Members in American Crime and Mystery Series, 1948–59.* Jefferson, NC: McFarland, 2011.

Abelman, R. *Reaching a Critical Mass: A Critical Analysis of Television Entertainment.* London: Routledge, 2013.

Allen, M., ed. *Reading CSI: Crime TV Under the Microscope.* London: I.B. Tauris, 2004.

Allen, R., ed. *Channels of Discourse, Reassembled.* Chapel Hill: University of North Carolina Press, 1992, 1987.

Allen, R., and T. van den Berg, eds. *Serialization in Popular Culture.* London: Routledge, 2013.

AlSayyad, N. *Cinematic Urbanism: A History of the Modern from Reel to Real.* London: Routledge, 2006.

Altman, R. *Film/Genre.* London: British Film Institute, 1999.

Alvarez, R. *The Wire: Truth Be Told.* New York: Pocket Books, 2004.

Ames, M., ed. *Time in Television Narrative: Exploring Temporality in Twenty-First Century Programming.* Jackson: University Press of Mississippi, 2012.

Anderson, C. *Hollywood TV: The Studio System in the Fifties.* Austin: University of Texas Press, 1994.

Anderson, R. *Consumer Culture and TV Programming.* Boulder, CO: Westview, 1995.

Balio, T., ed. *Hollywood in the Age of Television.* London: Unwin Hyman, 1990.

Banet-Weiser, S., C. Chris, and A. Freitas, eds. *Cable Visions: Television Beyond Broadcasting.* New York: New York University Press, 2007.

Barker, A., ed. *Television, Aesthetics and Reality.* Newcastle: Cambridge Scholars Press, 2006.

Barnouw, E. *Tube of Plenty: The Evolution of American Television,* 2d ed. New York: Oxford University Press, 1990.

Battles, K. *Calling All Cars: Radio Dragnets and the Technology of Policing.* Minneapolis: University of Minnesota Press, 2010.

Beahr H., and G. Dyer, eds. *Boxed In: Women and Television.* London: Pandora, 1987.

Bennett, J., and T. Brown, eds. *Film and Television after DVD.* London: Routledge, 2008.

Bennett, T. *Popular Television and Film.* London: British Film Institute, 1981.

Bernstein, L. *The Greatest Menace: Organized Crime in Cold War America.* Amherst: University of Massachusetts Press, 2002.

Beville, H.M., Jr. *Audience Ratings: Radio, Television, and Cable.* Hillsdale, NJ: Lawrence Erlbaum Associates, 1988.

Bianculli, D. *Teleliteracy: Taking Television Seriously.* Syracuse: Syracuse University Press, 2000.

Bignell, J. *An Introduction to Television Studies.* London: Routledge, 2004.

Billingham, P. *Sensing the City through Television.* Bristol: Intellect, 2000.

Blum, J. *Years of Discord: American Politics and Society, 1961–1974*. New York: Norton, 1991.

Blumenthal, H.J., and O. Goodenough. *The Business of Television*, 3d ed. New York: Billboard Books, 2006.

Bodroghkozy, A. *Groove Tube: Sixties Television and Youth Rebellion*. Durham: Duke University Press, 2001.

Brown, M.E, ed. *Television and Women's Culture*. London: Sage, 1990.

Busfield, S., and P. Owen, eds. *The Wire: Re-up*. London: Guardian Books, 2009.

Butler, J. *Television Style*. New York: Routledge, 2010.

Buxton, D. *Form and Ideology in Television Series*. Manchester: Manchester University Press, 1990.

_____. *From the Avengers to Miami Vice*. Manchester: Manchester University Press, 1990.

Byers, M., and V. Johnson, eds. *The CSI Effect: Television, Crime and Governance*. New York: Lexington Books, 2009.

Bzdak, D., ed. *The Wire and Philosophy*. Chicago: Open Court, 2013.

Caldwell, J.T. *Televisuality: Style, Crisis and Authority in American Television*. New Brunswick: Rutgers University Press, 1995.

Carrabine, E. *Crime, Culture and the Media*. Cambridge: Polity, 2008.

Castleman, H., and W. Podrazik. *Watching TV: Six Decades of American Television* expanded edition. Syracuse: Syracuse University Press, 2010.

Clarens, C. *Crime Movies: An Illustrated History*. New York: W.W. Norton, 1980.

Clarke, D.B., ed. *The Cinematic City*. London: Routledge, 1997.

Clarke, M.J. *Transmedia Television*. New York: Bloomsbury, 2013.

Cohan, S. *CSI: Crime Scene Investigation*. BFI TV Classics. London: BFI Publishing, 2008.

Connole, E., P. Ennis, and M. Masciandaro, eds. *True Detection*. Schism Press, 2014.

Corner, J. *Critical Ideas in Television Studies*. New York: Oxford University Press, 1999.

Couldry, N., and A. McCarthy, eds. *Media Space: Place, Scale and Culture in a Media Age*. London: Routledge, 2004.

Courrier, K., and S. Green. *Law & Order: The Unofficial Companion*. Los Angeles: Renaissance Books, 1998.

Creeber, G. *Fifty Key Television Programmes*. London: Arnold, 2004.

_____. *Serial Television: Big Drama on the Small Screen*. London: BFI Publishing, 2004.

_____, ed. *The Television Genre Book*. London: BFI Publishing, 2001.

Crisell, A. *A Study of Modern Television: Thinking Inside the Box*. Basingstoke: Palgrave Macmillan, 2006.

D'Acci, J. *Defining Women: Television and the Case of Cagney and Lacey*. Chapel Hill: University of North Carolina Press, 1994.

Davin, S., and R. Jackson, eds. *Television Criticism*. Bristol: Intellect, 2008.

Davis, M. *City of Quartz: Excavating the Future in Los Angeles*. London: Pimlico, 1998. London: Verso, 1990.

Dawidziak, M. *The Columbo Phile: A Casebook*. New York: Mysterious Press, 1989.

Dove, G.N. *The Police Procedural*. Bowling Green, OH: Bowling Green University Popular Press, 1982.

Dow, B.J. *Prime-Time Feminism: Television, Media Culture and the Women's Movement Since 1970*. Philadelphia: University of Pennsylvania Press, 1996.

Downing, J., and C. Husband. *Representing "Race": Racisms, Ethnicities and Media*. London: Sage, 2005.

Duffy, J. *Stay Tuned*. New York: Excelsior Music Publishing, 1997.

Dwyer, K., and J. Fiorillo. *True Stories of Law & Order: The Real Crimes Behind the Best Episodes of the Hit TV Show*. New York: Penguin/Berkley Trade, 2006.

Edgerton, G.R. *The Columbia History of American Television*. New York: Columbia University Press, 2007.

_____, and J.P. Jones, eds. *The Essential HBO Reader*. Lexington: University Press of Kentucky, 2008.

Edgerton, G.R., and B. Rose, eds. *Thinking Outside the Box: A Contemporary Television Genre Reader*. Lexington: University Press of Kentucky, 2008.

Ellis, J. *Seeing Things: Television in the Age of Uncertainty*. London: I.B. Tauris, 2002.

_____. *Visible Fictions*. London: Routledge & Kegan Paul, 1993, 1982.

_____, and E. McLane. *A New History of Documentary Film*. New York: Continuum, 2008.

Erickson, H. *Syndicated Television: The First 40 Years: 1947–1987*. Jefferson, NC: McFarland, 1989.

Etter, J. *Quinn Martin, Producer*. Jefferson, NC: McFarland, 2003.

Falk, P. *Just One More Thing*. London: Hutchinson, 2007.

Feasy, R. *Masculinity and Popular Television*. Edinburgh: Edinburgh University Press, 2008.

Feuer, J. *Seeing Through the Eighties.* Durham: Duke University Press, 1995.

_____, P. Kerr, and T. Vahimagi, eds. *MTM "Quality Television."* London: BFI Publishing, 1984.

Fishman, M., and G. Cavender, eds. *Entertaining Crime: Television Reality Programs.* New York: Walter de Gruyter, 1998.

Fiske, J. *Television Culture.* London: Routledge, 1993.

_____, and J. Hartley. *Reading Television.* London: Routledge, 2003, 1978.

Fletcher, C. *What Cops Know.* New York: Pocket Books/Simon & Schuster, 1990.

Friedman, J., ed. *Reality Squared: Televisual Discourse on the Real.* New Brunswick: Rutgers University Press, 2002.

Gabler, N. *Winchell: Gossip, Power, and the Culture of Celebrity.* New York: Vintage, 1994.

Gamman, L., and M. Marshment, eds. *The Female Gaze: Women as Viewers of Popular Culture.* London: Women's Press, 1988.

Gibbs, J., and D. Pye, eds. *Close-Up 03.* London: Wallflower, 2009.

Gill, R. *Gender and the Media.* Cambridge: Polity, 2007.

Gitlin, T. *Inside Prime Time.* London: Routledge, 1994, 1983.

Goldenson, L.H., and M. J. Wolf. *Beating the Odds: The Untold Story Behind the Rise of ABC.* New York: Scribner, 1991.

Grant, P., and C. Wood. *Blockbusters and Trade Wars: Popular Culture in a Globalized World.* Vancouver: Douglas & McIntyre, 2004.

Gray, H. *Cultural Moves: African Americans and the Politics of Representation.* Berkeley: University of California Press, 2005.

_____. *Watching Race: Television and the Struggle for Blackness.* Minneapolis: University of Minnesota Press, 2004.

Gray, J. *Television Entertainment.* London: Routledge, 2008.

Hammond, M., and L. Mazdon, eds. *The Contemporary Television Series.* Edinburgh: Edinburgh University Press, 2005.

Harris, G. *Beyond Representation: Television Drama and the Politics and Aesthetics of Identity.* Manchester: Manchester University Press, 2006.

Harrison, P., and N. Wardrip-Fruin, eds. *Third Person: Authoring and Exploring Vast Narratives.* Cambridge: MIT Press, 2009.

Haut, W. *Neon Noir: Contemporary American Crime Fiction.* London: Serpent's Tail, 1999.

Hayde, M.J. *My Name's Friday: The Unauthorized but True Story of Dragnet and the Films of Jack Webb.* Nashville: Cumberland House, 2001.

Hazard, P.D. *TV as Art.* Champaign, IL: National Council of Teachers of English, 1966.

Heil, D. *Primetime Authorship: Works About and by Three TV Dramatists.* Syracuse: Syracuse University Press, 2002.

Hills, M. *Fan Cultures.* London: Routledge, 2002.

Hilmes, M. *Only Connect: A Cultural History of Broadcasting in the United States.* London: Wadsworth, 2002.

_____, ed. *The Television History Book.* London: BFI Publishing, 2003.

Hoffman, T. *Homicide: Life on the Screen.* Toronto: ECW Press, 1998.

Holmes, S., and D. Jermyn, eds. *Understanding Reality Television.* London: Routledge, 2004.

Jancovich, M., and J. Lyons, eds. *Quality Popular Television.* London: British Film Institute, 2003.

Jarvis, R.M., and P. Joseph. *Prime Time Law: Fictional Television as Legal Narrative.* Durham: Carolina Academic Press, 1998.

Jenkins, H. *Convergence Culture: Where Old and New Media Collide.* New York: New York University Press, 2008.

_____. *Textual Poachers: Television Fans and Participatory Culture.* London: Routledge, 1992.

Jermyn, D. *Crime Watching: Investigating Real Crime TV.* London: I.B. Tauris, 2007.

Johnson, D. *Media Franchising: Creative License and Collaboration in the Culture Industries.* New York: New York University Press, 2013.

Joyrich, L. *Re-Viewing Reception: Television, Gender and Postmodern Culture.* Bloomington: Indiana University Press, 1996.

Kalat, D.P. *Homicide: Life on the Street: The Unofficial Companion.* Los Angeles: Renaissance Books, 1998.

Kaminsky, S.M., with J.H. Mahon. *American Television Genres.* Chicago: Nelson-Hall, 1985.

Kelleter, F. *Serial Agencies: The Wire and Its Readers.* Alresford: Zero Books, 2014.

Kellner, D. *Media Culture: Cultural Studies, Identity, and Politics Between the Modern and Postmodern.* New York: Routledge, 1995.

Kennedy, L., and S. Shapiro, eds. *The Wire: Race, Class, and Genre.* Ann Arbor: University of Michigan Press, 2012.

Kimmel, D. *The Fourth Network.* Chicago: Ivan R. Dee, 2004.

King, A.D., ed. *Re-presenting the City: Ethnicity, Capital and Culture in the Twenty-First Century Metropolis.* Basingstoke: Macmillan, 1996.

Klinger, B. *Beyond the Multiplex: Cinema, New Technologies and the Home.* Berkeley: University of California Press, 2006.

Kompare, D. *CSI.* Malden, MA: Wiley-Blackwell, 2010.

Kotsko, A. *Why We Love Sociopaths: A Guide to Late Capitalist Television.* Winchester, UK: Zero Books, 2012.

Lacey, N. *Narrative and Genre: Key Concepts in Media Studies.* Basingstoke: Palgrave, 2000.

Lawrence, R.G. *The Politics of Force: Media and the Construction of Police Brutality.* Berkeley: University of California Press, 2000.

Leverette, M., B.L. Ott, and C.L. Buckley, eds. *It's Not TV: Watching HBO in the Post-television Era.* London: Routledge, 2008.

Levinson, R., and W. Link. *Stay Tuned: An Inside Look at the Making of Prime Time Television.* New York: St. Martin's, 1981.

Lewis J., and E. Smoodin, eds. *Looking Past the Screen: Case Studies in American Film History and Method.* Durham: Duke University Press, 2007.

Lewis, L., ed. *The Adoring Audience.* London: Routledge, 1992.

Longhurst, D., ed. *Gender, Genre and Narrative Pleasure.* London: Unwin Hyman, 1989.

Lotz, A.D. *Cable Guys: Television and Masculinities in the 21st Century.* New York: New York University Press, 2014.

_____. *Redesigning Women: Television After the Network Era.* Champaign: University of Illinois Press, 2006.

_____. *The Television Will Be Revolutionized.* New York: New York University Press, 2007.

Lury, K. *Interpreting Television.* London: Hodder Arnold, 2005.

Lusted, D., and C. Geraghty, eds. *The Television Studies Book.* London: Bloomsbury, 1997.

Lyons, J. *Miami Vice: Wiley-Blackwell Studies in Film and Television.* Malden, MA: Wiley-Blackwell, 2010.

MacDonald, J.F. *One Nation Under Television: The Rise and Decline of Network TV.* New York: Pantheon, 1990.

Macek, S. *Urban Nightmares: The Media, the Right and the Moral Panic Over the City.* Minneapolis: University of Minnesota Press, 2006.

Mair, G. *Inside HBO.* New York: Dodd, Mead, 1988.

Marc, D., and R. Thompson. *Prime Time, Prime Movers.* Boston: Little, Brown, 1992.

Martin, B. *Difficult Men: From The Sopranos and The Wire to Mad Men and Breaking Bad.* New York: Penguin; London: Faber and Faber, 2013.

Martindale, D. *Television Detective Shows of the 1970s.* Jefferson, NC: McFarland, 1991.

Massoud, P.J. *Black City Cinema: African American Urban Experiences in Film.* Philadelphia: Temple University Press, 2003.

McCabe, J., and K. Akass, eds. *Quality TV: Contemporary American Television and Beyond.* London: I.B. Tauris, 2007.

McCarthy, A. *Ambient Television: Visual Culture and Public Space.* Durham: Duke University Press, 2001.

Messent, P., ed. *Criminal Proceedings: The Contemporary American Crime Novel.* London: Pluto Press, 1997.

Milch, D., and Clark, B. *True Blue: The Real Stories Behind NYPD Blue.* New York: William Morrow, 1995.

Miller, J. *Something Completely Different: British Television and American Culture.* Minneapolis: University of Minnesota Press, 2000.

Mittell, J. *Genre and Television: From Cop Shows to Cartoons in American Culture.* London: Routledge, 2004.

_____. *Television and American Culture.* New York: Oxford University Press, 2010.

Mizejewski, L. *Hardboiled and High-Heeled: The Woman Detective in Popular Culture.* London: Routledge, 2004.

Modleski, T., ed. *Studies in Entertainment: Critical Approaches to Mass Culture.* Bloomington: Indiana University Press, 1986.

Morley, D. *Television Audiences and Cultural Studies.* London: Routledge, 1992.

Moskos, P. *Cop in the Hood: My Year Policing Baltimore's Eastern District*. Princeton: Princeton University Press, 2008.

Moyer, D., and E. Alvarez. *The Authorized Biography of Jack Webb*. Santa Ana, CA: Seven Locks Press, 2001.

Murray, S., and L. Ouellette. *Reality TV: Remaking Television Culture*. New York: New York University Press, 2004.

Naremore, J. *More Thanks Night: Film Noir in Its Contexts*, updated ed. Berkeley: University of California Press, 2008.

Nelson, R. *State of Play: Contemporary "High-End" TV Drama*. Manchester: Manchester University Press, 2007.

_____. *TV Drama in Transition: Forms, Values and Cultural Change*. Basingstoke, UK: Macmillan, 1997.

Newcomb, H., ed. *Museum of Broadcast Communication: Encyclopedia of Television*, 2d ed. New York: Fitzroy Dearborn, 2004.

_____, ed. *Television: The Critical View*. Oxford: Oxford University Press, 1983, updated 2007.

_____, and R. Alley. *The Producer's Medium: Conversations with Creators of American TV*. New York: Oxford University Press, 1983.

Nichols-Pethick, J. *TV Cops: The Contemporary American Television Police Drama*. London: Routledge, 2012.

O'Donnell, V. *Television Criticism*, second edition. Thousand Oaks, CA: Sage, 2012.

Osgerby, B. *Playboys in Paradise: Masculinity, Youth and Leisure Style in Modern America*. New York: Berg, 2001.

_____, and A. Gough-Yates, eds. *Action TV: Tough Guys, Smooth Operators and Foxy Chicks*. London: Routledge, 2001.

Ott, B.L. *The Small Screen: How Television Equips Us to Live in the Information Age*. Oxford: Blackwell, 2007.

Palmer, G. *Discipline and Liberty: Television and Governance*. Manchester: Manchester University Press, 2003.

Parenti, C. *Lockdown America*. London: Verso, 2008, 1999.

Peacock, S., and J. Jacobs, eds. *Television Aesthetics and Style*. London: Bloomsbury, 2013.

Perlmutter, D.D. *Policing the Media: Street Cops and Public Perceptions of Law Enforcement*. London: Sage, 2000.

Potter, T., and C.W. Marshall, eds. *The Wire: Urban Decay and American Television*. London: Continuum, 2009.

Powers, R.G. *G-Men: Hoover's FBI in American Popular Culture*. Carbondale: Southern Illinois University Press, 1983.

Priestman, M., ed., *The Cambridge Companion to Crime Fiction*. Cambridge: Cambridge University Press, 2006.

Rapping, E. *Law and Justice as Seen on TV*. New York: New York University Press, 2003.

Renga, D., ed. *Mafia Movies: A Reader*, rev. ed. Toronto: University of Toronto Press, 2011.

Rhodes, Karen. *Booking Hawaii Five-O*. Jefferson, NC: McFarland, 1997.

Rixon, P. *American Television on British Screens*. Basingstoke, UK: Palgrave Macmillan, 2006.

Rose, B. *TV Genres: A Handbook and Reference Guide*. Westport, CT: Greenwood, 1985.

Rosenzweig, B. *Cagney & Lacey ... and Me: An Inside Hollywood Story or How I Learned to Stop Worrying and Love the Blonde*. Lincoln, NE: iUniverse, 2007.

Sanders, C.R., ed. *Marginal Conventions: Popular Culture, Mass Media and Social Deviance*. Bowling Green, OH: Bowling Green State University Popular Press, 1992.

Sanders, S., and A. Skoble, eds. *The Philosophy of TV Noir*. Lexington: University Press of Kentucky, 2008.

Sanders, Steven. *Miami Vice*. Detroit: Wayne State University Press, 2010.

Sepinwall, A. *The Revolution Was Televised: The Cops, Crooks, Slingers and Slayers Who Changed TV Drama Forever*. New York: Touchstone/Simon & Schuster, 2013.

Shimpach, S. *Television in Transition*. Chichester, UK: Wiley-Blackwell, 2010.

Silverstone, R. *Television and Everyday Life*. London: Routledge, 1994.

Simon, D. *Homicide: A Year on the Killing Streets*. New York: Random House, 1991.

_____, and E. Burns. *The Corner: A Year in the Life of an Inner-City Neighborhood*. New York: Broadway Books, 1997.

Slater, R. *This ... Is CBS: A Chronicle of 60 Years*. New York: Prentice Hall, 1988.

Snauffer, D. *Crime Television*. Westport, CT: Praeger, 2006.

Sparks, R. *Television and the Drama of Crime: Moral Tales and the Place of Crime in Public Life.* Buckingham: Open University Press, 1992.

Spigel, L. *The Revolution Wasn't Televised: Sixties Television and Social Conflict.* London: Routledge, 2001.

_____, and D. Mann, eds. *Private Screenings: Television and the Female Consumer.* Minneapolis: University of Minnesota Press, 1992.

Spigel, L., and J. Olsson, eds. *Television After TV: Essays on a Medium in Transition.* Durham: Duke University Press, 2004.

Stack, R., with M. Evans. *Straight Shooting.* New York: Macmillan, 1980.

Stempel, T. *Storytellers to the Nation: A History of American Television Writing.* Syracuse: Syracuse University Press, 1996.

Strinati, D. *An Introduction to Theories of Popular Culture.* London: Routledge, 1995, 2010.

Sumser, J. *Morality and Social Order in TV Crime Drama.* Jefferson, NC: McFarland, 1996.

Tagg, P. *Kojak—50 Seconds of Television Music: Towards the Analysis of Affect in Popular Music.* Larchmont: Mass Media Music Scholars' Press, e-book, 2009.

Tartikoff, B. *The Last Great Ride.* New York: Random House, 1992.

Tasker, Y., and D. Negra, eds. *Interrogating Post-Feminism: Gender and the Politics of Popular Culture.* Durham: Duke University Press, 2007.

Thompson, E., and J. Mittell, eds. *How to Watch Television.* New York: New York University Press, 2013.

Thompson, K. *Storytelling in Film and Television.* Cambridge: Harvard University Press, 2003.

Thompson, R.J. *Television's Second Golden Age: From Hill Street Blues to ER.* Syracuse: Syracuse University Press, 1997.

Thornham, S. *Women, Feminism and Media.* Edinburgh: Edinburgh University Press, 2007.

_____, and T. Purvis, eds. *Television Drama: Theories and Identities.* Basingstoke: Palgrave Macmillan, 2005.

Todreas, T. *Value Creation and Branding in Television's Digital Age.* Westport, CT: Greenwood Press, 1999.

Torres, S., ed. *Living Color: Race and Television in the United States.* Durham: Duke University Press, 1998.

Tropiano, S. *The Prime Time Closet: A History of Gays and Lesbians on TV.* New York: Applause Theatre and Cinema Books, 2002.

Trutnau, J-P. *Miami Vice: A One-Man Show? The Construction and Deconstruction of a Patriarchal Image in the Reagan Era: Reading the Audio-Visual Poetics of Miami Vice.* Bloomington: Trafford Publishing, 2006.

Tucker, K. *Eliot Ness and the Untouchables.* Jefferson, NC: McFarland, 2000.

Vahimagi, T. *The Untouchables.* London: BFI Publishing, 1998.

Vest, J.P. *The Wire, Deadwood, Homicide and NYPD Blue: Violence Is Power.* Oxford: Praeger, 2011.

Vint, S. *The Wire.* Detroit: Wayne State University Press, 2013.

Wasko, J., ed. *A Companion to Television.* Oxford: Blackwell, 2005.

Watson, M.A. *Expanding Vistas: American Television in the Kennedy Years.* Durham: Duke University Press, 1994.

Webber, A., and E. Wilson. *Cities in Transition: The Moving Image and the Modern Metropolis.* London: Wallflower, 2008.

Williams, L. *On The Wire.* Durham: Duke University Press, 2014.

Williams, R. *Television: Technology and Cultural Form.* London: Routledge, 2003.

Wilson, C.P. *Cop Knowledge: Police Power and Cultural Narrative in Twentieth-Century America.* Chicago: University of Chicago Press, 2000.

Wisker, A. *Crime Fiction: An Introduction.* London: Continuum, 2009.

Wolf, D., with J. Burstein. *Law & Order: Crime Scenes.* New York: Barnes & Noble, 2003.

Yeffeth, G., ed. *What Would Sipowicz Do? Race, Rights and Redemption in NYPD Blue.* Dallas: Benbella, 2004.

Zecker, R. *Metropolis: The American City in Popular Culture.* Westport CT: Praeger, 2008.

Zuiker, A. *Mr. CSI: How a Vegas Dreamer Made a Killing in Hollywood, One Body at a Time.* New York: Harper, 2011.

Journals

American Communication Journal

Cinema Journal

Clues

Continuum: Journal of Media and Cultural Studies

Crime Time
Criminology Studies
Critical Inquiry
Critical Studies in Mass Communication
Critical Studies in Television
Criticism
Cultural Studies
Film Quarterly
Film and TV Studies
International Journal of Digital Television
Journal of American and Comparative Cultures
Journal of American Culture
Journal of American Studies
Journal of Broadcasting and Electronic Media
Journal of Communication
Journal of Communication Inquiry
Journal of Popular Culture

Journal of Popular Film and Television
The Journal of Popular Television
Journalism Studies
Jump Cut
Media, Culture and Society
Media History
MELUS
Participations
Quarterly Review of Film and Video
Scope
Screen
Sight and Sound
Television and New Media
Television Quarterly
TV Studies
Velvet Light Trap

Index